THE RUST PROGRAMMING LANGUAGE

THE RUST PROGRAMMING LANGUAGE

by Steve Klabnik and Carol Nichols,
with contributions from
the Rust Community

**no starch
press**

San Francisco

Printed in USA

Third printing

22 21 20 19 18   3 4 5 6 7 8 9 10

ISBN-10: 1-59327-828-4
ISBN-13: 978-1-59327-828-1

Publisher: William Pollock
Production Editor: Janelle Ludowise
Cover Illustration: Karen Rustad Tölva
Interior Design: Octopod Studios
Developmental Editor: Liz Chadwick
Technical Reviewers: Eduard-Mihai "eddyb" Burtescu and Alex Crichton
Copyeditor: Anne Marie Walker
Compositors: Meg Sneeringer and Janelle Ludowise
Proofreader: Paula L. Fleming

For information on distribution, translations, or bulk sales, please contact No Starch Press, Inc. directly:
No Starch Press, Inc.
245 8th Street, San Francisco, CA 94103
phone: 1.415.863.9900; info@nostarch.com
www.nostarch.com

Library of Congress Cataloging-in-Publication Data

Names: Klabnik, Steve, author. | Nichols, Carol, 1983- eauthor.
Title: The Rust programming language / by Steve Klabnik and Carol Nichols ;
    with contributions from the Rust Community.
Description: San Francisco : No Starch Press, Inc., 2018. | Includes index.
Identifiers: LCCN 2018014097 (print) | LCCN 2018019844 (ebook) | ISBN
    9781593278519 (epub) | ISBN 1593278519 (epub) | ISBN 9781593278281
    (paperback) | ISBN 1593278284 (paperback)
Subjects: LCSH: Rust (Computer programming language) | BISAC: COMPUTERS /
    Programming / Open Source. | COMPUTERS / Programming Languages / General.
    | COMPUTERS / Programming / General.
Classification: LCC QA76.73.R87 (ebook) | LCC QA76.73.R87 K53 2018 (print) |
    DDC 005.13/3--dc23
LC record available at https://lccn.loc.gov/2018014097

About the Authors

Steve Klabnik leads the Rust documentation team and is one of Rust's core developers. A frequent speaker and a prolific open source contributor, he previously worked on projects such as Ruby and Ruby on Rails. Klabnik works at Mozilla.

Carol Nichols is a member of the Rust Core Team and co-founder of Integer 32, LLC, the world's first Rust-focused software consultancy. Nichols organizes the Rust Belt Rust Conference.

BRIEF CONTENTS

Foreword by Nicholas Matsakis and Aaron Turon xix

Acknowledgments xxi

Introduction xxiii

Chapter 1: Getting Started 1

Chapter 2: Programming a Guessing Game 13

Chapter 3: Common Programming Concepts 31

Chapter 4: Understanding Ownership 57

Chapter 5: Using Structs to Structure Related Data 81

Chapter 6: Enums and Pattern Matching 95

Chapter 7: Using Modules to Reuse and Organize Code 109

Chapter 8: Common Collections 129

Chapter 9: Error Handling 149

Chapter 10: Generic Types, Traits, and Lifetimes 167

Chapter 11: Writing Automated Tests 201

Chapter 12: An I/O Project: Building a Command Line Program 227

Chapter 13: Functional Language Features: Iterators and Closures 257

Chapter 14: More About Cargo and Crates.io 285

Chapter 15: Smart Pointers 305

Chapter 16: Fearless Concurrency 341

Chapter 17: Object-Oriented Programming Features of Rust 365

Chapter 18: Patterns and Matching 389

Chapter 19: Advanced Features 413

Chapter 20: Final Project: Building a Multithreaded Web Server 449

Appendix A: Keywords. 487

Appendix B: Operators and Symbols 491

Appendix C: Derivable Traits. 497

Appendix D: Macros 501

Index 511

CONTENTS IN DETAIL

FOREWORD by Nicholas Matsakis and Aaron Turon   **xix**

ACKNOWLEDGMENTS   **xxi**

INTRODUCTION   **xxiii**

Who Rust Is For xxiv
    Teams of Developers xxiv
    Students xxiv
    Companies xxiv
    Open Source Developers xxiv
    People Who Value Speed and Stability xxv
Who This Book Is For xxv
How to Use This Book xxv
Resources and How to Contribute to This Book xxvii

1
GETTING STARTED   **1**

Installation 1
    Installing rustup on Linux or macOS 2
    Installing rustup on Windows 3
    Updating and Uninstalling 3
    Troubleshooting 3
    Local Documentation 4
Hello, World! 4
    Creating a Project Directory 4
    Writing and Running a Rust Program 5
    Anatomy of a Rust Program 5
    Compiling and Running Are Separate Steps 6
Hello, Cargo! 7
    Creating a Project with Cargo 8
    Building and Running a Cargo Project 9
    Building for Release 10
    Cargo as Convention 11
Summary 11

2
PROGRAMMING A GUESSING GAME   **13**

Setting Up a New Project 14
Processing a Guess 14
    Storing Values with Variables 15
    Handling Potential Failure with the Result Type 17
    Printing Values with println! Placeholders 18
    Testing the First Part 18

Generating a Secret Number. 19
    Using a Crate to Get More Functionality 19
    Generating a Random Number. 21
Comparing the Guess to the Secret Number 23
Allowing Multiple Guesses with Looping. 26
    Quitting After a Correct Guess 27
    Handling Invalid Input 28
Summary 30

3
COMMON PROGRAMMING CONCEPTS   31

Variables and Mutability. 32
    Differences Between Variables and Constants. 34
    Shadowing. 34
Data Types 36
    Scalar Types. 36
    Compound Types 39
Functions. 42
    Function Parameters 43
    Statements and Expressions in Function Bodies 44
    Functions with Return Values. 46
Comments. 48
Control Flow 48
    if Expressions 48
    Repetition with Loops. 53
Summary 56

4
UNDERSTANDING OWNERSHIP   57

What Is Ownership? 57
    Ownership Rules. 59
    Variable Scope. 59
    The String Type. 60
    Memory and Allocation 61
    Ownership and Functions. 66
    Return Values and Scope. 66
References and Borrowing 68
    Mutable References. 70
    Dangling References 72
    The Rules of References 73
The Slice Type 73
    String Slices 75
    Other Slices 78
Summary 79

5
USING STRUCTS TO STRUCTURE RELATED DATA   81

Defining and Instantiating Structs 81
    Using the Field Init Shorthand When Variables and Fields
        Have the Same Name. 83

Creating Instances from Other Instances with Struct Update Syntax 84
Using Tuple Structs Without Named Fields to Create Different Types 84
Unit-Like Structs Without Any Fields 85
An Example Program Using Structs. 86
Refactoring with Tuples 87
Refactoring with Structs: Adding More Meaning 87
Adding Useful Functionality with Derived Traits. 88
Method Syntax 90
Defining Methods 90
Methods with More Parameters. 92
Associated Functions 93
Multiple impl Blocks. 94
Summary 94

6
ENUMS AND PATTERN MATCHING   95

Defining an Enum. 96
Enum Values. 96
The Option Enum and Its Advantages over Null Values 99
The match Control Flow Operator 102
Patterns That Bind to Values 104
Matching with Option<T> 105
Matches Are Exhaustive. 106
The _ Placeholder 106
Concise Control Flow with if let 107
Summary 108

7
USING MODULES TO REUSE AND ORGANIZE CODE   109

mod and the Filesystem. 110
Module Definitions 111
Moving Modules to Other Files. 112
Rules of Module Filesystems 117
Controlling Visibility with pub 118
Making a Function Public. 119
Privacy Rules 121
Privacy Examples 121
Referring to Names in Different Modules. 123
Bringing Names into Scope with the use Keyword. 123
Bringing All Names into Scope with a Glob 124
Using super to Access a Parent Module 125
Summary 127

8
COMMON COLLECTIONS   129

Storing Lists of Values with Vectors 130
Creating a New Vector 130
Updating a Vector. 131
Dropping a Vector Drops Its Elements 131
Reading Elements of Vectors. 131

Iterating over the Values in a Vector 133
Using an Enum to Store Multiple Types 134
Storing UTF-8 Encoded Text with Strings 135
What Is a String? 135
Creating a New String 135
Updating a String 136
Indexing into Strings 139
Slicing Strings. 140
Methods for Iterating over Strings 141
Strings Are Not So Simple 142
Storing Keys with Associated Values in Hash Maps 142
Creating a New Hash Map 142
Hash Maps and Ownership 143
Accessing Values in a Hash Map 144
Updating a Hash Map. 145
Hashing Functions. 147
Summary 147

9
ERROR HANDLING   149

Unrecoverable Errors with panic! 150
Using a panic! Backtrace. 151
Recoverable Errors with Result 153
Matching on Different Errors. 155
Shortcuts for Panic on Error: unwrap and expect. 157
Propagating Errors 158
To panic! or Not to panic! 161
Examples, Prototype Code, and Tests 162
Cases in Which You Have More Information Than the Compiler 162
Guidelines for Error Handling. 162
Creating Custom Types for Validation 164
Summary 166

10
GENERIC TYPES, TRAITS, AND LIFETIMES   167

Removing Duplication by Extracting a Function 168
Generic Data Types 170
In Function Definitions 170
In Struct Definitions 173
In Enum Definitions 174
In Method Definitions. 175
Performance of Code Using Generics 177
Traits: Defining Shared Behavior 178
Defining a Trait. 178
Implementing a Trait on a Type. 179
Default Implementations 181
Trait Bounds 182
Fixing the largest Function with Trait Bounds. 183
Using Trait Bounds to Conditionally Implement Methods. 185

Validating References with Lifetimes 187
    Preventing Dangling References with Lifetimes. 187
    The Borrow Checker 188
    Generic Lifetimes in Functions 189
    Lifetime Annotation Syntax 190
    Lifetime Annotations in Function Signatures. 191
    Thinking in Terms of Lifetimes 193
    Lifetime Annotations in Struct Definitions. 194
    Lifetime Elision 195
    Lifetime Annotations in Method Definitions 197
    The Static Lifetime 198
Generic Type Parameters, Trait Bounds, and Lifetimes Together 199
Summary 199

11
WRITING AUTOMATED TESTS   201

How to Write Tests. 202
    The Anatomy of a Test Function. 202
    Checking Results with the assert! Macro. 205
    Testing Equality with the assert_eq! and assert_ne! Macros 208
    Adding Custom Failure Messages 210
    Checking for Panics with should_panic 212
Controlling How Tests Are Run. 215
    Running Tests in Parallel or Consecutively. 215
    Showing Function Output. 216
    Running a Subset of Tests by Name. 218
    Ignoring Some Tests Unless Specifically Requested 219
Test Organization 220
    Unit Tests 221
    Integration Tests 222
Summary 226

12
AN I/O PROJECT: BUILDING A COMMAND LINE PROGRAM   227

Accepting Command Line Arguments 228
    Reading the Argument Values. 228
    Saving the Argument Values in Variables 230
Reading a File 231
Refactoring to Improve Modularity and Error Handling 232
    Separation of Concerns for Binary Projects. 233
    Fixing the Error Handling 237
    Extracting Logic from main 240
    Splitting Code into a Library Crate 242
Developing the Library's Functionality with Test-Driven Development 244
    Writing a Failing Test 244
    Writing Code to Pass the Test. 247
Working with Environment Variables 249
    Writing a Failing Test for the Case-Insensitive search Function 250
    Implementing the search_case_insensitive Function 251

Writing Error Messages to Standard Error Instead of Standard Output 254
    Checking Where Errors Are Written 254
    Printing Errors to Standard Error 255
Summary 256

13
FUNCTIONAL LANGUAGE FEATURES:
ITERATORS AND CLOSURES   257

Closures: Anonymous Functions That Can Capture Their Environment 258
    Creating an Abstraction of Behavior with Closures 258
    Closure Type Inference and Annotation 263
    Storing Closures Using Generic Parameters and the Fn Traits 264
    Limitations of the Cacher Implementation 267
    Capturing the Environment with Closures 268
Processing a Series of Items with Iterators 270
    The Iterator Trait and the next Method 271
    Methods That Consume the Iterator 272
    Methods That Produce Other Iterators 273
    Using Closures That Capture Their Environment. 274
    Creating Our Own Iterators with the Iterator Trait 275
Improving Our I/O Project 277
    Removing a clone Using an Iterator 278
    Making Code Clearer with Iterator Adaptors 280
Comparing Performance: Loops vs. Iterators 281
Summary 283

14
MORE ABOUT CARGO AND CRATES.IO   285

Customizing Builds with Release Profiles 286
Publishing a Crate to Crates.io 287
    Making Useful Documentation Comments. 287
    Exporting a Convenient Public API with pub use 290
    Setting Up a Crates.io Account. 294
    Adding Metadata to a New Crate 294
    Publishing to Crates.io. 295
    Publishing a New Version of an Existing Crate 296
    Removing Versions from Crates.io with cargo yank 296
Cargo Workspaces 297
    Creating a Workspace 297
    Creating the Second Crate in the Workspace. 298
Installing Binaries from Crates.io with cargo install. 302
Extending Cargo with Custom Commands. 303
Summary 303

15
SMART POINTERS   305

Using Box<T> to Point to Data on the Heap. 306
    Using a Box<T> to Store Data on the Heap 307
    Enabling Recursive Types with Boxes. 308

Treating Smart Pointers Like Regular References with the Deref Trait 311
    Following the Pointer to the Value with the Dereference Operator 312
    Using Box<T> Like a Reference. 312
    Defining Our Own Smart Pointer. 313
    Treating a Type Like a Reference by Implementing the Deref Trait 314
    Implicit Deref Coercions with Functions and Methods. 315
    How Deref Coercion Interacts with Mutability 316
Running Code on Cleanup with the Drop Trait. 317
    Dropping a Value Early with std::mem::drop 318
Rc<T>, the Reference Counted Smart Pointer 320
    Using Rc<T> to Share Data 320
    Cloning an Rc<T> Increases the Reference Count 322
RefCell<T> and the Interior Mutability Pattern 323
    Enforcing Borrowing Rules at Runtime with RefCell<T>. 324
    Interior Mutability: A Mutable Borrow to an Immutable Value 325
    Having Multiple Owners of Mutable Data
        by Combining Rc<T> and RefCell<T> 330
Reference Cycles Can Leak Memory. 332
    Creating a Reference Cycle 332
    Preventing Reference Cycles: Turning an Rc<T> into a Weak<T> 334
Summary 339

16
FEARLESS CONCURRENCY   341

Using Threads to Run Code Simultaneously 342
    Creating a New Thread with spawn 344
    Waiting for All Threads to Finish Using join Handles 345
    Using move Closures with Threads 347
Using Message Passing to Transfer Data Between Threads 349
    Channels and Ownership Transference 352
    Sending Multiple Values and Seeing the Receiver Waiting. 353
    Creating Multiple Producers by Cloning the Transmitter 354
Shared-State Concurrency. 355
    Using Mutexes to Allow Access to Data from One Thread at a Time 356
    Similarities Between RefCell<T>/Rc<T> and Mutex<T>/Arc<T> 362
Extensible Concurrency with the Sync and Send Traits 362
    Allowing Transference of Ownership Between Threads with Send 363
    Allowing Access from Multiple Threads with Sync 363
    Implementing Send and Sync Manually Is Unsafe 363
Summary 364

17
OBJECT-ORIENTED PROGRAMMING FEATURES OF RUST   365

Characteristics of Object-Oriented Languages 365
    Objects Contain Data and Behavior 366
    Encapsulation That Hides Implementation Details 366
    Inheritance as a Type System and as Code Sharing 368
Using Trait Objects That Allow for Values of Different Types 369
    Defining a Trait for Common Behavior. 369
    Implementing the Trait 371

Trait Objects Perform Dynamic Dispatch 374
Object Safety Is Required for Trait Objects 374
Implementing an Object-Oriented Design Pattern 376
Defining Post and Creating a New Instance in the Draft State 377
Storing the Text of the Post Content 378
Ensuring the Content of a Draft Post Is Empty 378
Requesting a Review of the Post Changes Its State 379
Adding the approve Method that Changes the Behavior of content 380
Trade-offs of the State Pattern 383
Summary 387

18
PATTERNS AND MATCHING   389

All the Places Patterns Can Be Used 390
match Arms 390
Conditional if let Expressions 390
while let Conditional Loops 392
for Loops 392
let Statements 393
Function Parameters 394
Refutability: Whether a Pattern Might Fail to Match 395
Pattern Syntax 396
Matching Literals 396
Matching Named Variables 397
Multiple Patterns 398
Matching Ranges of Values with the ... Syntax 398
Destructuring to Break Apart Values 399
Ignoring Values in a Pattern 403
Creating References in Patterns with ref and ref mut 407
Extra Conditionals with Match Guards 408
@ Bindings 410
Summary 411

19
ADVANCED FEATURES   413

Unsafe Rust 414
Unsafe Superpowers 414
Dereferencing a Raw Pointer 415
Calling an Unsafe Function or Method 417
Accessing or Modifying a Mutable Static Variable 421
Implementing an Unsafe Trait 422
When to Use Unsafe Code 423
Advanced Lifetimes 423
Ensuring One Lifetime Outlives Another with Lifetime Subtyping 423
Lifetime Bounds on References to Generic Types 428
Inference of Trait Object Lifetimes 429
Advanced Traits 430
Specifying Placeholder Types in Trait Definitions with Associated Types 431
Default Generic Type Parameters and Operator Overloading 432

Fully Qualified Syntax for Disambiguation:
  Calling Methods with the Same Name 434
  Using Supertraits to Require One Trait's Functionality Within Another Trait . . . 437
  Using the Newtype Pattern to Implement External Traits on External Types . . . 439
Advanced Types 440
  Using the Newtype Pattern for Type Safety and Abstraction 440
  Creating Type Synonyms with Type Aliases 441
  The Never Type That Never Returns. 443
  Dynamically Sized Types and the Sized Trait 445
Advanced Functions and Closures 446
  Function Pointers. 446
  Returning Closures 448
Summary 448

20
FINAL PROJECT: BUILDING A MULTITHREADED WEB SERVER   449

Building a Single-Threaded Web Server 450
  Listening to the TCP Connection 450
  Reading the Request 452
  A Closer Look at an HTTP Request. 454
  Writing a Response. 455
  Returning Real HTML 456
  Validating the Request and Selectively Responding 457
  A Touch of Refactoring 459
Turning Our Single-Threaded Server into a Multithreaded Server 460
  Simulating a Slow Request in the Current Server Implementation 460
  Improving Throughput with a Thread Pool 461
Graceful Shutdown and Cleanup. 479
  Implementing the Drop Trait on ThreadPool 479
  Signaling to the Threads to Stop Listening for Jobs. 481
Summary 485

A
KEYWORDS   487

Keywords Currently in Use 487
Keywords Reserved for Future Use 489

B
OPERATORS AND SYMBOLS   491

Operators 491
Non-operator Symbols 493

C
DERIVABLE TRAITS   497

Debug for Programmer Output. 498
PartialEq and Eq for Equality Comparisons 498
PartialOrd and Ord for Ordering Comparisons 499

Clone and Copy for Duplicating Values 499
Hash for Mapping a Value to a Value of Fixed Size. 500
Default for Default Values 500

D
MACROS   501

The Difference Between Macros and Functions. 502
Declarative Macros with macro_rules! for General Metaprogramming 502
Procedural Macros for Custom derive. 504
The Future of Macros 510

INDEX   511

FOREWORD

It wasn't always so clear, but the Rust programming language is fundamentally about *empowerment*: no matter what kind of code you are writing now, Rust empowers you to reach further, to program with confidence in a wider variety of domains than you did before.

Take, for example, "systems-level" work that deals with low-level details of memory management, data representation, and concurrency. Traditionally, this realm of programming is seen as arcane, accessible only to a select few who have devoted the necessary years learning to avoid its infamous pitfalls. And even those who practice it do so with caution, lest their code be open to exploits, crashes, or corruption.

Rust breaks down these barriers by eliminating the old pitfalls and providing a friendly, polished set of tools to help you along the way. Programmers who need to "dip down" into lower-level control can do so with Rust, without taking on the customary risk of crashes or security holes, and without having to learn the fine points of a fickle toolchain. Better yet, the language is designed to guide you naturally towards reliable code that is efficient in terms of speed and memory usage.

Programmers who are already working with low-level code can use Rust to raise their ambitions. For example, introducing parallelism in Rust is a relatively low-risk operation: the compiler will catch the classical mistakes for you. And you can tackle more aggressive optimizations in your code with the confidence that you won't accidentally introduce crashes or exploits.

But Rust isn't limited to low-level systems programming. It's expressive and ergonomic enough to make CLI apps, web servers, and many other kinds of code quite pleasant to write—you'll find simple examples of both later in the book. Working with Rust allows you to build skills that transfer from one domain to another; you can learn Rust by writing a web app and then apply those same skills to target your Raspberry Pi.

This book fully embraces the potential of Rust to empower its users. It's a friendly and approachable text intended to help you level up not just your knowledge of Rust but also your reach and confidence as a programmer in general. So dive in, get ready to learn—and welcome to the Rust community!

Nicholas Matsakis and Aaron Turon

ACKNOWLEDGMENTS

We would like to thank everyone who has worked on the Rust language for creating an amazing language worth writing a book about. We're grateful to everyone in the Rust community for being welcoming and creating an environment worth welcoming more folks into.

We're especially thankful for everyone who read early versions of this book online and provided feedback, bug reports, and pull requests. Special thanks to Eduard-Mihai Burtescu and Alex Crichton for providing technical review and Karen Rustad Tölva for the cover art. Thank you to our team at No Starch, including Bill Pollock, Liz Chadwick, and Janelle Ludowise, for improving this book and bringing it to print.

Steve would like to thank Carol for being an amazing co-author. Without her, this book would have been of much lesser quality and taken a lot more time. Additional thanks to Ashley Williams, who provided an incredible amount of support in the beginning, in the middle, and in the end <3.

Carol would like to thank Steve for piquing her interest in Rust and for the opportunity to work on this book. She's grateful to her family for their constant love and support, especially her husband Jake Goulding and her daughter Vivian.

INTRODUCTION

Welcome to *The Rust Programming Language*, an introductory book about Rust. The Rust programming language helps you write faster, more reliable software. High-level ergonomics and low-level control are often at odds in programming language design; Rust challenges that conflict. Through balancing powerful technical capacity and a great developer experience, Rust gives you the option to control low-level details (such as memory usage) without all the hassle traditionally associated with such control.

Who Rust Is For

Rust is ideal for many people for a variety of reasons. Let's look at a few of the most important groups.

Teams of Developers

Rust is proving to be a productive tool for collaboration among large teams of developers with varying levels of systems programming knowledge. Low-level code is prone to a variety of subtle bugs, which in most other languages can be caught only through extensive testing and careful code review by experienced developers. In Rust, the compiler plays a gatekeeper role by refusing to compile code with these elusive bugs, including concurrency bugs. By working alongside the compiler, the team can spend their time focusing on the program's logic rather than chasing down bugs.

Rust also brings contemporary developer tools to the systems programming world:

- Cargo, the included dependency manager and build tool, makes adding, compiling, and managing dependencies painless and consistent across the Rust ecosystem.
- Rustfmt ensures a consistent coding style across developers.
- The Rust Language Server powers Integrated Development Environment (IDE) integration for code completion and inline error messages.

By using these and other tools in the Rust ecosystem, developers can be productive while writing systems-level code.

Students

Rust is for students and those who are interested in learning about systems concepts. Using Rust, many people have learned about topics like operating systems development. The community is very welcoming and happy to answer student questions. Through efforts such as this book, the Rust teams want to make systems concepts more accessible to more people, especially those new to programming.

Companies

Hundreds of companies, large and small, use Rust in production for a variety of tasks. Those tasks include command line tools, web services, DevOps tooling, embedded devices, audio and video analysis and transcoding, cryptocurrencies, bioinformatics, search engines, Internet of Things applications, machine learning, and even major parts of the Firefox web browser.

Open Source Developers

Rust is for people who want to build the Rust programming language, community, developer tools, and libraries. We'd love to have you contribute to the Rust language.

People Who Value Speed and Stability

Rust is for people who crave speed and stability in a language. By speed, we mean the speed of the programs that you can create with Rust and the speed at which Rust lets you write them. The Rust compiler's checks ensure stability through feature additions and refactoring. This is in contrast to the brittle legacy code in languages without these checks, which developers are often afraid to modify. By striving for zero-cost abstractions, higher-level features that compile to lower-level code as fast as code written manually, Rust endeavors to make safe code be fast code as well.

The Rust language hopes to support many other users as well; those mentioned here are merely some of the biggest stakeholders. Overall, Rust's greatest ambition is to eliminate the trade-offs that programmers have accepted for decades by providing safety *and* productivity, speed *and* ergonomics. Give Rust a try and see if its choices work for you.

Who This Book Is For

This book assumes that you've written code in another programming language but doesn't make any assumptions about which one. We've tried to make the material broadly accessible to those from a wide variety of programming backgrounds. We don't spend a lot of time talking about what programming *is* or how to think about it. If you're entirely new to programming, you would be better served by reading a book that specifically provides an introduction to programming.

How to Use This Book

In general, this book assumes that you're reading it in sequence from front to back. Later chapters build on concepts in earlier chapters, and earlier chapters might not delve into details on a topic; we typically revisit the topic in a later chapter.

You'll find two kinds of chapters in this book: concept chapters and project chapters. In concept chapters, you'll learn about an aspect of Rust. In project chapters, we'll build small programs together, applying what you've learned so far. Chapters 2, 12, and 20 are project chapters; the rest are concept chapters.

Chapter 1 explains how to install Rust, how to write a Hello, World! program, and how to use Cargo, Rust's package manager and build tool. Chapter 2 is a hands-on introduction to the Rust language. Here we cover concepts at a high level, and later chapters will provide additional detail. If you want to get your hands dirty right away, Chapter 2 is the place for that. At first, you might even want to skip Chapter 3, which covers Rust features similar to those of other programming languages, and head straight to Chapter 4 to learn about Rust's ownership system. However, if you're a particularly meticulous learner who prefers to learn every detail before moving on to the next, you might want to skip Chapter 2 and go straight to Chapter 3, returning to Chapter 2 when you'd like to work on a project applying the details you've learned.

Chapter 5 discusses structs and methods, and Chapter 6 covers enums, `match` expressions, and the `if let` control flow construct. You'll use structs and enums to make custom types in Rust.

In Chapter 7, you'll learn about Rust's module system and about privacy rules for organizing your code and its public Application Programming Interface (API). Chapter 8 discusses some common collection data structures that the standard library provides, such as vectors, strings, and hash maps. Chapter 9 explores Rust's error-handling philosophy and techniques.

Chapter 10 digs into generics, traits, and lifetimes, which give you the power to define code that applies to multiple types. Chapter 11 is all about testing, which even with Rust's safety guarantees is necessary to ensure your program's logic is correct. In Chapter 12, we'll build our own implementation of a subset of functionality from the grep command line tool that searches for text within files. For this, we'll use many of the concepts we discussed in the previous chapters.

Chapter 13 explores closures and iterators: features of Rust that come from functional programming languages. In Chapter 14, we'll examine Cargo in more depth and talk about best practices for sharing your libraries with others. Chapter 15 discusses smart pointers that the standard library provides and the traits that enable their functionality.

In Chapter 16, we'll walk through different models of concurrent programming and talk about how Rust helps you to program in multiple threads fearlessly. Chapter 17 looks at how Rust idioms compare to object-oriented programming principles you might be familiar with.

Chapter 18 is a reference on patterns and pattern matching, which are powerful ways of expressing ideas throughout Rust programs. Chapter 19 contains a smorgasbord of advanced topics of interest, including unsafe Rust and more about lifetimes, traits, types, functions, and closures.

In Chapter 20, we'll complete a project in which we'll implement a low-level multithreaded web server!

Finally, some appendixes contain useful information about the language in a more reference-like format. Appendix A covers Rust's keywords, Appendix B covers Rust's operators and symbols, Appendix C covers derivable traits provided by the standard library, and Appendix D covers macros.

There is no wrong way to read this book: if you want to skip ahead, go for it! You might have to jump back to earlier chapters if you experience any confusion. But do whatever works for you.

An important part of the process of learning Rust is learning how to read the error messages the compiler displays: these will guide you toward working code. As such, we'll provide many examples of code that doesn't compile along with the error message the compiler will show you in each situation. Know that if you enter and run a random example, it may not compile! Make sure you read the surrounding text to see whether the example you're trying to run is meant to error. In most situations, we'll lead you to the correct version of any code that doesn't compile.

Resources and How to Contribute to This Book

This book is open source. If you find an error, please don't hesitate to file an issue or send a pull request on GitHub at *https://github.com/rust-lang/book/*. Please see *CONTRIBUTING.md* at *https://github.com/rust-lang/book/blob/master/CONTRIBUTING.md* for more details.

The source code for the examples in this book, errata, and other information are available at *https://www.nostarch.com/Rust/*.

1

GETTING STARTED

Let's start your Rust journey! There's a lot to learn, but every journey starts somewhere. In this chapter, we'll discuss:

- Installing Rust on Linux, macOS, and Windows
- Writing a program that prints `Hello, world!`
- Using `cargo`, Rust's package manager and build system

Installation

The first step is to install Rust. We'll download Rust through `rustup`, a command line tool for managing Rust versions and associated tools. You'll need an internet connection for the download.

NOTE   *If you prefer not to use* `rustup` *for some reason, please see the Rust installation page at* https://www.rust-lang.org/install.html *for other options.*

The following steps install the latest stable version of the Rust compiler. All the examples and output in this book use stable Rust 1.21.0. Rust's stability guarantees ensure that all the examples in the book that compile will continue to compile with newer Rust versions. The output might differ slightly between versions, because Rust often improves error messages and warnings. In other words, any newer, stable version of Rust you install using these steps should work as expected with the content of this book.

COMMAND LINE NOTATION

In this chapter and throughout the book, we'll show some commands used in the terminal. Lines that you should enter in a terminal all start with $. You don't need to type in the $ character; it indicates the start of each command. Lines that don't start with $ typically show the output of the previous command. Additionally, PowerShell-specific examples will use > rather than $.

Installing rustup on Linux or macOS

If you're using Linux or macOS, open a terminal and enter the following command:

```
$ curl https://sh.rustup.rs -sSf | sh
```

The command downloads a script and starts the installation of the rustup tool, which installs the latest stable version of Rust. You might be prompted for your password. If the install is successful, the following line will appear:

```
Rust is installed now. Great!
```

If you prefer, feel free to download the script and inspect it before running it.

The installation script automatically adds Rust to your system PATH after your next login. If you want to start using Rust right away instead of restarting your terminal, run the following command in your shell to add Rust to your system PATH manually:

```
$ source $HOME/.cargo/env
```

Alternatively, you can add the following line to your *~/.bash_profile*:

```
$ export PATH="$HOME/.cargo/bin:$PATH"
```

Additionally, you'll need a linker of some kind. It's likely one is already installed, but when you try to compile a Rust program and get errors indicating that a linker could not execute, that means a linker isn't installed on your system and you'll need to install one manually. C compilers usually come with the correct linker. Check your platform's documentation for how to install a C compiler. Also, some common Rust packages depend on C code and will need a C compiler. Therefore, it might be worth installing one now.

Installing rustup on Windows

On Windows, go to *https://www.rust-lang.org/install.html* and follow the instructions for installing Rust. At some point in the installation, you'll receive a message explaining that you'll also need the C++ build tools for Visual Studio 2013 or later. The easiest way to acquire the build tools is to install Build Tools for Visual Studio 2017 at *https://www.visualstudio.com/downloads/.* The tools are in the Other Tools and Frameworks section.

The rest of this book uses commands that work in both *cmd.exe* and PowerShell. If there are specific differences, we'll explain which to use.

Updating and Uninstalling

After you've installed Rust via rustup, updating to the latest version is easy. From your shell, run the following update script:

```
$ rustup update
```

To uninstall Rust and rustup, run the following uninstall script from your shell:

```
$ rustup self uninstall
```

Troubleshooting

To check whether you have Rust installed correctly, open a shell and enter this line:

```
$ rustc --version
```

You should see the version number, commit hash, and commit date for the latest stable version that has been released in the following format:

```
rustc x.y.z (abcabcabc yyyy-mm-dd)
```

If you see this information, you have installed Rust successfully! If you don't see this information and you're on Windows, check that Rust is in your %PATH% system variable. If that's all correct and Rust still isn't working, there are a number of places you can get help. The easiest is the #rust IRC channel on *irc.mozilla.org*, which you can access through Mibbit at *http://chat.mibbit.com/?server=irc.mozilla.org&channel=%23rust/.* At that address you can chat with other Rustaceans (a silly nickname we call ourselves) who can help you out. Other great resources include the Users forum at *https://users.rust-lang.org/* and Stack Overflow at *http://stackoverflow .com/questions/tagged/rust/*.

Local Documentation

The installer also includes a copy of the documentation locally, so you can read it offline. Run rustup doc to open the local documentation in your browser.

Any time a type or function is provided by the standard library and you're not sure what it does or how to use it, use the application programming interface (API) documentation to find out!

Hello, World!

Now that you've installed Rust, let's write your first Rust program. It's traditional when learning a new language to write a little program that prints the text Hello, world! to the screen, so we'll do the same here!

NOTE   *This book assumes basic familiarity with the command line. Rust makes no specific demands about your editing or tooling or where your code lives, so if you prefer to use an integrated development environment (IDE) instead of the command line, feel free to use your favorite IDE. Many IDEs now have some degree of Rust support; check the IDE's documentation for details. Recently, the Rust team has been focusing on enabling great IDE support, and progress has been made rapidly on that front!*

Creating a Project Directory

You'll start by making a directory to store your Rust code. It doesn't matter to Rust where your code lives, but for the exercises and projects in this book, we suggest making a *projects* directory in your home directory and keeping all your projects there.

Open a terminal and enter the following commands to make a *projects* directory and a directory for the Hello, world! project within the *projects* directory.

For Linux and macOS, enter this:

```
$ mkdir ~/projects
$ cd ~/projects
$ mkdir hello_world
$ cd hello_world
```

For Windows CMD, enter this:

```
> mkdir "%USERPROFILE%\projects"
> cd /d "%USERPROFILE%\projects"
> mkdir hello_world
> cd hello_world
```

For Windows PowerShell, enter this:

```
> mkdir $env:USERPROFILE\projects
> cd $env:USERPROFILE\projects
> mkdir hello_world
> cd hello_world
```

Writing and Running a Rust Program

Next, make a new source file and call it *main.rs*. Rust files always end with the *.rs* extension. If you're using more than one word in your filename, use an underscore to separate them. For example, use *hello_world.rs* rather than *helloworld.rs*.

Now open the *main.rs* file you just created and enter the code in Listing 1-1.

main.rs

```
fn main() {
    println!("Hello, world!");
}
```

Listing 1-1: A program that prints Hello, world!

Save the file and go back to your terminal window. On Linux or macOS, enter the following commands to compile and run the file:

```
$ rustc main.rs
$ ./main
Hello, world!
```

On Windows, enter the command .\main.exe instead of ./main:

```
> rustc main.rs
> .\main.exe
Hello, world!
```

Regardless of your operating system, the string Hello, world! should print to the terminal. If you don't see this output, refer to "Troubleshooting" on page 3 for ways to get help.

If Hello, world! did print, congratulations! You've officially written a Rust program. That makes you a Rust programmer—welcome!

Anatomy of a Rust Program

Let's review in detail what just happened in your Hello, world! program. Here's the first piece of the puzzle:

```
fn main() {

}
```

These lines define a function in Rust. The main function is special: it is always the first code that runs in every executable Rust program. The first line declares a function named main that has no parameters and returns nothing. If there were parameters, they would go inside the parentheses, ().

Also, note that the function body is wrapped in curly brackets, {}. Rust requires these around all function bodies. It's good style to place the opening curly bracket on the same line as the function declaration, adding one space in between.

At the time of this writing, an automatic formatter tool called rustfmt is under development. If you want to stick to a standard style across Rust projects, rustfmt will format your code in a particular style. The Rust team plans to eventually include this tool with the standard Rust distribution, like rustc. So depending on when you read this book, it might already be installed on your computer! Check the online documentation for more details.

Inside the main function is the following code:

```
println!("Hello, world!");
```

This line does all the work in this little program: it prints text to the screen. There are four important details to notice here. First, Rust style is to indent with four spaces, not a tab.

Second, println! calls a Rust macro. If it called a function instead, it would be entered as println (without the !). We'll discuss Rust macros in more detail in Appendix D. For now, you just need to know that using a ! means that you're calling a macro instead of a normal function.

Third, you see the "Hello, world!" string. We pass this string as an argument to println!, and the string is printed to the screen.

Fourth, we end the line with a semicolon (;), which indicates that this expression is over and the next one is ready to begin. Most lines of Rust code end with a semicolon.

Compiling and Running Are Separate Steps

You've just run a newly created program, so let's examine each step in the process.

Before running a Rust program, you must compile it using the Rust compiler by entering the rustc command and passing it the name of your source file, like this:

```
$ rustc main.rs
```

If you have a C or C++ background, you'll notice that this is similar to gcc or clang. After compiling successfully, Rust outputs a binary executable.

On Linux, macOS, and PowerShell on Windows, you can see the executable by entering the ls command in your shell as follows:

```
$ ls
main  main.rs
```

With CMD on Windows, you would enter the following:

```
> dir /B %= the /B option says to only show the file names =%
main.exe
main.pdb
main.rs
```

This shows the source code file with the *.rs* extension, the executable file (*main.exe* on Windows but *main* on all other platforms), and, when using CMD, a file containing debugging information with the *.pdb* extension. From here, you run the *main* or *main.exe* file, like this:

```
$ ./main  # or .\main.exe on Windows
```

If *main.rs* was your Hello, world! program, this line would print `Hello, world!` to your terminal.

If you're more familiar with a dynamic language, such as Ruby, Python, or JavaScript, you might not be used to compiling and running a program as separate steps. Rust is an *ahead-of-time compiled* language, meaning you can compile a program and give the executable to someone else, and they can run it even without having Rust installed. If you give someone a *.rb*, *.py*, or *.js* file, they need to have a Ruby, Python, or JavaScript implementation installed (respectively). But in those languages, you need only one command to compile and run your program. Everything is a trade-off in language design.

Just compiling with `rustc` is fine for simple programs, but as your project grows, you'll want to manage all the options and make it easy to share your code. Next, we'll introduce you to the Cargo tool, which will help you write real-world Rust programs.

Hello, Cargo!

Cargo is Rust's build system and package manager. Most Rustaceans use this tool to manage their Rust projects because Cargo handles a lot of tasks for you, such as building your code, downloading the libraries your code depends on, and building those libraries. (We call libraries your code needs *dependencies*.)

The simplest Rust programs, like the one we've written so far, don't have any dependencies. So if we had built the Hello, world! project with Cargo, it would only use the part of Cargo that handles building your code. As you write more complex Rust programs, you'll add dependencies, and if you start a project using Cargo, adding dependencies will be much easier to do.

Because the vast majority of Rust projects use Cargo, the rest of this book assumes that you're using Cargo, too. Cargo comes installed with Rust if you used the official installers discussed in "Installation" on page 1. If you installed Rust through some other means, check whether Cargo is installed by entering the following into your terminal:

```
$ cargo --version
```

If you see a version number, you have it! If you see an error, such as `command not found`, look at the documentation for your method of installation to determine how to install Cargo separately.

Creating a Project with Cargo

Let's create a new project using Cargo and look at how it differs from our original Hello, world! project. Navigate back to your *projects* directory (or wherever you decided to store your code). Then, on any operating system, run the following:

```
$ cargo new hello_cargo --bin
$ cd hello_cargo
```

The first command creates a new binary executable called *hello_cargo*. The `--bin` argument passed to `cargo new` makes an executable application (often just called a *binary*) as opposed to a library. We've named our project *hello_cargo*, and Cargo creates its files in a directory of the same name.

Go into the *hello_cargo* directory and list the files. You'll see that Cargo has generated two files and one directory for us: a *Cargo.toml* file and a *src* directory with a *main.rs* file inside. It has also initialized a new Git repository along with a *.gitignore* file.

NOTE *Git is a common version control system. You can change `cargo new` to use a different version control system or no version control system by using the `--vcs` flag. Run `cargo new --help` to see the available options.*

Open *Cargo.toml* in your text editor of choice. It should look similar to the code in Listing 1-2.

Cargo.toml

```
[package]
name = "hello_cargo"
version = "0.1.0"
authors = ["Your Name <you@example.com>"]

[dependencies]
```

Listing 1-2: Contents of Cargo.toml *generated by* `cargo new`

This file is in the *TOML* (*Tom's Obvious, Minimal Language*) format, which is Cargo's configuration format.

The first line, [package], is a section heading that indicates that the following statements are configuring a package. As we add more information to this file, we'll add other sections.

The next three lines set the configuration information Cargo needs to compile your program: the name, the version, and who wrote it. Cargo gets your name and email information from your environment, so if that information is not correct, fix the information now and then save the file.

The last line, [dependencies], is the start of a section for you to list any of your project's dependencies. In Rust, packages of code are referred to as *crates*. We won't need any other crates for this project, but we will in the first project in Chapter 2, so we'll use this dependencies section then.

Now open *src/main.rs* and take a look:

src/main.rs

```
fn main() {
    println!("Hello, world!");
}
```

Cargo has generated a Hello, world! program for you, just like the one we wrote in Listing 1-1! So far, the differences between our previous project and the project Cargo generates are that Cargo placed the code in the *src* directory and we have a *Cargo.toml* configuration file in the top directory.

Cargo expects your source files to live inside the *src* directory. The top-level project directory is just for README files, license information, configuration files, and anything else not related to your code. Using Cargo helps you organize your projects. There's a place for everything, and everything is in its place.

If you started a project that doesn't use Cargo, as we did with the Hello, world! project, you can convert it to a project that does use Cargo. Move the project code into the *src* directory and create an appropriate *Cargo.toml* file.

Building and Running a Cargo Project

Now let's look at what's different when we build and run the Hello, world! program with Cargo! From your *hello_cargo* directory, build your project by entering the following command:

```
$ cargo build
   Compiling hello_cargo v0.1.0 (file:///projects/hello_cargo)
    Finished dev [unoptimized + debuginfo] target(s) in 2.85 secs
```

This command creates an executable file in *target/debug/hello_cargo* (or *target\debug\hello_cargo.exe* on Windows) rather than in your current directory. You can run the executable with this command:

```
$ ./target/debug/hello_cargo # or .\target\debug\hello_cargo.exe on Windows
Hello, world!
```

If all goes well, Hello, world! should print to the terminal. Running cargo build for the first time also causes Cargo to create a new file at the top level: *Cargo.lock*. This file keeps track of the exact versions of dependencies in your project. This project doesn't have dependencies, so the file is a bit sparse. You won't ever need to change this file manually; Cargo manages its contents for you.

We just built a project with `cargo build` and ran it with `./target/debug/hello_cargo`, but we can also use `cargo run` to compile the code and then run the resulting executable all in one command:

```
$ cargo run
   Finished dev [unoptimized + debuginfo] target(s) in 0.0 secs
    Running `target/debug/hello_cargo`
Hello, world!
```

Notice that this time we didn't see output indicating that Cargo was compiling `hello_cargo`. Cargo figured out that the files hadn't changed, so it just ran the binary. If you had modified your source code, Cargo would have rebuilt the project before running it, and you would have seen this output:

```
$ cargo run
   Compiling hello_cargo v0.1.0 (file:///projects/hello_cargo)
   Finished dev [unoptimized + debuginfo] target(s) in 0.33 secs
    Running `target/debug/hello_cargo`
Hello, world!
```

Cargo also provides a command called `cargo check`. This command quickly checks your code to make sure it compiles but doesn't produce an executable:

```
$ cargo check
   Compiling hello_cargo v0.1.0 (file:///projects/hello_cargo)
   Finished dev [unoptimized + debuginfo] target(s) in 0.32 secs
```

Why would you not want an executable? Often, `cargo check` is much faster than `cargo build`, because it skips the step of producing an executable. If you're continually checking your work while writing the code, using `cargo check` will speed up the process! As such, many Rustaceans run `cargo check` periodically as they write their program to make sure it compiles. Then they run `cargo build` when they're ready to use the executable.

Let's recap what we've learned so far about Cargo:

- We can build a project using `cargo build` or `cargo check`.
- We can build and run a project in one step using `cargo run`.
- Instead of saving the result of the build in the same directory as our code, Cargo stores it in the *target/debug* directory.

An additional advantage of using Cargo is that the commands are the same no matter which operating system you're working on. So, at this point, we'll no longer provide specific instructions for Linux and macOS versus Windows.

Building for Release

When your project is finally ready for release, you can use `cargo build --release` to compile it with optimizations. This command will create an executable in *target/release* instead of *target/debug*. The optimizations make your Rust code run faster, but turning them on lengthens the time it takes for your program to compile. This is why there are two different profiles: one for development, when you want to rebuild quickly and often, and another for building the final program you'll give to a user that won't be rebuilt repeatedly and that will run as fast as possible. If you're benchmarking your code's running time, be sure to run `cargo build --release` and benchmark with the executable in *target/release*.

Cargo as Convention

With simple projects, Cargo doesn't provide a lot of value over just using rustc, but it will prove its worth as your programs become more intricate. With complex projects composed of multiple crates, it's much easier to let Cargo coordinate the build.

Even though the hello_cargo project is simple, it now uses much of the real tooling you'll use in the rest of your Rust career. In fact, to work on any existing projects, you can use the following commands to check out the code using Git, change to that project's directory, and build:

```
$ git clone someurl.com/someproject
$ cd someproject
$ cargo build
```

For more information about Cargo, check out its documentation at *https://doc.rust-lang.org/cargo/*.

Summary

You're already off to a great start on your Rust journey! In this chapter, you've learned how to:

- Install the latest stable version of Rust using rustup
- Update to a newer Rust version
- Open locally installed documentation
- Write and run a Hello, world! program using rustc directly
- Create and run a new project using the conventions of Cargo

This is a great time to build a more substantial program to get used to reading and writing Rust code. So, in Chapter 2, we'll build a guessing game program. If you would rather start by learning how common programming concepts work in Rust, see Chapter 3 and then return to Chapter 2.

2

PROGRAMMING A GUESSING GAME

Let's jump into Rust by working through a hands-on project together! This chapter introduces you to a few common Rust concepts by showing you how to use them in a real program. You'll learn about `let`, `match`, methods, associated functions, external crates, and more! The following chapters will explore these ideas in more detail. In this chapter, you'll practice the fundamentals.

We'll implement a classic beginner programming problem: a guessing game. Here's how it works: the program will generate a random integer between 1 and 100. It will then prompt the player to enter a guess. After a guess is entered, the program will indicate whether the guess is too low or too high. If the guess is correct, the game will print a congratulatory message and exit.

Setting Up a New Project

To set up a new project, go to the *projects* directory that you created in Chapter 1 and make a new project using Cargo, like so:

```
$ cargo new guessing_game --bin
$ cd guessing_game
```

The first command, cargo new, takes the name of the project (guessing_game) as the first argument. The --bin flag tells Cargo to make a binary project, like the one in Chapter 1. The second command changes to the new project's directory.

Look at the generated *Cargo.toml* file:

Cargo.toml
```
[package]
name = "guessing_game"
version = "0.1.0"
authors = ["Your Name <you@example.com>"]

[dependencies]
```

If the author information that Cargo obtained from your environment is not correct, fix that in the file and save it again.

As you saw in Chapter 1, cargo new generates a "Hello, world!" program for you. Check out the *src/main.rs* file:

src/main.rs
```
fn main() {
    println!("Hello, world!");
}
```

Now let's compile this "Hello, world!" program and run it in the same step using the cargo run command:

```
$ cargo run
   Compiling guessing_game v0.1.0 (file:///projects/guessing_game)
    Finished dev [unoptimized + debuginfo] target(s) in 1.50 secs
     Running `target/debug/guessing_game`
Hello, world!
```

The run command comes in handy when you need to rapidly iterate on a project, as we'll do in this game, quickly testing each iteration before moving on to the next one.

Reopen the *src/main.rs* file. You'll be writing all the code in this file.

Processing a Guess

The first part of the guessing game program will ask for user input, process that input, and check that the input is in the expected form. To start, we'll allow the player to input a guess. Enter the code in Listing 2-1 into *src/main.rs*.

```
use std::io;

fn main() {
    println!("Guess the number!");

    println!("Please input your guess.");

    let mut guess = String::new();

    io::stdin().read_line(&mut guess)
        .expect("Failed to read line");

    println!("You guessed: {}", guess);
}
```

Listing 2-1: Code that gets a guess from the user and prints it

This code contains a lot of information, so let's go over it line by line. To obtain user input and then print the result as output, we need to bring the io (input/output) library into scope. The io library comes from the standard library (which is known as std):

```
use std::io;
```

By default, Rust brings only a few types into the scope of every program in the *prelude*. If a type you want to use isn't in the prelude, you have to bring that type into scope explicitly with a use statement. Using the std::io library provides you with a number of useful features, including the ability to accept user input.

As you saw in Chapter 1, the main function is the entry point into the program:

```
fn main() {
```

The fn syntax declares a new function, the parentheses, (), indicate there are no parameters, and the curly bracket, {, starts the body of the function.

As you also learned in Chapter 1, println! is a macro that prints a string to the screen:

```
println!("Guess the number!");

println!("Please input your guess.");
```

This code is printing a prompt stating what the game is and requesting input from the user.

Storing Values with Variables

Next, we'll create a place to store the user input, like this:

```
let mut guess = String::new();
```

Now the program is getting interesting! There's a lot going on in this little line. Notice that this is a let statement, which is used to create a *variable*. Here's another example:

```
let foo = bar;
```

This line creates a new variable named foo and binds it to the value bar. In Rust, variables are immutable by default. We'll discuss this concept in detail in "Variables and Mutability" on page 32. The following example shows how to use mut before the variable name to make a variable mutable:

```
let foo = 5; // immutable
let mut bar = 5; // mutable
```

NOTE *The // syntax starts a comment that continues until the end of the line. Rust ignores everything in comments, which are discussed in more detail in Chapter 3.*

Let's return to the guessing game program. You now know that let mut guess will introduce a mutable variable named guess. On the other side of the equal sign (=) is the value that guess is bound to, which is the result of calling String::new, a function that returns a new instance of a String. String is a string type provided by the standard library that is a growable, UTF-8 encoded bit of text.

The :: syntax in the ::new line indicates that new is an *associated function* of the String type. An associated function is implemented on a type, in this case String, rather than on a particular instance of a String. Some languages call this a *static method*.

This new function creates a new, empty string. You'll find a new function on many types, because it's a common name for a function that makes a new value of some kind.

To summarize, the let mut guess = String::new(); line has created a mutable variable that is currently bound to a new, empty instance of a String. Whew!

Recall that we included the input/output functionality from the standard library with use std::io; on the first line of the program. Now we'll call an associated function, stdin, on io:

```
io::stdin().read_line(&mut guess)
    .expect("Failed to read line");
```

If we hadn't listed the use std::io line at the beginning of the program, we could have written this function call as std::io::stdin. The stdin function returns an instance of std::io::Stdin, which is a type that represents a handle to the standard input for your terminal.

The next part of the code, .read_line(&mut guess), calls the read_line method on the standard input handle to get input from the user. We're also passing one argument to read_line: &mut guess.

The job of read_line is to take whatever the user types into standard input and place that into a string, so it takes that string as an argument. The string argument needs to be mutable so the method can change the string's content by adding the user input.

The & indicates that this argument is a *reference*, which gives you a way to let multiple parts of your code access one piece of data without needing to copy that data into memory multiple times. References are a complex feature, and one of Rust's major advantages is how safe and easy it is to use references. You don't need to know a lot of those details to finish this program. For now, all you need to know is that like variables, references are immutable by default. Hence, you need to write &mut guess rather than &guess to make it mutable. (Chapter 4 will explain references more thoroughly.)

Handling Potential Failure with the Result Type

We're not quite done with this line of code. Although what we've discussed so far is a single line of text, it's only the first part of the single logical line of code. The second part is this method:

```
.expect("Failed to read line");
```

When you call a method with the .foo() syntax, it's often wise to introduce a newline and other whitespace to help break up long lines. We could have written this code as:

```
io::stdin().read_line(&mut guess).expect("Failed to read line");
```

However, one long line is difficult to read, so it's best to divide it: two lines for two method calls. Now let's discuss what this line does.

As mentioned earlier, read_line puts what the user types into the string we're passing it, but it also returns a value—in this case, an io::Result. Rust has a number of types named Result in its standard library: a generic Result as well as specific versions for submodules, such as io::Result.

The Result types are *enumerations*, often referred to as *enums*. An enumeration is a type that can have a fixed set of values, and those values are called the enum's *variants*. Chapter 6 will cover enums in more detail.

For Result, the variants are Ok or Err. The Ok variant indicates the operation was successful, and inside Ok is the successfully generated value. The Err variant means the operation failed, and Err contains information about how or why the operation failed.

The purpose of these Result types is to encode error-handling information. Values of the Result type, like values of any type, have methods defined on them. An instance of io::Result has an expect method that you can call. If this instance of io::Result is an Err value, expect will cause the program to crash and display the message that you passed as an argument to expect. If the read_line method returns an Err, it would likely be the result of an error coming from the underlying operating system. If this instance of io::Result is an Ok value, expect will take the return value that Ok is holding and return just that value to you so you can use it. In this case, that value is the number of bytes in what the user entered into standard input.

If you don't call expect, the program will compile, but you'll get a warning:

```
$ cargo build
   Compiling guessing_game v0.1.0 (file:///projects/guessing_game)
warning: unused `std::result::Result` which must be used
  --> src/main.rs:10:5
   |
10 |     io::stdin().read_line(&mut guess);
   |     ^^^^^^^^^^^^^^^^^^^^^^^^^^^^^^^^^^
   |
   = note: #[warn(unused_must_use)] on by default
```

Rust warns that you haven't used the Result value returned from read_line, indicating that the program hasn't handled a possible error.

The right way to suppress the warning is to actually write error handling, but because you just want to crash this program when a problem occurs, you can use expect. You'll learn about recovering from errors in Chapter 9.

Printing Values with println! Placeholders

Aside from the closing curly brackets, there's only one more line to discuss in the code added so far, which is the following:

```
println!("You guessed: {}", guess);
```

This line prints the string we saved the user's input in. The set of curly brackets, {}, is a placeholder: think of {} as little crab pincers that hold a value in place. You can print more than one value using curly brackets: the first set of curly brackets holds the first value listed after the format string, the second set holds the second value, and so on. Printing multiple values in one call to println! would look like this:

```
let x = 5;
let y = 10;

println!("x = {} and y = {}", x, y);
```

This code would print x = 5 and y = 10.

Testing the First Part

Let's test the first part of the guessing game. Run it using **cargo run**:

```
$ cargo run
   Compiling guessing_game v0.1.0 (file:///projects/guessing_game)
    Finished dev [unoptimized + debuginfo] target(s) in 1.50 secs
     Running `target/debug/guessing_game`
Guess the number!
```

```
Please input your guess.
6
You guessed: 6
```

At this point, the first part of the game is done: we're getting input from the keyboard and then printing it.

Generating a Secret Number

Next, we need to generate a secret number that the user will try to guess. The secret number should be different every time so the game is fun to play more than once. Let's use a random number between 1 and 100 so the game isn't too difficult. Rust doesn't yet include random number functionality in its standard library. However, the Rust team does provide a rand crate at *https://crates.io/crates/rand/*.

Using a Crate to Get More Functionality

Remember that a crate is a package of Rust code. The project we've been building is a *binary crate*, which is an executable. The rand crate is a *library crate*, which contains code intended to be used in other programs.

Cargo's use of external crates is where it really shines. Before we can write code that uses rand, we need to modify the *Cargo.toml* file to include the rand crate as a dependency. Open that file now and add the following line to the bottom beneath the [dependencies] section header that Cargo created for you:

Cargo.toml

```
[dependencies]

rand = "0.3.14"
```

In the *Cargo.toml* file, everything that follows a header is part of a section that continues until another section starts. The [dependencies] section is where you tell Cargo which external crates your project depends on and which versions of those crates you require. In this case, we'll specify the rand crate with the semantic version specifier 0.3.14. Cargo understands Semantic Versioning (sometimes called *SemVer*), which is a standard for writing version numbers. The number 0.3.14 is actually shorthand for ^0.3.14, which means "any version that has a public API compatible with version 0.3.14."

Now, without changing any of the code, let's build the project, as shown in Listing 2-2.

```
$ cargo build
    Updating registry `https://github.com/rust-lang/crates.io-index`
 Downloading rand v0.3.14
 Downloading libc v0.2.14
   Compiling libc v0.2.14
   Compiling rand v0.3.14
```

```
Compiling guessing_game v0.1.0 (file:///projects/guessing_game)
 Finished dev [unoptimized + debuginfo] target(s) in 1.50 secs
```

Listing 2-2: The output from running cargo build *after adding the rand crate as a dependency*

You may see different version numbers (but they will all be compatible with the code, thanks to SemVer!), and the lines may be in a different order.

Now that we have an external dependency, Cargo fetches the latest versions of everything from the *registry*, which is a copy of data from *https:// crates.io/*. Crates.io is where people in the Rust ecosystem post their open source Rust projects for others to use.

After updating the registry, Cargo checks the [dependencies] section and downloads any crates you don't have yet. In this case, although we only listed rand as a dependency, Cargo also grabbed a copy of libc, because rand depends on libc to work. After downloading the crates, Rust compiles them and then compiles the project with the dependencies available.

If you immediately run cargo build again without making any changes, you won't get any output aside from the Finished line. Cargo knows it has already downloaded and compiled the dependencies, and you haven't changed anything about them in your *Cargo.toml* file. Cargo also knows that you haven't changed anything about your code, so it doesn't recompile that either. With nothing to do, it simply exits.

If you open the *src/main.rs* file, make a trivial change, and then save it and build again, you'll only see two lines of output:

```
$ cargo build
  Compiling guessing_game v0.1.0 (file:///projects/guessing_game)
   Finished dev [unoptimized + debuginfo] target(s) in 1.50 secs
```

These lines show Cargo only updates the build with your tiny change to the *src/main.rs* file. Your dependencies haven't changed, so Cargo knows it can reuse what it has already downloaded and compiled for those. It just rebuilds your part of the code.

Ensuring Reproducible Builds with the Cargo.lock File

Cargo has a mechanism that ensures you can rebuild the same artifact every time you or anyone else builds your code: Cargo will use only the versions of the dependencies you specified until you indicate otherwise. For example, what happens if next week version 0.3.15 of the rand crate comes out and contains an important bug fix but also contains a regression that will break your code?

The answer to this problem is the *Cargo.lock* file, which was created the first time you ran cargo build and is now in your *guessing_game* directory. When you build a project for the first time, Cargo figures out all the versions of the dependencies that fit the criteria and then writes them to the *Cargo.lock* file. When you build your project in the future, Cargo will see that the *Cargo.lock* file exists and use the versions specified there rather than doing all the work of figuring out versions again. This lets you have a reproducible build automatically. In other words, your project will remain at 0.3.14 until you explicitly upgrade, thanks to the *Cargo.lock* file.

Updating a Crate to Get a New Version

When you *do* want to update a crate, Cargo provides another command, update, which will ignore the *Cargo.lock* file and figure out all the latest versions that fit your specifications in *Cargo.toml*. If that works, Cargo will write those versions to the *Cargo.lock* file.

But by default, Cargo will only look for versions larger than 0.3.0 and smaller than 0.4.0. If the rand crate has released two new versions, 0.3.15 and 0.4.0, you would see the following if you ran cargo update:

```
$ cargo update
    Updating registry `https://github.com/rust-lang/crates.io-index`
    Updating rand v0.3.14 -> v0.3.15
```

At this point, you would also notice a change in your *Cargo.lock* file noting that the version of the rand crate you are now using is 0.3.15.

If you wanted to use rand version 0.4.0 or any version in the 0.4.*x* series, you'd have to update the *Cargo.toml* file to look like this instead:

Cargo.toml
```
[dependencies]

rand = "0.4.0"
```

The next time you run cargo build, Cargo will update the registry of crates available and reevaluate your rand requirements according to the new version you have specified.

There's a lot more to say about Cargo and its ecosystem which we'll discuss in Chapter 14, but for now, that's all you need to know. Cargo makes it very easy to reuse libraries, so Rustaceans are able to write smaller projects that are assembled from a number of packages.

Generating a Random Number

Now that you've added the rand crate to *Cargo.toml*, let's start using rand. The next step is to update *src/main.rs*, as shown in Listing 2-3.

src/main.rs
```
❶ extern crate rand;

  use std::io;
❷ use rand::Rng;

  fn main() {
      println!("Guess the number!");

    ❸ let secret_number = rand::thread_rng().gen_range(1, 101);

      println!("The secret number is: {}", secret_number);
```

```
    println!("Please input your guess.");

    let mut guess = String::new();

    io::stdin().read_line(&mut guess)
        .expect("Failed to read line");

    println!("You guessed: {}", guess);
}
```

Listing 2-3: Adding code to generate a random number

First, we add a line that lets Rust know we'll be using the rand crate as an external dependency ❶. This also does the equivalent of calling use rand, so now we can call anything in the rand crate by placing rand:: before it.

Next, we add another use line: use rand::Rng ❷. The Rng trait defines methods that random number generators implement, and this trait must be in scope for us to use those methods. Chapter 10 will cover traits in detail.

Also, we're adding two more lines in the middle ❸. The rand::thread_rng function will give us the particular random number generator that we're going to use: one that is local to the current thread of execution and seeded by the operating system. Next, we call the gen_range method on the random number generator. This method is defined by the Rng trait that we brought into scope with the use rand::Rng statement. The gen_range method takes two numbers as arguments and generates a random number between them. It's inclusive on the lower bound but exclusive on the upper bound, so we need to specify 1 and 101 to request a number between 1 and 100.

NOTE   *You won't just know which traits to use and which functions and methods to call from a crate. Instructions for using a crate are in each crate's documentation. Another neat feature of Cargo is that you can run the cargo doc --open command, which will build documentation provided by all of your dependencies locally and open it in your browser. If you're interested in other functionality in the rand crate, for example, run cargo doc --open and click **rand** in the sidebar on the left.*

The second line that we added to the code prints the secret number. This is useful while we're developing the program to be able to test it, but we'll delete it from the final version. It's not much of a game if the program prints the answer as soon as it starts!

Try running the program a few times:

```
$ cargo run
   Compiling guessing_game v0.1.0 (file:///projects/guessing_game)
   Finished dev [unoptimized + debuginfo] target(s) in 1.50 secs
     Running `target/debug/guessing_game`
Guess the number!
The secret number is: 7
Please input your guess.
4
You guessed: 4
```

```
$ cargo run
    Running `target/debug/guessing_game`
Guess the number!
The secret number is: 83
Please input your guess.
5
You guessed: 5
```

You should get different random numbers, and they should all be numbers between 1 and 100. Great job!

Comparing the Guess to the Secret Number

Now that we have user input and a random number, we can compare them. That step is shown in Listing 2-4. Note that this code won't compile quite yet, as we will explain.

src/main.rs

```
extern crate rand;

use std::io;
❶ use std::cmp::Ordering;
use rand::Rng;

fn main() {

    // --snip--

    println!("You guessed: {}", guess);

    match❷ guess.cmp(&secret_number)❸ {
        Ordering::Less => println!("Too small!"),
        Ordering::Greater => println!("Too big!"),
        Ordering::Equal => println!("You win!"),
    }
}
```

Listing 2-4: Handling the possible return values of comparing two numbers

The first new bit here is another use statement ❶, bringing a type called std::cmp::Ordering into scope from the standard library. Like Result, Ordering is another enum, but the variants for Ordering are Less, Greater, and Equal. These are the three outcomes that are possible when you compare two values.

Then we add five new lines at the bottom that use the Ordering type. The cmp method ❸ compares two values and can be called on anything that can be compared. It takes a reference to whatever you want to compare with: here it's comparing the guess to the secret_number. Then it returns a variant of the Ordering enum we brought into scope with the use statement. We use a match expression ❷ to decide what to do next based on which variant of Ordering was returned from the call to cmp with the values in guess and secret_number.

A match expression is made up of *arms*. An arm consists of a *pattern* and the code that should be run if the value given to the beginning of the match expression fits that arm's pattern. Rust takes the value given to match and looks through each arm's pattern in turn. The match construct and patterns are powerful features in Rust that let you express a variety of situations your code might encounter and make sure that you handle them all. These features will be covered in detail in Chapter 6 and Chapter 18, respectively.

Let's walk through an example of what would happen with the match expression used here. Say that the user has guessed 50 and the randomly generated secret number this time is 38. When the code compares 50 to 38, the cmp method will return Ordering::Greater, because 50 is greater than 38. The match expression gets the Ordering::Greater value and starts checking each arm's pattern. It looks at the first arm's pattern, Ordering::Less, and sees that the value Ordering::Greater does not match Ordering::Less, so it ignores the code in that arm and moves to the next arm. The next arm's pattern, Ordering::Greater, *does* match Ordering::Greater! The associated code in that arm will execute and print Too big! to the screen. The match expression ends because it has no need to look at the last arm in this scenario.

However, the code in Listing 2-4 won't compile yet. Let's try it:

```
$ cargo build
   Compiling guessing_game v0.1.0 (file:///projects/guessing_game)
error[E0308]: mismatched types
  --> src/main.rs:23:21
   |
23 |     match guess.cmp(&secret_number) {
   |                     ^^^^^^^^^^^^^^ expected struct `std::string::String`,
found integral variable
   |
   = note: expected type `&std::string::String`
   = note:    found type `&{integer}`

error: aborting due to previous error
Could not compile `guessing_game`.
```

The core of the error states that there are *mismatched types*. Rust has a strong, static type system. However, it also has type inference. When we wrote let guess = String::new(), Rust was able to infer that guess should be a String and didn't make us write the type. The secret_number, on the other hand, is a number type. A few number types can have a value between 1 and 100: i32, a 32-bit number; u32, an unsigned 32-bit number; i64, a 64-bit number; as well as others. Rust defaults to an i32, which is the type of secret_number unless you add type information elsewhere that would cause Rust to infer a different numerical type. The reason for the error here is that Rust cannot compare a string and a number type.

Ultimately, we want to convert the String the program reads as input into a real number type so we can compare it numerically to the guess. We can do that by adding the following two lines to the main function body:

src/main.rs

```
// --snip--

    let mut guess = String::new();

    io::stdin().read_line(&mut guess)
        .expect("Failed to read line");

    let guess: u32 = guess.trim().parse()
        .expect("Please type a number!");

    println!("You guessed: {}", guess);

    match guess.cmp(&secret_number) {
        Ordering::Less => println!("Too small!"),
        Ordering::Greater => println!("Too big!"),
        Ordering::Equal => println!("You win!"),
    }
}
```

We create a variable named guess. But wait, doesn't the program already have a variable named guess? It does, but Rust allows us to *shadow* the previous value of guess with a new one. This feature is often used in situations in which you want to convert a value from one type to another type. Shadowing lets us reuse the guess variable name rather than forcing us to create two unique variables, such as guess_str and guess, for example. (Chapter 3 covers shadowing in more detail.)

We bind guess to the expression guess.trim().parse(). The guess in the expression refers to the original guess that was a String with the input in it. The trim method on a String instance will eliminate any whitespace at the beginning and end. Although u32 can contain only numerical characters, the user must press ENTER to satisfy read_line. When the user presses ENTER, a newline character is added to the string. For example, if the user types 5 and presses ENTER, guess looks like this: 5\n. The \n represents "newline," the result of pressing ENTER. The trim method eliminates \n, resulting in just 5.

The parse method on strings parses a string into some kind of number. Because this method can parse a variety of number types, we need to tell Rust the exact number type we want by using let guess: u32. The colon (:) after guess tells Rust we'll annotate the variable's type. Rust has a few built-in number types; the u32 seen here is an unsigned, 32-bit integer. It's a good default choice for a small positive number. You'll learn about other number types in Chapter 3. Additionally, the u32 annotation in this example program and the comparison with secret_number mean that Rust will infer that secret_number should be a u32 type as well. So now the comparison will be between two values of the same type!

The call to parse could easily cause an error. If, for example, the string contained A⌀%, there would be no way to convert that to a number. Because it might fail, the parse method returns a Result type, much as the read_line method does (discussed in "Handling Potential Failure with the Result Type" on page 17). We'll treat this Result the same way by using the expect method again. If parse returns an Err Result variant because it couldn't create a number from the string, the expect call will crash the game and print the message we give it. If parse can successfully convert the string to a number, it will return the Ok variant of Result, and expect will return the number that we want from the Ok value.

Let's run the program now!

```
$ cargo run
   Compiling guessing_game v0.1.0 (file:///projects/guessing_game)
   Finished dev[unoptimized + debuginfo] target(s) in 1.50 secs
    Running `target/debug/guessing_game`
Guess the number!
The secret number is: 58
Please input your guess.
  76
You guessed: 76
Too big!
```

Nice! Even though spaces were added before the guess, the program still figured out that the user guessed 76. Run the program a few times to verify the different behavior with different kinds of input: guess the number correctly, guess a number that is too high, and guess a number that is too low.

We have most of the game working now, but the user can make only one guess. Let's change that by adding a loop!

Allowing Multiple Guesses with Looping

The loop keyword creates an infinite loop. We'll add that now to give users more chances at guessing the number:

src/main.rs

```
// --snip--

    println!("The secret number is: {}", secret_number);

    loop {
        println!("Please input your guess.");

        // --snip--

        match guess.cmp(&secret_number) {
            Ordering::Less => println!("Too small!"),
            Ordering::Greater => println!("Too big!"),
            Ordering::Equal => println!("You win!"),
        }
    }
}
```

As you can see, we've moved everything into a loop from the guess input prompt onward. Be sure to indent the lines inside the loop another four spaces each and run the program again. Notice that there is a new problem because the program is doing exactly what we told it to do: ask for another guess forever! It doesn't seem like the user can quit!

The user could always halt the program by using the keyboard short-cut CTRL-C. But there's another way to escape this insatiable monster, as mentioned in the parse discussion in "Comparing the Guess to the Secret Number" on page 23: if the user enters a non-number answer, the program will crash. The user can take advantage of that in order to quit, as shown here:

```
$ cargo run
   Compiling guessing_game v0.1.0 (file:///projects/guessing_game)
    Finished dev [unoptimized + debuginfo] target(s) in 1.50 secs
     Running `target/debug/guessing_game`
Guess the number!
The secret number is: 59
Please input your guess.
45
You guessed: 45
Too small!
Please input your guess.
60
You guessed: 60
Too big!
Please input your guess.
59
You guessed: 59
You win!
Please input your guess.
quit
thread 'main' panicked at 'Please type a number!: ParseIntError { kind:
InvalidDigit }', src/libcore/result.rs:785
note: Run with `RUST_BACKTRACE=1` for a backtrace.
```

Typing quit actually quits the game, but so will any other non-number input. However, this is suboptimal to say the least. We want the game to automatically stop when the correct number is guessed.

Quitting After a Correct Guess

Let's program the game to quit when the user wins by adding a break statement:

src/main.rs

```
// --snip--

        match guess.cmp(&secret_number) {
            Ordering::Less => println!("Too small!"),
            Ordering::Greater => println!("Too big!"),
            Ordering::Equal => {
```

```
            println!("You win!");
            break;
        }
      }
    }
}
```

Adding the break line after You win! makes the program exit the loop when the user guesses the secret number correctly. Exiting the loop also means exiting the program, because the loop is the last part of main.

Handling Invalid Input

To further refine the game's behavior, rather than crashing the program when the user inputs a non-number, let's make the game ignore a non-number so the user can continue guessing. We can do that by altering the line where guess is converted from a String to a u32, as shown in Listing 2-5.

src/main.rs

```
// --snip--

io::stdin().read_line(&mut guess)
    .expect("Failed to read line");

let guess: u32 = match guess.trim().parse() {
    Ok(num) => num,
    Err(_) => continue,
};

println!("You guessed: {}", guess);

// --snip--
```

Listing 2-5: Ignoring a non-number guess and asking for another guess instead of crashing the program

Switching from an expect call to a match expression is how you generally move from crashing on an error to handling the error. Remember that parse returns a Result type and Result is an enum that has the variants Ok or Err. We're using a match expression here, as we did with the Ordering result of the cmp method.

If parse is able to successfully turn the string into a number, it will return an Ok value that contains the resulting number. That Ok value will match the first arm's pattern, and the match expression will just return the num value that parse produced and put inside the Ok value. That number will end up right where we want it in the new guess variable we're creating.

If parse is *not* able to turn the string into a number, it will return an Err value that contains more information about the error. The Err value does not match the Ok(num) pattern in the first match arm, but it does match the Err(_) pattern in the second arm. The underscore, _, is a catchall value; in this example, we're saying we want to match all Err values, no matter what information they have inside them. So the program will execute the second arm's code, continue, which tells the program to go to the next iteration of the loop and ask for another guess. So effectively, the program ignores all errors that parse might encounter!

Now everything in the program should work as expected. Let's try it:

```
$ cargo run
   Compiling guessing_game v0.1.0 (file:///projects/guessing_game)
    Finished dev [unoptimized + debuginfo] target(s) in 1.50 secs
     Running `target/debug/guessing_game`
Guess the number!
The secret number is: 61
Please input your guess.
10
You guessed: 10
Too small!
Please input your guess.
99
You guessed: 99
Too big!
Please input your guess.
foo
Please input your guess.
61
You guessed: 61
You win!
```

Awesome! With one tiny final tweak, we will finish the guessing game. Recall that the program is still printing the secret number. That worked well for testing, but it ruins the game. Let's delete the println! that outputs the secret number. Listing 2-6 shows the final code.

src/main.rs

```
extern crate rand;

use std::io;
use std::cmp::Ordering;
use rand::Rng;

fn main() {
    println!("Guess the number!");

    let secret_number = rand::thread_rng().gen_range(1, 101);

    loop {
        println!("Please input your guess.");

        let mut guess = String::new();

        io::stdin().read_line(&mut guess)
            .expect("Failed to read line");

        let guess: u32 = match guess.trim().parse() {
            Ok(num) => num,
            Err(_) => continue,
```

```
        };

        println!("You guessed: {}", guess);

        match guess.cmp(&secret_number) {
            Ordering::Less => println!("Too small!"),
            Ordering::Greater => println!("Too big!"),
            Ordering::Equal => {
                println!("You win!");
                break;
            }
        }
    }
}
```

Listing 2-6: Complete guessing game code

Summary

At this point, you've successfully built the guessing game. Congratulations!

This project was a hands-on way to introduce you to many new Rust concepts: let, match, methods, associated functions, external crates, and more. In the next few chapters, you'll learn about these concepts in more detail. Chapter 3 covers concepts that most programming languages have, such as variables, data types, and functions, and shows how to use them in Rust. Chapter 4 explores ownership, a feature that makes Rust different from other languages. Chapter 5 discusses structs and method syntax, and Chapter 6 explains how enums work.

3

COMMON PROGRAMMING CONCEPTS

This chapter covers concepts that appear in almost every programming language and how they work in Rust. Many programming languages have much in common at their core. None of the concepts presented in this chapter are unique to Rust, but we'll discuss them in the context of Rust and explain the conventions around using these concepts.

Specifically, you'll learn about variables, basic types, functions, comments, and control flow. These foundations will be in every Rust program, and learning them early will give you a strong core to start from.

Variables and Mutability

As mentioned in Chapter 2, by default variables are immutable. This is one of many nudges Rust gives you to write your code in a way that takes advantage of the safety and easy concurrency that Rust offers. However, you still have the option to make your variables mutable. Let's explore how and why Rust encourages you to favor immutability and why sometimes you might want to opt out.

When a variable is immutable, once a value is bound to a name, you can't change that value. To illustrate this, let's generate a new project called *variables* in your *projects* directory by using cargo new --bin variables.

Then, in your new *variables* directory, open *src/main.rs* and replace its code with the following code that won't compile just yet:

src/main.rs
```
fn main() {
    let x = 5;
    println!("The value of x is: {}", x);
    x = 6;
    println!("The value of x is: {}", x);
}
```

Save and run the program using cargo run. You should receive an error message, as shown in this output:

```
error[E0384]: cannot assign twice to immutable variable `x`
 --> src/main.rs:4:5
  |
2 |     let x = 5;
  |         - first assignment to `x`
3 |     println!("The value of x is: {}", x);
4 |     x = 6;
  |     ^^^^^ cannot assign twice to immutable variable
```

This example shows how the compiler helps you find errors in your programs. Even though compiler errors can be frustrating, they only mean your program isn't safely doing what you want it to do yet; they do *not* mean that you're not a good programmer! Experienced Rustaceans still get compiler errors.

The error message indicates that the cause of the error is that you cannot assign twice to immutable variable x, because you tried to assign a second value to the immutable x variable.

It's important that we get compile-time errors when we attempt to change a value that we previously designated as immutable because this very situation can lead to bugs. If one part of our code operates on the assumption that a value will never change and another part of our code changes that value, it's possible that the first part of the code won't do what it was designed to do. The cause of this kind of bug can be difficult to track down after the fact, especially when the second piece of code changes the value only *sometimes*.

In Rust, the compiler guarantees that when you state that a value won't change, it really won't change. That means that when you're reading and writing code, you don't have to keep track of how and where a value might change. Your code is thus easier to reason through.

But mutability can be very useful. Variables are immutable only by default; as you did in Chapter 2, you can make them mutable by adding mut in front of the variable name. In addition to allowing this value to change, mut conveys intent to future readers of the code by indicating that other parts of the code will be changing this variable value.

For example, let's change *src/main.rs* to the following:

src/main.rs

```
fn main() {
    let mut x = 5;
    println!("The value of x is: {}", x);
    x = 6;
    println!("The value of x is: {}", x);
}
```

When we run the program now, we get this:

```
$ cargo run
   Compiling variables v0.1.0 (file:///projects/variables)
    Finished dev [unoptimized + debuginfo] target(s) in 1.50 secs
     Running `target/debug/variables`
The value of x is: 5
The value of x is: 6
```

We're allowed to change the value that x binds to from 5 to 6 when mut is used. In some cases, you'll want to make a variable mutable because it makes the code more convenient to write than if it had only immutable variables.

There are multiple trade-offs to consider in addition to the prevention of bugs. For example, in cases where you're using large data structures, mutating an instance in place may be faster than copying and returning newly allocated instances. With smaller data structures, creating new instances and writing in a more functional programming style may be easier to think through, so lower performance might be a worthwhile penalty for gaining that clarity.

Differences Between Variables and Constants

Being unable to change the value of a variable might have reminded you of another programming concept that most other languages have: *constants.* Like immutable variables, constants are values that are bound to a name and are not allowed to change, but there are a few differences between constants and variables.

First, you aren't allowed to use `mut` with constants. Constants aren't just immutable by default—they're always immutable.

You declare constants using the `const` keyword instead of the `let` keyword, and the type of the value *must* be annotated. We're about to cover types and type annotations in "Data Types" on page 36, so don't worry about the details right now. Just know that you must always annotate the type.

Constants can be declared in any scope, including the global scope, which makes them useful for values that many parts of the code need to know about.

The last difference is that constants may be set only to a constant expression, not to the result of a function call or any other value that could only be computed at runtime.

Here's an example of a constant declaration where the constant's name is `MAX_POINTS` and its value is set to 100,000. (Rust's naming convention for constants is to use all uppercase with underscores between words):

```
const MAX_POINTS: u32 = 100_000;
```

Constants are valid for the entire time a program runs, within the scope they were declared in, making them a useful choice for values in your application domain that multiple parts of the program might need to know about, such as the maximum number of points any player of a game is allowed to earn or the speed of light.

Naming hardcoded values used throughout your program as constants is useful in conveying the meaning of that value to future maintainers of the code. It also helps to have only one place in your code you would need to change if the hardcoded value needed to be updated in the future.

Shadowing

As you saw in the guessing game tutorial in "Comparing the Guess to the Secret Number" on page 23, you can declare a new variable with the same name as a previous variable, and the new variable shadows the previous variable. Rustaceans say that the first variable is *shadowed* by the second, which means that the second variable's value is what appears when the variable is used. We can shadow a variable by using the same variable's name and repeating the use of the `let` keyword as follows:

src/main.rs

```
fn main() {
    let x = 5;

    let x = x + 1;
```

```
    let x = x * 2;

    println!("The value of x is: {}", x);
}
```

This program first binds x to a value of 5. Then it shadows x by repeating let x =, taking the original value and adding 1 so the value of x is then 6. The third let statement also shadows x, multiplying the previous value by 2 to give x a final value of 12. When we run this program, it will output the following:

```
$ cargo run
   Compiling variables v0.1.0 (file:///projects/variables)
    Finished dev [unoptimized + debuginfo] target(s) in 1.50 secs
     Running `target/debug/variables`
The value of x is: 12
```

Shadowing is different than marking a variable as mut, because we'll get a compile-time error if we accidentally try to reassign to this variable without using the let keyword. By using let, we can perform a few transformations on a value but have the variable be immutable after those transformations have been completed.

The other difference between mut and shadowing is that because we're effectively creating a new variable when we use the let keyword again, we can change the type of the value but reuse the same name. For example, say our program asks a user to show how many spaces they want between some text by inputting space characters, but we really want to store that input as a number:

```
let spaces = "   ";
let spaces = spaces.len();
```

This construct is allowed because the first spaces variable is a string type and the second spaces variable, which is a brand-new variable that happens to have the same name as the first one, is a number type. Shadowing thus spares us from having to come up with different names, such as spaces_str and spaces_num; instead, we can reuse the simpler spaces name. However, if we try to use mut for this, as shown here, we'll get a compile-time error:

```
let mut spaces = "   ";
spaces = spaces.len();
```

The error says we're not allowed to mutate a variable's type:

```
error[E0308]: mismatched types
 --> src/main.rs:3:14
  |
3 |     spaces = spaces.len();
  |              ^^^^^^^^^^^^ expected &str, found usize
  |
```

```
= note: expected type `&str`
          found type `usize`
```

Now that we've explored how variables work, let's look at more data types they can have.

Data Types

Every value in Rust is of a certain *data type*, which tells Rust what kind of data is being specified so it knows how to work with that data. We'll look at two data type subsets: scalar and compound.

Keep in mind that Rust is a *statically typed* language, which means that it must know the types of all variables at compile time. The compiler can usually infer what type we want to use based on the value and how we use it. In cases when many types are possible, such as when we converted a String to a numeric type using parse in "Comparing the Guess to the Secret Number" on page 23, we must add a type annotation, like this:

```
let guess: u32 = "42".parse().expect("Not a number!");
```

If we don't add the type annotation here, Rust will display the following error, which means the compiler needs more information from us to know which type we want to use:

```
error[E0282]: type annotations needed
 --> src/main.rs:2:9
  |
2 |     let guess = "42".parse().expect("Not a number!");
  |         ^^^^^
  |         |
  |         cannot infer type for `_`
  |         consider giving `guess` a type
```

You'll see different type annotations for other data types.

Scalar Types

A *scalar* type represents a single value. Rust has four primary scalar types: integers, floating-point numbers, Booleans, and characters. You may recognize these from other programming languages. Let's jump into how they work in Rust.

Integer Types

An *integer* is a number without a fractional component. We used one integer type in Chapter 2, the u32 type. This type declaration indicates that the value it's associated with should be an unsigned integer (signed integer types start with i, instead of u) that takes up 32 bits of space. Table 3-1 shows the built-in integer types in Rust. Each variant in the Signed and Unsigned columns (for example, i16) can be used to declare the type of an integer value.

Table 3-1: Integer Types in Rust

Length	Signed	Unsigned
8-bit	i8	u8
16-bit	i16	u16
32-bit	i32	u32
64-bit	i64	u64
arch	isize	usize

Each variant can be either signed or unsigned and has an explicit size. *Signed* and *unsigned* refer to whether it's possible for the number to be negative or positive—in other words, whether the number needs to have a sign with it (signed) or whether it will only ever be positive and can therefore be represented without a sign (unsigned). It's like writing numbers on paper: when the sign matters, a number is shown with a plus sign or a minus sign; however, when it's safe to assume the number is positive, it's shown with no sign. Signed numbers are stored using two's complement representation (if you're unsure what this is, you can search for it online; an explanation is outside the scope of this book).

Each signed variant can store numbers from $-(2^{n-1})$ to $2^{n-1} - 1$ inclusive, where n is the number of bits that variant uses. So an i8 can store numbers from $-(2^7)$ to $2^7 - 1$, which equals −128 to 127. Unsigned variants can store numbers from 0 to $2^n - 1$, so a u8 can store numbers from 0 to $2^8 - 1$, which equals 0 to 255.

Additionally, the isize and usize types depend on the kind of computer your program is running on: 64 bits if you're on a 64-bit architecture and 32 bits if you're on a 32-bit architecture.

You can write integer literals in any of the forms shown in Table 3-2. Note that all number literals except the byte literal allow a type suffix, such as 57u8, and _ as a visual separator, such as 1_000.

Table 3-2: Integer Literals in Rust

Number literals	Example
Decimal	98_222
Hex	0xff
Octal	0o77
Binary	0b1111_0000
Byte (u8 only)	b'A'

So how do you know which type of integer to use? If you're unsure, Rust's defaults are generally good choices, and integer types default to i32: this type is generally the fastest, even on 64-bit systems. The primary situation in which you'd use isize or usize is when indexing some sort of collection.

Floating-Point Types

Rust also has two primitive types for *floating-point numbers*, which are numbers with decimal points. Rust's floating-point types are f32 and f64, which are 32 bits and 64 bits in size, respectively. The default type is f64 because on modern CPUs it's roughly the same speed as f32 but is capable of more precision.

Here's an example that shows floating-point numbers in action:

src/main.rs

```
fn main() {
    let x = 2.0; // f64

    let y: f32 = 3.0; // f32
}
```

Floating-point numbers are represented according to the IEEE-754 standard. The f32 type is a single-precision float, and f64 has double precision.

Numeric Operations

Rust supports the basic mathematical operations you'd expect for all of the number types: addition, subtraction, multiplication, division, and remainder. The following code shows how you'd use each one in a let statement:

src/main.rs

```
fn main() {
    // addition
    let sum = 5 + 10;

    // subtraction
    let difference = 95.5 - 4.3;

    // multiplication
    let product = 4 * 30;

    // division
    let quotient = 56.7 / 32.2;

    // remainder
    let remainder = 43 % 5;
}
```

Each expression in these statements uses a mathematical operator and evaluates to a single value, which is then bound to a variable. Appendix B contains a list of all operators that Rust provides.

The Boolean Type

As in most other programming languages, a Boolean type in Rust has two
possible values: true and false. The Boolean type in Rust is specified using
bool. For example:

```
fn main() {
    let t = true;

    let f: bool = false; // with explicit type annotation
}
```

The main way to use Boolean values is through conditionals, such as an
if expression. We'll cover how if expressions work in Rust in "Control Flow"
on page 48.

The Character Type

So far we've worked only with numbers, but Rust supports letters too. Rust's
char type is the language's most primitive alphabetic type, and the following
code shows one way to use it. (Note that the char type is specified with single
quotes, as opposed to strings, which use double quotes.)

```
fn main() {
    let c = 'z';
    let z = 'z';
    let heart_eyed_cat = '😻';
}
```

Rust's char type represents a Unicode Scalar Value, which means it can
represent a lot more than just ASCII. Accented letters; Chinese, Japanese,
and Korean characters; emoji; and zero-width spaces are all valid char
values in Rust. Unicode Scalar Values range from U+0000 to U+D7FF and
U+E000 to U+10FFFF inclusive. However, a "character" isn't really a concept in
Unicode, so your human intuition for what a "character" is may not match
up with what a char is in Rust. We'll discuss this topic in detail in "Storing
UTF-8 Encoded Text with Strings" on page 135.

Compound Types

Compound types can group multiple values into one type. Rust has two
primitive compound types: tuples and arrays.

The Tuple Type

A tuple is a general way of grouping together some number of other values
with a variety of types into one compound type.

We create a tuple by writing a comma-separated list of values inside parentheses. Each position in the tuple has a type, and the types of the different values in the tuple don't have to be the same. We've added optional type annotations in this example:

src/main.rs

```rust
fn main() {
    let tup: (i32, f64, u8) = (500, 6.4, 1);
}
```

The variable tup binds to the entire tuple, because a tuple is considered a single compound element. To get the individual values out of a tuple, we can use pattern matching to destructure a tuple value, like this:

src/main.rs

```rust
fn main() {
    let tup = (500, 6.4, 1);

    let (x, y, z) = tup;

    println!("The value of y is: {}", y);
}
```

This program first creates a tuple and binds it to the variable tup. It then uses a pattern with let to take tup and turn it into three separate variables, x, y, and z. This is called *destructuring*, because it breaks the single tuple into three parts. Finally, the program prints the value of y, which is 6.4.

In addition to destructuring through pattern matching, we can access a tuple element directly by using a period (.) followed by the index of the value we want to access. For example:

src/main.rs

```rust
fn main() {
    let x: (i32, f64, u8) = (500, 6.4, 1);

    let five_hundred = x.0;

    let six_point_four = x.1;

    let one = x.2;
}
```

This program creates a tuple, x, and then makes new variables for each element by using their index. As with most programming languages, the first index in a tuple is 0.

The Array Type

Another way to have a collection of multiple values is with an *array*. Unlike a tuple, every element of an array must have the same type. Arrays in Rust are different from arrays in some other languages because arrays in Rust have a fixed length: once declared, they cannot grow or shrink in size.

In Rust, the values going into an array are written as a comma-separated list inside square brackets:

```
fn main() {
    let a = [1, 2, 3, 4, 5];
}
```

Arrays are useful when you want your data allocated on the stack rather than the heap (we will discuss the stack and the heap more in Chapter 4) or when you want to ensure you always have a fixed number of elements. An array isn't as flexible as the vector type, though. A vector is a similar collection type provided by the standard library that *is* allowed to grow or shrink in size. If you're unsure whether to use an array or a vector, you should probably use a vector. Chapter 8 discusses vectors in more detail.

An example of when you might want to use an array rather than a vector is in a program that needs to know the names of the months of the year. It's very unlikely that such a program will need to add or remove months, so you can use an array because you know it will always contain 12 items:

```
let months = ["January", "February", "March", "April", "May", "June", "July",
              "August", "September", "October", "November", "December"];
```

Accessing Array Elements

An array is a single chunk of memory allocated on the stack. You can access elements of an array using indexing, like this:

```
fn main() {
    let a = [1, 2, 3, 4, 5];

    let first = a[0];
    let second = a[1];
}
```

In this example, the variable named first will get the value 1, because that is the value at index [0] in the array. The variable named second will get the value 2 from index [1] in the array.

Invalid Array Element Access

What happens if you try to access an element of an array that is past the end of the array? Say you change the example to the following code, which will compile but exit with an error when it runs:

```
fn main() {
    let a = [1, 2, 3, 4, 5];
    let index = 10;

    let element = a[index];
```

```
        println!("The value of element is: {}", element);
}
```

Running this code using cargo run produces the following result:

```
$ cargo run
   Compiling arrays v0.1.0 (file:///projects/arrays)
    Finished dev [unoptimized + debuginfo] target(s) in 1.50 secs
     Running `target/debug/arrays`
thread '<main>' panicked at 'index out of bounds: the len is 5 but the index
is 10', src/main.rs:6
note: Run with `RUST_BACKTRACE=1` for a backtrace.
```

The compilation didn't produce any errors, but the program resulted in a *runtime* error and didn't exit successfully. When you attempt to access an element using indexing, Rust will check that the index you've specified is less than the array length. If the index is greater than the length, Rust will *panic*, which is the term Rust uses when a program exits with an error.

This is the first example of Rust's safety principles in action. In many low-level languages, this kind of check is not done, and when you provide an incorrect index, invalid memory can be accessed. Rust protects you against this kind of error by immediately exiting instead of allowing the memory access and continuing. Chapter 9 discusses more of Rust's error handling.

Functions

Functions are pervasive in Rust code. You've already seen one of the most important functions in the language: the main function, which is the entry point of many programs. You've also seen the fn keyword, which allows you to declare new functions.

Rust code uses *snake case* as the conventional style for function and variable names. In snake case, all letters are lowercase and underscores separate words. Here's a program that contains an example function definition:

src/main.rs

```
fn main() {
    println!("Hello, world!");

    another_function();
}

fn another_function() {
    println!("Another function.");
}
```

Function definitions in Rust start with fn and have a set of parentheses after the function name. The curly brackets tell the compiler where the function body begins and ends.

We can call any function we've defined by entering its name followed by a set of parentheses. Because another_function is defined in the program, it can be called from inside the `main` function. Note that we defined `another _function` *after* the main function in the source code; we could have defined it before as well. Rust doesn't care where you define your functions, only that they're defined somewhere.

Let's start a new binary project named *functions* to explore functions further. Place the `another_function` example in *src/main.rs* and run it. You should see the following output:

```
$ cargo run
   Compiling functions v0.1.0 (file:///projects/functions)
    Finished dev [unoptimized + debuginfo] target(s) in 1.50 secs
     Running `target/debug/functions`
Hello, world!
Another function.
```

The lines execute in the order in which they appear in the `main` function. First, the "Hello, world!" message prints, and then `another_function` is called and its message is printed.

Function Parameters

Functions can also be defined to have *parameters*, which are special variables that are part of a function's signature. When a function has parameters, you can provide it with concrete values for those parameters. Technically, the concrete values are called *arguments*, but in casual conversation, people tend to use the words *parameter* and *argument* interchangeably for either the variables in a function's definition or the concrete values passed in when you call a function.

The following rewritten version of `another_function` shows what parameters look like in Rust:

src/main.rs

```
fn main() {
    another_function(5);
}

fn another_function(x: i32) {
    println!("The value of x is: {}", x);
}
```

Try running this program; you should get the following output:

```
$ cargo run
   Compiling functions v0.1.0 (file:///projects/functions)
    Finished dev [unoptimized + debuginfo] target(s) in 1.50 secs
     Running `target/debug/functions`
The value of x is: 5
```

The declaration of `another_function` has one parameter named x. The type of x is specified as i32. When 5 is passed to `another_function`, the `println!` macro puts 5 where the pair of curly brackets were in the format string.

In function signatures, you *must* declare the type of each parameter. This is a deliberate decision in Rust's design: requiring type annotations in function definitions means the compiler almost never needs you to use them elsewhere in the code to figure out what you mean.

When you want a function to have multiple parameters, separate the parameter declarations with commas, like this:

src/main.rs

```
fn main() {
    another_function(5, 6);
}

fn another_function(x: i32, y: i32) {
    println!("The value of x is: {}", x);
    println!("The value of y is: {}", y);
}
```

This example creates a function with two parameters, both of which are i32 types. The function then prints the values in both of its parameters. Note that function parameters don't all need to be the same type; they just happen to be in this example.

Let's try running this code. Replace the program currently in your *functions* project's *src/main.rs* file with the preceding example and run it using cargo run:

```
$ cargo run
   Compiling functions v0.1.0 (file:///projects/functions)
    Finished dev [unoptimized + debuginfo] target(s) in 1.50 secs
     Running `target/debug/functions`
The value of x is: 5
The value of y is: 6
```

Because we called the function with 5 as the value for x and 6 is passed as the value for y, the two strings are printed with these values.

Statements and Expressions in Function Bodies

Function bodies are made up of a series of statements optionally ending in an expression. So far, we've only covered functions without an ending expression, but you have seen an expression as part of a statement. Because Rust is an expression-based language, this is an important distinction to understand. Other languages don't have the same distinctions, so let's look at what statements and expressions are and how their differences affect the bodies of functions.

We've actually already used statements and expressions. *Statements* are instructions that perform some action and do not return a value. *Expressions* evaluate to a resulting value. Let's look at some examples.

Creating a variable and assigning a value to it with the let keyword is a statement. In Listing 3-1, let y = 6; is a statement.

```
fn main() {
    let y = 6;
}
```

Listing 3-1: A main function declaration containing one statement

Function definitions are also statements; the entire preceding example is a statement in itself.

Statements do not return values. Therefore, you can't assign a let statement to another variable, as the following code tries to do; you'll get an error:

```
fn main() {
    let x = (let y = 6);
}
```

When you run this program, the error you'll get looks like this:

```
$ cargo run
   Compiling functions v0.1.0 (file:///projects/functions)
error: expected expression, found statement (`let`)
 --> src/main.rs:2:14
  |
2 |     let x = (let y = 6);
  |                  ^^^
  |
  = note: variable declaration using `let` is a statement
```

The let y = 6 statement does not return a value, so there isn't anything for x to bind to. This is different from what happens in other languages, such as C and Ruby, where the assignment returns the value of the assignment. In those languages, you can write x = y = 6 and have both x and y contain the value 6; that is not the case in Rust.

Expressions evaluate to something and make up most of the rest of the code that you'll write in Rust. Consider a simple math operation, such as 5 + 6, which is an expression that evaluates to the value 11. Expressions can be part of statements: in Listing 3-1, the 6 in the statement let y = 6; is an expression that evaluates to the value 6. Calling a function is an expression. Calling a macro is an expression. The block that we use to create new scopes, {}, is an expression, for example:

```
fn main() {
    let x = 5;

 ❶ let y = {❷
        let x = 3;
      ❸ x + 1
    };

    println!("The value of y is: {}", y);
}
```

The expression ❷ is a block that, in this case, evaluates to 4. That value gets bound to y as part of the let statement ❶. Note the line without a semicolon at the end ❸, which is unlike most of the lines you've seen so far. Expressions do not include ending semicolons. If you add a semicolon to the end of an expression, you turn it into a statement, which will then not return a value. Keep this in mind as you explore function return values and expressions next.

Functions with Return Values

Functions can return values to the code that calls them. We don't name return values, but we do declare their type after an arrow (->). In Rust, the return value of the function is synonymous with the value of the final expression in the block of the body of a function. You can return early from a function by using the return keyword and specifying a value, but most functions return the last expression implicitly. Here's an example of a function that returns a value:

src/main.rs

```
fn five() -> i32 {
    5
}

fn main() {
    let x = five();

    println!("The value of x is: {}", x);
}
```

There are no function calls, macros, or even let statements in the five function—just the number 5 by itself. That's a perfectly valid function in Rust. Note that the function's return type is specified, too, as -> i32. Try running this code; the output should look like this:

```
$ cargo run
   Compiling functions v0.1.0 (file:///projects/functions)
    Finished dev [unoptimized + debuginfo] target(s) in 1.50 secs
     Running `target/debug/functions`
The value of x is: 5
```

The 5 in five is the function's return value, which is why the return type is i32. Let's examine this in more detail. There are two important bits: first, the line let x = five(); shows that we're using the return value of a function to initialize a variable. Because the function five returns a 5, that line is the same as the following:

```
let x = 5;
```

Second, the five function has no parameters and defines the type of the return value, but the body of the function is a lonely 5 with no semicolon because it's an expression whose value we want to return.

Let's look at another example:

src/main.rs

```rust
fn main() {
    let x = plus_one(5);

    println!("The value of x is: {}", x);
}

fn plus_one(x: i32) -> i32 {
    x + 1
}
```

Running this code will print The value of x is: 6. But if we place a semi-colon at the end of the line containing x + 1, changing it from an expression to a statement, we'll get an error.

src/main.rs

```rust
fn main() {
    let x = plus_one(5);

    println!("The value of x is: {}", x);
}

fn plus_one(x: i32) -> i32 {
    x + 1;
}
```

Running this code produces an error, as follows:

```
error[E0308]: mismatched types
 --> src/main.rs:7:28
  |
7 |   fn plus_one(x: i32) -> i32 {
  |   _____^
8 | |     x + 1;
  | |          = help: consider removing this semicolon
9 | | }
  | |_^ expected i32, found ()
  |
  = note: expected type `i32`
             found type `()`
```

The main error message, "mismatched types," reveals the core issue with this code. The definition of the function plus_one says that it will return an i32, but statements don't evaluate to a value, which is expressed by (), the empty tuple. Therefore, nothing is returned, which contradicts the function definition and results in an error. In this output, Rust provides a message to possibly help rectify this issue: it suggests removing the semicolon, which would fix the error.

Comments

All programmers strive to make their code easy to understand, but some-times extra explanation is warranted. In these cases, programmers leave notes, or *comments*, in their source code that the compiler will ignore but people reading the source code may find useful.

Here's a simple comment:

```
// hello, world
```

In Rust, comments must start with two slashes and continue until the end of the line. For comments that extend beyond a single line, you'll need to include // on each line, like this:

```
// So we're doing something complicated here, long enough that we need
// multiple lines of comments to do it! Whew! Hopefully, this comment will
// explain what's going on.
```

Comments can also be placed at the end of lines containing code:

src/main.rs
```
fn main() {
    let lucky_number = 7; // I'm feeling lucky today
}
```

But you'll more often see them used in this format, with the comment on a separate line above the code it's annotating:

src/main.rs
```
fn main() {
    // I'm feeling lucky today
    let lucky_number = 7;
}
```

Rust also has another kind of comment, documentation comments, which we'll discuss in Chapter 14.

Control Flow

Deciding whether or not to run some code depending on whether a condi-tion is true and deciding to run some code repeatedly while a condition is true are basic building blocks in most programming languages. The most common constructs that let you control the flow of execution of Rust code are if expressions and loops.

if Expressions

An if expression allows you to branch your code depending on conditions. You provide a condition and then state, "If this condition is met, run this block of code. If the condition is not met, do not run this block of code."

Create a new project called *branches* in your *projects* directory to explore the if expression. In the *src/main.rs* file, input the following:

src/main.rs

```
fn main() {
    let number = 3;

    if number < 5 {
        println!("condition was true");
    } else {
        println!("condition was false");
    }
}
```

All if expressions start with the keyword if, which is followed by a condition. In this case, the condition checks whether or not the variable number has a value less than 5. The block of code we want to execute if the condition is true is placed immediately after the condition inside curly brackets. Blocks of code associated with the conditions in if expressions are sometimes called *arms*, just like the arms in match expressions that we discussed in "Comparing the Guess to the Secret Number" on page 23.

Optionally, we can also include an else expression, which we chose to do here, to give the program an alternative block of code to execute should the condition evaluate to false. If you don't provide an else expression and the condition is false, the program will just skip the if block and move on to the next bit of code.

Try running this code; you should see the following output:

```
$ cargo run
   Compiling branches v0.1.0 (file:///projects/branches)
    Finished dev [unoptimized + debuginfo] target(s) in 1.50 secs
     Running `target/debug/branches`
condition was true
```

Let's try changing the value of number to a value that makes the condition false to see what happens:

```
let number = 7;
```

Run the program again, and look at the output:

```
$ cargo run
   Compiling branches v0.1.0 (file:///projects/branches)
    Finished dev [unoptimized + debuginfo] target(s) in 1.50 secs
     Running `target/debug/branches`
condition was false
```

It's also worth noting that the condition in this code *must* be a bool. If the condition isn't a bool, we'll get an error. For example, try running the following code:

src/main.rs

```
fn main() {
    let number = 3;

    if number {
        println!("number was three");
    }
}
```

The if condition evaluates to a value of 3 this time, and Rust throws an error:

```
error[E0308]: mismatched types
 --> src/main.rs:4:8
  |
4 |     if number {
  |        ^^^^^^ expected bool, found integral variable
  |
  = note: expected type `bool`
             found type `{integer}`
```

The error indicates that Rust expected a bool but got an integer. Unlike languages such as Ruby and JavaScript, Rust will not automatically try to convert non-Boolean types to a Boolean. You must be explicit and always provide if with a Boolean as its condition. If we want the if code block to run only when a number is not equal to 0, for example, we can change the if expression to the following:

src/main.rs

```
fn main() {
    let number = 3;

    if number != 0 {
        println!("number was something other than zero");
    }
}
```

Running this code will print number was something other than zero.

Handling Multiple Conditions with else if

You can have multiple conditions by combining if and else in an else if expression. For example:

src/main.rs

```
fn main() {
    let number = 6;

    if number % 4 == 0 {
        println!("number is divisible by 4");
    } else if number % 3 == 0 {
```

```
        println!("number is divisible by 3");
    } else if number % 2 == 0 {
        println!("number is divisible by 2");
    } else {
        println!("number is not divisible by 4, 3, or 2");
    }
}
```

This program has four possible paths it can take. After running it, you should see the following output:

```
$ cargo run
   Compiling branches v0.1.0 (file:///projects/branches)
    Finished dev [unoptimized + debuginfo] target(s) in 1.50 secs
     Running `target/debug/branches`
number is divisible by 3
```

When this program executes, it checks each if expression in turn and executes the first body for which the condition holds true. Note that even though 6 is divisible by 2, we don't see the output number is divisible by 2, nor do we see the number is not divisible by 4, 3, or 2 text from the else block. That's because Rust only executes the block for the first true condition, and once it finds one, it doesn't even check the rest.

Using too many else if expressions can clutter your code, so if you have more than one, you might want to refactor your code. Chapter 6 describes a powerful Rust branching construct called match for these cases.

Using if in a let Statement

Because if is an expression, we can use it on the right side of a let statement, as in Listing 3-2.

src/main.rs
```
fn main() {
    let condition = true;
    let number = if condition {
        5
    } else {
        6
    };

    println!("The value of number is: {}", number);
}
```

Listing 3-2: Assigning the result of an if expression to a variable

The number variable will be bound to a value based on the outcome of the if expression. Run this code to see what happens:

```
$ cargo run
   Compiling branches v0.1.0 (file:///projects/branches)
    Finished dev [unoptimized + debuginfo] target(s) in 1.50 secs
```

```
    Running `target/debug/branches`
The value of number is: 5
```

Remember that blocks of code evaluate to the last expression in them, and numbers by themselves are also expressions. In this case, the value of the whole if expression depends on which block of code executes. This means the values that have the potential to be results from each arm of the if must be the same type; in Listing 3-2, the results of both the if arm and the else arm were i32 integers. If the types are mismatched, as in the following example, we'll get an error:

```rust
fn main() {
    let condition = true;

    let number = if condition {
        5
    } else {
        "six"
    };

    println!("The value of number is: {}", number);
}
```

When we try to compile this code, we'll get an error. The if and else arms have value types that are incompatible, and Rust indicates exactly where to find the problem in the program:

```
error[E0308]: if and else have incompatible types
  --> src/main.rs:4:18
   |
4  |         let number = if condition {
   |  _____^
5  | |             5
6  | |         } else {
7  | |             "six"
8  | |         };
   | |_____^ expected integral variable, found &str
   |
   = note: expected type `{integer}`
              found type `&str`
```

The expression in the if block evaluates to an integer, and the expression in the else block evaluates to a string. This won't work because variables must have a single type. Rust needs to know at compile time what type the number variable is, definitively, so it can verify at compile time that its type is valid everywhere we use number. Rust wouldn't be able to do that if the type of number was only determined at runtime; the compiler would be more complex and would make fewer guarantees about the code if it had to keep track of multiple hypothetical types for any variable.

Repetition with Loops

It's often useful to execute a block of code more than once. For this task, Rust provides several *loops*. A loop runs through the code inside the loop body to the end and then starts immediately back at the beginning. To experiment with loops, let's make a new project called *loops*.

Rust has three kinds of loops: loop, while, and for. Let's try each one.

Repeating Code with loop

The loop keyword tells Rust to execute a block of code over and over again forever or until you explicitly tell it to stop.

As an example, change the *src/main.rs* file in your *loops* directory to look like this:

src/main.rs

```
fn main() {
    loop {
        println!("again!");
    }
}
```

When we run this program, we'll see again! printed over and over continuously until we stop the program manually. Most terminals support a keyboard shortcut, CTRL-C, to halt a program that is stuck in a continual loop. Give it a try:

```
$ cargo run
   Compiling loops v0.1.0 (file:///projects/loops)
    Finished dev [unoptimized + debuginfo] target(s) in 1.50 secs
     Running `target/debug/loops`
again!
again!
again!
again!
^Cagain!
```

The symbol ^C represents where you pressed CTRL-C. You may or may not see the word again! printed after the ^C, depending on where the code was in the loop when it received the halt signal.

Fortunately, Rust provides another, more reliable way to break out of a loop. You can place the break keyword within the loop to tell the program when to stop executing the loop. Recall that we did this in the guessing game in "Quitting After a Correct Guess" on page 27 to exit the program when the user won the game by guessing the correct number.

Conditional Loops with while

It's often useful for a program to evaluate a condition within a loop. While the condition is true, the loop runs. When the condition ceases to be true, the program calls break, stopping the loop. This loop type could be implemented using a combination of loop, if, else, and break; you could try that now in a program, if you'd like.

However, this pattern is so common that Rust has a built-in language construct for it, called a while loop. Listing 3-3 uses while: the program loops three times, counting down each time, and then, after the loop, it prints another message and exits.

src/main.rs

```
fn main() {
    let mut number = 3;

    while number != 0  {
        println!("{}!", number);

        number = number - 1;
    }

    println!("LIFTOFF!!!");
}
```

Listing 3-3: Using a while loop to run code while a condition holds true

This construct eliminates a lot of nesting that would be necessary if you used loop, if, else, and break, and it's clearer. While a condition holds true, the code runs; otherwise, it exits the loop.

Looping Through a Collection with for

You could use the while construct to loop over the elements of a collection, such as an array. For example, let's look at Listing 3-4.

src/main.rs

```
fn main() {
    let a = [10, 20, 30, 40, 50];
    let mut index = 0;

    while index < 5 {
        println!("the value is: {}", a[index]);

        index = index + 1;
    }
}
```

Listing 3-4: Looping through each element of a collection using a while loop

Here, the code counts up through the elements in the array. It starts at index 0, and then loops until it reaches the final index in the array (that is, when index < 5 is no longer true). Running this code will print every element in the array:

```
$ cargo run
   Compiling loops v0.1.0 (file:///projects/loops)
    Finished dev [unoptimized + debuginfo] target(s) in 1.50 secs
     Running `target/debug/loops`
the value is: 10
```

```
the value is: 20
the value is: 30
the value is: 40
the value is: 50
```

All five array values appear in the terminal, as expected. Even though index will reach a value of 5 at some point, the loop stops executing before trying to fetch a sixth value from the array.

But this approach is error prone; we could cause the program to panic if the index length is incorrect. It's also slow, because the compiler adds runtime code to perform the conditional check on every element on every iteration through the loop.

As a more concise alternative, you can use a for loop and execute some code for each item in a collection. A for loop looks like the code in Listing 3-5.

src/main.rs

```rust
fn main() {
    let a = [10, 20, 30, 40, 50];

    for element in a.iter() {
        println!("the value is: {}", element);
    }
}
```

Listing 3-5: Looping through each element of a collection using a for loop

When we run this code, we'll see the same output as in Listing 3-4. More importantly, we've now increased the safety of the code and eliminated the chance of bugs that might result from going beyond the end of the array or not going far enough and missing some items.

For example, in the code in Listing 3-4, if you removed an item from the a array but forgot to update the condition to while index < 4, the code would panic. Using the for loop, you wouldn't need to remember to change any other code if you changed the number of values in the array.

The safety and conciseness of for loops make them the most commonly used loop construct in Rust. Even in situations in which you want to run some code a certain number of times, as in the countdown example that used a while loop in Listing 3-3, most Rustaceans would use a for loop. The way to do that would be to use a Range, which is a type provided by the standard library that generates all numbers in sequence starting from one number and ending before another number.

Here's what the countdown would look like using a for loop and another method we've not yet talked about, rev, to reverse the range:

src/main.rs

```rust
fn main() {
    for number in (1..4).rev() {
        println!("{}!", number);
    }
    println!("LIFTOFF!!!");
}
```

This code is a bit nicer, isn't it?

Summary

You made it! That was a sizable chapter: you learned about variables, scalar and compound data types, functions, comments, if expressions, and loops! If you want to practice with the concepts discussed in this chapter, try building programs to do the following:

- Convert temperatures between Fahrenheit and Celsius.
- Generate the *n*th Fibonacci number.
- Print the lyrics to the Christmas carol "The Twelve Days of Christmas," taking advantage of the repetition in the song.

When you're ready to move on, we'll talk about a concept in Rust that *doesn't* commonly exist in other programming languages: ownership.

4

UNDERSTANDING OWNERSHIP

Ownership is Rust's most unique feature, and it enables Rust to make memory safety guarantees without needing a garbage collector. Therefore, it's important to understand how ownership works in Rust. In this chapter, we'll talk about ownership as well as several related features: borrowing, slices, and how Rust lays data out in memory.

What Is Ownership?

Rust's central feature is *ownership*. Although the feature is straightforward to explain, it has deep implications for the rest of the language.

All programs have to manage the way they use a computer's memory while running. Some languages have garbage collection that constantly looks for no longer used memory as the program runs; in other languages, the programmer must explicitly allocate and free the memory. Rust uses a third approach: memory is managed through a system of ownership with a set of rules that the compiler checks at compile time. None of the ownership features slow down your program while it's running.

Because ownership is a new concept for many programmers, it does take some time to get used to. The good news is that the more experienced you become with Rust and the rules of the ownership system, the more you'll be able to naturally develop code that is safe and efficient. Keep at it!

When you understand ownership, you'll have a solid foundation for understanding the features that make Rust unique. In this chapter, you'll learn ownership by working through some examples that focus on a very common data structure: strings.

THE STACK AND THE HEAP

In many programming languages, you don't have to think about the stack and the heap very often. But in a systems programming language like Rust, whether a value is on the stack or the heap has more of an effect on how the language behaves and why you have to make certain decisions. Parts of ownership will be described in relation to the stack and the heap later in this chapter, so here is a brief explanation in preparation.

Both the stack and the heap are parts of memory that is available to your code to use at runtime, but they are structured in different ways. The stack stores values in the order it gets them and removes the values in the opposite order. This is referred to as *last in, first out*. Think of a stack of plates: when you add more plates, you put them on top of the pile, and when you need a plate, you take one off the top. Adding or removing plates from the middle or bottom wouldn't work as well! Adding data is called *pushing onto the stack*, and removing data is called *popping off the stack*.

The stack is fast because of the way it accesses the data: it never has to search for a place to put new data or a place to get data from because that place is always the top. Another property that makes the stack fast is that all data on the stack must take up a known, fixed size.

Data with a size unknown at compile time or a size that might change can be stored on the heap instead. The heap is less organized: when you put data on the heap, you ask for some amount of space. The operating system finds an empty spot somewhere in the heap that is big enough, marks it as being in use, and returns a *pointer*, which is the address of that location. This process is called *allocating on the heap*, sometimes abbreviated as just "allocating." Pushing values onto the stack is not considered allocating. Because the pointer is a known, fixed size, you can store the pointer on the stack, but when you want the actual data, you have to follow the pointer.

Think of being seated at a restaurant. When you enter, you state the number of people in your group, and the staff finds an empty table that fits everyone and leads you there. If someone in your group comes late, they can ask where you've been seated to find you.

Accessing data in the heap is slower than accessing data on the stack because you have to follow a pointer to get there. Contemporary processors are faster if they jump around less in memory. Continuing the analogy, consider a server at a restaurant taking orders from many tables. It's most efficient to get all the orders at one table before moving on to the next table. Taking an order from table A, then an order from table B, then one from A again, and then one from B again would be a much slower process. By the same token, a processor can do its job better if it works on data that's close to other data (as it is on the stack) rather than farther away (as it can be on the heap). Allocating a large amount of space on the heap can also take time.

When your code calls a function, the values passed into the function (including, potentially, pointers to data on the heap) and the function's local variables get pushed onto the stack. When the function is over, those values get popped off the stack.

Keeping track of what parts of code are using what data on the heap, minimizing the amount of duplicate data on the heap, and cleaning up unused data on the heap so you don't run out of space are all problems that ownership addresses. Once you understand ownership, you won't need to think about the stack and the heap very often, but knowing that managing heap data is why ownership exists can help explain why it works the way it does.

Ownership Rules

First, let's take a look at the ownership rules. Keep these rules in mind as we work through the examples that illustrate them:

- Each value in Rust has a variable that's called its *owner*.
- There can be only one owner at a time.
- When the owner goes out of scope, the value will be dropped.

Variable Scope

We've walked through an example of a Rust program already in Chapter 2. Now that we're past basic syntax, we won't include all the `fn main() {` code in examples, so if you're following along, you'll have to put the following examples inside a `main` function manually. As a result, our examples will be a bit more concise, letting us focus on the details rather than boilerplate code.

As a first example of ownership, we'll look at the *scope* of some variables. A scope is the range within a program for which an item is valid. Let's say we have a variable that looks like this:

```
let s = "hello";
```

The variable s refers to a string literal, where the value of the string is hardcoded into the text of our program. The variable is valid from the point at which it's declared until the end of the current *scope*. Listing 4-1 has comments annotating where the variable s is valid.

```
{                      // s is not valid here; it's not yet declared
    let s = "hello";   // s is valid from this point forward

    // do stuff with s
}                      // this scope is now over, and s is no longer valid
```

Listing 4-1: A variable and the scope in which it is valid

In other words, there are two important points in time here:

- When s comes *into scope*, it is valid.
- It remains valid until it goes *out of scope*.

At this point, the relationship between scopes and when variables are valid is similar to that in other programming languages. Now we'll build on top of this understanding by introducing the String type.

The String Type

To illustrate the rules of ownership, we need a data type that is more complex than the ones we covered in "Data Types" on page 36. The types covered previously are all stored on the stack and popped off the stack when their scope is over, but we want to look at data that is stored on the heap and explore how Rust knows when to clean up that data.

We'll use String as the example here and concentrate on the parts of String that relate to ownership. These aspects also apply to other complex data types provided by the standard library and that you create. We'll discuss String in more depth in Chapter 8.

We've already seen string literals, where a string value is hardcoded into our program. String literals are convenient, but they aren't suitable for every situation in which we may want to use text. One reason is that they're immutable. Another is that not every string value can be known when we write our code: for example, what if we want to take user input and store it? For these situations, Rust has a second string type, String. This type is allocated on the heap and as such is able to store an amount of text that is unknown to us at compile time. You can create a String from a string literal using the from function, like so:

```
let s = String::from("hello");
```

The double colon (::) is an operator that allows us to namespace this particular from function under the String type rather than using some sort of name like string_from. We'll discuss this syntax more in "Method Syntax" on page 90 and when we talk about namespacing with modules in "Module Definitions" on page 111.

This kind of string *can* be mutated:

```
let mut s = String::from("hello");

s.push_str(", world!"); // push_str() appends a literal to a String

println!("{}", s); // this will print `hello, world!`
```

So, what's the difference here? Why can String be mutated but literals cannot? The difference is how these two types deal with memory.

Memory and Allocation

In the case of a string literal, we know the contents at compile time, so the text is hardcoded directly into the final executable. This is why string literals are fast and efficient. But these properties only come from the string literal's immutability. Unfortunately, we can't put a blob of memory into the binary for each piece of text whose size is unknown at compile time and whose size might change while running the program.

With the String type, in order to support a mutable, growable piece of text, we need to allocate an amount of memory on the heap, unknown at compile time, to hold the contents. This means:

- The memory must be requested from the operating system at runtime.
- We need a way of returning this memory to the operating system when we're done with our String.

That first part is done by us: when we call String::from, its implementation requests the memory it needs. This is pretty much universal in programming languages.

However, the second part is different. In languages with a *garbage collector (GC)*, the GC keeps track and cleans up memory that isn't being used anymore, and we don't need to think about it. Without a GC, it's our responsibility to identify when memory is no longer being used and call code to explicitly return it, just as we did to request it. Doing this correctly has historically been a difficult programming problem. If we forget, we'll waste memory. If we do it too early, we'll have an invalid variable. If we do it twice, that's a bug too. We need to pair exactly one allocate with exactly one free.

Rust takes a different path: the memory is automatically returned once the variable that owns it goes out of scope. Here's a version of our scope example from Listing 4-1 using a String instead of a string literal:

```
{
    let s = String::from("hello"); // s is valid from this point forward
```

```
        // do stuff with s
}                                       // this scope is now over, and s is no
                                        // longer valid
```

There is a natural point at which we can return the memory our String needs to the operating system: when s goes out of scope. When a variable goes out of scope, Rust calls a special function for us. This function is called drop, and it's where the author of String can put the code to return the memory. Rust calls drop automatically at the closing curly bracket.

NOTE   *In C++, this pattern of deallocating resources at the end of an item's lifetime is some-times called* Resource Acquisition Is Initialization (RAII). *The drop function in Rust will be familiar to you if you've used RAII patterns.*

This pattern has a profound impact on the way Rust code is written. It may seem simple right now, but the behavior of code can be unexpected in more complicated situations when we want to have multiple variables use the data we've allocated on the heap. Let's explore some of those situations now.

Ways That Variables and Data Interact: Move

Multiple variables can interact with the same data in different ways in Rust. Let's look at an example using an integer in Listing 4-2.

```
let x = 5;
let y = x;
```

Listing 4-2: Assigning the integer value of variable x to y

We can probably guess what this is doing: "bind the value 5 to x; then make a copy of the value in x and bind it to y." We now have two variables, x and y, and both equal 5. This is indeed what is happening, because integers are simple values with a known, fixed size and these two 5 values are pushed onto the stack.

Now let's look at the String version:

```
let s1 = String::from("hello");
let s2 = s1;
```

This looks very similar to the previous code, so we might assume that the way it works would be the same: that is, the second line would make a copy of the value in s1 and bind it to s2. But this isn't quite what happens.

Take a look at Figure 4-1 to see what is happening to String under the covers. A String is made up of three parts, shown on the left: a pointer to the memory that holds the contents of the string, a length, and a capacity. This group of data is stored on the stack. On the right is the memory on the heap that holds the contents.

The length is how much memory, in bytes, the contents of the `String` is currently using. The capacity is the total amount of memory, in bytes, that the `String` has received from the operating system. The difference between length and capacity matters, but not in this context, so for now, it's fine to ignore the capacity.

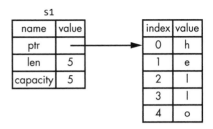

Figure 4-1: Representation in memory of a `String` holding the value `"hello"` bound to `s1`

When we assign `s1` to `s2`, the `String` data is copied, meaning we copy the pointer, the length, and the capacity that are on the stack. We do not copy the data on the heap that the pointer refers to. In other words, the data representation in memory looks like Figure 4-2.

The representation does *not* look like Figure 4-3, which is what memory would look like if Rust instead copied the heap data as well. If Rust did this, the operation `s2 = s1` could be very expensive in terms of runtime performance if the data on the heap were large.

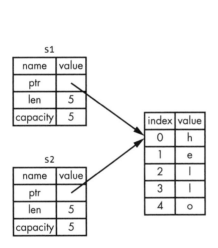

Figure 4-2: Representation in memory of the variable `s2` that has a copy of the pointer, length, and capacity of `s1`

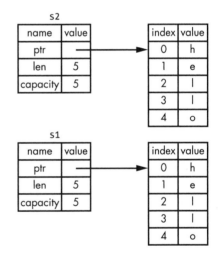

Figure 4-3: Another possibility for what `s2 = s1` might do if Rust copied the heap data as well

Earlier, we said that when a variable goes out of scope, Rust automatically calls the `drop` function and cleans up the heap memory for that variable. But Figure 4-2 shows both data pointers pointing to the same location. This is a problem: when `s2` and `s1` go out of scope, they will both try to free the same memory. This is known as a *double free* error and is one of the memory safety bugs we mentioned previously. Freeing memory twice can lead to memory corruption, which can potentially lead to security vulnerabilities.

To ensure memory safety, there's one more detail to what happens in this situation in Rust. Instead of trying to copy the allocated memory, Rust considers s1 to no longer be valid and, therefore, Rust doesn't need to free anything when s1 goes out of scope. Check out what happens when you try to use s1 after s2 is created; it won't work:

```
let s1 = String::from("hello");
let s2 = s1;

println!("{}, world!", s1);
```

You'll get an error like this because Rust prevents you from using the invalidated reference:

```
error[E0382]: use of moved value: `s1`
 --> src/main.rs:5:28
  |
3 |     let s2 = s1;
  |              -- value moved here
4 |
5 |     println!("{}, world!", s1);
  |                            ^^ value used here after move
  |
  = note: move occurs because `s1` has type `std::string::String`, which does
not implement the `Copy` trait
```

If you've heard the terms *shallow copy* and *deep copy* while working with other languages, the concept of copying the pointer, length, and capacity without copying the data probably sounds like making a shallow copy. But because Rust also invalidates the first variable, instead of being called a shallow copy, it's known as a *move*. In this example, we would say that s1 was *moved* into s2. So what actually happens is shown in Figure 4-4.

That solves our problem! With only s2 valid, when it goes out of scope, it alone will free the memory, and we're done.

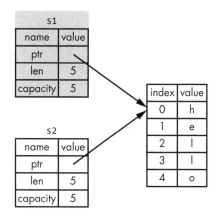

Figure 4-4: Representation in memory after s1 has been invalidated

In addition, there's a design choice that's implied by this: Rust will never automatically create "deep" copies of your data. Therefore, any *automatic* copying can be assumed to be inexpensive in terms of runtime performance.

Ways That Variables and Data Interact: Clone

If we *do* want to deeply copy the heap data of the String, not just the stack data, we can use a common method called clone. We'll discuss method syntax in Chapter 5, but because methods are a common feature in many programming languages, you've probably seen them before.

Here's an example of the clone method in action:

```
let s1 = String::from("hello");
let s2 = s1.clone();

println!("s1 = {}, s2 = {}", s1, s2);
```

This works just fine and explicitly produces the behavior shown in Figure 4-3, where the heap data *does* get copied.

When you see a call to clone, you know that some arbitrary code is being executed and that code may be expensive. It's a visual indicator that something different is going on.

Stack-Only Data: Copy

There's another wrinkle we haven't talked about yet. This code using integers, part of which was shown in Listing 4-2, works and is valid:

```
let x = 5;
let y = x;

println!("x = {}, y = {}", x, y);
```

But this code seems to contradict what we just learned: we don't have a call to clone, but x is still valid and wasn't moved into y.

The reason is that types such as integers that have a known size at compile time are stored entirely on the stack, so copies of the actual values are quick to make. That means there's no reason we would want to prevent x from being valid after we create the variable y. In other words, there's no difference between deep and shallow copying here, so calling clone wouldn't do anything different from the usual shallow copying and we can leave it out.

Rust has a special annotation called the Copy trait that we can place on types like integers that are stored on the stack (we'll talk more about traits in Chapter 10). If a type has the Copy trait, an older variable is still usable after assignment. Rust won't let us annotate a type with the Copy trait if the type, or any of its parts, has implemented the Drop trait. If the type needs something special to happen when the value goes out of scope and we add the Copy annotation to that type, we'll get a compile-time error. To learn about how to add the Copy annotation to your type, see Appendix C.

So what types are Copy? You can check the documentation for the given type to be sure, but as a general rule, any group of simple scalar values can be Copy, and nothing that requires allocation or is some form of resource is Copy. Here are some of the types that are Copy:

- All the integer types, such as u32.
- The Boolean type, bool, with values true and false.
- The character type, char.
- All the floating point types, such as f64.
- Tuples, but only if they contain types that are also Copy. For example, (i32, i32) is Copy, but (i32, String) is not.

Ownership and Functions

The semantics for passing a value to a function are similar to those for assigning a value to a variable. Passing a variable to a function will move or copy, just as assignment does. Listing 4-3 has an example with some annotations showing where variables go into and out of scope.

src/main.rs

```
fn main() {
    let s = String::from("hello");  // s comes into scope

    takes_ownership(s);             // s's value moves into the function...
                                    // ... and so is no longer valid here

    let x = 5;                      // x comes into scope

    makes_copy(x);                  // x would move into the function,
                                    // but i32 is Copy, so it's okay to
                                    // still use x afterward

} // Here, x goes out of scope, then s. But because s's value was moved,
  // nothing special happens.

fn takes_ownership(some_string: String) { // some_string comes into scope
    println!("{}", some_string);
} // Here, some_string goes out of scope and `drop` is called. The backing
  // memory is freed.

fn makes_copy(some_integer: i32) { // some_integer comes into scope
    println!("{}", some_integer);
} // Here, some_integer goes out of scope. Nothing special happens.
```

Listing 4-3: Functions with ownership and scope annotated

If we tried to use s after the call to takes_ownership, Rust would throw a compile-time error. These static checks protect us from mistakes. Try adding code to main that uses s and x to see where you can use them and where the ownership rules prevent you from doing so.

Return Values and Scope

Returning values can also transfer ownership. Listing 4-4 is an example with similar annotations to those in Listing 4-3.

```
fn main() {
    let s1 = gives_ownership();         // gives_ownership moves its return
                                        // value into s1

    let s2 = String::from("hello");     // s2 comes into scope

    let s3 = takes_and_gives_back(s2);  // s2 is moved into
                                        // takes_and_gives_back, which also
                                        // moves its return value into s3
} // Here, s3 goes out of scope and is dropped. s2 goes out of scope but was
  // moved, so nothing happens. s1 goes out of scope and is dropped.

fn gives_ownership() -> String {        // gives_ownership will move its
                                        // return value into the function
                                        // that calls it

    let some_string = String::from("hello"); // some_string comes into scope

    some_string                         // some_string is returned and
                                        // moves out to the calling
                                        // function
}

// takes_and_gives_back will take a String and return one
fn takes_and_gives_back(a_string: String) -> String { // a_string comes into
                                                      // scope

    a_string  // a_string is returned and moves out to the calling function
}
```

Listing 4-4: Transferring ownership of return values

The ownership of a variable follows the same pattern every time: assigning a value to another variable moves it. When a variable that includes data on the heap goes out of scope, the value will be cleaned up by drop unless the data has been moved to be owned by another variable.

Taking ownership and then returning ownership with every function is a bit tedious. What if we want to let a function use a value but not take ownership? It's quite annoying that anything we pass in also needs to be passed back if we want to use it again, in addition to any data resulting from the body of the function that we might want to return as well.

It's possible to return multiple values using a tuple, as shown in Listing 4-5.

```
fn main() {
    let s1 = String::from("hello");

    let (s2, len) = calculate_length(s1);

    println!("The length of '{}' is {}.", s2, len);
}
```

```
fn calculate_length(s: String) -> (String, usize) {
    let length = s.len(); // len() returns the length of a String

    (s, length)
}
```

Listing 4-5: Returning ownership of parameters

But this is too much ceremony and a lot of work for a concept that should be common. Luckily for us, Rust has a feature for this concept, called *references*.

References and Borrowing

The issue with the tuple code in Listing 4-5 is that we have to return the String to the calling function so we can still use the String after the call to calculate_length, because the String was moved into calculate_length.

Here is how you would define and use a calculate_length function that has a reference to an object as a parameter instead of taking ownership of the value:

src/main.rs

```
fn main() {
    let s1 = String::from("hello");

    let len = calculate_length(&s1);

    println!("The length of '{}' is {}.", s1, len);
}

fn calculate_length(s: &String) -> usize {
    s.len()
}
```

First, notice that all the tuple code in the variable declaration and the function return value is gone. Second, note that we pass &s1 into calculate_length and, in its definition, we take &String rather than String.

These ampersands are *references*, and they allow you to refer to some value without taking ownership of it. Figure 4-5 shows a diagram.

Figure 4-5: A diagram of &String s pointing at String s1

NOTE *The opposite of referencing by using & is* dereferencing, *which is accomplished with the dereference operator, *. We'll see some uses of the dereference operator in Chapter 8 and discuss details of dereferencing in Chapter 15.*

Let's take a closer look at the function call here:

```
let s1 = String::from("hello");

let len = calculate_length(&s1);
```

The &s1 syntax lets us create a reference that *refers* to the value of s1 but does not own it. Because it does not own it, the value it points to will not be dropped when the reference goes out of scope.

Likewise, the signature of the function uses & to indicate that the type of the parameter s is a reference. Let's add some explanatory annotations:

```
fn calculate_length(s: &String) -> usize { // s is a reference to a String
    s.len()
} // Here, s goes out of scope. But because it does not have ownership of
  // what it refers to, nothing happens.
```

The scope in which the variable s is valid is the same as any function parameter's scope, but we don't drop what the reference points to when it goes out of scope because we don't have ownership. When functions have references as parameters instead of the actual values, we don't need to return the values in order to give back ownership, because we never had ownership.

We call having references as function parameters *borrowing*. As in real life, if a person owns something, you can borrow it from them. When you're done, you have to give it back.

So what happens if we try to modify something we're borrowing? Try the code in Listing 4-6. Spoiler alert: it doesn't work!

src/main.rs

```
fn main() {
    let s = String::from("hello");

    change(&s);
}

fn change(some_string: &String) {
    some_string.push_str(", world");
}
```

Listing 4-6: Attempting to modify a borrowed value

Here's the error:

```
error[E0596]: cannot borrow immutable borrowed content `*some_string` as
mutable
 --> error.rs:8:5
  |
7 | fn change(some_string: &String) {
  |                        ------- use `&mut String` here to make mutable
8 |     some_string.push_str(", world");
  |     ^^^^^^^^^^^ cannot borrow as mutable
```

Just as variables are immutable by default, so are references. We're not allowed to modify something we have a reference to.

Mutable References

We can fix the error in the code from Listing 4-6 with just a small tweak:

src/main.rs

```
fn main() {
    let mut s = String::from("hello");

    change(&mut s);
}

fn change(some_string: &mut String) {
    some_string.push_str(", world");
}
```

First, we had to change s to be mut. Then we had to create a mutable reference with &mut s and accept a mutable reference with some_string: &mut String.

But mutable references have one big restriction: you can have only one mutable reference to a particular piece of data in a particular scope. This code will fail:

```
let mut s = String::from("hello");

let r1 = &mut s;
let r2 = &mut s;

println!("{}, {}", r1, r2);
```

Here's the error:

```
error[E0499]: cannot borrow `s` as mutable more than once at a time
  --> borrow_twice.rs:5:19
   |
4 |      let r1 = &mut s;
   |                    - first mutable borrow occurs here
5 |      let r2 = &mut s;
   |                    ^ second mutable borrow occurs here
8 | }
   | - first borrow ends here
```

This restriction allows for mutation but in a very controlled fashion. It's something that new Rustaceans struggle with, because most languages let you mutate whenever you'd like.

The benefit of having this restriction is that Rust can prevent data races at compile time. A *data race* is similar to a race condition and happens when these three behaviors occur:

- Two or more pointers access the same data at the same time.
- At least one of the pointers is being used to write to the data.
- There's no mechanism being used to synchronize access to the data.

Data races cause undefined behavior and can be difficult to diagnose and fix when you're trying to track them down at runtime; Rust prevents this problem from happening because it won't even compile code with data races!

As always, we can use curly brackets to create a new scope, allowing for multiple mutable references, just not *simultaneous* ones:

```
let mut s = String::from("hello");

{
    let r1 = &mut s;

} // r1 goes out of scope here, so we can make a new reference with no
  // problems.

let r2 = &mut s;
```

A similar rule exists for combining mutable and immutable references. This code results in an error:

```
let mut s = String::from("hello");

let r1 = &s; // no problem
let r2 = &s; // no problem
let r3 = &mut s; // BIG PROBLEM

println!("{}, {}, and {}", r1, r2, r3);
```

Here's the error:

```
error[E0502]: cannot borrow `s` as mutable because it is also borrowed as
immutable
 --> borrow_thrice.rs:6:19
  |
4 |     let r1 = &s; // no problem
  |               - immutable borrow occurs here
5 |     let r2 = &s; // no problem
6 |     let r3 = &mut s; // BIG PROBLEM
  |                   ^ mutable borrow occurs here
9 | }
  | - immutable borrow ends here
```

Whew! We *also* cannot have a mutable reference while we have an immutable one. Users of an immutable reference don't expect the values to suddenly change out from under them! However, multiple immutable references are okay because no one who is just reading the data has the ability to affect anyone else's reading of the data.

Even though these errors may be frustrating at times, remember that it's the Rust compiler pointing out a potential bug early (at compile time rather than at runtime) and showing you exactly where the problem is. Then you don't have to track down why your data isn't what you thought it was.

Dangling References

In languages with pointers, it's easy to erroneously create a *dangling pointer*, a pointer that references a location in memory that may have been given to someone else, by freeing some memory while preserving a pointer to that memory. In Rust, by contrast, the compiler guarantees that references will never be dangling references: if you have a reference to some data, the compiler will ensure that the data will not go out of scope before the reference to the data does.

Let's try to create a dangling reference, which Rust will prevent with a compile-time error:

src/main.rs
```
fn main() {
    let reference_to_nothing = dangle();
}

fn dangle() -> &String {
    let s = String::from("hello");

    &s
}
```

Here's the error:

```
error[E0106]: missing lifetime specifier
 --> main.rs:5:16
  |
5 | fn dangle() -> &String {
  |                ^expected lifetime parameter
  |
  = help: this function's return type contains a borrowed value, but there is
    no value for it to be borrowed from
  = help: consider giving it a 'static lifetime
```

This error message refers to a feature we haven't covered yet: lifetimes. We'll discuss lifetimes in detail in Chapter 10. But, if you disregard the parts about lifetimes, the message does contain the key to why this code is a problem:

```
this function's return type contains a borrowed value, but there is
no value for it to be borrowed from.
```

Let's take a closer look at exactly what's happening at each stage of our dangle code:

src/main.rs
```
fn dangle() -> &String { // dangle returns a reference to a String

    let s = String::from("hello"); // s is a new String

    &s // we return a reference to the String, s
} // Here, s goes out of scope, and is dropped. Its memory goes away.
  // Danger!
```

Because s is created inside dangle, when the code of dangle is finished, s will be deallocated. But we tried to return a reference to it. That means this reference would be pointing to an invalid String. That's no good! Rust won't let us do this.

The solution here is to return the String directly:

src/main.rs

```
fn no_dangle() -> String {
    let s = String::from("hello");

    s
}
```

This works without any problems. Ownership is moved out, and nothing is deallocated.

The Rules of References

Let's recap what we've discussed about references:

- At any given time, you can have *either* but not both of the following: one mutable reference *or* any number of immutable references.
- References must always be valid.

Next, we'll look at a different kind of reference: slices.

The Slice Type

Another data type that does not have ownership is the *slice*. Slices let you reference a contiguous sequence of elements in a collection rather than the whole collection.

Here's a small programming problem: write a function that takes a string and returns the first word it finds in that string. If the function doesn't find a space in the string, the whole string must be one word, so the entire string should be returned.

Let's think about the signature of this function:

```
fn first_word(s: &String) -> ?
```

This function, first_word, has a &String as a parameter. We don't want ownership, so this is fine. But what should we return? We don't really have a way to talk about *part* of a string. However, we could return the index of the end of the word. Let's try that, as shown in Listing 4-7.

src/main.rs

```
fn first_word(s: &String) -> usize {
❶ let bytes = s.as_bytes();

    for (i, &item)❷ in bytes.iter()❸.enumerate() {
    ❹ if item == b' ' {
            return i;
        }
```

```
    }

❺ s.len()
}
```

Listing 4-7: The `first_word` function that returns a byte index value into the `String` parameter

Because we need to go through the `String` element by element and check whether a value is a space, we'll convert our `String` to an array of bytes using the as_bytes method ❶. Next, we create an iterator over the array of bytes using the iter method ❸.

We'll discuss iterators in more detail in Chapter 13. For now, know that iter is a method that returns each element in a collection and that enumerate wraps the result of iter and returns each element as part of a tuple instead. The first element of the tuple returned from enumerate is the index, and the second element is a reference to the element. This is a bit more convenient than calculating the index ourselves.

Because the enumerate method returns a tuple, we can use patterns to destructure that tuple, just like everywhere else in Rust. So in the for loop, we specify a pattern that has i for the index in the tuple and &item for the single byte in the tuple ❷. Because we get a reference to the element from .iter().enumerate(), we use & in the pattern.

Inside the for loop, we search for the byte that represents the space by using the byte literal syntax ❹. If we find a space, we return the position. Otherwise, we return the length of the string by using s.len() ❺.

We now have a way to find out the index of the end of the first word in the string, but there's a problem. We're returning a usize on its own, but it's only a meaningful number in the context of the &String. In other words, because it's a separate value from the String, there's no guarantee that it will still be valid in the future. Consider the program in Listing 4-8 that uses the first_word function from Listing 4-7.

src/main.rs

```
fn main() {
    let mut s = String::from("hello world");

    let word = first_word(&s); // word will get the value 5

    s.clear(); // this empties the String, making it equal to ""

    // word still has the value 5 here, but there's no more string that
    // we could meaningfully use the value 5 with. word is now totally
    // invalid!
}
```

Listing 4-8: Storing the result from calling the `first_word` function and then changing the `String` contents

This program compiles without any errors and would also do so if we used `word` after calling `s.clear()`. Because `word` isn't connected to the state of `s` at all, `word` still contains the value 5. We could use that value 5 with the variable `s` to try to extract the first word, but this would be a bug because the contents of `s` have changed since we saved 5 in `word`.

Having to worry about the index in `word` getting out of sync with the data in `s` is tedious and error prone! Managing these indices is even more brittle if we write a `second_word` function. Its signature would have to look like this:

```
fn second_word(s: &String) -> (usize, usize) {
```

Now we're tracking a starting *and* an ending index, and we have even more values that were calculated from data in a particular state but aren't tied to that state at all. We now have three unrelated variables floating around that need to be kept in sync.

Luckily, Rust has a solution to this problem: string slices.

String Slices

A *string slice* is a reference to part of a `String`, and it looks like this:

```
let s = String::from("hello world");

let hello = &s[0..5];
❶ let world = &s[6..11];
```

This is similar to taking a reference to the whole `String` but with the extra `[0..5]` bit. Rather than a reference to the entire `String`, it's a reference to a portion of the `String`. The `start..end` syntax is a range that begins at start and continues up to, but not including, end.

We can create slices using a range within brackets by specifying `[starting_index..ending_index]`, where `starting_index` is the first position in the slice and `ending_index` is one more than the last position in the slice. Internally, the slice data structure stores the starting position and the length of the slice, which corresponds to `ending_index` minus `starting_index`. So at ❶, `world` would be a slice that contains a pointer to the 7th byte of `s` with a length value of 5.

Figure 4-6 shows this in a diagram.

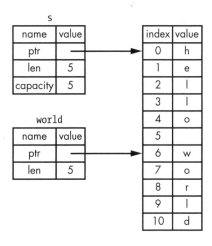

Figure 4-6: String slice referring to part of a String

With Rust's .. range syntax, if you want to start at the first index (zero), you can drop the value before the two periods. In other words, these are equal:

```
let s = String::from("hello");

let slice = &s[0..2];
let slice = &s[..2];
```

By the same token, if your slice includes the last byte of the String, you can drop the trailing number. That means these are equal:

```
let s = String::from("hello");

let len = s.len();

let slice = &s[3..len];
let slice = &s[3..];
```

You can also drop both values to take a slice of the entire string. So these are equal:

```
let s = String::from("hello");

let len = s.len();

let slice = &s[0..len];
let slice = &s[..];
```

NOTE *String slice range indices must occur at valid UTF-8 character boundaries. If you attempt to create a string slice in the middle of a multibyte character, your program will exit with an error. For the purposes of introducing string slices, we are assuming ASCII only in this section; a more thorough dicussion of UTF-8 handling is in "Storing UTF-8 Encoded Text with Strings" on page 135.*

With all this information in mind, let's rewrite first_word to return a slice. The type that signifies "string slice" is written as &str:

src/main.rs
```
fn first_word(s: &String) -> &str {
    let bytes = s.as_bytes();

    for (i, &item) in bytes.iter().enumerate() {
        if item == b' ' {
            return &s[0..i];
        }
    }

    &s[..]
}
```

We get the index for the end of the word in the same way as we did in Listing 4-7, by looking for the first occurrence of a space. When we find a space, we return a string slice using the start of the string and the index of the space as the starting and ending indices.

Now when we call first_word, we get back a single value that is tied to the underlying data. The value is made up of a reference to the starting point of the slice and the number of elements in the slice.

Returning a slice would also work for a second_word function:

```
fn second_word(s: &String) -> &str {
```

We now have a straightforward API that's much harder to mess up, because the compiler will ensure the references into the String remain valid. Remember the bug in the program in Listing 4-8, when we got the index to the end of the first word but then cleared the string so our index was invalid? That code was logically incorrect but didn't show any immediate errors. The problems would show up later if we kept trying to use the first word index with an emptied string. Slices make this bug impossible and let us know we have a problem with our code much sooner. Using the slice version of first_word will throw a compile-time error:

src/main.rs

```
fn main() {
    let mut s = String::from("hello world");

    let word = first_word(&s);

    s.clear(); // error!

    println!("the first word is: {}", word);
}
```

Here's the compiler error:

```
error[E0502]: cannot borrow `s` as mutable because it is also borrowed as
immutable
 --> src/main.rs:6:5
  |
4 |     let word = first_word(&s);
  |                           - immutable borrow occurs here
5 |
6 |     s.clear(); // error!
  |     ^ mutable borrow occurs here
9 | }
  | - immutable borrow ends here
```

Recall from the borrowing rules that if we have an immutable reference to something, we cannot also take a mutable reference. Because clear needs to truncate the String, it tries to take a mutable reference, which fails. Not only has Rust made our API easier to use, but it has also eliminated an entire class of errors at compile time!

String Literals Are Slices

Recall that we talked about string literals being stored inside the binary. Now that we know about slices, we can properly understand string literals:

```
let s = "Hello, world!";
```

The type of s here is &str: it's a slice pointing to that specific point of the binary. This is also why string literals are immutable; &str is an immutable reference.

String Slices as Parameters

Knowing that you can take slices of literals and String values leads us to one more improvement on first_word, and that's its signature:

```
fn first_word(s: &String) -> &str {
```

A more experienced Rustacean would write the signature shown in Listing 4-9 instead because it allows us to use the same function on both String and &str values.

```
fn first_word(s: &str) -> &str {
```

Listing 4-9: Improving the first_word function by using a string slice for the type of the s parameter

If we have a string slice, we can pass that directly. If we have a String, we can pass a slice of the entire String. Defining a function to take a string slice instead of a reference to a String makes our API more general and useful without losing any functionality:

src/main.rs
```
fn main() {
    let my_string = String::from("hello world");

    // first_word works on slices of `String`s
    let word = first_word(&my_string[..]);

    let my_string_literal = "hello world";

    // first_word works on slices of string literals
    let word = first_word(&my_string_literal[..]);

    // Because string literals *are* string slices already,
    // this works too, without the slice syntax!
    let word = first_word(my_string_literal);
}
```

Other Slices

String slices, as you might imagine, are specific to strings. But there's a more general slice type, too. Consider this array:

```
let a = [1, 2, 3, 4, 5];
```

Just as we might want to refer to a part of a string, we might want to refer to part of an array. We'd do so like this:

```
let a = [1, 2, 3, 4, 5];

let slice = &a[1..3];
```

This slice has the type &[i32]. It works the same way as string slices do, by storing a reference to the first element and a length. You'll use this kind of slice for all sorts of other collections. We'll discuss these collections in detail when we talk about vectors in Chapter 8.

Summary

The concepts of ownership, borrowing, and slices ensure memory safety in Rust programs at compile time. The Rust language gives you control over your memory usage in the same way as other systems programming languages, but having the owner of data automatically clean up that data when the owner goes out of scope means you don't have to write and debug extra code to get this control.

Ownership affects how lots of other parts of Rust work, so we'll talk about these concepts further throughout the rest of the book. Let's move on to Chapter 5 and look at grouping pieces of data together in a struct.

5

USING STRUCTS TO STRUCTURE RELATED DATA

A *struct*, or *structure*, is a custom data type that lets you name and package together multiple related values that make up a meaningful group. If you're familiar with an object-oriented language, a *struct* is like an object's data attributes. In this chapter, we'll compare and contrast tuples with structs, demonstrate how to use structs, and discuss how to define methods and associated functions to specify behavior associated with a struct's data. Structs and enums (discussed in Chapter 6) are the building blocks for creating new types in your program's domain to take full advantage of Rust's compile time type checking.

Defining and Instantiating Structs

Structs are similar to tuples, which were discussed in Chapter 3. Like tuples, the pieces of a struct can be different types. Unlike with tuples, you'll name each piece of data so it's clear what the values mean. As a result of these names, structs are more flexible than tuples: you don't have to rely on the order of the data to specify or access the values of an instance.

To define a struct, we enter the keyword struct and name the entire struct. A struct's name should describe the significance of the pieces of data being grouped together. Then, inside curly brackets, we define the names and types of the pieces of data, which we call *fields*. For example, Listing 5-1 shows a struct that stores information about a user account.

```
struct User {
    username: String,
    email: String,
    sign_in_count: u64,
    active: bool,
}
```

Listing 5-1: A User struct definition

To use a struct after we've defined it, we create an *instance* of that struct by specifying concrete values for each of the fields. We create an instance by stating the name of the struct and then add curly brackets containing key: value pairs, where the keys are the names of the fields and the values are the data we want to store in those fields. We don't have to specify the fields in the same order in which we declared them in the struct. In other words, the struct definition is like a general template for the type, and instances fill in that template with particular data to create values of the type. For example, we can declare a particular user as shown in Listing 5-2.

```
let user1 = User {
    email: String::from("someone@example.com"),
    username: String::from("someusername123"),
    active: true,
    sign_in_count: 1,
};
```

Listing 5-2: Creating an instance of the User struct

To get a specific value from a struct, we can use dot notation. If we wanted just this user's email address, we could use user1.email wherever we wanted to use this value. If the instance is mutable, we can change a value by using the dot notation and assigning into a particular field. Listing 5-3 shows how to change the value in the email field of a mutable User instance.

```
let mut user1 = User {
    email: String::from("someone@example.com"),
    username: String::from("someusername123"),
    active: true,
    sign_in_count: 1,
};

user1.email = String::from("anotheremail@example.com");
```

Listing 5-3: Changing the value in the email field of a User instance

Note that the entire instance must be mutable; Rust doesn't allow us to mark only certain fields as mutable. As with any expression, we can construct a new instance of the struct as the last expression in the function body to implicitly return that new instance.

Listing 5-4 shows a build_user function that returns a User instance with the given email and username. The active field gets a value of true, and the sign_in_count gets a value of 1.

```
fn build_user(email: String, username: String) -> User {
    User {
        email: email,
        username: username,
        active: true,
        sign_in_count: 1,
    }
}
```

Listing 5-4: A build_user function that takes an email and username and returns a User instance

It makes sense to name the function parameters with the same name as the struct fields, but having to repeat the email and username field names and variables is a bit tedious. If the struct had more fields, repeating each name would get even more annoying. Luckily, there's a convenient shorthand!

Using the Field Init Shorthand When Variables and Fields Have the Same Name

Because the parameter names and the struct field names are exactly the same in Listing 5-4, we can use the *field init shorthand* syntax to rewrite build_user so that it behaves exactly the same but doesn't have the repetition of email and username, as shown in Listing 5-5.

```
fn build_user(email: String, username: String) -> User {
    User {
        email,
        username,
        active: true,
        sign_in_count: 1,
    }
}
```

Listing 5-5: A build_user function that uses field init shorthand because the email and username parameters have the same name as struct fields

Here, we're creating a new instance of the User struct, which has a field named email. We want to set the email field's value to the value in the email parameter of the build_user function. Because the email field and the email parameter have the same name, we only need to write email rather than email: email.

Creating Instances from Other Instances with Struct Update Syntax

It's often useful to create a new instance of a struct that uses most of an old instance's values but changes some. You'll do this using *struct update syntax*.

First, Listing 5-6 shows how we create a new User instance in user2 without the update syntax. We set new values for email and username but otherwise use the same values from user1 that we created in Listing 5-2.

```
let user2 = User {
    email: String::from("another@example.com"),
    username: String::from("anotherusername567"),
    active: user1.active,
    sign_in_count: user1.sign_in_count,
};
```

Listing 5-6: Creating a new User instance using some of the values from user1

Using struct update syntax, we can achieve the same effect with less code, as shown in Listing 5-7. The syntax .. specifies that the remaining fields not explicitly set should have the same value as the fields in the given instance.

```
let user2 = User {
    email: String::from("another@example.com"),
    username: String::from("anotherusername567"),
    ..user1
};
```

Listing 5-7: Using struct update syntax to set new email and username values for a User instance but use the rest of the values from the fields of the instance in the user1 variable

The code in Listing 5-7 also creates an instance in user2 that has a different value for email and username but has the same values for the active and sign_in_count fields from user1.

Using Tuple Structs Without Named Fields to Create Different Types

You can also define structs that look similar to tuples, called *tuple structs*. Tuple structs have the added meaning the struct name provides but don't have names associated with their fields; rather, they just have the types of the fields. Tuple structs are useful when you want to give the whole tuple a name and make the tuple be a different type than other tuples, and naming each field as in a regular struct would be verbose or redundant.

To define a tuple struct, start with the struct keyword and the struct name followed by the types in the tuple. For example, here are definitions and usages of two tuple structs named Color and Point:

```
struct Color(i32, i32, i32);
struct Point(i32, i32, i32);

let black = Color(0, 0, 0);
let origin = Point(0, 0, 0);
```

Note that the black and origin values are different types, because they're instances of different tuple structs. Each struct you define is its own type, even though the fields within the struct have the same types. For example, a function that takes a parameter of type Color cannot take a Point as an argument, even though both types are made up of three i32 values. Otherwise, tuple struct instances behave like tuples: you can destructure them into their individual pieces, you can use a . followed by the index to access an individual value, and so on.

Unit-Like Structs Without Any Fields

You can also define structs that don't have any fields! These are called *unit-like structs* because they behave similarly to (), the unit type. Unit-like structs can be useful in situations in which you need to implement a trait on some type but don't have any data that you want to store in the type itself. We'll discuss traits in Chapter 10.

OWNERSHIP OF STRUCT DATA

In the User struct definition in Listing 5-1, we use the owned String type rather than the &str string slice type. This is a deliberate choice because we want instances of this struct to own all of its data and for that data to be valid for as long as the entire struct is valid.

It's possible for structs to store references to data owned by something else, but to do so requires the use of *lifetimes*, a Rust feature that we'll discuss in Chapter 10. Lifetimes ensure that the data referenced by a struct is valid for as long as the struct is. Let's say you try to store a reference in a struct without specifying lifetimes, like this, which won't work:

src/main.rs
```
struct User {
    username: &str,
    email: &str,
    sign_in_count: u64,
    active: bool,
}

fn main() {
    let user1 = User {
        email: "someone@example.com",
        username: "someusername123",
        active: true,
        sign_in_count: 1,
    };
}
```

(continued)

The compiler will complain that it needs lifetime specifiers:

```
error[E0106]: missing lifetime specifier
 -->
  |
2 |     username: &str,
  |               ^ expected lifetime parameter

error[E0106]: missing lifetime specifier
 -->
  |
3 |     email: &str,
  |            ^ expected lifetime parameter
```

In Chapter 10, we'll discuss how to fix these errors so you can store references in structs, but for now, we'll fix errors like these using owned types like String instead of references like &str.

An Example Program Using Structs

To understand when we might want to use structs, let's write a program that calculates the area of a rectangle. We'll start with single variables, and then refactor the program until we're using structs instead.

Let's make a new binary project with Cargo called *rectangles* that will take the width and height of a rectangle specified in pixels and calculate the area of the rectangle. Listing 5-8 shows a short program with one way of doing exactly that in our project's *src/main.rs*.

src/main.rs
```
fn main() {
    let width1 = 30;
    let height1 = 50;

    println!(
        "The area of the rectangle is {} square pixels.",
        area(width1, height1)
    );
}

fn area(width: u32, height: u32) -> u32 {
    width * height
}
```

Listing 5-8: Calculating the area of a rectangle specified by separate width and height variables

Now, run this program using cargo run:

```
The area of the rectangle is 1500 square pixels.
```

Even though Listing 5-8 works and figures out the area of the rectangle by calling the area function with each dimension, we can do better. The width and the height are related to each other because together they describe one rectangle.

The issue with this code is evident in the signature of area:

```
fn area(width: u32, height: u32) -> u32 {
```

The area function is supposed to calculate the area of one rectangle, but the function we wrote has two parameters. The parameters are related, but that's not expressed anywhere in our program. It would be more readable and more manageable to group width and height together. We've already discussed one way we might do that in "The Tuple Type" on page 39: by using tuples.

Refactoring with Tuples

Listing 5-9 shows another version of our program that uses tuples.

src/main.rs
```
fn main() {
    let rect1 = (30, 50);

    println!(
        "The area of the rectangle is {} square pixels.",
    ❶ area(rect1)
    );
}

fn area(dimensions: (u32, u32)) -> u32 {
❷ dimensions.0 * dimensions.1
}
```

Listing 5-9: Specifying the width and height of the rectangle with a tuple

In one way, this program is better. Tuples let us add a bit of structure, and we're now passing just one argument ❶. But in another way, this version is less clear: tuples don't name their elements, so our calculation has become more confusing because we have to index into the parts of the tuple ❷.

It doesn't matter if we mix up width and height for the area calculation, but if we want to draw the rectangle on the screen, it would matter! We would have to keep in mind that width is the tuple index 0 and height is the tuple index 1. If someone else worked on this code, they would have to figure this out and keep it in mind as well. It would be easy to forget or mix up these values and cause errors, because we haven't conveyed the meaning of our data in our code.

Refactoring with Structs: Adding More Meaning

We use structs to add meaning by labeling the data. We can transform the tuple we're using into a data type with a name for the whole as well as names for the parts, as shown in Listing 5-10.

```
❶ struct Rectangle {
   ❷ width: u32,
      height: u32,
   }

   fn main() {
   ❸ let rect1 = Rectangle { width: 30, height: 50 };

      println!(
          "The area of the rectangle is {} square pixels.",
          area(&rect1)
      );
   }

❹ fn area(rectangle: &Rectangle) -> u32 {
   ❺ rectangle.width * rectangle.height
   }
```

Listing 5-10: Defining a Rectangle struct

Here we've defined a struct and named it Rectangle ❶. Inside the curly brackets, we defined the fields as width and height, both of which have type u32 ❷. Then in main, we created a particular instance of Rectangle that has a width of 30 and a height of 50 ❸.

Our area function is now defined with one parameter, which we've named rectangle, whose type is an immutable borrow of a struct Rectangle instance ❹. As mentioned in Chapter 4, we want to borrow the struct rather than take ownership of it. This way, main retains its ownership and can continue using rect1, which is the reason we use the & in the function signature and where we call the function.

The area function accesses the width and height fields of the Rectangle instance ❺. Our function signature for area now says exactly what we mean: calculate the area of Rectangle, using its width and height fields. This conveys that the width and height are related to each other, and it gives descriptive names to the values rather than using the tuple index values of 0 and 1. This is a win for clarity.

Adding Useful Functionality with Derived Traits

It'd be nice to be able to print an instance of Rectangle while we're debugging our program and see the values for all its fields. Listing 5-11 tries using the println! macro as we have used in previous chapters. This won't work, however.

```
struct Rectangle {
    width: u32,
    height: u32,
}

fn main() {
    let rect1 = Rectangle { width: 30, height: 50 };
```

```
    println!("rect1 is {}", rect1);
}
```

Listing 5-11: Attempting to print a Rectangle instance

When we run this code, we get an error with this core message:

```
error[E0277]: the trait bound `Rectangle: std::fmt::Display` is not satisfied
```

The println! macro can do many kinds of formatting, and by default, the curly brackets tell println! to use formatting known as Display: output intended for direct end user consumption. The primitive types we've seen so far implement Display by default, because there's only one way you'd want to show a 1 or any other primitive type to a user. But with structs, the way println! should format the output is less clear because there are more display possibilities: Do you want commas or not? Do you want to print the curly brackets? Should all the fields be shown? Due to this ambiguity, Rust doesn't try to guess what we want, and structs don't have a provided implementation of Display.

If we continue reading the errors, we'll find this helpful note:

```
`Rectangle` cannot be formatted with the default formatter; try using
`:?` instead if you are using a format string
```

Let's try it! The println! macro call will now look like println!("rect1 is {:?}", rect1);. Putting the specifier :? inside the curly brackets tells println! we want to use an output format called Debug. The Debug trait enables us to print our struct in a way that is useful for developers so we can see its value while we're debugging our code.

Run the code with this change. Drat! We still get an error:

```
error[E0277]: the trait bound `Rectangle: std::fmt::Debug` is not satisfied
```

But again, the compiler gives us a helpful note:

```
`Rectangle` cannot be formatted using `:?`; if it is defined in your
crate, add `#[derive(Debug)]` or manually implement it
```

Rust *does* include functionality to print debugging information, but we have to explicitly opt in to make that functionality available for our struct. To do that, we add the annotation #[derive(Debug)] just before the struct definition, as shown in Listing 5-12.

src/main.rs

```
#[derive(Debug)]
struct Rectangle {
    width: u32,
    height: u32,
}

fn main() {
    let rect1 = Rectangle { width: 30, height: 50 };
```

```
        println!("rect1 is {:?}", rect1);
}
```

Listing 5-12: Adding the annotation to derive the Debug trait and printing the Rectangle instance using debug formatting

Now when we run the program, we won't get any errors, and we'll see the following output:

```
rect1 is Rectangle { width: 30, height: 50 }
```

Nice! It's not the prettiest output, but it shows the values of all the fields for this instance, which would definitely help during debugging. When we have larger structs, it's useful to have output that's a bit easier to read; in those cases, we can use {:#?} instead of {:?} in the println! string. When we use the {:#?} style in the example, the output will look like this:

```
rect1 is Rectangle {
    width: 30,
    height: 50
}
```

Rust has provided a number of traits for us to use with the derive annotation that can add useful behavior to our custom types. Those traits and their behaviors are listed in Appendix C. We'll cover how to implement these traits with custom behavior as well as how to create your own traits in Chapter 10.

Our area function is very specific: it only computes the area of rectangles. It would be helpful to tie this behavior more closely to our Rectangle struct, because it won't work with any other type. Let's look at how we can continue to refactor this code by turning the area function into an area *method* defined on our Rectangle type.

Method Syntax

Methods are similar to functions: they're declared with the fn keyword and their name, they can have parameters and a return value, and they contain some code that is run when they're called from somewhere else. However, methods are different from functions in that they're defined within the context of a struct (or an enum or a trait object, which we cover in Chapters 6 and 17, respectively), and their first parameter is always self, which represents the instance of the struct the method is being called on.

Defining Methods

Let's change the area function that has a Rectangle instance as a parameter and instead make an area method defined on the Rectangle struct, as shown in Listing 5-13.

```
#[derive(Debug)]
struct Rectangle {
    width: u32,
    height: u32,
}

❶ impl Rectangle {
  ❷ fn area(&self) -> u32 {
        self.width * self.height
    }
}

fn main() {
    let rect1 = Rectangle { width: 30, height: 50 };

    println!(
        "The area of the rectangle is {} square pixels.",
      ❸ rect1.area()
    );
}
```

Listing 5-13: Defining an area method on the Rectangle struct

To define the function within the context of Rectangle, we start an impl (implementation) block ❶. Then we move the area function within the impl curly brackets ❷ and change the first (and in this case, only) parameter to be self in the signature and everywhere within the body. In main, where we called the area function and passed rect1 as an argument, we can instead use *method syntax* to call the area method on our Rectangle instance ❸. The method syntax goes after an instance: we add a dot followed by the method name, parentheses, and any arguments.

In the signature for area, we use &self instead of rectangle: &Rectangle because Rust knows the type of self is Rectangle due to this method's being inside the impl Rectangle context. Note that we still need to use the & before self, just as we did in &Rectangle. Methods can take ownership of self, borrow self immutably as we've done here, or borrow self mutably, just as they can any other parameter.

We've chosen &self here for the same reason we used &Rectangle in the function version: we don't want to take ownership, and we just want to read the data in the struct, not write to it. If we wanted to change the instance that we've called the method on as part of what the method does, we'd use &mut self as the first parameter. Having a method that takes ownership of the instance by using just self as the first parameter is rare; this technique is usually used when the method transforms self into something else and you want to prevent the caller from using the original instance after the transformation.

The main benefit of using methods instead of functions, in addition to using method syntax and not having to repeat the type of self in every method's signature, is for organization. We've put all the things we can do with an instance of a type in one impl block rather than making future users of our code search for capabilities of Rectangle in various places in the library we provide.

WHERE'S THE -> OPERATOR?

In C and C++, two different operators are used for calling methods: you use the . operator if you're calling a method on the object directly and the -> operator if you're calling the method on a pointer to the object and need to dereference the pointer first. In other words, if object is a pointer, object->something() is similar to (*object).something().

Rust doesn't have an equivalent to the -> operator; instead, Rust has a feature called *automatic referencing and dereferencing*. Calling methods is one of the few places in Rust that has this behavior.

Here's how it works: when you call a method with object.something(), Rust automatically adds in &, &mut, or * so object matches the signature of the method. In other words, the following are the same:

```
p1.distance(&p2);
(&p1).distance(&p2);
```

The first one looks much cleaner. This automatic referencing behavior works because methods have a clear receiver—the type of self. Given the receiver and name of a method, Rust can figure out definitively whether the method is reading (&self), mutating (&mut self), or consuming (self). The fact that Rust makes borrowing implicit for method receivers is a big part of making ownership ergonomic in practice.

Methods with More Parameters

Let's practice using methods by implementing a second method on the Rectangle struct. This time, we want an instance of Rectangle to take another instance of Rectangle and return true if the second Rectangle can fit completely within self; otherwise it should return false. That is, we want to be able to write the program shown in Listing 5-14, once we've defined the can_hold method.

src/main.rs

```rust
fn main() {
    let rect1 = Rectangle { width: 30, height: 50 };
    let rect2 = Rectangle { width: 10, height: 40 };
    let rect3 = Rectangle { width: 60, height: 45 };

    println!("Can rect1 hold rect2? {}", rect1.can_hold(&rect2));
    println!("Can rect1 hold rect3? {}", rect1.can_hold(&rect3));
}
```

Listing 5-14: Using the as-yet-unwritten can_hold method

And the expected output would look like the following, because both dimensions of rect2 are smaller than the dimensions of rect1 but rect3 is wider than rect1:

```
Can rect1 hold rect2? true
Can rect1 hold rect3? false
```

We know we want to define a method, so it will be within the impl Rectangle block. The method name will be can_hold, and it will take an immutable borrow of another Rectangle as a parameter. We can tell what the type of the parameter will be by looking at the code that calls the method: rect1.can_hold(&rect2) passes in &rect2, which is an immutable borrow to rect2, an instance of Rectangle. This makes sense because we only need to read rect2 (rather than write, which would mean we'd need a mutable borrow), and we want main to retain ownership of rect2 so we can use it again after calling the can_hold method. The return value of can_hold will be a Boolean, and the implementation will check whether the width and height of self are both greater than the width and height of the other Rectangle, respectively. Let's add the new can_hold method to the impl block from Listing 5-13, shown in Listing 5-15.

src/main.rs

```
impl Rectangle {
    fn area(&self) -> u32 {
        self.width * self.height
    }

    fn can_hold(&self, other: &Rectangle) -> bool {
        self.width > other.width && self.height > other.height
    }
}
```

Listing 5-15: Implementing the can_hold method on Rectangle that takes another Rectangle instance as a parameter

When we run this code with the main function in Listing 5-14, we'll get our desired output. Methods can take multiple parameters that we add to the signature after the self parameter, and those parameters work just like parameters in functions.

Associated Functions

Another useful feature of impl blocks is that we're allowed to define functions within impl blocks that *don't* take self as a parameter. These are called *associated functions* because they're associated with the struct. They're still functions, not methods, because they don't have an instance of the struct to work with. You've already used the String::from associated function.

Associated functions are often used for constructors that will return a new instance of the struct. For example, we could provide an associated function that would have one dimension parameter and use that as both width and height, thus making it easier to create a square Rectangle rather than having to specify the same value twice:

src/main.rs

```
impl Rectangle {
    fn square(size: u32) -> Rectangle {
        Rectangle { width: size, height: size }
    }
}
```

To call this associated function, we use the `::` syntax with the struct name; `let sq = Rectangle::square(3);` is an example. This function is name-spaced by the struct: the `::` syntax is used for both associated functions and namespaces created by modules. We'll discuss modules in Chapter 7.

Multiple impl Blocks

Each struct is allowed to have multiple `impl` blocks. For example, Listing 5-15 is equivalent to the code shown in Listing 5-16, which has each method in its own `impl` block.

src/main.rs

```
impl Rectangle {
    fn area(&self) -> u32 {
        self.width * self.height
    }
}

impl Rectangle {
    fn can_hold(&self, other: &Rectangle) -> bool {
        self.width > other.width && self.height > other.height
    }
}
```

Listing 5-16: Rewriting Listing 5-15 using multiple `impl` blocks

There's no reason to separate these methods into multiple `impl` blocks here, but this is valid syntax. We'll see a case in which multiple `impl` blocks are useful in Chapter 10, where we discuss generic types and traits.

Summary

Structs let you create custom types that are meaningful for your domain. By using structs, you can keep associated pieces of data connected to each other and name each piece to make your code clear. Methods let you specify the behavior that instances of your structs have, and associated functions let you namespace functionality that is particular to your struct without having an instance available.

But structs aren't the only way you can create custom types: let's turn to Rust's enum feature to add another tool to your toolbox.

6

ENUMS AND PATTERN MATCHING

In this chapter, we'll look at *enumerations,* also referred to as *enums.* Enums allow you to define a type by enumerating its possible values. First, we'll define and use an enum to show how an enum can encode meaning along with data. Next, we'll explore a particularly useful enum, called Option, which expresses that a value can be either something or nothing. Then we'll look at how pattern matching in the match expression makes it easy to run different code for different values of an enum. Finally, we'll cover how the if let construct is another convenient and concise idiom available to you to handle enums in your code.

Enums are a feature in many languages, but their capabilities differ in each language. Rust's enums are most similar to *algebraic data types* in functional languages, such as F#, OCaml, and Haskell.

Defining an Enum

Let's look at a situation we might want to express in code and see why enums are useful and more appropriate than structs in this case. Say we need to work with IP addresses. Currently, two major standards are used for IP addresses: version four and version six. These are the only possibilities for an IP address that our program will come across: we can *enumerate* all possible values, which is where enumeration gets its name.

Any IP address can be either a version four or a version six address, but not both at the same time. That property of IP addresses makes the enum data structure appropriate, because enum values can only be one of the variants. Both version four and version six addresses are still fundamentally IP addresses, so they should be treated as the same type when the code is handling situations that apply to any kind of IP address.

We can express this concept in code by defining an IpAddrKind enumeration and listing the possible kinds an IP address can be, V4 and V6. These are known as the *variants* of the enum:

```
enum IpAddrKind {
    V4,
    V6,
}
```

IpAddrKind is now a custom data type that we can use elsewhere in our code.

Enum Values

We can create instances of each of the two variants of IpAddrKind like this:

```
let four = IpAddrKind::V4;
let six = IpAddrKind::V6;
```

Note that the variants of the enum are namespaced under its identifier, and we use a double colon to separate the two. The reason this is useful is that now both values IpAddrKind::V4 and IpAddrKind::V6 are of the same type: IpAddrKind. We can then, for instance, define a function that takes any IpAddrKind:

```
fn route(ip_type: IpAddrKind) { }
```

And we can call this function with either variant:

```
route(IpAddrKind::V4);
route(IpAddrKind::V6);
```

Using enums has even more advantages. Thinking more about our IP address type, at the moment we don't have a way to store the actual IP address *data*; we only know what *kind* it is. Given that you just learned about structs in Chapter 5, you might tackle this problem as shown in Listing 6-1.

```
❶ enum IpAddrKind {
      V4,
      V6,
  }

❷ struct IpAddr {
    ❸ kind: IpAddrKind,
    ❹ address: String,
  }

❺ let home = IpAddr {
      kind: IpAddrKind::V4,
      address: String::from("127.0.0.1"),
  };

❻ let loopback = IpAddr {
      kind: IpAddrKind::V6,
      address: String::from("::1"),
  };
```

Listing 6-1: Storing the data and IpAddrKind variant of an IP address using a struct

Here, we've defined a struct IpAddr ❷ that has two fields: a kind field ❸ that is of type IpAddrKind (the enum we defined previously ❶) and an address field ❹ of type String. We have two instances of this struct. The first, home ❺, has the value IpAddrKind::V4 as its kind with associated address data of 127.0.0.1. The second instance, loopback ❻, has the other variant of IpAddrKind as its kind value, V6, and has address ::1 associated with it. We've used a struct to bundle the kind and address values together, so now the variant is associated with the value.

We can represent the same concept in a more concise way using just an enum, rather than an enum inside a struct, by putting data directly into each enum variant. This new definition of the IpAddr enum says that both V4 and V6 variants will have associated String values:

```
enum IpAddr {
    V4(String),
    V6(String),
}

let home = IpAddr::V4(String::from("127.0.0.1"));

let loopback = IpAddr::V6(String::from("::1"));
```

We attach data to each variant of the enum directly, so there is no need for an extra struct.

There's another advantage to using an enum rather than a struct: each variant can have different types and amounts of associated data. Version four type IP addresses will always have four numeric components that will have values between 0 and 255. If we wanted to store V4 addresses as four u8 values but still express V6 addresses as one String value, we wouldn't be able to with a struct. Enums handle this case with ease.

```
enum IpAddr {
    V4(u8, u8, u8, u8),
    V6(String),
}

let home = IpAddr::V4(127, 0, 0, 1);

let loopback = IpAddr::V6(String::from("::1"));
```

We've shown several different ways to define data structures to store version four and version six IP addresses. However, as it turns out, wanting to store IP addresses and encode which kind they are is so common that the standard library has a definition we can use! Let's look at how the standard library defines IpAddr: it has the exact enum and variants that we've defined and used, but it embeds the address data inside the variants in the form of two different structs, which are defined differently for each variant:

```
struct Ipv4Addr {
    // --snip--
}

struct Ipv6Addr {
    // --snip--
}

enum IpAddr {
    V4(Ipv4Addr),
    V6(Ipv6Addr),
}
```

This code illustrates that you can put any kind of data inside an enum variant: strings, numeric types, or structs, for example. You can even include another enum! Also, standard library types are often not much more complicated than what you might come up with.

Note that even though the standard library contains a definition for IpAddr, we can still create and use our own definition without conflict because we haven't brought the standard library's definition into our scope. We'll talk more about bringing types into scope in Chapter 7.

Let's look at another example of an enum in Listing 6-2: this one has a wide variety of types embedded in its variants.

```
enum Message {
    Quit,
    Move { x: i32, y: i32 },
    Write(String),
    ChangeColor(i32, i32, i32),
}
```

Listing 6-2: A Message *enum whose variants each store different amounts and types of values*

This enum has four variants with different types:

- Quit has no data associated with it at all.
- Move includes an anonymous struct inside it.
- Write includes a single String.
- ChangeColor includes three i32 values.

Defining an enum with variants such as the ones in Listing 6-2 is similar to defining different kinds of struct definitions, except the enum doesn't use the struct keyword and all the variants are grouped together under the Message type. The following structs could hold the same data that the preceding enum variants hold:

```
struct QuitMessage; // unit struct
struct MoveMessage {
    x: i32,
    y: i32,
}
struct WriteMessage(String); // tuple struct
struct ChangeColorMessage(i32, i32, i32); // tuple struct
```

But if we used the different structs, which each have their own type, we couldn't as easily define a function to take any of these kinds of messages as we could with the Message enum defined in Listing 6-2, which is a single type.

There is one more similarity between enums and structs: just as we're able to define methods on structs using impl, we're also able to define methods on enums. Here's a method named call that we could define on our Message enum:

```
impl Message {
    fn call(&self) {
        ❶ // method body would be defined here
    }
}

❷ let m = Message::Write(String::from("hello"));
m.call();
```

The body of the method would use self to get the value that we called the method on. In this example, we've created a variable m ❷ that has the value Message::Write(String::from("hello")), and that is what self will be in the body of the call method ❶ when m.call() runs.

Let's look at another enum in the standard library that is very common and useful: Option.

The Option Enum and Its Advantages over Null Values

In the previous section, we looked at how the IpAddr enum let us use Rust's type system to encode more information than just the data into our program. This section explores a case study of Option, which is another enum defined by the standard library. The Option type is used in many places because it encodes the very common scenario in which a value could be something or it could be nothing. Expressing this concept in terms of the type system means the compiler can check whether you've handled all the cases you should be handling; this functionality can prevent bugs that are extremely common in other programming languages.

Programming language design is often thought of in terms of which features you include, but the features you exclude are important too. Rust doesn't have the null feature that many other languages have. *Null* is a value that means there is no value there. In languages with null, variables can always be in one of two states: null or not-null.

In his 2009 presentation "Null References: The Billion Dollar Mistake," Tony Hoare, the inventor of null, has this to say:

> I call it my billion dollar mistake. At that time, I was design-
> ing the first comprehensive type system for references in an
> object-oriented language. My goal was to ensure that all use of
> references should be absolutely safe, with checking performed
> automatically by the compiler. But I couldn't resist the temptation
> to put in a null reference, simply because it was so easy to imple-
> ment. This has led to innumerable errors, vulnerabilities, and
> system crashes, which have probably caused a billion dollars of
> pain and damage in the last forty years.

The problem with null values is that if you try to use a null value as a not-null value, you'll get an error of some kind. Because this null or not-null property is pervasive, it's extremely easy to make this kind of error.

However, the concept that null is trying to express is still a useful one: a null is a value that is currently invalid or absent for some reason.

The problem isn't really with the concept but with the particular imple-mentation. As such, Rust does not have nulls, but it does have an enum that can encode the concept of a value being present or absent. This enum is Option<T>, and it is defined by the standard library as follows:

```
enum Option<T> {
    Some(T),
    None,
}
```

The Option<T> enum is so useful that it's even included in the prelude; you don't need to bring it into scope explicitly. In addition, so are its vari-ants: you can use Some and None directly without the Option:: prefix. The Option<T> enum is still just a regular enum, and Some(T) and None are still variants of type Option<T>.

The <T> syntax is a feature of Rust we haven't talked about yet. It's a generic type parameter, and we'll cover generics in more detail in Chapter 10. For now, all you need to know is that <T> means the Some variant of the Option enum can hold one piece of data of any type. Here are some examples of using `Option` values to hold number types and string types:

```
let some_number = Some(5);
let some_string = Some("a string");

let absent_number: Option<i32> = None;
```

If we use `None` rather than `Some`, we need to tell Rust what type of `Option<T>` we have, because the compiler can't infer the type that the `Some` variant will hold by looking only at a `None` value.

When we have a `Some` value, we know that a value is present and the value is held within the `Some`. When we have a `None` value, in some sense, it means the same thing as null: we don't have a valid value. So why is having `Option<T>` any better than having null?

In short, because `Option<T>` and `T` (where `T` can be any type) are different types, the compiler won't let us use an `Option<T>` value as if it were definitely a valid value. For example, this code won't compile because it's trying to add an `i8` to an `Option<i8>`:

```
let x: i8 = 5;
let y: Option<i8> = Some(5);

let sum = x + y;
```

If we run this code, we get an error message like this:

```
error[E0277]: the trait bound `i8: std::ops::Add<std::option::Option<i8>>` is
not satisfied
  -->
   |
5  |     let sum = x + y;
   |                 ^ no implementation for `i8 + std::option::Option<i8>`
   |
```

Intense! In effect, this error message means that Rust doesn't understand how to add an `i8` and an `Option<i8>`, because they're different types. When we have a value of a type like `i8` in Rust, the compiler will ensure that we always have a valid value. We can proceed confidently without having to check for null before using that value. Only when we have an `Option<i8>` (or whatever type of value we're working with) do we have to worry about possibly not having a value, and the compiler will make sure we handle that case before using the value.

In other words, you have to convert an `Option<T>` to a `T` before you can perform `T` operations with it. Generally, this helps catch one of the most common issues with null: assuming that something isn't null when it actually is.

Not having to worry about incorrectly assuming a not-null value helps you to be more confident in your code. In order to have a value that can possibly be null, you must explicitly opt in by making the type of that value

Option<T>. Then, when you use that value, you are required to explicitly handle the case when the value is null. Everywhere that a value has a type that isn't an Option<T>, you *can* safely assume that the value isn't null. This was a deliberate design decision for Rust to limit null's pervasiveness and increase the safety of Rust code.

So, how do you get the T value out of a Some variant when you have a value of type Option<T> so you can use that value? The Option<T> enum has a large number of methods that are useful in a variety of situations; you can check them out in its documentation. Becoming familiar with the methods on Option<T> will be extremely useful in your journey with Rust.

In general, in order to use an Option<T> value, you want to have code that will handle each variant. You want some code that will run only when you have a Some(T) value, and this code is allowed to use the inner T. You want some other code to run if you have a None value, and that code doesn't have a T value available. The match expression is a control flow construct that does just this when used with enums: it will run different code depending on which variant of the enum it has, and that code can use the data inside the matching value.

The match Control Flow Operator

Rust has an extremely powerful control flow operator called match that allows you to compare a value against a series of patterns and then execute code based on which pattern matches. Patterns can be made up of literal values, variable names, wildcards, and many other things; Chapter 18 covers all the different kinds of patterns and what they do. The power of match comes from the expressiveness of the patterns and the fact that the compiler confirms that all possible cases are handled.

Think of a match expression as being like a coin-sorting machine: coins slide down a track with variously sized holes along it, and each coin falls through the first hole it encounters that it fits into. In the same way, values go through each pattern in a match, and at the first pattern the value "fits," the value falls into the associated code block to be used during execution.

Because we just mentioned coins, let's use them as an example of using match! We can write a function that can take an unknown United States coin and, in a similar way as the counting machine, determine which coin it is and return its value in cents, as shown here in Listing 6-3.

```
❶ enum Coin {
      Penny,
      Nickel,
      Dime,
      Quarter,
  }
```

```
fn value_in_cents(coin: Coin) -> u32 {
  ❷ match coin {
      ❸ Coin::Penny => 1,
        Coin::Nickel => 5,
        Coin::Dime => 10,
        Coin::Quarter => 25,
    }
}
```

Listing 6-3: An enum and a match expression that has the variants of the enum as its patterns

Let's break down the match in the value_in_cents function. First, we list
the match keyword followed by an expression, which in this case is the value
coin ❷. This seems very similar to an expression used with if, but there's a
big difference: with if, the expression needs to return a Boolean value, but
here, it can be any type. The type of coin in this example is the Coin enum
that we defined at ❶.

Next are the match arms. An arm has two parts: a pattern and some code.
The first arm here has a pattern that is the value Coin::Penny and then the =>
operator that separates the pattern and the code to run ❸. The code in this
case is just the value 1. Each arm is separated from the next with a comma.

When the match expression executes, it compares the resulting value
against the pattern of each arm, in order. If a pattern matches the value, the
code associated with that pattern is executed. If that pattern doesn't match
the value, execution continues to the next arm, much as in a coin-sorting
machine. We can have as many arms as we need: in Listing 6-3, our match has
four arms.

The code associated with each arm is an expression, and the resulting
value of the expression in the matching arm is the value that gets returned
for the entire match expression.

Curly brackets typically aren't used if the match arm code is short,
as it is in Listing 6-3 where each arm just returns a value. If you want to
run multiple lines of code in a match arm, you can use curly brackets. For
example, the following code would print "Lucky penny!" every time the
method was called with a Coin::Penny but would still return the last value
of the block, 1:

```
fn value_in_cents(coin: Coin) -> u32 {
    match coin {
        Coin::Penny => {
            println!("Lucky penny!");
            1
        },
        Coin::Nickel => 5,
        Coin::Dime => 10,
        Coin::Quarter => 25,
    }
}
```

Patterns That Bind to Values

Another useful feature of match arms is that they can bind to the parts of the values that match the pattern. This is how we can extract values out of enum variants.

As an example, let's change one of our enum variants to hold data inside it. From 1999 through 2008, the United States minted quarters with different designs for each of the 50 states on one side. No other coins got state designs, so only quarters have this extra value. We can add this information to our enum by changing the Quarter variant to include a UsState value stored inside it, which we've done here in Listing 6-4.

```
#[derive(Debug)] // so we can inspect the state in a minute
enum UsState {
    Alabama,
    Alaska,
    // --snip--
}

enum Coin {
    Penny,
    Nickel,
    Dime,
    Quarter(UsState),
}
```

Listing 6-4: A Coin enum in which the Quarter variant also holds a UsState value

Let's imagine that a friend of ours is trying to collect all 50 state quarters. While we sort our loose change by coin type, we'll also call out the name of the state associated with each quarter so if it's one our friend doesn't have, they can add it to their collection.

In the match expression for this code, we add a variable called state to the pattern that matches values of the variant Coin::Quarter. When a Coin::Quarter matches, the state variable will bind to the value of that quarter's state. Then we can use state in the code for that arm, like so:

```
fn value_in_cents(coin: Coin) -> u32 {
    match coin {
        Coin::Penny => 1,
        Coin::Nickel => 5,
        Coin::Dime => 10,
        Coin::Quarter(state) => {
            println!("State quarter from {:?}!", state);
            25
        },
    }
}
```

If we were to call value_in_cents(Coin::Quarter(UsState::Alaska)), coin would be Coin::Quarter(UsState::Alaska). When we compare that value with each of the match arms, none of them match until we reach

`Coin::Quarter(state)`. At that point, the binding for `state` will be the value `UsState::Alaska`. We can then use that binding in the `println!` expression, thus getting the inner state value out of the `Coin` enum variant for `Quarter`.

Matching with Option<T>

In the previous section, we wanted to get the inner `T` value out of the `Some` case when using `Option<T>`; we can also handle `Option<T>` using `match` as we did with the `Coin` enum! Instead of comparing coins, we'll compare the variants of `Option<T>`, but the way that the `match` expression works remains the same.

Let's say we want to write a function that takes an `Option<i32>` and, if there's a value inside, adds 1 to that value. If there isn't a value inside, the function should return the `None` value and not attempt to perform any operations.

This function is very easy to write, thanks to `match`, and will look like Listing 6-5.

```
fn plus_one(x: Option<i32>) -> Option<i32> {
    match x {
      ❶ None => None,
      ❷ Some(i) => Some(i + 1),
    }
}

let five = Some(5);
let six = plus_one(five); ❸
let none = plus_one(None); ❹
```

Listing 6-5: A function that uses a match expression on an Option<i32>

Let's examine the first execution of `plus_one` in more detail. When we call `plus_one(five)` ❸, the variable `x` in the body of `plus_one` will have the value `Some(5)`. We then compare that against each match arm.

The `Some(5)` value doesn't match the pattern `None` ❶, so we continue to the next arm. Does `Some(5)` match `Some(i)` ❷? Why yes it does! We have the same variant. The `i` binds to the value contained in `Some`, so `i` takes the value 5. The code in the match arm is then executed, so we add 1 to the value of `i` and create a new `Some` value with our total 6 inside.

Now let's consider the second call of `plus_one` in Listing 6-5, where `x` is `None` ❹. We enter the `match` and compare to the first arm ❶.

It matches! There's no value to add to, so the program stops and returns the `None` value on the right side of `=>`. Because the first arm matched, no other arms are compared.

Combining `match` and enums is useful in many situations. You'll see this pattern a lot in Rust code: match against an enum, bind a variable to the data inside, and then execute code based on it. It's a bit tricky at first, but once you get used to it, you'll wish you had it in all languages. It's consistently a user favorite.

Matches Are Exhaustive

There's one other aspect of match we need to discuss. Consider this version of our plus_one function that has a bug and won't compile:

```
fn plus_one(x: Option<i32>) -> Option<i32> {
    match x {
        Some(i) => Some(i + 1),
    }
}
```

We didn't handle the None case, so this code will cause a bug. Luckily, it's a bug Rust knows how to catch. If we try to compile this code, we'll get this error:

```
error[E0004]: non-exhaustive patterns: `None` not covered
  -->
   |
6  |          match x {
   |                ^ pattern `None` not covered
```

Rust knows that we didn't cover every possible case and even knows which pattern we forgot! Matches in Rust are *exhaustive*: we must exhaust every last possibility in order for the code to be valid. Especially in the case of Option<T>, when Rust prevents us from forgetting to explicitly handle the None case, it protects us from assuming that we have a value when we might have null, thus making the billion-dollar mistake discussed earlier.

The _ Placeholder

Rust also has a pattern we can use when we don't want to list all possible values. For example, a u8 can have valid values of 0 through 255. If we only care about the values 1, 3, 5, and 7, we don't want to have to list out 0, 2, 4, 6, 8, 9 all the way up to 255. Fortunately, we don't have to: we can use the special pattern _ instead:

```
let some_u8_value = 0u8;
match some_u8_value {
    1 => println!("one"),
    3 => println!("three"),
    5 => println!("five"),
    7 => println!("seven"),
    _ => (),
}
```

The _ pattern will match any value. By putting it after our other arms, the _ will match all the possible cases that aren't specified before it. The ()

is just the unit value, so nothing will happen in the _ case. As a result, we can say that we want to do nothing for all the possible values that we don't list before the _ placeholder.

However, the match expression can be a bit wordy in a situation in which we care about only *one* of the cases. For this situation, Rust provides if let.

Concise Control Flow with if let

The if let syntax lets you combine if and let into a less verbose way to handle values that match one pattern while ignoring the rest. Consider the program in Listing 6-6 that matches on an Option<u8> value but only wants to execute code if the value is 3.

```
let some_u8_value = Some(0u8);
match some_u8_value {
    Some(3) => println!("three"),
    _ => (),
}
```

Listing 6-6: A match that only cares about executing code when the value is Some(3)

We want to do something with the Some(3) match but do nothing with any other Some<u8> value or the None value. To satisfy the match expression, we have to add _ => () after processing just one variant, which is a lot of boilerplate code to add.

Instead, we could write this in a shorter way using if let. The following code behaves the same as the match in Listing 6-6:

```
if let Some(3) = some_u8_value {
    println!("three");
}
```

The syntax if let takes a pattern and an expression separated by an equal sign. It works the same way as a match, where the expression is given to the match and the pattern is its first arm.

Using if let means less typing, less indentation, and less boilerplate code. However, you lose the exhaustive checking that match enforces. Choosing between match and if let depends on what you're doing in your particular situation and whether gaining conciseness is an appropriate trade-off for losing exhaustive checking.

In other words, you can think of if let as syntax sugar for a match that runs code when the value matches one pattern and then ignores all other values.

We can include an else with an if let. The block of code that goes with the else is the same as the block of code that would go with the _ case in the match expression that is equivalent to the if let and else. Recall the

Coin enum definition in Listing 6-4, where the Quarter variant also held a UsState value. If we wanted to count all non-quarter coins we see while also announcing the state of the quarters, we could do that with a match expression like this:

```
let mut count = 0;
match coin {
    Coin::Quarter(state) => println!("State quarter from {:?}!", state),
    _ => count += 1,
}
```

Or we could use an if let and else expression like this:

```
let mut count = 0;
if let Coin::Quarter(state) = coin {
    println!("State quarter from {:?}!", state);
} else {
    count += 1;
}
```

If you have a situation in which your program has logic that is too verbose to express using a match, remember that if let is in your Rust toolbox as well.

Summary

We've now covered how to use enums to create custom types that can be one of a set of enumerated values. We've shown how the standard library's Option<T> type helps you use the type system to prevent errors. When enum values have data inside them, you can use match or if let to extract and use those values, depending on how many cases you need to handle.

Your Rust programs can now express concepts in your domain using structs and enums. Creating custom types to use in your API ensures type safety: the compiler will make certain your functions get only values of the type each function expects.

In order to provide a well-organized API to your users that is straightforward to use and only exposes exactly what your users will need, let's now turn to Rust's modules.

7

USING MODULES TO REUSE
AND ORGANIZE CODE

When you start writing programs in Rust, your code might live solely in the `main` function. As your code grows, you'll eventually move functionality into other functions for reuse and better organization. By splitting your code into smaller chunks, you make each chunk easier to understand on its own. But what happens if you have too many functions? Rust has a module system that enables the reuse of code in an organized fashion.

In the same way that you extract lines of code into a function, you can extract functions (and other code, like structs and enums) into different modules. A *module* is a namespace that contains definitions of functions or types, and you can choose whether those definitions are visible outside their module (public) or not (private). Here's an overview of how modules work:

- The mod keyword declares a new module. Code within the module appears either immediately following this declaration within curly brackets or in another file.
- By default, functions, types, constants, and modules are private. The pub keyword makes an item public and therefore visible outside its namespace.
- The use keyword brings modules, or the definitions inside modules, into scope so it's easier to refer to them.

We'll look at each of these parts to see how they fit into the whole.

mod and the Filesystem

We'll start our module example by making a new project with Cargo, but instead of creating a binary crate, we'll make a library crate: a project that other people can pull into their projects as a dependency. For example, the rand crate discussed in Chapter 2 is a library crate that we used as a dependency in the guessing game project.

We'll create a skeleton of a library that provides some general networking functionality; we'll concentrate on the organization of the modules and functions, but we won't worry about what code goes in the function bodies. We'll call our library communicator. To create a library, pass the --lib option instead of --bin:

```
$ cargo new communicator --lib
$ cd communicator
```

Notice that Cargo generated *src/lib.rs* instead of *src/main.rs*. Inside *src/lib.rs* we'll find the following:

src/lib.rs
```
#[cfg(test)]
mod tests {
    #[test]
    fn it_works() {
        assert_eq!(2 + 2, 4);
    }
}
```

Cargo creates an example test to help us get our library started, rather than the "Hello, world!" binary that we get when we use the --bin option. We'll look at the #[] and mod tests syntax in "Using super to Access a Parent Module" on page 125, but for now, leave this code at the bottom of *src/lib.rs*.

Because we don't have a *src/main.rs* file, there's nothing for Cargo to execute with the cargo run command. Therefore, we'll use the cargo build command to compile our library crate's code.

We'll look at different options for organizing your library's code that will be suitable in a variety of situations, depending on the intent of the code.

Module Definitions

For our communicator networking library, we'll first define a module named network that contains the definition of a function called connect. Every module definition in Rust starts with the mod keyword. Add this code to the beginning of the *src/lib.rs* file, above the test code:

src/lib.rs

```
mod network {
    fn connect() {
    }
}
```

After the mod keyword, we put the name of the module, network, and then a block of code in curly brackets. Everything inside this block is inside the namespace network. In this case, we have a single function, connect. If we wanted to call this function from code outside the network module, we would need to specify the module and use the :: namespace syntax like so: network::connect().

We can also have multiple modules, side by side, in the same *src/lib.rs* file. For example, to also have a client module that has a function named connect, we can add it as shown in Listing 7-1.

src/lib.rs

```
mod network {
    fn connect() {
    }
}

mod client {
    fn connect() {
    }
}
```

Listing 7-1: The network module and the client module defined side by side in src/lib.rs

Now we have a network::connect function and a client::connect function. These can have completely different functionality, and the function names do not conflict with each other because they're in different modules.

In this case, because we're building a library, the file that serves as the entry point for building our library is *src/lib.rs*. However, in respect to creating modules, there's nothing special about *src/lib.rs*. We could also create modules in *src/main.rs* for a binary crate in the same way as we're creating modules in *src/lib.rs* for the library crate. In fact, we can put modules inside of modules, which can be useful as your modules grow to keep related functionality organized together and separate functionality apart. The way you choose to organize your code depends on how you think about the relationship between the parts of your code. For instance, the client code and its connect function might make more sense to users of our library if they were inside the network namespace instead, as in Listing 7-2.

```
mod network {
    fn connect() {
    }

    mod client {
        fn connect() {
        }
    }
}
```

Listing 7-2: Moving the `client` module inside the `network` module

In your *src/lib.rs* file, replace the existing `mod network` and `mod client` definitions with the ones in Listing 7-2, which have the `client` module as an inner module of `network`. The functions `network::connect` and `network::client::connect` are both named `connect`, but they don't conflict with each other because they're in different namespaces.

In this way, modules form a hierarchy. The contents of *src/lib.rs* are at the topmost level, and the submodules are at lower levels. Here's what the organization of our example in Listing 7-1 looks like when thought of as a hierarchy:

```
communicator
 ├── network
 └── client
```

And here's the hierarchy corresponding to the example in Listing 7-2:

```
communicator
 └── network
      └── client
```

The hierarchy shows that in Listing 7-2, `client` is a child of the `network` module rather than a sibling. More complicated projects can have many modules, and they'll need to be organized logically in order for you to keep track of them. What "logically" means in your project is up to you and depends on how you and your library's users think about your project's domain. Use the techniques shown here to create side-by-side modules and nested modules in whatever structure you would like.

Moving Modules to Other Files

Modules form a hierarchical structure, much like another structure in computing that you're used to: filesystems! We can use Rust's module system along with multiple files to split up Rust projects so not everything lives in *src/lib.rs* or *src/main.rs*. For this example, let's start with the code in Listing 7-3.

src/lib.rs

```
mod client {
    fn connect() {
    }
}

mod network {
    fn connect() {
    }

    mod server {
        fn connect() {
        }
    }
}
```

Listing 7-3: Three modules, `client`, `network`, and `network::server`, all defined in src/lib.rs

The file *src/lib.rs* has this module hierarchy:

```
communicator
 ├── client
 └── network
      └── server
```

If these modules had many functions, and those functions were becoming lengthy, it would be difficult to scroll through this file to find the code we wanted to work with. Because the functions are nested inside one or more mod blocks, the lines of code inside the functions will start getting lengthy as well. These would be good reasons to separate the client, network, and server modules from *src/lib.rs* and place them into their own files.

First, let's replace the client module code with only the declaration of the client module so that *src/lib.rs* looks like the code shown in Listing 7-4.

src/lib.rs

```
mod client;

mod network {
    fn connect() {
    }

    mod server {
        fn connect() {
        }
    }
}
```

Listing 7-4: Extracting the contents of the `client` module but leaving the declaration in src/lib.rs

We're still *declaring* the client module here, but by replacing the block with a semicolon, we're telling Rust to look in another location for the code

defined within the scope of the client module. In other words, the line mod
client; means this:

```
mod client {
    // contents of client.rs
}
```

Now we need to create the external file with that module name. Create
a *client.rs* file in your *src/* directory and open it. Then enter the following,
which is the connect function in the client module that we removed in the
previous step:

```
fn connect() {
}
```

Note that we don't need a mod declaration in this file because we already
declared the client module with mod in *src/lib.rs*. This file just provides the
contents of the client module. If we put a mod client here, we'd be giving the
client module its own submodule named client!

Rust only knows to look in *src/lib.rs* by default. If we want to add more
files to our project, we need to tell Rust in *src/lib.rs* to look in other files;
this is why mod client needs to be defined in *src/lib.rs* and can't be defined
in *src/client.rs*.

Now the project should compile successfully, although you'll get a few
warnings. Remember to use cargo build instead of cargo run because we have
a library crate rather than a binary crate:

```
$ cargo build
   Compiling communicator v0.1.0 (file:///projects/communicator)
warning: function is never used: `connect`
 --> src/client.rs:1:1
  |
1 | / fn connect() {
2 | | }
  | |_^
  |
  = note: #[warn(dead_code)] on by default

warning: function is never used: `connect`
 --> src/lib.rs:4:5
  |
4 | /     fn connect() {
5 | |     }
  | |_____^

warning: function is never used: `connect`
 --> src/lib.rs:8:9
  |
8 | /         fn connect() {
9 | |         }
  | |_____^
```

These warnings tell us that we have functions that are never used. Don't worry about these warnings for now; we'll address them in "Controlling Visibility with pub" on page 118. The good news is that they're just warnings; our project built successfully!

Next, let's extract the network module into its own file using the same pattern. In *src/lib.rs*, delete the body of the network module and add a semi-colon to the declaration, like so:

src/lib.rs

```
mod client;

mod network;
```

Then create a new *src/network.rs* file and enter the following:

src/network.rs

```
fn connect() {
}

mod server {
    fn connect() {
    }
}
```

Notice that we still have a mod declaration within this module file; this is because we still want server to be a submodule of network.

Run cargo build again. Success! We have one more module to extract: server. Because it's a submodule—that is, a module within a module—our current tactic of extracting a module into a file named after that module won't work. We'll try anyway so you can see the error. First, change *src/network.rs* to have mod server; instead of the server module's contents:

src/network.rs

```
fn connect() {
}

mod server;
```

Then create a *src/server.rs* file and enter the contents of the server module that we extracted:

src/server.rs

```
fn connect() {
}
```

When we try to run cargo build, we'll get the error shown in Listing 7-5.

```
$ cargo build
   Compiling communicator v0.1.0 (file:///projects/communicator)
error: cannot declare a new module at this location
 --> src/network.rs:4:5
  |
4 | mod server;
  |     ^^^^^^
  |
```

```
note: maybe move this module `src/network.rs` to its own directory via `src/
network/mod.rs`
 --> src/network.rs:4:5
  |
4 | mod server;
  |     ^^^^^^
note: ... or maybe `use` the module `server` instead of possibly redeclaring
it
 --> src/network.rs:4:5
  |
4 | mod server;
  |     ^^^^^^
```

Listing 7-5: Error when trying to extract the server submodule into src/server.rs

The error says we cannot declare a new module at this location and is pointing to the mod server; line in *src/network.rs*. So *src/network.rs* is different from *src/lib.rs* somehow: keep reading to understand why.

The note in the middle of Listing 7-5 is actually very helpful because it points out something we haven't yet talked about doing:

```
note: maybe move this module `network` to its own directory via
`network/mod.rs`
```

Instead of continuing to follow the same file-naming pattern we used previously, we can do what the note suggests:

1. Make a new *directory* named *network*, the parent module's name.

2. Move the *src/network.rs* file into the new *network* directory and rename it *src/network/mod.rs*.

3. Move the submodule file *src/server.rs* into the *network* directory.

Here are commands to carry out these steps:

```
$ mkdir src/network
$ mv src/network.rs src/network/mod.rs
$ mv src/server.rs src/network
```

Now when we try to run cargo build, compilation will work (we'll still have warnings, though). Our module layout still looks exactly the same as it did when we had all the code in *src/lib.rs* in Listing 7-3:

```
communicator
├── client
└── network
    └── server
```

The corresponding file layout now looks like this:

```
└── src
    ├── client.rs
    ├── lib.rs
    └── network
        ├── mod.rs
        └── server.rs
```

So when we wanted to extract the network::server module, why did we have to also change the *src/network.rs* file to the *src/network/mod.rs* file and put the code for network::server in the *network* directory in *src/network/server.rs*? Why couldn't we just extract the network::server module into *src/server.rs*? The reason is that Rust wouldn't be able to recognize that server was supposed to be a submodule of network if the *server.rs* file was in the *src* directory. To clarify Rust's behavior here, let's consider a different example with the following module hierarchy, where all the definitions are in *src/lib.rs*:

```
communicator
├── client
└── network
    └── client
```

In this example, we have three modules again: client, network, and network::client. Following the same steps we did earlier for extracting modules into files, we would create *src/client.rs* for the client module. For the network module, we would create *src/network.rs*. But we wouldn't be able to extract the network::client module into a *src/client.rs* file because that already exists for the top-level client module! If we could put the code for *both* the client and network::client modules in the *src/client.rs* file, Rust wouldn't have any way to know whether the code was for client or for network::client.

Therefore, in order to extract a file for the network::client submodule of the network module, we needed to create a directory for the network module instead of a *src/network.rs* file. The code that is in the network module then goes into the *src/network/mod.rs* file, and the submodule network::client can have its own *src/network/client.rs* file. Now the top-level *src/client.rs* is unambiguously the code that belongs to the client module.

Rules of Module Filesystems

Let's summarize the rules of modules with regard to files:

- If a module named foo has no submodules, you should put the declarations for foo in a file named *foo.rs*.

- If a module named foo does have submodules, you should put the declarations for foo in a file named *foo/mod.rs*.

These rules apply recursively, so if a module named foo has a submodule named bar and bar does not have submodules, you should have the following files in your *src* directory:

```
└── foo
    ├── bar.rs (contains the declarations in `foo::bar`)
    └── mod.rs (contains the declarations in `foo`, including `mod bar`)
```

The modules should be declared in their parent module's file using the mod keyword.

Next, we'll talk about the pub keyword and get rid of those warnings!

Controlling Visibility with pub

We resolved the error messages shown in Listing 7-5 by moving the network and network::server code into the *src/network/mod.rs* and *src/network/server.rs* files, respectively. At that point, cargo build was able to build our project, but we still get warning messages saying that the client::connect, network::connect, and network::server::connect functions are not being used.

So why are we receiving these warnings? After all, we're building a library with functions that are intended to be used by our *users*, not necessarily by us within our own project, so it shouldn't matter that these connect functions go unused. The point of creating them is that they will be used by another project, not our own.

To understand why this program invokes these warnings, let's try using the communicator library from another project, calling it externally. To do that, we'll create a binary crate in the same directory as our library crate by making a *src/main.rs* file containing this code:

src/main.rs
```
extern crate communicator;

fn main() {
    communicator::client::connect();
}
```

We use the extern crate command to bring the communicator library crate into scope. Our package now contains *two* crates. Cargo treats *src/main.rs* as the root file of a binary crate, which is separate from the existing library crate whose root file is *src/lib.rs*. This pattern is quite common for executable projects: most functionality is in a library crate, and the binary crate uses that library crate. As a result, other programs can also use the library crate, and it's a nice separation of concerns.

From the point of view of a crate outside the communicator library looking in, all the modules we've been creating are within a module that has the same name as the crate, communicator. We call the top-level module of a crate the *root module*.

Also note that even if we're using an external crate within a submodule of our project, the extern crate should go in our root module (so in *src/main.rs* or *src/lib.rs*). Then, in our submodules, we can refer to items from external crates as if the items are top-level modules.

Right now, our binary crate just calls our library's connect function from the client module. However, invoking cargo build will now give us an error after the warnings:

```
error[E0603]: module `client` is private
 --> src/main.rs:4:5
  |
4 |     communicator::client::connect();
  |     ^^^^^^^^^^^^^^^^^^^^^^^^^^^^^^^
```

Ah ha! This error tells us that the client module is private, which is the crux of the warnings. It's also the first time we've run into the concepts of *public* and *private* in the context of Rust. The default state of all code in Rust is private: no one else is allowed to use the code. If you don't use a private function within your program, because your program is the only code allowed to use that function, Rust will warn you that the function has gone unused.

After you specify that a function such as client::connect is public, not only will your call to that function from your binary crate be allowed, but also the warning that the function is unused will go away. Marking a function as public lets Rust know that the function will be used by code outside of your program. Rust considers the theoretical external usage that's now possible as the function "being used." Thus, when a function is marked public, Rust will not require that it be used in your program and will stop warning that the function is unused.

Making a Function Public

To tell Rust to make a function public, we add the pub keyword to the start of the declaration. We'll focus on fixing the warning that indicates client::connect has gone unused for now, as well as the module `client` is private error from our binary crate. Modify *src/lib.rs* to make the client module public, like so:

src/lib.rs

```
pub mod client;

mod network;
```

The pub keyword is placed right before mod. Let's try building again:

```
error[E0603]: function `connect` is private
 --> src/main.rs:4:5
  |
4 |     communicator::client::connect();
  |     ^^^^^^^^^^^^^^^^^^^^^^^^^^^^^^^
```

Hooray! We have a different error! Yes, different error messages are a cause for celebration. The new error shows function `connect` is private, so let's edit *src/client.rs* to make client::connect public, too:

src/client.rs

```
pub fn connect() {
}
```

Now run cargo build again:

```
warning: function is never used: `connect`
--> src/network/mod.rs:1:1
  |
1 | / fn connect() {
2 | | }
  | |_^
  |
  = note: #[warn(dead_code)] on by default

warning: function is never used: `connect`
 --> src/network/server.rs:1:1
  |
1 | / fn connect() {
2 | | }
  | |_^
```

The code compiled, and the warning that client::connect is not being used is gone!

Unused code warnings don't always indicate that an item in your code needs to be made public: if you *didn't* want these functions to be part of your public API, unused code warnings could be alerting you to code you no longer need that you can safely delete. They could also be alerting you to a bug if you had just accidentally removed all places within your library where this function is called.

But in this case, we *do* want the other two functions to be part of our crate's public API, so let's mark them as pub as well to get rid of the remaining warnings. Modify *src/network/mod.rs* to look like the following:

src/network/mod.rs

```
pub fn connect() {
}

mod server;
```

Then compile the code:

```
warning: function is never used: `connect`
 --> src/network/mod.rs:1:1
  |
1 | / pub fn connect() {
2 | | }
  | |_^
  |
  = note: #[warn(dead_code)] on by default
```

```
warning: function is never used: `connect`
 --> src/network/server.rs:1:1
  |
1 | / fn connect() {
2 | | }
  | |_^
```

Hmmm, we're still getting an unused function warning, even though
network::connect is set to pub. The reason is that the function is public within
the module, but the network module that the function resides in is not public. We're working from the interior of the library out this time, whereas
with client::connect, we worked from the outside in. We need to change *src/
lib.rs* to make network public too, like so:

src/lib.rs

```
pub mod client;

pub mod network;
```

Now when we compile, that warning is gone:

```
warning: function is never used: `connect`
 --> src/network/server.rs:1:1
  |
1 | / fn connect() {
2 | | }
  | |_^
  |
  = note: #[warn(dead_code)] on by default
```

Only one warning is left—try to fix this one on your own!

Privacy Rules

Overall, these are the rules for item visibility:

- If an item is public, it can be accessed through any of its parent modules.
- If an item is private, it can be accessed only by its immediate parent
  module and any of the parent's child modules.

Privacy Examples

Let's look at a few more privacy examples to get some practice. Create a
new library project and enter the code in Listing 7-6 into your new project's
src/lib.rs.

src/lib.rs

```
mod outermost {
    pub fn middle_function() {}

    fn middle_secret_function() {}

    mod inside {
        pub fn inner_function() {}
```

```
            fn secret_function() {}
        }
    }

    fn try_me() {
        outermost::middle_function();
        outermost::middle_secret_function();
        outermost::inside::inner_function();
        outermost::inside::secret_function();
    }
```

Listing 7-6: Examples of private and public functions, some of which are incorrect

Before you try to compile this code, make a guess about which lines in the try_me function will have errors. Then, try compiling the code to see whether you were right—and read on for the discussion of the errors!

Looking at the Errors

The try_me function is in the root module of our project. The module named outermost is private, but the second privacy rule states that the try_me function is allowed to access the outermost module because outermost is in the current (root) module, as is try_me.

The call to outermost::middle_function will work because middle_function is public and try_me is accessing middle_function through its parent module outermost. We already determined that this module is accessible.

The call to outermost::middle_secret_function will cause a compilation error. Because middle_secret_function is private, the second rule applies. The root module is neither the current module of middle_secret_function (outermost is), nor is it a child module of the current module of middle_secret_function.

The module named inside is private and has no child modules, so it can be accessed only by its current module outermost. That means the try_me function is not allowed to call outermost::inside::inner_function or outermost::inside::secret_function.

Fixing the Errors

Here are some suggestions for changing the code in an attempt to fix the errors. Make a guess as to whether it will fix the errors before you try each one. Then compile the code to see whether or not you're right, using the privacy rules to understand why. Feel free to design more experiments and try them out!

- What if the inside module were public?
- What if outermost were public and inside were private?
- What if, in the body of inner_function, you called ::outermost::middle_secret_function()? (The two colons at the beginning mean that we want to refer to the modules starting from the root module.)

Next, let's talk about bringing items into scope with the use keyword.

Referring to Names in Different Modules

We've covered how to call functions defined within a module using the module name as part of the call, as in the call to the nested_modules function shown here in Listing 7-7.

src/main.rs

```
pub mod a {
    pub mod series {
        pub mod of {
            pub fn nested_modules() {}
        }
    }
}

fn main() {
    a::series::of::nested_modules();
}
```

Listing 7-7: Calling a function by fully specifying its enclosing module's path

As you can see, referring to the fully qualified name can get quite lengthy. Fortunately, Rust has a keyword to make these calls more concise.

Bringing Names into Scope with the use Keyword

Rust's use keyword shortens lengthy function calls by bringing the modules of the function you want to call into scope. Here's an example of bringing the a::series::of module into a binary crate's root scope:

src/main.rs

```
pub mod a {
    pub mod series {
        pub mod of {
            pub fn nested_modules() {}
        }
    }
}

use a::series::of;

fn main() {
    of::nested_modules();
}
```

The line use a::series::of; means that rather than using the full a::series::of path wherever we want to refer to the of module, we can use of.

The use keyword brings only what we've specified into scope; it does not bring children of modules into scope. That's why we still have to use of::nested_modules when we want to call the nested_modules function.

We could have chosen to bring the function into scope by instead specifying the function in the use as follows:

```
pub mod a {
    pub mod series {
```

```
        pub mod of {
            pub fn nested_modules() {}
        }
    }
}

use a::series::of::nested_modules;

fn main() {
    nested_modules();
}
```

Doing so allows us to exclude all the modules and reference the function directly.

Because enums also form a sort of namespace like modules, we can bring an enum's variants into scope with use as well. For any kind of use statement, if you're bringing multiple items from one namespace into scope, you can list them using curly brackets and commas in the last position, like so:

```
enum TrafficLight {
    Red,
    Yellow,
    Green,
}

use TrafficLight::{Red, Yellow};

fn main() {
    let red = Red;
    let yellow = Yellow;
    let green = TrafficLight::Green;
}
```

We're still specifying the TrafficLight namespace for the Green variant because we didn't include Green in the use statement.

Bringing All Names into Scope with a Glob

To bring all the items in a namespace into scope at once, we can use the * syntax, which is called the *glob operator*. This example brings all the variants of an enum into scope without having to list each specifically:

```
enum TrafficLight {
    Red,
    Yellow,
    Green,
}

use TrafficLight::*;

fn main() {
    let red = Red;
    let yellow = Yellow;
```

```
    let green = Green;
}
```

The * operator will bring into scope all the visible items in the TrafficLight namespace. You should use globs sparingly: they are convenient, but a glob might also pull in more items than you expected and cause naming conflicts.

Using super to Access a Parent Module

As you saw at the beginning of this chapter, when you create a library crate, Cargo makes a tests module for you. Let's go into more detail about that now. In your communicator project, open *src/lib.rs*:

src/lib.rs

```
pub mod client;

pub mod network;

#[cfg(test)]
mod tests {
    #[test]
    fn it_works() {
        assert_eq!(2 + 2, 4);
    }
}
```

Chapter 11 explains more about testing, but parts of this example should make sense now: we have a module named tests that lives next to our other modules and contains one function named it_works. Even though there are special annotations, the tests module is just another module! So our module hierarchy looks like this:

```
communicator
 ├── client
 ├── network
 │   └── client
 └── tests
```

Tests are for exercising the code within our library, so let's try to call our client::connect function from this it_works function, even though we won't be checking any functionality right now. This won't work yet:

src/lib.rs

```
#[cfg(test)]
mod tests {
    #[test]
    fn it_works() {
        client::connect();
    }
}
```

Run the tests by invoking the cargo test command:

```
$ cargo test
   Compiling communicator v0.1.0 (file:///projects/communicator)
error[E0433]: failed to resolve. Use of undeclared type or module `client`
 --> src/lib.rs:9:9
  |
9 |         client::connect();
  |         ^^^^^^ Use of undeclared type or module `client`
```

The compilation failed, but why? We don't need to place communicator:: in front of the function, as we did in *src/main.rs*, because we are definitely within the communicator library crate here. The reason is that paths are always relative to the current module, which here is tests. The only exception is in a use statement, where paths are relative to the crate root by default. Our tests module needs the client module in its scope!

So how do we get back up one module in the module hierarchy to call the client::connect function in the tests module? In the tests module, we can either use leading colons to let Rust know that we want to start from the root and list the whole path, like this:

```
::client::connect();
```

Or, we can use super to move up one module in the hierarchy from our current module, like this:

```
super::client::connect();
```

These two options don't look that different in this example, but if you're deeper in a module hierarchy, starting from the root every time would make your code lengthy. In those cases, using super to get from the current module to sibling modules is a good shortcut. Plus, if you've specified the path from the root in many places in your code and then rearrange your modules by moving a subtree to another place, you'll end up needing to update the path in several places, which would be tedious.

It would also be annoying to have to type super:: in each test, but you've already seen the tool for that solution: use! The super:: functionality changes the path you give to use so it is relative to the parent module instead of to the root module.

For these reasons, in the tests module especially, use super::*something* is usually the best solution. So now our test looks like this:

src/lib.rs
```
#[cfg(test)]
mod tests {
    use super::client;

    #[test]
    fn it_works() {
        client::connect();
```

```
        }
}
```

When we run cargo test again, the test will pass, and the first part of
the test result output will be the following:

```
$ cargo test
   Compiling communicator v0.1.0 (file:///projects/communicator)
     Running target/debug/communicator-92007ddb5330fa5a

running 1 test
test tests::it_works ... ok

test result: ok. 1 passed; 0 failed; 0 ignored; 0 measured; 0 filtered out
```

Summary

Now you know some new techniques for organizing your code! Use these
techniques to group related functionality together, keep files from becoming
too long, and present a tidy public API to your library users.

Next, we'll look at some collection data structures in the standard
library that you can use in your nice, neat code.

8

COMMON COLLECTIONS

Rust's standard library includes a number of very useful data structures called *collections*. Most other data types represent one specific value, but collections can contain multiple values. Unlike the built-in array and tuple types, the data these collections point to is stored on the heap, which means the amount of data does not need to be known at compile time and can grow or shrink as the program runs. Each kind of collection has different capabilities and costs, and choosing an appropriate one for your current situation is a skill you'll develop over time. In this chapter, we'll discuss three collections that are used very often in Rust programs:

- A *vector* allows you to store a variable number of values next to each other.
- A *string* is a collection of characters. We've mentioned the String type previously, but in this chapter we'll talk about it in depth.

- A *hash map* allows you to associate a value with a particular key. It's a particular implementation of the more general data structure called a *map*.

To learn about the other kinds of collections provided by the standard library, see the documentation at *https://doc.rust-lang.org/stable/std/collections/*.

We'll discuss how to create and update vectors, strings, and hash maps, as well as what makes each special.

Storing Lists of Values with Vectors

The first collection type we'll look at is Vec<T>, also known as a *vector*. Vectors allow you to store more than one value in a single data structure that puts all the values next to each other in memory. Vectors can only store values of the same type. They are useful when you have a list of items, such as the lines of text in a file or the prices of items in a shopping cart.

Creating a New Vector

To create a new, empty vector, we can call the Vec::new function, as shown in Listing 8-1.

```
let v: Vec<i32> = Vec::new();
```

Listing 8-1: Creating a new, empty vector to hold values of type i32

Note that we added a type annotation here. Because we aren't inserting any values into this vector, Rust doesn't know what kind of elements we intend to store. This is an important point. Vectors are implemented using generics; we'll cover how to use generics with your own types in Chapter 10. For now, know that the Vec<T> type provided by the standard library can hold any type, and when a specific vector holds a specific type, the type is specified within angle brackets. In Listing 8-1, we've told Rust that the Vec<T> in v will hold elements of the i32 type.

In more realistic code, Rust can often infer the type of value you want to store once you insert values, so you rarely need to do this type annotation. It's more common to create a Vec<T> that has initial values, and Rust provides the vec! macro for convenience. The macro will create a new vector that holds the values you give it. Listing 8-2 creates a new Vec<i32> that holds the values 1, 2, and 3.

```
let v = vec![1, 2, 3];
```

Listing 8-2: Creating a new vector containing values

Because we've given initial i32 values, Rust can infer that the type of v is Vec<i32>, and the type annotation isn't necessary. Next, we'll look at how to modify a vector.

Updating a Vector

To create a vector and then add elements to it, we can use the push method, as shown in Listing 8-3.

```
let mut v = Vec::new();

v.push(5);
v.push(6);
v.push(7);
v.push(8);
```

Listing 8-3: Using the push method to add values to a vector

As with any variable, if we want to be able to change its value, we need to make it mutable using the mut keyword, as discussed in Chapter 3. The numbers we place inside are all of type i32, and Rust infers this from the data, so we don't need the Vec<i32> annotation.

Dropping a Vector Drops Its Elements

Like any other struct, a vector is freed when it goes out of scope, as annotated in Listing 8-4.

```
{
    let v = vec![1, 2, 3, 4];

    // do stuff with v

} // <- v goes out of scope and is freed here
```

Listing 8-4: Showing where the vector and its elements are dropped

When the vector gets dropped, all of its contents are also dropped, meaning those integers it holds will be cleaned up. This may seem like a straightforward point but can get a bit more complicated when you start to introduce references to the elements of the vector. Let's tackle that next!

Reading Elements of Vectors

Now that you know how to create, update, and destroy vectors, knowing how to read their contents is a good next step. There are two ways to reference a value stored in a vector. In the examples, we've annotated the types of the values that are returned from these functions for extra clarity.

Listing 8-5 shows both methods of accessing a value in a vector, either with indexing syntax or the get method.

```
let v = vec![1, 2, 3, 4, 5];

let third: &i32 = &v[2];
let third: Option<&i32> = v.get(2);
```

Listing 8-5: Using indexing syntax or the get method to access an item in a vector

Note two details here. First, we use the index value of 2 to get the third element: vectors are indexed by number, starting at zero. Second, the two ways to get the third element are by using & and [], which gives us a reference, or by using the get method with the index passed as an argument, which gives us an Option<&T>.

Rust has two ways to reference an element so you can choose how the program behaves when you try to use an index value that the vector doesn't have an element for. As an example, let's see what a program will do if it has a vector that holds five elements and then tries to access an element at index 100, as shown in Listing 8-6.

```
let v = vec![1, 2, 3, 4, 5];

let does_not_exist = &v[100];
let does_not_exist = v.get(100);
```

Listing 8-6: Attempting to access the element at index 100 in a vector containing five elements

When we run this code, the first [] method will cause the program to panic because it references a nonexistent element. This method is best used when you want your program to crash if there's an attempt to access an element past the end of the vector.

When the get method is passed an index that is outside the vector, it returns None without panicking. You would use this method if accessing an element beyond the range of the vector happens occasionally under normal circumstances. Your code will then have logic to handle having either Some(&element) or None, as discussed in Chapter 6. For example, the index could be coming from a person entering a number. If they accidentally enter a number that's too large and the program gets a None value, you could tell the user how many items are in the current vector and give them another chance to enter a valid value. That would be more user-friendly than crashing the program due to a typo!

When the program has a valid reference, the borrow checker enforces the ownership and borrowing rules (covered in Chapter 4) to ensure this reference and any other references to the contents of the vector remain valid. Recall the rule that states you can't have mutable and immutable references in the same scope. That rule applies in Listing 8-7, where we hold an immutable reference to the first element in a vector and try to add an element to the end, which won't work.

```
let mut v = vec![1, 2, 3, 4, 5];

let first = &v[0];

v.push(6);

println!("The first element is: {}", first);
```

Listing 8-7: Attempting to add an element to a vector while holding a reference to an item

Compiling this code will result in this error:

```
error[E0502]: cannot borrow `v` as mutable because it is also borrowed as
immutable
  |
4 |     let first = &v[0];
  |                      - immutable borrow occurs here
5 |
6 |     v.push(6);
  |     ^ mutable borrow occurs here
9 | }
  | - immutable borrow ends here
```

The code in Listing 8-7 might look like it should work: why should a reference to the first element care about what changes at the end of the vector? This error is due to the way vectors work: adding a new element onto the end of the vector might require allocating new memory and copying the old elements to the new space, if there isn't enough room to put all the elements next to each other where the vector currently is. In that case, the reference to the first element would be pointing to deallocated memory. The borrowing rules prevent programs from ending up in that situation.

NOTE *For more on the implementation details of the Vec<T> type, see "The Rustonomicon" at https://doc.rust-lang.org/stable/nomicon/vec.html.*

Iterating over the Values in a Vector

If we want to access each element in a vector in turn, we can iterate through all of the elements rather than use indexes to access one at a time. Listing 8-8 shows how to use a for loop to get immutable references to each element in a vector of i32 values and print them.

```
let v = vec![100, 32, 57];
for i in &v {
    println!("{}", i);
}
```

Listing 8-8: Printing each element in a vector by iterating over the elements using a for loop

We can also iterate over mutable references to each element in a mutable vector in order to make changes to all the elements. The for loop in Listing 8-9 will add 50 to each element.

```
let mut v = vec![100, 32, 57];
for i in &mut v {
    *i += 50;
}
```

Listing 8-9: Iterating over mutable references to elements in a vector

To change the value that the mutable reference refers to, we have to use the dereference operator (*) to get to the value in i before we can use the += operator.

Using an Enum to Store Multiple Types

At the beginning of this chapter, we said that vectors can only store values that are the same type. This can be inconvenient; there are definitely use cases for needing to store a list of items of different types. Fortunately, the variants of an enum are defined under the same enum type, so when we need to store elements of a different type in a vector, we can define and use an enum!

For example, say we want to get values from a row in a spreadsheet in which some of the columns in the row contain integers, some floating-point numbers, and some strings. We can define an enum whose variants will hold the different value types, and then all the enum variants will be considered the same type: that of the enum. Then we can create a vector that holds that enum and so, ultimately, holds different types. We've demonstrated this in Listing 8-10.

```
enum SpreadsheetCell {
    Int(i32),
    Float(f64),
    Text(String),
}

let row = vec![
    SpreadsheetCell::Int(3),
    SpreadsheetCell::Text(String::from("blue")),
    SpreadsheetCell::Float(10.12),
];
```

Listing 8-10: Defining an enum to store values of different types in one vector

Rust needs to know what types will be in the vector at compile time so it knows exactly how much memory on the heap will be needed to store each element. A secondary advantage is that we can be explicit about what types are allowed in this vector. If Rust allowed a vector to hold any type, there would be a chance that one or more of the types would cause errors with the operations performed on the elements of the vector. Using an enum plus a match expression means that Rust will ensure at compile time that every possible case is handled, as discussed in Chapter 6.

When you're writing a program, if you don't know the exhaustive set of types the program will get at runtime to store in a vector, the enum technique won't work. Instead, you can use a trait object, which we'll cover in Chapter 17.

Now that we've discussed some of the most common ways to use vectors, be sure to review the API documentation for all the many useful methods defined on Vec<T> by the standard library. For example, in addition to push, a pop method removes and returns the last element. Let's move on to the next collection type: String!

Storing UTF-8 Encoded Text with Strings

We talked about strings in Chapter 4, but we'll look at them in more depth now. New Rustaceans commonly get stuck on strings for a combination of three reasons: Rust's propensity for exposing possible errors, strings being a more complicated data structure than many programmers give them credit for, and UTF-8. These factors combine in a way that can seem difficult when you're coming from other programming languages.

It's useful to discuss strings in the context of collections because strings are implemented as a collection of bytes, plus some methods to provide useful functionality when those bytes are interpreted as text. In this section, we'll talk about the operations on String that every collection type has, such as creating, updating, and reading. We'll also discuss the ways in which String is different from the other collections, namely how indexing into a String is complicated by the differences between how people and computers interpret String data.

What Is a String?

We'll first define what we mean by the term *string*. Rust has only one string type in the core language, which is the string slice str that is usually seen in its borrowed form &str. In Chapter 4, we talked about *string slices*, which are references to some UTF-8 encoded string data stored elsewhere. String literals, for example, are stored in the binary output of the program and are therefore string slices.

The String type, which is provided by Rust's standard library rather than coded into the core language, is a growable, mutable, owned, UTF-8 encoded string type. When Rustaceans refer to "strings" in Rust, they usually mean the String and the string slice &str types, not just one of those types. Although this section is largely about String, both types are used heavily in Rust's standard library, and both String and string slices are UTF-8 encoded.

Rust's standard library also includes a number of other string types, such as OsString, OsStr, CString, and CStr. Library crates can provide even more options for storing string data. See how those names all end in String or Str? They refer to owned and borrowed variants, just like the String and str types you've seen previously. These string types can store text in different encodings or be represented in memory in a different way, for example. We won't discuss these other string types in this chapter; see their API documentation for more about how to use them and when each is appropriate.

Creating a New String

Many of the same operations available with Vec<T> are available with String as well, starting with the new function to create a string, shown in Listing 8-11.

```
let mut s = String::new();
```

Listing 8-11: Creating a new, empty String

This line creates a new, empty string called s, which we can then load data into. Often, we'll have some initial data that we want to start the string with. For that, we use the to_string method, which is available on any type that implements the Display trait, as string literals do. Listing 8-12 shows two examples.

```
let data = "initial contents";

let s = data.to_string();

// the method also works on a literal directly:
let s = "initial contents".to_string();
```

Listing 8-12: Using the to_string method to create a String from a string literal

This code creates a string containing initial contents.

We can also use the function String::from to create a String from a string literal. The code in Listing 8-13 is equivalent to the code from Listing 8-12 that uses to_string.

```
let s = String::from("initial contents");
```

Listing 8-13: Using the String::from function to create a String from a string literal

Because strings are used for so many things, we can use many different generic APIs for strings, providing us with a lot of options. Some of them can seem redundant, but they all have their place! In this case, String::from and to_string do the same thing, so which you choose is a matter of style.

Remember that strings are UTF-8 encoded, so we can include any properly encoded data in them, as shown in Listing 8-14.

```
let hello = String::from("السلام عليكم");
let hello = String::from("Dobrý den");
let hello = String::from("Hello");
let hello = String::from("שלום");
let hello = String::from("नमस्ते");
let hello = String::from("こんにちは");
let hello = String::from("안녕하세요");
let hello = String::from("你好");
let hello = String::from("Olá");
let hello = String::from("Здравствуйте");
let hello = String::from("Hola");
```

Listing 8-14: Storing greetings in different languages in strings

All of these are valid String values.

Updating a String

A String can grow in size and its contents can change, just like the contents of a Vec<T>, if you push more data into it. In addition, you can conveniently use the + operator or the format! macro to concatenate String values.

Appending to a String with push_str and push

We can grow a String by using the push_str method to append a string slice, as shown in Listing 8-15.

```
let mut s = String::from("foo");
s.push_str("bar");
```

Listing 8-15: Appending a string slice to a String using the push_str method

After these two lines, s will contain foobar. The push_str method takes a string slice because we don't necessarily want to take ownership of the parameter. For example, the code in Listing 8-16 shows that it would be unfortunate if we weren't able to use s2 after appending its contents to s1.

```
let mut s1 = String::from("foo");
let s2 = "bar";
s1.push_str(s2);
println!("s2 is {}", s2);
```

Listing 8-16: Using a string slice after appending its contents to a String

If the push_str method took ownership of s2, we wouldn't be able to print its value on the last line. However, this code works as we'd expect!

The push method takes a single character as a parameter and adds it to the String. Listing 8-17 shows code that adds the letter *l* to a String using the push method.

```
let mut s = String::from("lo");
s.push('l');
```

Listing 8-17: Adding one character to a String value using push

As a result of this code, s will contain lol.

Concatenation with the + Operator or the format! Macro

Often, you'll want to combine two existing strings. One way is to use the + operator, as shown in Listing 8-18.

```
let s1 = String::from("Hello, ");
let s2 = String::from("world!");
let s3 = s1 + &s2; // note s1 has been moved here and can no longer be used
```

Listing 8-18: Using the + operator to combine two String values into a new String value

The string s3 will contain Hello, world! as a result of this code. The reason s1 is no longer valid after the addition and the reason we used a reference to s2 has to do with the signature of the method that gets called when we use the + operator. The + operator uses the add method, whose signature looks something like this:

```
fn add(self, s: &str) -> String {
```

This isn't the exact signature that's in the standard library: in the standard library, add is defined using generics. Here, we're looking at the signature of add with concrete types substituted for the generic ones, which is what happens when we call this method with String values. We'll discuss generics in Chapter 10. This signature gives us the clues we need to understand the tricky bits of the + operator.

First, s2 has an &, meaning that we're adding a *reference* of the second string to the first string because of the s parameter in the add function: we can only add a &str to a String; we can't add two String values together. But wait—the type of &s2 is &String, not &str, as specified in the second parameter to add. So why does Listing 8-18 compile?

The reason we're able to use &s2 in the call to add is that the compiler can *coerce* the &String argument into a &str. When we call the add method, Rust uses a *deref coercion*, which here turns &s2 into &s2[..]. We'll discuss deref coercion in more depth in Chapter 15. Because add does not take ownership of the s parameter, s2 will still be a valid String after this operation.

Second, we can see in the signature that add takes ownership of self, because self does *not* have an &. This means s1 in Listing 8-18 will be moved into the add call and no longer be valid after that. So although let s3 = s1 + &s2; looks like it will copy both strings and create a new one, this statement actually takes ownership of s1, appends a copy of the contents of s2, and then returns ownership of the result. In other words, it looks like it's making a lot of copies but isn't; the implementation is more efficient than copying.

If we need to concatenate multiple strings, the behavior of the + operator gets unwieldy:

```
let s1 = String::from("tic");
let s2 = String::from("tac");
let s3 = String::from("toe");

let s = s1 + "-" + &s2 + "-" + &s3;
```

At this point, s will be tic-tac-toe. With all of the + and " characters, it's difficult to see what's going on. For more complicated string combining, we can use the format! macro:

```
let s1 = String::from("tic");
let s2 = String::from("tac");
let s3 = String::from("toe");

let s = format!("{}-{}-{}", s1, s2, s3);
```

This code also sets s to tic-tac-toe. The format! macro works in the same way as println!, but instead of printing the output to the screen, it returns a String with the contents. The version of the code using format! is much easier to read and doesn't take ownership of any of its parameters.

Indexing into Strings

In many other programming languages, accessing individual characters in a string by referencing them by index is a valid and common operation. However, if you try to access parts of a `String` using indexing syntax in Rust, you'll get an error. Consider the invalid code in Listing 8-19.

```
let s1 = String::from("hello");
let h = s1[0];
```

Listing 8-19: Attempting to use indexing syntax with a String

This code will result in the following error:

```
error[E0277]: the trait bound `std::string::String: std::ops::Index<{integer}>` is not satisfied
 -->
  |
3 |     let h = s1[0];
  |             ^^^^^ the type `std::string::String` cannot be indexed by `{integer}`
  |
  = help: the trait `std::ops::Index<{integer}>` is not implemented for `std::string::String`
```

The error and the note tell the story: Rust strings don't support indexing. But why not? To answer that question, we need to discuss how Rust stores strings in memory.

Internal Representation

A `String` is a wrapper over a `Vec<u8>`. Let's look at some of our properly encoded UTF-8 example strings from Listing 8-14. First, this one:

```
let len = String::from("Hola").len();
```

In this case, `len` will be 4, which means the vector storing the string "Hola" is 4 bytes long. Each of these letters takes 1 byte when encoded in UTF-8. But what about the following line? (Note that this string begins with the capital Cyrillic letter Ze, not the Arabic number 3.)

```
let len = String::from("Здравствуйте").len();
```

Asked how long the string is, you might say 12. However, Rust's answer is 24: that's the number of bytes it takes to encode "Здравствуйте" in UTF-8, because each Unicode scalar value takes 2 bytes of storage. Therefore, an index into the string's bytes will not always correlate to a valid Unicode scalar value. To demonstrate, consider this invalid Rust code:

```
let hello = "Здравствуйте";
let answer = &hello[0];
```

What should the value of `answer` be? Should it be 3, the first letter? When encoded in UTF-8, the first byte of 3 is 208 and the second is 151, so answer should in fact be 208, but 208 is not a valid character on its own. Returning 208 is likely not what a user would want if they asked for the first letter of this string; however, that's the only data that Rust has at byte index 0. Users generally don't want the byte value returned, even if the string contains only Latin letters: if &"hello"[0] were valid code that returned the byte value, it would return 104, not h. To avoid returning an unexpected value and causing bugs that might not be discovered immediately, Rust doesn't compile this code at all and prevents misunderstandings early in the development process.

Bytes and Scalar Values and Grapheme Clusters! Oh My!

Another point about UTF-8 is that there are actually three relevant ways to look at strings from Rust's perspective: as bytes, scalar values, and grapheme clusters (the closest thing to what we would call *letters*).

If we look at the Hindi word "नमस्ते" written in the Devanagari script, it is stored as a vector of u8 values that looks like this:

```
[224, 164, 168, 224, 164, 174, 224, 164, 184, 224, 165, 141, 224, 164, 164,
224, 165, 135]
```

That's 18 bytes and is how computers ultimately store this data. If we look at them as Unicode scalar values, which are what Rust's char type is, those bytes look like this:

```
['न', 'म', 'स', '्', 'त', 'े']
```

There are six char values here, but the fourth and sixth are not letters: they're diacritics that don't make sense on their own. Finally, if we look at them as grapheme clusters, we'd get what a person would call the four letters that make up the Hindi word:

```
["न", "म", "स्", "ते"]
```

Rust provides different ways of interpreting the raw string data that computers store so that each program can choose the interpretation it needs, no matter what human language the data is in.

A final reason Rust doesn't allow us to index into a String to get a character is that indexing operations are expected to always take constant time (O(1)). But it isn't possible to guarantee that performance with a String, because Rust would have to walk through the contents from the beginning to the index to determine how many valid characters there were.

Slicing Strings

Indexing into a string is often a bad idea because it's not clear what the return type of the string-indexing operation should be: a byte value, a character, a grapheme cluster, or a string slice. Therefore, Rust asks you to be more specific if you really need to use indices to create string slices. To be more specific in your indexing and indicate that you want a string slice, rather than indexing using [] with a single number, you can use [] with a range to create a string slice containing particular bytes:

```
let hello = "Здравствуйте";

let s = &hello[0..4];
```

Here, s will be a &str that contains the first 4 bytes of the string. Earlier, we mentioned that each of these characters was 2 bytes, which means s will be Зд.

What would happen if we used &hello[0..1]? The answer: Rust would panic at runtime in the same way as if an invalid index were accessed in a vector:

```
thread 'main' panicked at 'byte index 1 is not a char boundary; it is inside
'З' (bytes 0..2) of `Здравствуйте`', src/libcore/str/mod.rs:2188:4
```

You should use ranges to create string slices with caution, because doing so can crash your program.

Methods for Iterating over Strings

Fortunately, you can access elements in a string in other ways.

If you need to perform operations on individual Unicode scalar values, the best way to do so is to use the chars method. Calling chars on "नमस्ते" separates out and returns six values of type char, and you can iterate over the result to access each element:

```
for c in "नमस्ते".chars() {
    println!("{}", c);
}
```

This code will print the following:

```
न
म
स
्
त
े
```

The bytes method returns each raw byte, which might be appropriate for your domain:

```
for b in "नमस्ते".bytes() {
    println!("{}", b);
}
```

This code will print the 18 bytes that make up this `String`:

```
224
164
// --snip--
165
135
```

But be sure to remember that valid Unicode scalar values may be made up of more than 1 byte.

Getting grapheme clusters from strings is complex, so this functionality is not provided by the standard library. Crates are available on *https://crates.io/* if this is the functionality you need.

Strings Are Not So Simple

To summarize, strings are complicated. Different programming languages make different choices about how to present this complexity to the programmer. Rust has chosen to make the correct handling of `String` data the default behavior for all Rust programs, which means programmers have to put more thought into handling UTF-8 data up front. This trade-off exposes more of the complexity of strings than is apparent in other programming languages, but it prevents you from having to handle errors involving non-ASCII characters later in your development life cycle.

Let's switch to something a bit less complex: hash maps!

Storing Keys with Associated Values in Hash Maps

The last of our common collections is the *hash map*. The type `HashMap<K, V>` stores a mapping of keys of type `K` to values of type `V`. It does this via a *hashing function*, which determines how it places these keys and values into memory. Many programming languages support this kind of data structure, but they often use a different name, such as hash, map, object, hash table, or associative array, just to name a few.

Hash maps are useful when you want to look up data not by using an index, as you can with vectors, but by using a key that can be of any type. For example, in a game, you could keep track of each team's score in a hash map in which each key is a team's name and the values are each team's score. Given a team name, you can retrieve its score.

We'll go over the basic API of hash maps in this section, but many more goodies are hiding in the functions defined on `HashMap<K, V>` by the standard library. As always, check the standard library documentation for more information.

Creating a New Hash Map

You can create an empty hash map with `new` and add elements with `insert`. In Listing 8-20, we're keeping track of the scores of two teams whose names are Blue and Yellow. The Blue team starts with 10 points, and the Yellow team starts with 50.

```
use std::collections::HashMap;

let mut scores = HashMap::new();

scores.insert(String::from("Blue"), 10);
scores.insert(String::from("Yellow"), 50);
```

Listing 8-20: Creating a new hash map and inserting some keys and values

Note that we need to first use the `HashMap` from the collections portion of the standard library. Of our three common collections, this one is the least often used, so it's not included in the features brought into scope automatically in the prelude. Hash maps also have less support from the standard library; there's no built-in macro to construct them, for example.

Just like vectors, hash maps store their data on the heap. This `HashMap` has keys of type `String` and values of type `i32`. Like vectors, hash maps are homogeneous: all of the keys must have the same type, and all of the values must have the same type.

Another way of constructing a hash map is by using the `collect` method on a vector of tuples, where each tuple consists of a key and its value. The collect method gathers data into a number of collection types, including `HashMap`. For example, if we had the team names and initial scores in two separate vectors, we could use the `zip` method to create a vector of tuples where `"Blue"` is paired with `10`, and so forth. Then we could use the `collect` method to turn that vector of tuples into a hash map. as shown in Listing 8-21.

```
use std::collections::HashMap;

let teams  = vec![String::from("Blue"), String::from("Yellow")];
let initial_scores = vec![10, 50];

let scores: HashMap<_, _> = teams.iter().zip(initial_scores.iter()).collect();
```

Listing 8-21: Creating a hash map from a list of teams and a list of scores

The type annotation `HashMap<_, _>` is needed here because it's possible to collect into many different data structures and Rust doesn't know which you want unless you specify. For the parameters for the key and value types, however, we use underscores, and Rust can infer the types that the hash map contains based on the types of the data in the vectors.

Hash Maps and Ownership

For types that implement the `Copy` trait, such as `i32`, the values are copied into the hash map. For owned values such as `String`, the values will be moved and the hash map will be the owner of those values, as demonstrated in Listing 8-22.

```
use std::collections::HashMap;

let field_name = String::from("Favorite color");
let field_value = String::from("Blue");

let mut map = HashMap::new();
map.insert(field_name, field_value);
// field_name and field_value are invalid at this point, try using them and
// see what compiler error you get!
```

Listing 8-22: Showing that keys and values are owned by the hash map once they're inserted

We aren't able to use the variables field_name and field_value after they've been moved into the hash map with the call to insert.

If we insert references to values into the hash map, the values won't be moved into the hash map. The values that the references point to must be valid for at least as long as the hash map is valid. We'll talk more about these issues in "Validating References with Lifetimes" on page 187.

Accessing Values in a Hash Map

We can get a value out of the hash map by providing its key to the get method, as shown in Listing 8-23.

```
use std::collections::HashMap;

let mut scores = HashMap::new();

scores.insert(String::from("Blue"), 10);
scores.insert(String::from("Yellow"), 50);

let team_name = String::from("Blue");
let score = scores.get(&team_name);
```

Listing 8-23: Accessing the score for the Blue team stored in the hash map

Here, score will have the value that's associated with the Blue team, and the result will be Some(&10). The result is wrapped in Some because get returns an Option<&V>; if there's no value for that key in the hash map, get will return None. The program will need to handle the Option in one of the ways that we covered in Chapter 6.

We can iterate over each key/value pair in a hash map in a similar manner as we do with vectors, using a for loop:

```
use std::collections::HashMap;

let mut scores = HashMap::new();

scores.insert(String::from("Blue"), 10);
scores.insert(String::from("Yellow"), 50);
```

```
for (key, value) in &scores {
    println!("{}: {}", key, value);
}
```

This code will print each pair in an arbitrary order:

```
Yellow: 50
Blue: 10
```

Updating a Hash Map

Although the number of keys and values is growable, each key can only have one value associated with it at a time. When you want to change the data in a hash map, you have to decide how to handle the case when a key already has a value assigned. You could replace the old value with the new value, completely disregarding the old value. You could keep the old value and ignore the new value, only adding the new value if the key *doesn't* already have a value. Or you could combine the old value and the new value. Let's look at how to do each of these!

Overwriting a Value

If we insert a key and a value into a hash map and then insert that same key with a different value, the value associated with that key will be replaced. Even though the code in Listing 8-24 calls insert twice, the hash map will only contain one key/value pair because we're inserting the value for the Blue team's key both times.

```
use std::collections::HashMap;

let mut scores = HashMap::new();

scores.insert(String::from("Blue"), 10);
scores.insert(String::from("Blue"), 25);

println!("{:?}", scores);
```

Listing 8-24: Replacing a value stored with a particular key

This code will print {"Blue": 25}. The original value of 10 has been overwritten.

Only Inserting a Value If the Key Has No Value

It's common to check whether a particular key has a value and, if it doesn't, insert a value for it. Hash maps have a special API for this called entry that takes the key you want to check as a parameter. The return value of the entry method is an enum called Entry that represents a value that might or might not exist. Let's say we want to check whether the key for the Yellow team has a value associated with it. If it doesn't, we want to insert the value 50, and the same for the Blue team. Using the entry API, the code looks like Listing 8-25.

```
use std::collections::HashMap;

let mut scores = HashMap::new();
scores.insert(String::from("Blue"), 10);

scores.entry(String::from("Yellow")).or_insert(50);
scores.entry(String::from("Blue")).or_insert(50);

println!("{:?}", scores);
```

Listing 8-25: Using the entry method to only insert if the key does not already have a value

The or_insert method on Entry is defined to return a mutable reference to the value for the corresponding Entry key if that key exists, and if not, inserts the parameter as the new value for this key and returns a mutable reference to the new value. This technique is much cleaner than writing the logic ourselves and, in addition, plays more nicely with the borrow checker.

Running the code in Listing 8-25 will print {"Yellow": 50, "Blue": 10}. The first call to entry will insert the key for the Yellow team with the value 50 because the Yellow team doesn't have a value already. The second call to entry will not change the hash map because the Blue team already has the value 10.

Updating a Value Based on the Old Value

Another common use case for hash maps is to look up a key's value and then update it based on the old value. For instance, Listing 8-26 shows code that counts how many times each word appears in some text. We use a hash map with the words as keys and increment the value to keep track of how many times we've seen that word. If it's the first time we've seen a word, we'll first insert the value 0.

```
use std::collections::HashMap;

let text = "hello world wonderful world";

let mut map = HashMap::new();

for word in text.split_whitespace() {
    let count = map.entry(word).or_insert(0);
    *count += 1;
}

println!("{:?}", map);
```

Listing 8-26: Counting occurrences of words using a hash map that stores words and counts

This code will print {"world": 2, "hello": 1, "wonderful": 1}. The or_insert method actually returns a mutable reference (&mut V) to the value for this key. Here we store that mutable reference in the count variable, so in order to assign to that value, we must first dereference count using the asterisk (*). The mutable reference goes out of scope at the end of the for loop, so all of these changes are safe and allowed by the borrowing rules.

Hashing Functions

By default, `HashMap` uses a cryptographically secure hashing function that can provide resistance to Denial of Service (DoS) attacks. This is not the fastest hashing algorithm available, but the trade-off for better security that comes with the drop in performance is worth it. If you profile your code and find that the default hash function is too slow for your purposes, you can switch to another function by specifying a different *hasher*. A hasher is a type that implements the `BuildHasher` trait. We'll talk about traits and how to implement them in Chapter 10. You don't necessarily have to implement your own hasher from scratch; *https://crates.io/* has libraries shared by other Rust users that provide hashers implementing many common hashing algorithms.

Summary

Vectors, strings, and hash maps will provide a large amount of functionality necessary in programs when you need to store, access, and modify data. Here are some exercises you should now be equipped to solve:

- Given a list of integers, use a vector and return the mean (the average value), median (when sorted, the value in the middle position), and mode (the value that occurs most often; a hash map will be helpful here) of the list.

- Convert strings to pig latin. The first consonant of each word is moved to the end of the word and "ay" is added, so "first" becomes "irst-fay." Words that start with a vowel have "hay" added to the end instead ("apple" becomes "apple-hay"). Keep in mind the details about UTF-8 encoding!

- Using a hash map and vectors, create a text interface to allow a user to add employee names to a department in a company. For example, "Add Sally to Engineering" or "Add Amir to Sales." Then let the user retrieve a list of all people in a department or all people in the company by department, sorted alphabetically.

The standard library API documentation describes methods that vectors, strings, and hash maps have that will be helpful for these exercises!

We're getting into more complex programs in which operations can fail, so, it's a perfect time to discuss error handling. We'll do that next!

9

ERROR HANDLING

Rust's commitment to reliability extends to error handling. Errors are a fact of life in software, so Rust has a number of features for handling situations in which something goes wrong. In many cases, Rust requires you to acknowledge the possibility of an error and take some action before your code will compile. This requirement makes your program more robust by ensuring that you'll discover errors and handle them appropriately before you've deployed your code to production!

Rust groups errors into two major categories: *recoverable* and *unrecoverable* errors. For a recoverable error, such as a file not found error, it's reasonable to report the problem to the user and retry the operation. Unrecoverable errors are always symptoms of bugs, like trying to access a location beyond the end of an array.

Most languages don't distinguish between these two kinds of errors and handle both in the same way, using mechanisms such as exceptions. Rust doesn't have exceptions. Instead, it has the type Result<T, E> for recoverable errors and the panic! macro that stops execution when the program encounters an unrecoverable error. This chapter covers calling panic! first and then talks about returning Result<T, E> values. Additionally, we'll explore considerations when deciding whether to try to recover from an error or to stop execution.

Unrecoverable Errors with panic!

Sometimes, bad things happen in your code, and there's nothing you can do about it. In these cases, Rust has the panic! macro. When the panic! macro executes, your program will print a failure message, unwind and clean up the stack, and then quit. This most commonly occurs when a bug of some kind has been detected and it's not clear to the programmer how to handle the error.

UNWINDING THE STACK OR ABORTING IN RESPONSE TO A PANIC

By default, when a panic occurs, the program starts *unwinding*, which means Rust walks back up the stack and cleans up the data from each function it encounters. But this walking back and cleanup is a lot of work. The alternative is to immediately *abort*, which ends the program without cleaning up. Memory that the program was using will then need to be cleaned up by the operating system. If in your project you need to make the resulting binary as small as possible, you can switch from unwinding to aborting upon a panic by adding panic = 'abort' to the appropriate [profile] sections in your *Cargo.toml* file. For example, if you want to abort on panic in release mode, add this:

```
[profile.release]
panic = 'abort'
```

Let's try calling panic! in a simple program:

src/main.rs

```
fn main() {
    panic!("crash and burn");
}
```

When you run the program, you'll see something like this:

```
$ cargo run
   Compiling panic v0.1.0 (file:///projects/panic)
    Finished dev [unoptimized + debuginfo] target(s) in 0.25 secs
     Running 'target/debug/panic'
```

```
thread 'main' panicked at 'crash and burn', src/main.rs:2:4
note: Run with 'RUST_BACKTRACE=1' for a backtrace.
```

The call to panic! causes the error message contained in the last two
lines. The first line shows our panic message and the place in our source
code where the panic occurred: *src/main.rs:2:4* indicates that it's the second
line, fourth character of our *src/main.rs* file.

In this case, the line indicated is part of our code, and if we go to that
line, we see the panic! macro call. In other cases, the panic! call might be in
code that our code calls, and the filename and line number reported by the
error message will be someone else's code where the panic! macro is called,
not the line of our code that eventually led to the panic! call. We can use
the backtrace of the functions the panic! call came from to figure out the
part of our code that is causing the problem. We'll discuss what a backtrace
is in more detail next.

Using a panic! Backtrace

Let's look at another example to see what it's like when a panic! call comes
from a library because of a bug in our code instead of from our code calling
the macro directly. Listing 9-1 has some code that attempts to access an element by index in a vector.

src/main.rs

```
fn main() {
    let v = vec![1, 2, 3];

    v[99];
}
```

*Listing 9-1: Attempting to access an element beyond the end of a vector, which will cause
a call to panic!*

Here, we're attempting to access the 100th element of our vector (which
is at index 99 because indexing starts at zero), but it has only 3 elements. In
this situation, Rust will panic. Using [ ] is supposed to return an element,
but if you pass an invalid index, there's no element that Rust could return
here that would be correct.

Other languages, like C, will attempt to give you exactly what you asked
for in this situation, even though it isn't what you want: you'll get whatever
is at the location in memory that would correspond to that element in the
vector, even though the memory doesn't belong to the vector. This is called
a *buffer overread* and can lead to security vulnerabilities if an attacker is able
to manipulate the index in such a way as to read data they shouldn't be
allowed to that is stored after the array.

To protect your program from this sort of vulnerability, if you try to
read an element at an index that doesn't exist, Rust will stop execution and
refuse to continue. Let's try it and see:

```
$ cargo run
   Compiling panic v0.1.0 (file:///projects/panic)
```

```
    Finished dev [unoptimized + debuginfo] target(s) in 0.27 secs
        Running 'target/debug/panic'
thread 'main' panicked at 'index out of bounds: the len is 3 but the index is
99', /checkout/src/liballoc/vec.rs:1555:10
note: Run with 'RUST_BACKTRACE=1' for a backtrace.
```

This error points at a file we didn't write, *vec.rs*. That's the implementation of Vec<T> in the standard library. The code that gets run when we use [ ] on our vector v is in *vec.rs*, and that is where the panic! is actually happening.

The next note line tells us that we can set the RUST_BACKTRACE environment variable to get a backtrace of exactly what happened to cause the error. A *backtrace* is a list of all the functions that have been called to get to this point. Backtraces in Rust work as they do in other languages: the key to reading the backtrace is to start from the top and read until you see files you wrote. That's the spot where the problem originated. The lines above the lines mentioning your files are code that your code called; the lines below are code that called your code. These lines might include core Rust code, standard library code, or crates that you're using. Let's try getting a backtrace by setting the RUST_BACKTRACE environment variable to any value except 0. Listing 9-2 shows output similar to what you'll see.

```
$ RUST_BACKTRACE=1 cargo run
    Finished dev [unoptimized + debuginfo] target(s) in 0.0 secs
        Running `target/debug/panic`
thread 'main' panicked at 'index out of bounds: the len is 3 but the index is 99', /checkout/
src/liballoc/vec.rs:1555:10
stack backtrace:
   0: std::sys::imp::backtrace::tracing::imp::unwind_backtrace
             at /checkout/src/libstd/sys/unix/backtrace/tracing/gcc_s.rs:49
   1: std::sys_common::backtrace::_print
             at /checkout/src/libstd/sys_common/backtrace.rs:71
   2: std::panicking::default_hook::{{closure}}
             at /checkout/src/libstd/sys_common/backtrace.rs:60
             at /checkout/src/libstd/panicking.rs:381
   3: std::panicking::default_hook
             at /checkout/src/libstd/panicking.rs:397
   4: std::panicking::rust_panic_with_hook
             at /checkout/src/libstd/panicking.rs:611
   5: std::panicking::begin_panic
             at /checkout/src/libstd/panicking.rs:572
   6: std::panicking::begin_panic_fmt
             at /checkout/src/libstd/panicking.rs:522
   7: rust_begin_unwind
             at /checkout/src/libstd/panicking.rs:498
   8: core::panicking::panic_fmt
             at /checkout/src/libcore/panicking.rs:71
   9: core::panicking::panic_bounds_check
             at /checkout/src/libcore/panicking.rs:58
  10: <alloc::vec::Vec<T> as core::ops::index::Index<usize>>::index
             at /checkout/src/liballoc/vec.rs:1555
  11: panic::main
             at src/main.rs:4
```

```
12: __rust_maybe_catch_panic
          at /checkout/src/libpanic_unwind/lib.rs:99
13: std::rt::lang_start
          at /checkout/src/libstd/panicking.rs:459
          at /checkout/src/libstd/panic.rs:361
          at /checkout/src/libstd/rt.rs:61
14: main
15: __libc_start_main
16: <unknown>
```

Listing 9-2: The backtrace generated by a call to panic! displayed when the environment variable RUST_BACKTRACE is set

That's a lot of output! The exact output you see might be different depending on your operating system and Rust version. In order to get backtraces with this information, debug symbols must be enabled. Debug symbols are enabled by default when using cargo build or cargo run without the --release flag, as we have here.

In the output in Listing 9-2, line 11 of the backtrace points to the line in our project that's causing the problem: line 4 of *src/main.rs*. If we don't want our program to panic, the location pointed to by the first line mentioning a file we wrote is where we should start investigating. In Listing 9-1, where we deliberately wrote code that would panic in order to demonstrate how to use backtraces, the way to fix the panic is to not request an element at index 99 from a vector that only contains 3 items. When your code panics in the future, you'll need to figure out what action the code is taking with what values to cause the panic and what the code should do instead.

We'll come back to panic! and when we should and should not use panic! to handle error conditions in "To panic! or Not to panic!" on page 161. Next, we'll look at how to recover from an error using Result.

Recoverable Errors with Result

Most errors aren't serious enough to require the program to stop entirely. Sometimes, when a function fails, it's for a reason that you can easily interpret and respond to. For example, if you try to open a file and that operation fails because the file doesn't exist, you might want to create the file instead of terminating the process.

Recall from "Handling Potential Failure with the Result Type" on page 17 that the Result enum is defined as having two variants, Ok and Err, as follows:

```
enum Result<T, E> {
    Ok(T),
    Err(E),
}
```

The T and E are generic type parameters: we'll discuss generics in more detail in Chapter 10. What you need to know right now is that T represents the type of the value that will be returned in a success case within the Ok variant, and E represents the type of the error that will be returned in a failure case within the Err variant. Because Result has these generic type parameters, we can use the Result type and the functions that the standard library has defined on it in many different situations where the successful value and error value we want to return may differ.

Let's call a function that returns a Result value because the function could fail. In Listing 9-3 we try to open a file.

```
use std::fs::File;

fn main() {
    let f = File::open("hello.txt");
}
```

Listing 9-3: Opening a file

How do we know File::open returns a Result? We could look at the standard library API documentation, or we could ask the compiler! If we give f a type annotation that we know is *not* a return type of the function and then try to compile the code, the compiler will tell us that the types don't match. The error message will then tell us what the type of f *is*. Let's try it! We know that the return type of File::open isn't of type u32, so let's change the let f statement to this:

```
let f: u32 = File::open("hello.txt");
```

Attempting to compile now gives us the following output:

```
error[E0308]: mismatched types
 --> src/main.rs:4:18
  |
4 |     let f: u32 = File::open("hello.txt");
  |                  ^^^^^^^^^^^^^^^^^^^^^^^^ expected u32, found enum
`std::result::Result`
  |
  = note: expected type `u32`
             found type `std::result::Result<std::fs::File, std::io::Error>`
```

This tells us the return type of the File::open function is a Result<T, E>. The generic parameter T has been filled in here with the type of the success value, std::fs::File, which is a file handle. The type of E used in the error value is std::io::Error.

This return type means the call to File::open might succeed and return a file handle that we can read from or write to. The function call also might fail: for example, the file might not exist, or we might not have permission to access the file. The File::open function needs to have a way to tell us whether it succeeded or failed and at the same time give us either the file handle or error information. This information is exactly what the Result enum conveys.

In the case where `File::open` succeeds, the value in the variable `f` will be an instance of `Ok` that contains a file handle. In the case where it fails, the value in `f` will be an instance of `Err` that contains more information about the kind of error that happened.

We need to add to the code in Listing 9-3 to take different actions depending on the value `File::open` returns. Listing 9-4 shows one way to handle the `Result` using a basic tool, the `match` expression that we discussed in Chapter 6.

src/main.rs

```
use std::fs::File;

fn main() {
    let f = File::open("hello.txt");

    let f = match f {
        Ok(file) => file,
        Err(error) => {
            panic!("There was a problem opening the file: {:?}", error)
        },
    };
}
```

Listing 9-4: Using a match expression to handle the `Result` variants that might be returned

Note that, like the `Option` enum, the `Result` enum and its variants have been imported in the prelude, so we don't need to specify `Result::` before the `Ok` and `Err` variants in the `match` arms.

Here we tell Rust that when the result is `Ok`, return the inner `file` value out of the `Ok` variant, and we then assign that file handle value to the variable `f`. After the `match`, we can use the file handle for reading or writing.

The other arm of the `match` handles the case where we get an `Err` value from `File::open`. In this example, we've chosen to call the `panic!` macro. If there's no file named *hello.txt* in our current directory and we run this code, we'll see the following output from the `panic!` macro:

```
thread 'main' panicked at 'There was a problem opening the file: Error { repr:
Os { code: 2, message: "No such file or directory" } }', src/main.rs:9:12
```

As usual, this output tells us exactly what has gone wrong.

Matching on Different Errors

The code in Listing 9-4 will `panic!` no matter why `File::open` failed. What we want to do instead is take different actions for different failure reasons: if `File::open` failed because the file doesn't exist, we want to create the file and return the handle to the new file. If `File::open` failed for any other reason—for example, because we didn't have permission to open the file—we still want the code to `panic!` in the same way as it did in Listing 9-4. Look at Listing 9-5, which adds another arm to the `match`.

```
use std::fs::File;
use std::io::ErrorKind;

fn main() {
    let f = File::open("hello.txt");

    let f = match f {
        Ok(file) => file,
        Err(ref error) if error.kind() == ErrorKind::NotFound => {
            match File::create("hello.txt") {
                Ok(fc) => fc,
                Err(e) => {
                    panic!(
                        "Tried to create file but there was a problem: {:?}",
                        e
                    )
                },
            }
        },
        Err(error) => {
            panic!(
                "There was a problem opening the file: {:?}",
                error
            )
        },
    };
}
```

Listing 9-5: Handling different kinds of errors in different ways

The type of the value that File::open returns inside the Err variant is io::Error, which is a struct provided by the standard library. This struct has a method kind that we can call to get an io::ErrorKind value. The enum io::ErrorKind is provided by the standard library and has variants representing the different kinds of errors that might result from an io operation. The variant we want to use is ErrorKind::NotFound, which indicates the file we're trying to open doesn't exist yet.

The condition if error.kind() == ErrorKind::NotFound is called a *match guard*: it's an extra condition on a match arm that further refines the arm's pattern. This condition must be true for that arm's code to be run; otherwise, the pattern matching will move on to consider the next arm in the match. The ref in the pattern is needed so error is not moved into the guard condition but is merely referenced by it. The reason you use ref to create a reference in a pattern instead of & will be covered in detail in Chapter 18. In short, in the context of a pattern, & matches a reference and gives you its value, but ref matches a value and gives you a reference to it.

The condition we want to check in the match guard is whether the value returned by error.kind() is the NotFound variant of the ErrorKind enum. If it is, we try to create the file with File::create. However, because File::create could also fail, we need to add an inner match expression as well. When the file can't be opened, a different error message will be printed. The last arm of the outer match stays the same so the program panics on any error besides the missing file error.

Shortcuts for Panic on Error: unwrap and expect

Using match works well enough, but it can be a bit verbose and doesn't always communicate intent well. The Result<T, E> type has many helper methods defined on it to do various tasks. One of those methods, called unwrap, is a shortcut method that is implemented just like the match expression we wrote in Listing 9-4. If the Result value is the Ok variant, unwrap will return the value inside the Ok. If the Result is the Err variant, unwrap will call the panic! macro for us. Here is an example of unwrap in action:

src/main.rs

```
use std::fs::File;

fn main() {
    let f = File::open("hello.txt").unwrap();
}
```

If we run this code without a *hello.txt* file, we'll see an error message from the panic! call that the unwrap method makes:

```
thread 'main' panicked at 'called 'Result::unwrap()' on an 'Err' value: Error
{ repr: Os { code: 2, message: "No such file or directory" } }', /src/libcore/
result.rs:906:4
```

Another method, expect, which is similar to unwrap, lets us also choose the panic! error message. Using expect instead of unwrap and providing good error messages can convey your intent and make tracking down the source of a panic easier. The syntax of expect looks like this:

src/main.rs

```
use std::fs::File;

fn main() {
    let f = File::open("hello.txt").expect("Failed to open hello.txt");
}
```

We use expect in the same way as unwrap: to return the file handle or call the panic! macro. The error message used by expect in its call to panic! will be the parameter that we pass to expect, rather than the default panic! message that unwrap uses. Here's what it looks like:

```
thread 'main' panicked at 'Failed to open hello.txt: Error { repr: Os { code:
2, message: "No such file or directory" } }', /src/libcore/result.rs:906:4
```

Because this error message starts with the text we specified, Failed to open hello.txt, it will be easier to find where in the code this error message is coming from. If we use unwrap in multiple places, it can take more time to figure out exactly which unwrap is causing the panic because all unwrap calls that panic print the same message.

Propagating Errors

When you're writing a function whose implementation calls something that might fail, instead of handling the error within this function, you can return the error to the calling code so that it can decide what to do. This is known as *propagating* the error and gives more control to the calling code, where there might be more information or logic that dictates how the error should be handled than what you have available in the context of your code.

For example, Listing 9-6 shows a function that reads a username from a file. If the file doesn't exist or can't be read, this function will return those errors to the code that called this function.

src/main.rs

```
use std::io;
use std::io::Read;
use std::fs::File;

fn read_username_from_file() -> Result<String, io::Error>❶ {
  ❷ let f = File::open("hello.txt");

  ❸ let mut f = match f {
        Ok(file) => file,
        Err(e) => return Err(e),
    };

  ❹ let mut s = String::new();

  ❺ match f.read_to_string(&mut s)❻ {
        Ok(_) => Ok(s)❼,
        Err(e) => Err(e)❽,
    }
}
```

Listing 9-6: A function that returns errors to the calling code using match

Look at the return type of the function first: Result<String, io::Error> ❶. This means the function is returning a value of the type Result<T, E> where the generic parameter T has been filled in with the concrete type String and the generic type E has been filled in with the concrete type io::Error. If this function succeeds without any problems, the code that calls this function will receive an Ok value that holds a String—the username that this function read from the file ❼. If this function encounters any problems, the code that calls this function will receive an Err value that holds an instance of io::Error that contains more information about what the problems were. We chose io::Error as the return type of this function because that happens to be the type of the error value returned from both of the operations we're calling in this function's body that might fail: the File::open function and the read_to_string method.

The body of the function starts by calling the File::open function ❷. Then we handle the Result value returned with a match ❸ similar to the match in Listing 9-4, only instead of calling panic! in the Err case, we return early from this function and pass the error value from File::open back to the calling code as this function's error value ❹. If File::open succeeds, we store the file handle in the variable f and continue.

Then we create a new String in variable s ❺ and call the read_to_string method on the file handle in f to read the contents of the file into s ❻. The read_to_string method also returns a Result because it might fail, even though File::open succeeded. So we need another match to handle that Result: if read_to_string succeeds, then our function has succeeded, and we return the username from the file that's now in s wrapped in an Ok ❼. If read_to_string fails, we return the error value in the same way that we returned the error value in the match that handled the return value of File::open ❽. However, we don't need to explicitly say return, because this is the last expression in the function.

The code that calls this code will then handle getting either an Ok value that contains a username or an Err value that contains an io::Error. We don't know what the calling code will do with those values. If the calling code gets an Err value, it could call panic! and crash the program, use a default username, or look up the username from somewhere other than a file, for example. We don't have enough information on what the calling code is actually trying to do, so we propagate all the success or error information upward for it to handle appropriately.

This pattern of propagating errors is so common in Rust that Rust provides the question mark operator ? to make this easier.

A Shortcut for Propagating Errors: the ? Operator

Listing 9-7 shows an implementation of read_username_from_file that has the same functionality as it had in Listing 9-6, but this implementation uses the ? operator.

src/main.rs

```
use std::io;
use std::io::Read;
use std::fs::File;

fn read_username_from_file() -> Result<String, io::Error> {
    let mut f = File::open("hello.txt")?;
    let mut s = String::new();
    f.read_to_string(&mut s)?;
    Ok(s)
}
```

Listing 9-7: A function that returns errors to the calling code using the ? operator

The ? placed after a Result value is defined to work in almost the same way as the match expressions we defined to handle the Result values in Listing 9-6. If the value of the Result is an Ok, the value inside the Ok will get returned from this expression, and the program will continue. If the value is an `Err`, the value inside the `Err` will be returned from the whole function as if we had used the `return` keyword so the error value gets propagated to the calling code.

There is a difference between what the `match` expression from Listing 9-6 and the ? operator do: error values used with ? go through the `from` function, defined in the `From` trait in the standard library, which is used to convert errors from one type into another. When the ? operator calls the `from` function, the error type received is converted into the error type defined in the return type of the current function. This is useful when a function returns one error type to represent all the ways a function might fail, even if parts might fail for many different reasons. As long as each error type implements the `from` function to define how to convert itself to the returned error type, the ? operator takes care of the conversion automatically.

In the context of Listing 9-7, the ? at the end of the `File::open` call will return the value inside an `Ok` to the variable `f`. If an error occurs, the ? operator will return early out of the whole function and give any `Err` value to the calling code. The same thing applies to the ? at the end of the `read_to_string` call.

The ? operator eliminates a lot of boilerplate and makes this function's implementation simpler. We could even shorten this code further by chaining method calls immediately after the ?, as shown in Listing 9-8.

src/main.rs

```
use std::io;
use std::io::Read;
use std::fs::File;

fn read_username_from_file() -> Result<String, io::Error> {
    let mut s = String::new();

    File::open("hello.txt")?.read_to_string(&mut s)?;

    Ok(s)
}
```

Listing 9-8: Chaining method calls after the ? operator

We've moved the creation of the new `String` in `s` to the beginning of the function; that part hasn't changed. Instead of creating a variable `f`, we've chained the call to `read_to_string` directly onto the result of `File::open("hello .txt")?`. We still have a ? at the end of the `read_to_string` call, and we still return an `Ok` value containing the username in `s` when both `File::open` and `read_to_string` succeed rather than returning errors. The functionality is again the same as in Listing 9-6 and Listing 9-7; this is just a different, more ergonomic way to write it.

The ? Operator Can Only Be Used in Functions That Return Result

The ? operator can only be used in functions that have a return type of `Result`, because it is defined to work in the same way as the `match` expression we defined in Listing 9-6. The part of the match that requires a return type of Result is return Err(e), so the return type of the function must be a Result to be compatible with this return.

Let's look at what happens if we use the ? operator in the main function, which you'll recall has a return type of ():

```
use std::fs::File;

fn main() {
    let f = File::open("hello.txt")?;
}
```

When we compile this code, we get the following error message:

```
error[E0277]: the trait bound `(): std::ops::Try` is not satisfied
  --> src/main.rs:4:13
   |
4  |      let f = File::open("hello.txt")?;
   |              -----------------------
   |              |
   |              the `?` operator can only be used in a function that returns
`Result` (or another type that implements `std::ops::Try`)
   |              in this macro invocation
   |
   = help: the trait `std::ops::Try` is not implemented for `()`
   = note: required by `std::ops::Try::from_error
```

This error points out that we're only allowed to use the ? operator in a function that returns Result. In functions that don't return Result, when you call other functions that return Result, you'll need to use a match or one of the Result methods to handle the Result instead of using the ? operator to potentially propagate the error to the calling code.

Now that we've discussed the details of calling panic! or returning Result, let's return to the topic of how to decide which is appropriate to use in which cases.

To panic! or Not to panic!

So how do you decide when you should call panic! and when you should return Result? When code panics, there's no way to recover. You could call panic! for any error situation, whether there's a possible way to recover or not, but then you're making the decision on behalf of the code calling your code that a situation is unrecoverable. When you choose to return a Result value, you give the calling code options rather than making the decision for it. The calling code could choose to attempt to recover in a way that's appropriate for its situation, or it could decide that an Err value in this case is unrecoverable, so it can call panic! and turn your recoverable error into an unrecoverable one. Therefore, returning Result is a good default choice when you're defining a function that might fail.

In rare situations, it's more appropriate to write code that panics instead of returning a Result. Let's explore why it's appropriate to panic in examples, prototype code, and tests. Then we'll discuss situations in which the compiler can't tell that failure is impossible, but you as a human can. The chapter will conclude with some general guidelines on how to decide whether to panic in library code.

Examples, Prototype Code, and Tests

When you're writing an example to illustrate some concept, having robust error-handling code in the example as well can make the example less clear. In examples, it's understood that a call to a method like unwrap that could panic is meant as a placeholder for the way you'd want your application to handle errors, which can differ based on what the rest of your code is doing.

Similarly, the unwrap and expect methods are very handy when prototyping, before you're ready to decide how to handle errors. They leave clear markers in your code for when you're ready to make your program more robust.

If a method call fails in a test, you'd want the whole test to fail, even if that method isn't the functionality under test. Because panic! is how a test is marked as a failure, calling unwrap or expect is exactly what should happen.

Cases in Which You Have More Information Than the Compiler

It would also be appropriate to call unwrap when you have some other logic that ensures the Result will have an Ok value, but the logic isn't something the compiler understands. You'll still have a Result value that you need to handle: whatever operation you're calling still has the possibility of failing in general, even though it's logically impossible in your particular situation. If you can ensure by manually inspecting the code that you'll never have an Err variant, it's perfectly acceptable to call unwrap. Here's an example:

```
use std::net::IpAddr;

let home: IpAddr = "127.0.0.1".parse().unwrap();
```

We're creating an IpAddr instance by parsing a hardcoded string. We can see that 127.0.0.1 is a valid IP address, so it's acceptable to use unwrap here. However, having a hardcoded, valid string doesn't change the return type of the parse method: we still get a Result value, and the compiler will still make us handle the Result as if the Err variant is a possibility because the compiler isn't smart enough to see that this string is always a valid IP address. If the IP address string came from a user rather than being hardcoded into the program and therefore *did* have a possibility of failure, we'd definitely want to handle the Result in a more robust way instead.

Guidelines for Error Handling

It's advisable to have your code panic when it's possible that your code could end up in a bad state. In this context, a *bad state* is when some assumption, guarantee, contract, or invariant has been broken, such as when invalid values, contradictory values, or missing values are passed to your code—plus one or more of the following:

- The bad state is not something that's *expected* to happen occasionally.
- Your code after this point needs to rely on not being in this bad state.
- There's not a good way to encode this information in the types you use.

If someone calls your code and passes in values that don't make sense, the best choice might be to call panic! and alert the person using your library to the bug in their code so they can fix it during development. Similarly, panic! is often appropriate if you're calling external code that is out of your control and it returns an invalid state that you have no way of fixing.

When a bad state is reached, but it's expected to happen no matter how well you write your code, it's still more appropriate to return a Result than to make a panic! call. Examples include a parser being given malformed data or an HTTP request returning a status that indicates you have hit a rate limit. In these cases, you should indicate that failure is an expected possibility by returning a Result to propagate these bad states upward so the calling code can decide how to handle the problem. To call panic! wouldn't be the best way to handle these cases.

When your code performs operations on values, your code should verify the values are valid first and panic if the values aren't valid. This is mostly for safety reasons: attempting to operate on invalid data can expose your code to vulnerabilities. This is the main reason the standard library will call panic! if you attempt an out-of-bounds memory access: trying to access memory that doesn't belong to the current data structure is a common security problem. Functions often have *contracts*: their behavior is only guaranteed if the inputs meet particular requirements. Panicking when the contract is violated makes sense because a contract violation always indicates a caller-side bug and it's not a kind of error you want the calling code to have to explicitly handle. In fact, there's no reasonable way for calling code to recover; the calling *programmers* need to fix the code. Contracts for a function, especially when a violation will cause a panic, should be explained in the API documentation for the function.

However, having lots of error checks in all of your functions would be verbose and annoying. Fortunately, you can use Rust's type system (and thus the type checking the compiler does) to do many of the checks for you. If your function has a particular type as a parameter, you can proceed with your code's logic knowing that the compiler has already ensured you have a valid value. For example, if you have a type rather than an Option, your program expects to have *something* rather than *nothing*. Your code then doesn't have to handle two cases for the Some and None variants: it will only have one case for definitely having a value. Code trying to pass nothing to your function won't even compile, so your function doesn't have to check for that case at runtime. Another example is using an unsigned integer type such as u32, which ensures the parameter is never negative.

Creating Custom Types for Validation

Let's take the idea of using Rust's type system to ensure we have a valid value one step further and look at creating a custom type for validation. Recall the guessing game in Chapter 2 in which our code asked the user to guess a number between 1 and 100. We never validated that the user's guess was between those numbers before checking it against our secret number; we only validated that the guess was positive. In this case, the consequences were not very dire: our output of "Too high" or "Too low" would still be correct. But it would be a useful enhancement to guide the user toward valid guesses and have different behavior when a user guesses a number that's out of range versus when a user types, for example, letters instead.

One way to do this would be to parse the guess as an i32 instead of only a u32 to allow potentially negative numbers, and then add a check for the number being in range, like so:

```
loop {
    // --snip--

    let guess: i32 = match guess.trim().parse() {
        Ok(num) => num,
        Err(_) => continue,
    };

    if guess < 1 || guess > 100 {
        println!("The secret number will be between 1 and 100.");
        continue;
    }

    match guess.cmp(&secret_number) {
        // --snip--
}
```

The if expression checks whether our value is out of range, tells the user about the problem, and calls continue to start the next iteration of the loop and ask for another guess. After the if expression, we can proceed with the comparisons between guess and the secret number knowing that guess is between 1 and 100.

However, this is not an ideal solution: if it were absolutely critical that the program only operated on values between 1 and 100, and it had many functions with this requirement, having a check like this in every function would be tedious (and might impact performance).

Instead, we can make a new type and put the validations in a function to create an instance of the type rather than repeating the validations everywhere. That way, it's safe for functions to use the new type in their signatures and confidently use the values they receive. Listing 9-9 shows one way to define a Guess type that will only create an instance of Guess if the new function receives a value between 1 and 100.

```
❶ pub struct Guess {
      value: u32,
  }

  impl Guess {
  ❷   pub fn new(value: u32) -> Guess {
  ❸       if value < 1 || value > 100 {
  ❹           panic!("Guess value must be between 1 and 100, got {}.", value);
          }

  ❺       Guess {
              value
          }
      }

  ❻   pub fn value(&self) -> u32 {
          self.value
      }
  }
```

Listing 9-9: A Guess type that will only continue with values between 1 and 100

First, we define a struct named Guess that has a field named value that holds a u32 ❶. This is where the number will be stored.

Then we implement an associated function named new on Guess that creates instances of Guess values ❷. The new function is defined to have one parameter named value of type u32 and to return a Guess. The code in the body of the new function tests value to make sure it's between 1 and 100 ❸. If value doesn't pass this test, we make a panic! call ❹, which will alert the programmer who is writing the calling code that they have a bug they need to fix, because creating a Guess with a value outside this range would violate the contract that Guess::new is relying on. The conditions in which Guess::new might panic should be discussed in its public-facing API documentation; we'll cover documentation conventions indicating the possibility of a panic! in the API documentation that you create in Chapter 14. If value does pass the test, we create a new Guess with its value field set to the value parameter and return the Guess ❺.

Next, we implement a method named value that borrows self, doesn't have any other parameters, and returns a u32 ❻. This kind of method is sometimes called a *getter*, because its purpose is to get some data from its fields and return it. This public method is necessary because the value field of the Guess struct is private. It's important that the value field be private so code using the Guess struct is not allowed to set value directly: code outside the module *must* use the Guess::new function to create an instance of Guess, thereby ensuring there's no way for a Guess to have a value that hasn't been checked by the conditions in the Guess::new function.

A function that has a parameter or returns only numbers between 1 and 100 could then declare in its signature that it takes or returns a Guess rather than a u32 and wouldn't need to do any additional checks in its body.

Summary

Rust's error-handling features are designed to help you write more robust code. The panic! macro signals that your program is in a state it can't handle and lets you tell the process to stop instead of trying to proceed with invalid or incorrect values. The Result enum uses Rust's type system to indicate that operations might fail in a way that your code could recover from. You can use Result to tell code that calls your code that it needs to handle potential success or failure as well. Using panic! and Result in the appropriate situations will make your code more reliable in the face of inevitable problems.

Now that you've seen useful ways that the standard library uses generics with the Option and Result enums, we'll talk about how generics work and how you can use them in your code.

10

GENERIC TYPES, TRAITS, AND LIFETIMES

Every programming language has tools for effectively handling the duplication of concepts. In Rust, one such tool is *generics*. Generics are abstract stand-ins for concrete types or other properties. When we're writing code, we can express the behavior of generics or how they relate to other generics without knowing what will be in their place when compiling and running the code.

Similar to the way a function takes parameters with unknown values to run the same code on multiple concrete values, functions can take parameters of some generic type instead of a concrete type, like i32 or String. In fact, we've already used generics in Chapter 6 with Option<T>, Chapter 8 with Vec<T> and HashMap<K, V>, and Chapter 9 with Result<T, E>. In this chapter, you'll explore how to define your own types, functions, and methods with generics!

First, we'll review how to extract a function to reduce code duplication. Next, we'll use the same technique to make a generic function from two functions that differ only in the types of their parameters. We'll also explain how to use generic types in struct and enum definitions.

Then you'll learn how to use *traits* to define behavior in a generic way. You can combine traits with generic types to constrain a generic type to only those types that have a particular behavior, as opposed to just any type.

Finally, we'll discuss *lifetimes*, a variety of generics that give the compiler information about how references relate to each other. Lifetimes allow us to borrow values in many situations while still enabling the compiler to check that the references are valid.

Removing Duplication by Extracting a Function

Before diving into generics syntax, let's first look at how to remove duplication that doesn't involve generic types by extracting a function. Then we'll apply this technique to extract a generic function! In the same way that you recognize duplicated code to extract into a function, you'll start to recognize duplicated code that can use generics.

Consider a short program that finds the largest number in a list, as shown in Listing 10-1.

src/main.rs

```
fn main() {
❶ let number_list = vec![34, 50, 25, 100, 65];

❷ let mut largest = number_list[0];

❸ for number in number_list {
    ❹ if number > largest {
        ❺ largest = number;
        }
    }

    println!("The largest number is {}", largest);
}
```

Listing 10-1: Code to find the largest number in a list of numbers

This code stores a list of integers in the variable number_list ❶ and places the first number in the list in a variable named largest ❷. Then it iterates through all the numbers in the list ❸, and if the current number is greater than the number stored in largest ❹, it replaces the number in that variable ❺. However, if the current number is less than the largest number seen so far, the variable doesn't change, and the code moves on to the next number in the list. After considering all the numbers in the list, largest should hold the largest number, which in this case is 100.

To find the largest number in two different lists of numbers, we can duplicate the code in Listing 10-1 and use the same logic at two different places in the program, as shown in Listing 10-2.

```
fn main() {
    let number_list = vec![34, 50, 25, 100, 65];

    let mut largest = number_list[0];

    for number in number_list {
        if number > largest {
            largest = number;
        }
    }

    println!("The largest number is {}", largest);

    let number_list = vec![102, 34, 6000, 89, 54, 2, 43, 8];

    let mut largest = number_list[0];

    for number in number_list {
        if number > largest {
            largest = number;
        }
    }

    println!("The largest number is {}", largest);
}
```

Listing 10-2: Code to find the largest number in two lists of numbers

Although this code works, duplicating code is tedious and error prone. We also have to update the code in multiple places when we want to change it.

To eliminate this duplication, we can create an abstraction by defining a function that operates on any list of integers given to it in a parameter. This solution makes our code clearer and lets us express the concept of finding the largest number in a list abstractly.

In Listing 10-3, we extracted the code that finds the largest number into a function named largest. Unlike the code in Listing 10-1, which can find the largest number in only one particular list, this program can find the largest number in two different lists.

```
fn largest(list: &[i32]) -> i32 {
    let mut largest = list[0];

    for &item in list.iter() {
        if item > largest {
            largest = item;
        }
    }

    largest
}
```

```
fn main() {
    let number_list = vec![34, 50, 25, 100, 65];

    let result = largest(&number_list);
    println!("The largest number is {}", result);

    let number_list = vec![102, 34, 6000, 89, 54, 2, 43, 8];

    let result = largest(&number_list);
    println!("The largest number is {}", result);
}
```

Listing 10-3: Abstracted code to find the largest number in two lists

The largest function has a parameter called list, which represents any concrete slice of i32 values that we might pass into the function. As a result, when we call the function, the code runs on the specific values that we pass in.

In sum, here are the steps we took to change the code from Listing 10-2 to Listing 10-3:

1. Identify duplicate code.
2. Extract the duplicate code into the body of the function and specify the inputs and return values of that code in the function signature.
3. Update the two instances of duplicated code to call the function instead.

Next, we'll use these same steps with generics to reduce code duplication in different ways. In the same way that the function body can operate on an abstract list instead of specific values, generics allow code to operate on abstract types.

For example, say we had two functions: one that finds the largest item in a slice of i32 values and one that finds the largest item in a slice of char values. How would we eliminate that duplication? Let's find out!

Generic Data Types

We can use generics to create definitions for items like function signatures or structs, which we can then use with many different concrete data types. Let's first look at how to define functions, structs, enums, and methods using generics. Then we'll discuss how generics affect code performance.

In Function Definitions

When defining a function that uses generics, we place the generics in the signature of the function where we would usually specify the data types of the parameters and return value. Doing so makes our code more flexible and provides more functionality to callers of our function while preventing code duplication.

Continuing with our largest function, Listing 10-4 shows two functions that both find the largest value in a slice.

src/main.rs

```
fn largest_i32(list: &[i32]) -> i32 {
    let mut largest = list[0];

    for &item in list.iter() {
        if item > largest {
            largest = item;
        }
    }

    largest
}

fn largest_char(list: &[char]) -> char {
    let mut largest = list[0];

    for &item in list.iter() {
        if item > largest {
            largest = item;
        }
    }

    largest
}

fn main() {
    let number_list = vec![34, 50, 25, 100, 65];

    let result = largest_i32(&number_list);
    println!("The largest number is {}", result);

    let char_list = vec!['y', 'm', 'a', 'q'];

    let result = largest_char(&char_list);
    println!("The largest char is {}", result);
}
```

Listing 10-4: Two functions that differ only in their names and the types in their signatures

The largest_i32 function is the one we extracted in Listing 10-3 that finds the largest i32 in a slice. The largest_char function finds the largest char in a slice. The function bodies have the same code, so let's eliminate the duplication by introducing a generic type parameter in a single function.

To parameterize the types in the new function we'll define, we need to name the type parameter, just as we do for the value parameters to a function. You can use any identifier as a type parameter name. But we'll use T because, by convention, parameter names in Rust are short, often just a letter, and Rust's type-naming convention is CamelCase. Short for "type," T is the default choice of most Rust programmers.

When we use a parameter in the body of the function, we have to declare the parameter name in the signature so the compiler knows what that name means. Similarly, when we use a type parameter name in a function signature, we have to declare the type parameter name before we use it. To define the generic largest function, place type name declarations inside angle brackets, <>, between the name of the function and the parameter list, like this:

```
fn largest<T>(list: &[T]) -> T {
```

We read this definition as: the function largest is generic over some type T. This function has one parameter named list, which is a slice of values of type T. The largest function will return a value of the same type T.

Listing 10-5 shows the combined largest function definition using the generic data type in its signature. The listing also shows how we can call the function with either a slice of i32 values or char values. Note that this code won't compile yet, but we'll fix it later in this chapter.

src/main.rs
```
fn largest<T>(list: &[T]) -> T {
    let mut largest = list[0];

    for &item in list.iter() {
        if item > largest {
            largest = item;
        }
    }

    largest
}

fn main() {
    let number_list = vec![34, 50, 25, 100, 65];

    let result = largest(&number_list);
    println!("The largest number is {}", result);

    let char_list = vec!['y', 'm', 'a', 'q'];

    let result = largest(&char_list);
    println!("The largest char is {}", result);
}
```

Listing 10-5: A definition of the largest function that uses generic type parameters but doesn't compile yet

If we compile this code right now, we'll get this error:

```
error[E0369]: binary operation `>` cannot be applied to type `T`
 --> src/main.rs:5:12
  |
5 |         if item > largest {
  |            ^^^^^^^^^^^^^^^
  |
  = note: an implementation of `std::cmp::PartialOrd` might be missing for `T`
```

The note mentions `std::cmp::PartialOrd`, which is a *trait*. We'll talk about traits in "Traits: Defining Shared Behavior" on page 178. For now, this error states that the body of `largest` won't work for all possible types that `T` could be. Because we want to compare values of type `T` in the body, we can only use types whose values can be ordered. To enable comparisons, the standard library has the `std::cmp::PartialOrd` trait that you can implement on types (see Appendix C for more on this trait). You'll learn how to specify that a generic type has a particular trait in "Trait Bounds" on page 182, but let's first explore other ways of using generic type parameters.

In Struct Definitions

We can also define structs to use a generic type parameter in one or more fields using the `<>` syntax. Listing 10-6 shows how to define a `Point<T>` struct to hold x and y coordinate values of any type.

src/main.rs

```
struct Point<T>❶ {
    x: T❷,
    y: T❸,
}

fn main() {
    let integer = Point { x: 5, y: 10 };
    let float = Point { x: 1.0, y: 4.0 };
}
```

Listing 10-6: A `Point<T>` struct that holds x and y values of type T

The syntax for using generics in struct definitions is similar to that used in function definitions. First, we declare the name of the type parameter inside angle brackets just after the name of the struct ❶. Then we can use the generic type in the struct definition where we would otherwise specify concrete data types ❷ ❸.

Note that because we've used only one generic type to define `Point<T>`, this definition says that the `Point<T>` struct is generic over some type `T`, and the fields x and y are *both* that same type, whatever that type may be. If we create an instance of a `Point<T>` that has values of different types, as in Listing 10-7, our code won't compile.

src/main.rs

```
struct Point<T> {
    x: T,
    y: T,
}

fn main() {
    let wont_work = Point { x: 5, y: 4.0 };
}
```

Listing 10-7: The fields x and y must be the same type because both have the same generic data type T.

In this example, when we assign the integer value 5 to x, we let the compiler know that the generic type T will be an integer for this instance of Point<T>. Then when we specify 4.0 for y, which we've defined to have the same type as x, we'll get a type mismatch error like this:

```
error[E0308]: mismatched types
 --> src/main.rs:7:38
  |
7 |     let wont_work = Point { x: 5, y: 4.0 };
  |                                      ^^^ expected integral variable, found
floating-point variable
  |
  = note: expected type `{integer}`
             found type `{float}`
```

To define a Point struct where x and y are both generics but could have different types, we can use multiple generic type parameters. For example, in Listing 10-8, we can change the definition of Point to be generic over types T and U where x is of type T and y is of type U.

src/main.rs

```
struct Point<T, U> {
    x: T,
    y: U,
}

fn main() {
    let both_integer = Point { x: 5, y: 10 };
    let both_float = Point { x: 1.0, y: 4.0 };
    let integer_and_float = Point { x: 5, y: 4.0 };
}
```

Listing 10-8: A Point<T, U> generic over two types so that x and y can be values of different types

Now all the instances of Point shown are allowed! You can use as many generic type parameters in a definition as you want, but using more than a few makes your code hard to read. When you need lots of generic types in your code, it could indicate that your code needs restructuring into smaller pieces.

In Enum Definitions

As we did with structs, we can define enums to hold generic data types in their variants. Let's take another look at the Option<T> enum that the standard library provides, which we used in Chapter 6:

```
enum Option<T> {
    Some(T),
    None,
}
```

This definition should now make more sense to you. As you can see, Option<T> is an enum that is generic over type T and has two variants: Some, which holds one value of type T, and a None variant that doesn't hold any value. By using the Option<T> enum, we can express the abstract concept of having an optional value, and because Option<T> is generic, we can use this abstraction no matter what the type of the optional value is.

Enums can use multiple generic types as well. The definition of the Result enum that we used in Chapter 9 is one example:

```
enum Result<T, E> {
    Ok(T),
    Err(E),
}
```

The Result enum is generic over two types, T and E, and has two variants: Ok, which holds a value of type T, and Err, which holds a value of type E. This definition makes it convenient to use the Result enum anywhere we have an operation that might succeed (return a value of some type T) or fail (return an error of some type E). In fact, this is what we used to open a file in Listing 9-3 on page 154, where T was filled in with the type std::fs::File when the file was opened successfully and E was filled in with the type std::io::Error when there were problems opening the file.

When you recognize situations in your code with multiple struct or enum definitions that differ only in the types of the values they hold, you can avoid duplication by using generic types instead.

In Method Definitions

We can implement methods on structs and enums (as we did in Chapter 5) and use generic types in their definitions, too. Listing 10-9 shows the Point<T> struct we defined in Listing 10-6 with a method named x implemented on it.

src/main.rs

```
struct Point<T> {
    x: T,
    y: T,
}

impl<T> Point<T> {
    fn x(&self) -> &T {
        &self.x
    }
}

fn main() {
    let p = Point { x: 5, y: 10 };

    println!("p.x = {}", p.x());
}
```

Listing 10-9: Implementing a method named x on the Point<T> struct that will return a reference to the x field of type T

Here, we've defined a method named x on Point<T> that returns a reference to the data in the field x.

Note that we have to declare T just after impl so we can use it to specify that we're implementing methods on the type Point<T>. By declaring T as a generic type after impl, Rust can identify that the type in the angle brackets in Point is a generic type rather than a concrete type.

We could, for example, implement methods only on Point<f32> instances rather than on Point<T> instances with any generic type. In Listing 10-10, we use the concrete type f32, meaning we don't declare any types after impl.

```
impl Point<f32> {
    fn distance_from_origin(&self) -> f32 {
        (self.x.powi(2) + self.y.powi(2)).sqrt()
    }
}
```

Listing 10-10: An impl block that only applies to a struct with a particular concrete type for the generic type parameter T

This code means the type Point<f32> will have a method named distance_from_origin and other instances of Point<T> where T is not of type f32 will not have this method defined. The method measures how far our point is from the point at coordinates (0.0, 0.0) and uses mathematical operations that are available only for floating point types.

Generic type parameters in a struct definition aren't always the same as those you use in that struct's method signatures. For example, Listing 10-11 defines the method mixup on the Point<T, U> struct from Listing 10-8. The method takes another Point as a parameter, which might have different types than the self Point we're calling mixup on. The method creates a new Point instance with the x value from the self Point (of type T) and the y value from the passed-in Point (of type W).

src/main.rs

```
struct Point<T, U> {
    x: T,
    y: U,
}

impl<T, U>❶ Point<T, U> {
    fn mixup<V, W>❷(self, other: Point<V, W>) -> Point<T, W> {
        Point {
            x: self.x,
            y: other.y,
        }
    }
}

fn main() {
  ❸ let p1 = Point { x: 5, y: 10.4 };
  ❹ let p2 = Point { x: "Hello", y: 'c'};

  ❺ let p3 = p1.mixup(p2);
```

```
❻  println!("p3.x = {}, p3.y = {}", p3.x, p3.y);
}
```

Listing 10-11: A method that uses different generic types than its struct's definition

In main, we've defined a Point that has an i32 for x (with value 5) and an f64 for y (with value 10.4 ❸). The p2 variable is a Point struct that has a string slice for x (with value "Hello") and a char for y (with value c ❹). Calling mixup on p1 with the argument p2 gives us p3 ❺, which will have an i32 for x, because x came from p1. The p3 variable will have a char for y, because y came from p2. The println! macro call ❻ will print p3.x = 5, p3.y = c.

The purpose of this example is to demonstrate a situation in which some generic parameters are declared with impl and some are declared with the method definition. Here, the generic parameters T and U are declared after impl ❶, because they go with the struct definition. The generic parameters V and W are declared after fn mixup ❷, because they're only relevant to the method.

Performance of Code Using Generics

You might be wondering whether there is a runtime cost when you're using generic type parameters. The good news is that Rust implements generics in such a way that your code doesn't run any slower using generic types than it would with concrete types.

Rust accomplishes this by performing monomorphization of the code that is using generics at compile time. *Monomorphization* is the process of turning generic code into specific code by filling in the concrete types that are used when compiled.

In this process, the compiler does the opposite of the steps we used to create the generic function in Listing 10-5: the compiler looks at all the places where generic code is called and generates code for the concrete types the generic code is called with.

Let's look at how this works with an example that uses the standard library's Option<T> enum:

```
let integer = Some(5);
let float = Some(5.0);
```

When Rust compiles this code, it performs monomorphization. During that process, the compiler reads the values that have been used in Option<T> instances and identifies two kinds of Option<T>: one is i32 and the other is f64. As such, it expands the generic definition of Option<T> into Option_i32 and Option_f64, thereby replacing the generic definition with the specific ones.

The monomorphized version of the code looks like the following. The generic Option<T> is replaced with the specific definitions created by the compiler:

src/main.rs
```
enum Option_i32 {
    Some(i32),
    None,
}
```

```
enum Option_f64 {
    Some(f64),
    None,
}

fn main() {
    let integer = Option_i32::Some(5);
    let float = Option_f64::Some(5.0);
}
```

Because Rust compiles generic code into code that specifies the type in each instance, we pay no runtime cost for using generics. When the code runs, it performs just as it would if we had duplicated each definition by hand. The process of monomorphization makes Rust's generics extremely efficient at runtime.

Traits: Defining Shared Behavior

A *trait* tells the Rust compiler about functionality a particular type has and can share with other types. We can use traits to define shared behavior in an abstract way. We can use trait bounds to specify that a generic can be any type that has certain behavior.

> **NOTE** *Traits are similar to a feature often called* interfaces *in other languages, although with some differences.*

Defining a Trait

A type's behavior consists of the methods we can call on that type. Different types share the same behavior if we can call the same methods on all of those types. Trait definitions are a way to group method signatures together to define a set of behaviors necessary to accomplish some purpose.

For example, let's say we have multiple structs that hold various kinds and amounts of text: a NewsArticle struct that holds a news story filed in a particular location and a Tweet that can have at most 280 characters along with metadata that indicates whether it was a new tweet, a retweet, or a reply to another tweet.

We want to make a media aggregator library that can display summaries of data that might be stored in a NewsArticle or Tweet instance. To do this, we need a summary from each type, and we need to request that summary by calling a summarize method on an instance. Listing 10-12 shows the definition of a Summary trait that expresses this behavior.

src/lib.rs
```
pub trait Summary {
    fn summarize(&self) -> String;
}
```

Listing 10-12: A Summary trait that consists of the behavior provided by a summarize method

Here, we declare a trait using the `trait` keyword and then the trait's name, which is `Summary` in this case. Inside the curly brackets, we declare the method signatures that describe the behaviors of the types that implement this trait, which in this case is `fn summarize(&self) -> String`.

After the method signature, instead of providing an implementation within curly brackets, we use a semicolon. Each type implementing this trait must provide its own custom behavior for the body of the method. The compiler will enforce that any type that has the `Summary` trait will have the method `summarize` defined with this signature exactly.

A trait can have multiple methods in its body: the method signatures are listed one per line and each line ends in a semicolon.

Implementing a Trait on a Type

Now that we've defined the desired behavior using the `Summary` trait, we can implement it on the types in our media aggregator. Listing 10-13 shows an implementation of the `Summary` trait on the `NewsArticle` struct that uses the headline, the author, and the location to create the return value of `summarize`. For the `Tweet` struct, we define `summarize` as the username followed by the entire text of the tweet, assuming that tweet content is already limited to 280 characters.

src/lib.rs

```
pub struct NewsArticle {
    pub headline: String,
    pub location: String,
    pub author: String,
    pub content: String,
}

impl Summary for NewsArticle {
    fn summarize(&self) -> String {
        format!("{}, by {} ({})", self.headline, self.author, self.location)
    }
}

pub struct Tweet {
    pub username: String,
    pub content: String,
    pub reply: bool,
    pub retweet: bool,
}

impl Summary for Tweet {
    fn summarize(&self) -> String {
        format!("{}: {}", self.username, self.content)
    }
}
```

Listing 10-13: Implementing the `Summary` trait on the `NewsArticle` and `Tweet` types

Implementing a trait on a type is similar to implementing regular methods. The difference is that after `impl`, we put the trait name that we want to implement, then use the for keyword, and then specify the name of the type we want to implement the trait for. Within the impl block, we put the method signatures that the trait definition has defined. Instead of adding a semicolon after each signature, we use curly brackets and fill in the method body with the specific behavior that we want the methods of the trait to have for the particular type.

After implementing the trait, we can call the methods on instances of NewsArticle and Tweet in the same way we call regular methods, like this:

```
let tweet = Tweet {
    username: String::from("horse_ebooks"),
    content: String::from("of course, as you probably already know, people"),
    reply: false,
    retweet: false,
};

println!("1 new tweet: {}", tweet.summarize());
```

This code prints 1 new tweet: horse_ebooks: of course, as you probably already know, people.

Note that because we defined the Summary trait and the NewsArticle and Tweet types in the same *lib.rs* in Listing 10-13, they're all in the same scope. Let's say this *lib.rs* is for a crate we've called aggregator and someone else wants to use our crate's functionality to implement the Summary trait on a struct defined within their library's scope. They would need to import the trait into their scope first. They would do so by specifying use aggregator::Summary;, which then would enable them to implement Summary for their type. The Summary trait would also need to be a public trait for another crate to implement it, which it is because we put the pub keyword before trait in Listing 10-12.

One restriction to note with trait implementations is that we can implement a trait on a type only if either the trait or the type is local to our crate. For example, we can implement standard library traits like Display on a custom type like Tweet as part of our aggregator crate functionality, because the type Tweet is local to our aggregator crate. We can also implement Summary on Vec<T> in our aggregator crate, because the trait Summary is local to our aggregator crate.

But we can't implement external traits on external types. For example, we can't implement the Display trait on Vec<T> within our aggregator crate, because Display and Vec<T> are defined in the standard library and aren't local to our aggregator crate. This restriction is part of a property of programs called *coherence*, and more specifically the *orphan rule*, so named because the parent type is not present. This rule ensures that other people's code can't break your code and vice versa. Without the rule, two crates could implement the same trait for the same type, and Rust wouldn't know which implementation to use.

Default Implementations

Sometimes it's useful to have default behavior for some or all of the methods in a trait instead of requiring implementations for all methods on every type. Then, as we implement the trait on a particular type, we can keep or override each method's default behavior.

Listing 10-14 shows how to specify a default string for the summarize method of the Summary trait instead of only defining the method signature, as we did in Listing 10-12.

src/lib.rs

```
pub trait Summary {
    fn summarize(&self) -> String {
        String::from("(Read more...)")
    }
}
```

Listing 10-14: Definition of a Summary trait with a default implementation of the summarize method

To use a default implementation to summarize instances of NewsArticle instead of defining a custom implementation, we specify an empty impl block with impl Summary for NewsArticle {}.

Even though we're no longer defining the summarize method on NewsArticle directly, we've provided a default implementation and specified that NewsArticle implements the Summary trait. As a result, we can still call the summarize method on an instance of NewsArticle, like this:

```
let article = NewsArticle {
    headline: String::from("Penguins win the Stanley Cup Championship!"),
    location: String::from("Pittsburgh, PA, USA"),
    author: String::from("Iceburgh"),
    content: String::from("The Pittsburgh Penguins once again are the best
    hockey team in the NHL."),
};

println!("New article available! {}", article.summarize());
```

This code prints New article available! (Read more...).

Creating a default implementation for summarize doesn't require us to change anything about the implementation of Summary on Tweet in Listing 10-13. The reason is that the syntax for overriding a default implementation is the same as the syntax for implementing a trait method that doesn't have a default implementation.

Default implementations can call other methods in the same trait, even if those other methods don't have a default implementation. In this way, a trait can provide a lot of useful functionality and only require implementors to specify a small part of it. For example, we could define the Summary trait to have a summarize_author method whose implementation is required, and then define a `summarize` method that has a default implementation that calls the `summarize_author` method:

```
pub trait Summary {
    fn summarize_author(&self) -> String;

    fn summarize(&self) -> String {
        format!("(Read more from {}...)", self.summarize_author())
    }
}
```

To use this version of `Summary`, we only need to define `summarize_author` when we implement the trait on a type:

```
impl Summary for Tweet {
    fn summarize_author(&self) -> String {
        format!("@{}", self.username)
    }
}
```

After we define `summarize_author`, we can call `summarize` on instances of the `Tweet` struct, and the default implementation of `summarize` will call the definition of `summarize_author` that we've provided. Because we've implemented `summarize_author`, the `Summary` trait has given us the behavior of the `summarize` method without requiring us to write any more code.

```
let tweet = Tweet {
    username: String::from("horse_ebooks"),
    content: String::from("of course, as you probably already know, people"),
    reply: false,
    retweet: false,
};

println!("1 new tweet: {}", tweet.summarize());
```

This code prints `1 new tweet: (Read more from @horse_ebooks...)`.

Note that it isn't possible to call the default implementation from an overriding implementation of that same method.

Trait Bounds

Now that you know how to define traits and implement those traits on types, we can explore how to use traits with generic type parameters. We can use *trait bounds* to constrain generic types to ensure the type will be limited to those that implement a particular trait and behavior.

For example, in Listing 10-13, we implemented the `Summary` trait on the types `NewsArticle` and `Tweet`. We can define a function `notify` that calls the `summarize` method on its parameter `item`, which is of the generic type `T`. To be able to call `summarize` on `item` without getting an error telling us that the generic type T doesn't implement the method summarize, we can use trait bounds on T to specify that item must be of a type that implements the Summary trait:

```
pub fn notify<T: Summary>(item: T) {
    println!("Breaking news! {}", item.summarize());
}
```

We place trait bounds with the declaration of the generic type parameter, after a colon and inside angle brackets. Because of the trait bound on T, we can call notify and pass in any instance of NewsArticle or Tweet. Code that calls the function with any other type, like a String or an i32, won't compile, because those types don't implement Summary.

We can specify multiple trait bounds on a generic type using the + syntax. For example, to use display formatting on the type T in a function as well as the summarize method, we can use T: Summary + Display to say T can be any type that implements Summary and Display.

However, there are downsides to using too many trait bounds. Each generic has its own trait bounds, so functions with multiple generic type parameters can have lots of trait bound information between a function's name and its parameter list, making the function signature hard to read. For this reason, Rust has alternate syntax for specifying trait bounds inside a where clause after the function signature. So instead of writing this:

```
fn some_function<T: Display + Clone, U: Clone + Debug>(t: T, u: U) -> i32 {
```

we can use a where clause, like this:

```
fn some_function<T, U>(t: T, u: U) -> i32
    where T: Display + Clone,
          U: Clone + Debug
{
```

This function's signature is less cluttered in that the function name, parameter list, and return type are close together, similar to a function without lots of trait bounds.

Fixing the largest Function with Trait Bounds

Now that you know how to specify the behavior you want to use using the generic type parameter's bounds, let's return to Listing 10-5 to fix the definition of the largest function that uses a generic type parameter! Last time we tried to run that code, we received this error:

```
error[E0369]: binary operation `>` cannot be applied to type `T`
 --> src/main.rs:5:12
  |
5 |         if item > largest {
  |            ^^^^^^^^^^^^^^^
```

```
      |
      = note: an implementation of `std::cmp::PartialOrd` might be missing for `T`
```

In the body of largest, we wanted to compare two values of type T using the greater than (>) operator. Because that operator is defined as a default method on the standard library trait std::cmp::PartialOrd, we need to specify PartialOrd in the trait bounds for T so the largest function can work on slices of any type that we can compare. We don't need to bring PartialOrd into scope because it's in the prelude. Change the signature of largest to look like this:

```
fn largest<T: PartialOrd>(list: &[T]) -> T {
```

This time when we compile the code, we get a different set of errors:

```
error[E0508]: cannot move out of type `[T]`, a non-copy slice
  --> src/main.rs:2:23
   |
2  |      let mut largest = list[0];
   |                        ^^^^^^^
   |                            |
   |                            cannot move out of here
   |                            help: consider using a reference instead: `&list[0]`

error[E0507]: cannot move out of borrowed content
  --> src/main.rs:4:9
   |
4  |      for &item in list.iter() {
   |          ^----
   |          ||
   |          |hint: to prevent move, use `ref item` or `ref mut item`
   |          cannot move out of borrowed content
```

The key line in this error is cannot move out of type [T], a non-copy slice. With our non-generic versions of the largest function, we were only trying to find the largest i32 or char. As discussed in "Stack-Only Data: Copy" on page 65, types like i32 and char that have a known size can be stored on the stack, so they implement the Copy trait. But when we made the largest function generic, it became possible for the list parameter to have types in it that don't implement the Copy trait. Consequently, we wouldn't be able to move the value out of list[0] and into the largest variable, resulting in this error.

To call this code with only those types that implement the Copy trait, we can add Copy to the trait bounds of T! Listing 10-15 shows the complete code of a generic largest function that will compile as long as the types of the values in the slice that we pass into the function implement the PartialOrd *and* Copy traits, as i32 and char do.

src/main.rs

```
fn largest<T: PartialOrd + Copy>(list: &[T]) -> T {
    let mut largest = list[0];

    for &item in list.iter() {
        if item > largest {
```

```
            largest = item;
        }
    }

    largest
}

fn main() {
    let number_list = vec![34, 50, 25, 100, 65];

    let result = largest(&number_list);
    println!("The largest number is {}", result);

    let char_list = vec!['y', 'm', 'a', 'q'];

    let result = largest(&char_list);
    println!("The largest char is {}", result);
}
```

Listing 10-15: A working definition of the largest *function that works on any generic type that implements the* PartialOrd *and* Copy *traits*

If we don't want to restrict the largest function to the types that implement the Copy trait, we could specify that T has the trait bound Clone instead of Copy. Then we could clone each value in the slice when we want the largest function to have ownership. Using the clone function means we're potentially making more heap allocations in the case of types that own heap data like String, and heap allocations can be slow if we're working with large amounts of data.

Another way we could implement largest is for the function to return a reference to a T value in the slice. If we change the return type to &T instead of T, thereby changing the body of the function to return a reference, we wouldn't need the Clone or Copy trait bounds and we could avoid heap allocations. Try implementing these alternate solutions on your own!

Using Trait Bounds to Conditionally Implement Methods

By using a trait bound with an impl block that uses generic type parameters, we can implement methods conditionally for types that implement the specified traits. For example, the type Pair<T> in Listing 10-16 always implements the new function. But Pair<T> only implements the cmp_display method if its inner type T implements the PartialOrd trait that enables comparison *and* the Display trait that enables printing.

```
use std::fmt::Display;

struct Pair<T> {
    x: T,
    y: T,
}
```

```
impl<T> Pair<T> {
    fn new(x: T, y: T) -> Self {
        Self {
            x,
            y,
        }
    }
}

impl<T: Display + PartialOrd> Pair<T> {
    fn cmp_display(&self) {
        if self.x >= self.y {
            println!("The largest member is x = {}", self.x);
        } else {
            println!("The largest member is y = {}", self.y);
        }
    }
}
```

Listing 10-16: Conditionally implement methods on a generic type depending on trait bounds

We can also conditionally implement a trait for any type that implements another trait. Implementations of a trait on any type that satisfies the trait bounds are called *blanket implementations* and are extensively used in the Rust standard library. For example, the standard library implements the ToString trait on any type that implements the Display trait. The impl block in the standard library looks similar to this code:

```
impl<T: Display> ToString for T {
    // --snip--
}
```

Because the standard library has this blanket implementation, we can call the to_string method defined by the ToString trait on any type that implements the Display trait. For example, we can turn integers into their corresponding String values like this because integers implement Display:

```
let s = 3.to_string();
```

Blanket implementations appear in the documentation for the trait in the "Implementors" section.

Traits and trait bounds let us write code that uses generic type parameters to reduce duplication but also specify to the compiler that we want the generic type to have particular behavior. The compiler can then use the trait bound information to check that all the concrete types used with our code provide the correct behavior. In dynamically typed languages, we would get an error at runtime if we called a method on a type that the type didn't implement. But Rust moves these errors to compile time so we're forced to fix the problems before our code is even able to run. Additionally, we don't have to write code that checks for behavior at runtime because we've already checked at compile time. Doing so improves performance without having to give up the flexibility of generics.

Another kind of generic that we've already been using is called *lifetimes*. Rather than ensuring that a type has the behavior we want, lifetimes ensure that references are valid as long as we need them to be. Let's look at how lifetimes do that.

Validating References with Lifetimes

One detail we didn't discuss in "References and Borrowing" on page 68 is that every reference in Rust has a *lifetime*, which is the scope for which that reference is valid. Most of the time, lifetimes are implicit and inferred, just like most of the time, types are inferred. We must annotate types when multiple types are possible. In a similar way, we must annotate lifetimes when the lifetimes of references could be related in a few different ways. Rust requires us to annotate the relationships using generic lifetime parameters to ensure the actual references used at runtime will definitely be valid.

The concept of lifetimes is somewhat different from tools in other programming languages, arguably making lifetimes Rust's most distinctive feature. Although we won't cover lifetimes in their entirety in this chapter, we'll discuss common ways you might encounter lifetime syntax so you can become familiar with the concepts. See "Advanced Lifetimes" on page 423 for more detailed information.

Preventing Dangling References with Lifetimes

The main aim of lifetimes is to prevent dangling references, which cause a program to reference data other than the data it's intended to reference. Consider the program in Listing 10-17, which has an outer scope and an inner scope.

```
{
❶ let r;

    {
    ❷ let x = 5;
    ❸ r = &x;
❹ }

❺ println!("r: {}", r);
}
```

Listing 10-17: An attempt to use a reference whose value has gone out of scope

NOTE   *The examples in Listings 10-17, 10-18, and 10-24 declare variables without giving them an initial value, so the variable name exists in the outer scope. At first glance, this might appear to be in conflict with Rust's having no null values. However, if we try to use a variable before giving it a value, we'll get a compile-time error, which shows that Rust indeed does not allow null values.*

The outer scope declares a variable named r with no initial value ❶, and the inner scope declares a variable named x with the initial value of 5 ❷. Inside the inner scope, we attempt to set the value of r as a reference to x ❸. Then the inner scope ends ❹, and we attempt to print the value in r ❺. This code won't compile because the value r is referring to has gone out of scope before we try to use it. Here is the error message:

```
error[E0597]: `x` does not live long enough
  --> src/main.rs:7:5
   |
6  |          r = &x;
   |                - borrow occurs here
7  |      }
   |      ^ `x` dropped here while still borrowed
...
10 | }
   | - borrowed value needs to live until here
```

The variable x doesn't "live long enough." The reason is that x will be out of scope when the inner scope ends at ❹. But r is still valid for the outer scope; because its scope is larger, we say that it "lives longer." If Rust allowed this code to work, r would be referencing memory that was deallocated when x went out of scope, and anything we tried to do with r wouldn't work correctly. So how does Rust determine that this code is invalid? It uses a borrow checker.

The Borrow Checker

The Rust compiler has a *borrow checker* that compares scopes to determine whether all borrows are valid. Listing 10-18 shows the same code as Listing 10-17 but with annotations showing the lifetimes of the variables.

```
{
    let r;                // ---------+-- 'a
                          // |
    {                     // |
        let x = 5;        // -+-- 'b  |
        r = &x;           // |        |
    }                     // -+       |
                          // |
    println!("r: {}", r); // |
}                         // ---------+
```

Listing 10-18: Annotations of the lifetimes of r and x, named 'a and 'b, respectively

Here, we've annotated the lifetime of r with 'a and the lifetime of x with 'b. As you can see, the inner 'b block is much smaller than the outer 'a lifetime block. At compile time, Rust compares the size of the two lifetimes and sees that r has a lifetime of 'a but that it refers to memory with a lifetime of 'b. The program is rejected because 'b is shorter than 'a: the subject of the reference doesn't live as long as the reference.

Listing 10-19 fixes the code so it doesn't have a dangling reference and compiles without any errors.

```
{
    let x = 5;            // ----------+-- 'b
                          //           |
    let r = &x;           // --+-- 'a  |
                          //   |       |
    println!("r: {}", r); //   |       |
                          // --+        |
}                         // ----------+
```

Listing 10-19: A valid reference because the data has a longer lifetime than the reference

Here, x has the lifetime 'b, which in this case is larger than 'a. This means r can reference x because Rust knows that the reference in r will always be valid while x is valid.

Now that you know where the lifetimes of references are and how Rust analyzes lifetimes to ensure references will always be valid, let's explore generic lifetimes of parameters and return values in the context of functions.

Generic Lifetimes in Functions

Let's write a function that returns the longer of two string slices. This function will take two string slices and return a string slice. After we've implemented the longest function, the code in Listing 10-20 should print The longest string is abcd.

src/main.rs

```
fn main() {
    let string1 = String::from("abcd");
    let string2 = "xyz";

    let result = longest(string1.as_str(), string2);
    println!("The longest string is {}", result);
}
```

Listing 10-20: A main function that calls the longest function to find the longer of two string slices

Note that we want the function to take string slices, which are references, because we don't want the longest function to take ownership of its parameters. We want to allow the function to accept slices of a String (the type stored in the variable string1) as well as string literals (which is what variable string2 contains).

Refer to "String Slices as Parameters" on page 78 for more discussion about why the parameters we use in Listing 10-20 are the ones we want.

If we try to implement the longest function as shown in Listing 10-21, it won't compile.

src/main.rs

```
fn longest(x: &str, y: &str) -> &str {
    if x.len() > y.len() {
        x
```

```
        } else {
            y
        }
}
```

Listing 10-21: An implementation of the longest *function that returns the longer of two string slices but does not yet compile*

Instead, we get the following error that talks about lifetimes:

```
error[E0106]: missing lifetime specifier
 --> src/main.rs:1:33
  |
1 | fn longest(x: &str, y: &str) -> &str {
  |                                 ^ expected lifetime parameter
  |
  = help: this function's return type contains a borrowed value, but the
signature does not say whether it is borrowed from `x` or `y`
```

The help text reveals that the return type needs a generic lifetime parameter on it because Rust can't tell whether the reference being returned refers to x or y. Actually, we don't know either, because the if block in the body of this function returns a reference to x and the else block returns a reference to y!

When we're defining this function, we don't know the concrete values that will be passed into this function, so we don't know whether the if case or the else case will execute. We also don't know the concrete lifetimes of the references that will be passed in, so we can't look at the scopes as we did in Listings 10-18 and 10-19 to determine whether the reference we return will always be valid. The borrow checker can't determine this either, because it doesn't know how the lifetimes of x and y relate to the lifetime of the return value. To fix this error, we'll add generic lifetime parameters that define the relationship between the references so the borrow checker can perform its analysis.

Lifetime Annotation Syntax

Lifetime annotations don't change how long any of the references live. Just as functions can accept any type when the signature specifies a generic type parameter, functions can accept references with any lifetime by specifying a generic lifetime parameter. Lifetime annotations describe the relationships of the lifetimes of multiple references to each other without affecting the lifetimes.

Lifetime annotations have a slightly unusual syntax: the names of lifetime parameters must start with a single quote (') and are usually all lowercase and very short, like generic types. Most people use the name 'a. We place lifetime parameter annotations after the & of a reference, using a space to separate the annotation from the reference's type.

Here are some examples: a reference to an i32 without a lifetime parameter, a reference to an i32 that has a lifetime parameter named 'a, and a mutable reference to an i32 that also has the lifetime 'a.

```
&i32       // a reference
&'a i32    // a reference with an explicit lifetime
&'a mut i32 // a mutable reference with an explicit lifetime
```

One lifetime annotation by itself doesn't have much meaning, because the annotations are meant to tell Rust how generic lifetime parameters of multiple references relate to each other. For example, let's say we have a function with the parameter first that is a reference to an i32 with lifetime 'a. The function also has another parameter named second that is another reference to an i32 that also has the lifetime 'a. The lifetime annotations indicate that the references first and second must both live as long as that generic lifetime.

Lifetime Annotations in Function Signatures

Now let's examine lifetime annotations in the context of the longest function. As with generic type parameters, we need to declare generic lifetime parameters inside angle brackets between the function name and the parameter list. The constraint we want to express in this signature is that all the references in the parameters and the return value must have the same lifetime. We'll name the lifetime 'a and then add it to each reference, as shown in Listing 10-22.

src/main.rs

```
fn longest<'a>(x: &'a str, y: &'a str) -> &'a str {
    if x.len() > y.len() {
        x
    } else {
        y
    }
}
```

Listing 10-22: The longest function definition specifying that all the references in the signature must have the same lifetime 'a

This code should compile and produce the result we want when we use it with the main function in Listing 10-20.

The function signature now tells Rust that for some lifetime 'a, the function takes two parameters, both of which are string slices that live at least as long as lifetime 'a. The function signature also tells Rust that the string slice returned from the function will live at least as long as lifetime 'a. These constraints are what we want Rust to enforce. Remember, when we specify the lifetime parameters in this function signature, we're not changing the lifetimes of any values passed in or returned. Rather, we're specifying that the borrow checker should reject any values that don't adhere to these constraints. Note that the longest function doesn't need to know exactly how long x and y will live, only that some scope can be substituted for 'a that will satisfy this signature.

When annotating lifetimes in functions, the annotations go in the function signature, not in the function body. Rust can analyze the code within the function without any help. However, when a function has references to or from code outside that function, it becomes almost impossible for Rust to figure out the lifetimes of the parameters or return values on its own. The lifetimes might be different each time the function is called. This is why we need to annotate the lifetimes manually.

When we pass concrete references to longest, the concrete lifetime that is substituted for 'a is the part of the scope of x that overlaps with the scope of y. In other words, the generic lifetime 'a will get the concrete lifetime that is equal to the smaller of the lifetimes of x and y. Because we've annotated the returned reference with the same lifetime parameter 'a, the returned reference will also be valid for the length of the smaller of the lifetimes of x and y.

Let's look at how the lifetime annotations restrict the longest function by passing in references that have different concrete lifetimes. Listing 10-23 is a straightforward example.

src/main.rs

```
fn main() {
    let string1 = String::from("long string is long");

    {
        let string2 = String::from("xyz");
        let result = longest(string1.as_str(), string2.as_str());
        println!("The longest string is {}", result);
    }
}
```

Listing 10-23: Using the longest function with references to String values that have different concrete lifetimes

In this example, string1 is valid until the end of the outer scope, string2 is valid until the end of the inner scope, and result references something that is valid until the end of the inner scope. Run this code, and you'll see that the borrow checker approves of this code; it will compile and print The longest string is long string is long.

Next, let's try an example that shows that the lifetime of the reference in result must be the smaller lifetime of the two arguments. We'll move the declaration of the result variable outside the inner scope but leave the assignment of the value to the result variable inside the scope with string2. Then we'll move the println! that uses result outside the inner scope, after the inner scope has ended. The code in Listing 10-24 will not compile.

src/main.rs

```
fn main() {
    let string1 = String::from("long string is long");
    let result;
    {
        let string2 = String::from("xyz");
        result = longest(string1.as_str(), string2.as_str());
    }
    println!("The longest string is {}", result);
}
```

Listing 10-24: Attempting to use result after string2 has gone out of scope

When we try to compile this code, we'll get this error:

```
error[E0597]: `string2` does not live long enough
  --> src/main.rs:15:5
   |
14 |         result = longest(string1.as_str(), string2.as_str());
   |                                             ------- borrow occurs here
15 |     }
   |     ^ `string2` dropped here while still borrowed
16 |     println!("The longest string is {}", result);
17 | }
   | - borrowed value needs to live until here
```

The error shows that for result to be valid for the println! statement, string2 would need to be valid until the end of the outer scope. Rust knows this because we annotated the lifetimes of the function parameters and return values using the same lifetime parameter 'a.

As humans, we can look at this code and see that string1 is longer than string2 and therefore result will contain a reference to string1. Because string1 has not gone out of scope yet, a reference to string1 will still be valid for the println! statement. However, the compiler can't see that the reference is valid in this case. We've told Rust that the lifetime of the reference returned by the longest function is the same as the smaller of the lifetimes of the references passed in. Therefore, the borrow checker disallows the code in Listing 10-24 as possibly having an invalid reference.

Try designing more experiments that vary the values and lifetimes of the references passed in to the longest function and how the returned reference is used. Make hypotheses about whether or not your experiments will pass the borrow checker before you compile; then check to see if you're right!

Thinking in Terms of Lifetimes

The way in which you need to specify lifetime parameters depends on what your function is doing. For example, if we changed the implementation of the longest function to always return the first parameter rather than the longest string slice, we wouldn't need to specify a lifetime on the y parameter. The following code will compile:

src/main.rs

```
fn longest<'a>(x: &'a str, y: &str) -> &'a str {
    x
}
```

In this example, we've specified a lifetime parameter 'a for the parameter x and the return type, but not for the parameter y, because the lifetime of y does not have any relationship with the lifetime of x or the return value.

When returning a reference from a function, the lifetime parameter for the return type needs to match the lifetime parameter for one of the parameters. If the reference returned does *not* refer to one of the parameters, it must refer to a value created within this function, which would be a dangling reference because the value will go out of scope at the end of the function. Consider this attempted implementation of the longest function that won't compile:

src/main.rs

```
fn longest<'a>(x: &str, y: &str) -> &'a str {
    let result = String::from("really long string");
    result.as_str()
}
```

Here, even though we've specified a lifetime parameter 'a for the return type, this implementation will fail to compile because the return value lifetime is not related to the lifetime of the parameters at all. Here is the error message we get:

```
error[E0597]: `result` does not live long enough
  --> src/main.rs:3:5
   |
3  |     result.as_str()
   |     ^^^^^^ does not live long enough
4  | }
   | - borrowed value only lives until here
   |
note: borrowed value must be valid for the lifetime 'a as defined on the
function body at 1:1...
  --> src/main.rs:1:1
   |
1  | / fn longest<'a>(x: &str, y: &str) -> &'a str {
2  | |     let result = String::from("really long string");
3  | |     result.as_str()
4  | | }
   | |_^
```

The problem is that result goes out of scope and gets cleaned up at the end of the longest function. We're also trying to return a reference to result from the function. There is no way we can specify lifetime parameters that would change the dangling reference, and Rust won't let us create a dangling reference. In this case, the best fix would be to return an owned data type rather than a reference so the calling function is then responsible for cleaning up the value.

Ultimately, lifetime syntax is about connecting the lifetimes of various parameters and return values of functions. Once they're connected, Rust has enough information to allow memory-safe operations and disallow operations that would create dangling pointers or otherwise violate memory safety.

Lifetime Annotations in Struct Definitions

So far, we've only defined structs to hold owned types. It's possible for structs to hold references, but in that case we would need to add a lifetime annotation on every reference in the struct's definition. Listing 10-25 has a struct named ImportantExcerpt that holds a string slice.

```
❶ struct ImportantExcerpt<'a> {
     ❷ part: &'a str,
   }

   fn main() {
     ❸ let novel = String::from("Call me Ishmael. Some years ago...");
     ❹ let first_sentence = novel.split('.')
           .next()
           .expect("Could not find a '.'");
     ❺ let i = ImportantExcerpt { part: first_sentence };
   }
```

Listing 10-25: A struct that holds a reference, so its definition needs a lifetime annotation

This struct has one field, part, that holds a string slice, which is a reference ❷. As with generic data types, we declare the name of the generic lifetime parameter inside angle brackets after the name of the struct so we can use the lifetime parameter in the body of the struct definition ❶. This annotation means an instance of ImportantExcerpt can't outlive the reference it holds in its part field.

The main function here creates an instance of the ImportantExcerpt struct ❺ that holds a reference to the first sentence of the String ❹ owned by the variable novel ❸. The data in novel exists before the ImportantExcerpt instance is created. In addition, novel doesn't go out of scope until after the ImportantExcerpt goes out of scope, so the reference in the ImportantExcerpt instance is valid.

Lifetime Elision

You've learned that every reference has a lifetime and that you need to specify lifetime parameters for functions or structs that use references. However, we had a function in Listing 4-9 on page 78, which is shown again in Listing 10-26, that compiled without lifetime annotations.

```
fn first_word(s: &str) -> &str {
    let bytes = s.as_bytes();

    for (i, &item) in bytes.iter().enumerate() {
        if item == b' ' {
            return &s[0..i];
        }
    }

    &s[..]
}
```

Listing 10-26: A function we defined in Listing 4-9 that compiled without lifetime annotations, even though the parameter and return type are references

The reason this function compiles without lifetime annotations is historical: in early versions (pre-1.0) of Rust, this code wouldn't have compiled because every reference needed an explicit lifetime. At that time, the function signature would have been written like this:

```
fn first_word<'a>(s: &'a str) -> &'a str {
```

After writing a lot of Rust code, the Rust team found that Rust programmers were entering the same lifetime annotations over and over in particular situations. These situations were predictable and followed a few deterministic patterns. The developers programmed these patterns into the compiler's code so the borrow checker could infer the lifetimes in these situations and wouldn't need explicit annotations.

This piece of Rust history is relevant because it's possible that more deterministic patterns will emerge and be added to the compiler. In the future, even fewer lifetime annotations might be required.

The patterns programmed into Rust's analysis of references are called the *lifetime elision rules*. These aren't rules for programmers to follow; they're a set of particular cases that the compiler will consider, and if your code fits these cases, you don't need to write the lifetimes explicitly.

The elision rules don't provide full inference. If Rust deterministically applies the rules but there is still ambiguity as to what lifetimes the references have, the compiler won't guess what the lifetime of the remaining references should be. In this case, instead of guessing, the compiler will give you an error that you can resolve by adding the lifetime annotations that specify how the references relate to each other.

Lifetimes on function or method parameters are called *input lifetimes*, and lifetimes on return values are called *output lifetimes*.

The compiler uses three rules to figure out what lifetimes references have when there aren't explicit annotations. The first rule applies to input lifetimes, and the second and third rules apply to output lifetimes. If the compiler gets to the end of the three rules and there are still references for which it can't figure out lifetimes, the compiler will stop with an error.

The first rule is that each parameter that is a reference gets its own lifetime parameter. In other words, a function with one parameter gets one lifetime parameter: fn foo<'a>(x: &'a i32); a function with two parameters gets two separate lifetime parameters: fn foo<'a, 'b>(x: &'a i32, y: &'b i32); and so on.

The second rule is if there is exactly one input lifetime parameter, that lifetime is assigned to all output lifetime parameters: fn foo<'a>(x: &'a i32) -> &'a i32.

The third rule is if there are multiple input lifetime parameters, but one of them is &self or &mut self because this is a method, the lifetime of self is assigned to all output lifetime parameters. This third rule makes methods much nicer to read and write because fewer symbols are necessary.

Let's pretend we're the compiler. We'll apply these rules to figure out what the lifetimes of the references in the signature of the first_word function in Listing 10-26 are. The signature starts without any lifetimes associated with the references:

```
fn first_word(s: &str) -> &str {
```

Then the compiler applies the first rule, which specifies that each parameter gets its own lifetime. We'll call it 'a as usual, so now the signature is this:

```
fn first_word<'a>(s: &'a str) -> &str {
```

The second rule applies because there is exactly one input lifetime. The second rule specifies that the lifetime of the one input parameter gets assigned to the output lifetime, so the signature is now this:

```
fn first_word<'a>(s: &'a str) -> &'a str {
```

Now all the references in this function signature have lifetimes, and the compiler can continue its analysis without needing the programmer to annotate the lifetimes in this function signature.

Let's look at another example, this time using the longest function that had no lifetime parameters when we started working with it in Listing 10-21:

```
fn longest(x: &str, y: &str) -> &str {
```

Let's apply the first rule: each parameter gets its own lifetime. This time we have two parameters instead of one, so we have two lifetimes:

```
fn longest<'a, 'b>(x: &'a str, y: &'b str) -> &str {
```

You can see that the second rule doesn't apply because there is more than one input lifetime. The third rule doesn't apply either, because longest is a function rather than a method, so none of the parameters are self. After working through all three rules, we still haven't figured out what the return type's lifetime is. This is why we got an error trying to compile the code in Listing 10-21: the compiler worked through the lifetime elision rules but still couldn't figure out all the lifetimes of the references in the signature.

Because the third rule really only applies in method signatures, we'll look at lifetimes in that context next to see why the third rule means we don't have to annotate lifetimes in method signatures very often.

Lifetime Annotations in Method Definitions

When we implement methods on a struct with lifetimes, we use the same syntax as that of generic type parameters shown in Listing 10-11. Where we declare and use the lifetime parameters depends on whether they're related to the struct fields or the method parameters and return values.

Lifetime names for struct fields always need to be declared after the `impl` keyword and then used after the struct's name, because those lifetimes are part of the struct's type.

In method signatures inside the `impl` block, references might be tied to the lifetime of references in the struct's fields, or they might be independent. In addition, the lifetime elision rules often make it so that lifetime annotations aren't necessary in method signatures. Let's look at some examples using the struct named `ImportantExcerpt` that we defined in Listing 10-25.

First, we'll use a method named `level` whose only parameter is a reference to `self` and whose return value is an `i32`, which is not a reference to anything:

```
impl<'a> ImportantExcerpt<'a> {
    fn level(&self) -> i32 {
        3
    }
}
```

The lifetime parameter declaration after `impl` and use after the type name is required, but we're not required to annotate the lifetime of the reference to `self` because of the first elision rule.

Here is an example where the third lifetime elision rule applies:

```
impl<'a> ImportantExcerpt<'a> {
    fn announce_and_return_part(&self, announcement: &str) -> &str {
        println!("Attention please: {}", announcement);
        self.part
    }
}
```

There are two input lifetimes, so Rust applies the first lifetime elision rule and gives both `&self` and `announcement` their own lifetimes. Then, because one of the parameters is `&self`, the return type gets the lifetime of `&self`, and all lifetimes have been accounted for.

The Static Lifetime

One special lifetime we need to discuss is `'static`, which denotes the entire duration of the program. All string literals have the `'static` lifetime, which we can annotate as follows:

```
let s: &'static str = "I have a static lifetime.";
```

The text of this string is stored directly in the binary of your program, which is always available. Therefore, the lifetime of all string literals is `'static`.

You might see suggestions to use the `'static` lifetime in error messages. But before specifying `'static` as the lifetime for a reference, think about whether the reference you have actually lives the entire lifetime of your program or not. You might consider whether you want it to live that long, even if it could. Most of the time, the problem results from attempting to create a dangling reference or a mismatch of the available lifetimes. In such cases, the solution is fixing those problems, not specifying the 'static lifetime.

Generic Type Parameters, Trait Bounds, and Lifetimes Together

Let's briefly look at the syntax of specifying generic type parameters, trait bounds, and lifetimes all in one function!

```
use std::fmt::Display;

fn longest_with_an_announcement<'a, T>(x: &'a str, y: &'a str, ann: T) -> &'a str
    where T: Display
{
    println!("Announcement! {}", ann);
    if x.len() > y.len() {
        x
    } else {
        y
    }
}
```

This is the longest function from Listing 10-22 that returns the longer of two string slices. But now it has an extra parameter named ann of the generic type T, which can be filled in by any type that implements the Display trait as specified by the where clause. This extra parameter will be printed before the function compares the lengths of the string slices, which is why the Display trait bound is necessary. Because lifetimes are a type of generic, the declarations of the lifetime parameter 'a and the generic type parameter T go in the same list inside the angle brackets after the function name.

Summary

We covered a lot in this chapter! Now that you know about generic type parameters, traits and trait bounds, and generic lifetime parameters, you're ready to write code without repetition that works in many different situations. Generic type parameters let you apply the code to different types. Traits and trait bounds ensure that even though the types are generic, they'll have the behavior the code needs. You learned how to use lifetime annotations to ensure that this flexible code won't have any dangling references. And all of this analysis happens at compile time, which doesn't affect runtime performance!

Believe it or not, there is much more to learn on the topics we discussed in this chapter: Chapter 17 discusses trait objects, which are another way to use traits. Chapter 19 covers more complex scenarios involving lifetime annotations as well as some advanced type system features. But next, you'll learn how to write tests in Rust so you can make sure your code is working the way it should.

11

WRITING AUTOMATED TESTS

In his 1972 essay "The Humble Programmer," Edsger W. Dijkstra said that "Program testing can be a very effective way to show the presence of bugs, but it is hopelessly inadequate for showing their absence." That doesn't mean we shouldn't try to test as much as we can!

Correctness in our programs is the extent to which our code does what we intend it to do. Rust is designed with a high degree of concern about the correctness of programs, but correctness is complex and not easy to prove. Rust's type system shoulders a huge part of this burden, but the type system cannot catch every kind of incorrectness. As such, Rust includes support for writing automated software tests within the language.

As an example, say we write a function called add_two that adds 2 to whatever number is passed to it. This function's signature accepts an integer as a parameter and returns an integer as a result. When we implement and compile that function, Rust does all the type checking and borrow checking that you've learned so far to ensure that, for instance, we aren't passing a String value or an invalid reference to this function. But Rust *can't* check that this function will do precisely what we intend, which is return the parameter plus 2 rather than, say, the parameter plus 10 or the parameter minus 50! That's where tests come in.

We can write tests that assert, for example, that when we pass 3 to the add_two function, the returned value is 5. We can run these tests whenever we make changes to our code to make sure any existing correct behavior has not changed.

Testing is a complex skill: although we can't cover every detail about how to write good tests in one chapter, we'll discuss the mechanics of Rust's testing facilities. We'll talk about the annotations and macros available to you when writing your tests, the default behavior and options provided for running your tests, and how to organize tests into unit tests and integration tests.

How to Write Tests

Tests are Rust functions that verify that the non-test code is functioning in the expected manner. The bodies of test functions typically perform these three actions:

1. Set up any needed data or state.
2. Run the code you want to test.
3. Assert the results are what you expect.

Let's look at the features Rust provides specifically for writing tests that take these actions, which include the test attribute, a few macros, and the should_panic attribute.

The Anatomy of a Test Function

At its simplest, a test in Rust is a function that's annotated with the test attribute. Attributes are metadata about pieces of Rust code; one example is the derive attribute we used with structs in Chapter 5. To change a function into a test function, add #[test] on the line before fn. When you run your tests with the cargo test command, Rust builds a test runner binary that runs the functions annotated with the test attribute and reports on whether each test function passes or fails.

In Chapter 7, we saw that when we make a new library project with Cargo, a test module with a test function in it is automatically generated for us. This module helps you start writing your tests so you don't have to look up the exact structure and syntax of test functions every time you start a new project. You can add as many additional test functions and as many test modules as you want!

We'll explore some aspects of how tests work by experimenting with the template test generated for us without actually testing any code. Then we'll write some real-world tests that call some code that we've written and assert that its behavior is correct.

Let's create a new library project called adder:

```
$ cargo new adder --lib
     Created library `adder` project
$ cd adder
```

The contents of the *src/lib.rs* file in your adder library should look like Listing 11-1.

src/lib.rs

```
#[cfg(test)]
mod tests {
  ❶ #[test]
    fn it_works() {
      ❷ assert_eq!(2 + 2, 4);
    }
}
```

Listing 11-1: The test module and function generated automatically by cargo new

For now, let's ignore the top two lines and focus on the function to see how it works. Note the #[test] annotation ❶: this attribute indicates this is a test function, so the test runner knows to treat this function as a test. We could also have non-test functions in the tests module to help set up common scenarios or perform common operations, so we need to indicate which functions are tests by using the #[test] attribute.

The function body uses the assert_eq! macro ❷ to assert that $2 + 2$ equals 4. This assertion serves as an example of the format for a typical test. Let's run it to see that this test passes.

The cargo test command runs all tests in our project, as shown in Listing 11-2.

```
$ cargo test
   Compiling adder v0.1.0 (file:///projects/adder)
    Finished dev [unoptimized + debuginfo] target(s) in 0.22 secs
     Running target/debug/deps/adder-ce99bcc2479f4607

❶ running 1 test
❷ test tests::it_works ... ok

❸ test result: ok. 1 passed; 0 failed; 0 ignored; 0 measured; 0 filtered out

  ❹ Doc-tests adder

running 0 tests

test result: ok. 0 passed; 0 failed; 0 ignored; 0 measured; 0 filtered out
```

Listing 11-2: The output from running the automatically generated test

Cargo compiled and ran the test. After the Compiling, Finished, and Running lines is the line running 1 test ❶. The next line shows the name of the generated test function, called it_works, and the result of running that test, ok ❷. The overall summary of running the tests appears next. The text test result: ok. ❸ means that all the tests passed, and the portion that reads 1 passed; 0 failed totals the number of tests that passed or failed.

Because we don't have any tests we've marked as ignored, the summary shows 0 ignored. We also haven't filtered the tests being run, so the end of the summary shows 0 filtered out. We'll talk about ignoring and filtering out tests in "Controlling How Tests Are Run" on page 215.

The 0 measured statistic is for benchmark tests that measure performance. Benchmark tests are, as of this writing, only available in nightly Rust. See the documentation about benchmark tests at *https://doc.rust-lang.org/nightly/unstable-book/library-features/test.html* to learn more.

The next part of the test output, which starts with Doc-tests adder ❹, is for the results of any documentation tests. We don't have any documentation tests yet, but Rust can compile any code examples that appear in our API documentation. This feature helps us keep our docs and our code in sync! We'll discuss how to write documentation tests in "Documentation Comments as Tests" on page 289. For now, we'll ignore the Doc-tests output.

Let's change the name of our test to see how that changes the test output. Change the it_works function to a different name, such as exploration, like so:

src/lib.rs

```
#[cfg(test)]
mod tests {
    #[test]
    fn exploration() {
        assert_eq!(2 + 2, 4);
    }
}
```

Then run cargo test again. The output now shows exploration instead of it_works:

```
running 1 test
test tests::exploration ... ok

test result: ok. 1 passed; 0 failed; 0 ignored; 0 measured; 0 filtered out
```

Let's add another test, but this time we'll make a test that fails! Tests fail when something in the test function panics. Each test is run in a new thread, and when the main thread sees that a test thread has died, the test is marked as failed. We talked about the simplest way to cause a panic in Chapter 9, which is to call the panic! macro. Enter the new test, another, so your *src/lib.rs* file looks like Listing 11-3.

src/lib.rs

```
#[cfg(test)]
mod tests {
    #[test]
    fn exploration() {
        assert_eq!(2 + 2, 4);
    }
```

```
    #[test]
    fn another() {
        panic!("Make this test fail");
    }
}
```

Listing 11-3: Adding a second test that will fail because we call the panic! macro

Run the tests again using cargo test. The output should look like Listing 11-4, which shows that our exploration test passed and another failed.

```
running 2 tests
test tests::exploration ... ok
❶ test tests::another ... FAILED

❷ failures:

---- tests::another stdout ----
    thread 'tests::another' panicked at 'Make this test fail', src/lib.rs:10:8
note: Run with `RUST_BACKTRACE=1` for a backtrace.

❸ failures:
    tests::another

❹ test result: FAILED. 1 passed; 1 failed; 0 ignored; 0 measured; 0 filtered out

error: test failed
```

Listing 11-4: Test results when one test passes and one test fails

Instead of ok, the line test tests::another shows FAILED ❶. Two new sections appear between the individual results and the summary: the first section ❷ displays the detailed reason for each test failure. In this case, another failed because it panicked at 'Make this test fail', which happened on line 10 in the *src/lib.rs* file. The next section ❸ lists just the names of all the failing tests, which is useful when there are lots of tests and lots of detailed failing test output. We can use the name of a failing test to run just that test to more easily debug it; we'll talk more about ways to run tests in "Controlling How Tests Are Run" on page 215.

The summary line displays at the end ❹: overall, our test result is FAILED. We had one test pass and one test fail.

Now that you've seen what the test results look like in different scenarios, let's look at some macros other than panic! that are useful in tests.

Checking Results with the assert! Macro

The assert! macro, provided by the standard library, is useful when you want to ensure that some condition in a test evaluates to true. We give the assert! macro an argument that evaluates to a Boolean. If the value is true, assert! does nothing and the test passes. If the value is false, the assert! macro calls the panic! macro, which causes the test to fail. Using the assert! macro helps us check that our code is functioning in the way we intend.

In Listing 5-15 on page 93, we used a Rectangle struct and a can_hold method, which are repeated here in Listing 11-5. Let's put this code in the *src/lib.rs* file and write some tests for it using the assert! macro.

src/lib.rs

```
#[derive(Debug)]
pub struct Rectangle {
    length: u32,
    width: u32,
}

impl Rectangle {
    pub fn can_hold(&self, other: &Rectangle) -> bool {
        self.length > other.length && self.width > other.width
    }
}
```

Listing 11-5: Using the Rectangle struct and its can_hold method from Chapter 5

The can_hold method returns a Boolean, which means it's a perfect use case for the assert! macro. In Listing 11-6, we write a test that exercises the can_hold method by creating a Rectangle instance that has a length of 8 and a width of 7 and asserting that it can hold another Rectangle instance that has a length of 5 and a width of 1.

src/lib.rs

```
#[cfg(test)]
mod tests {
 ❶ use super::*;

    #[test]
 ❷ fn larger_can_hold_smaller() {
     ❸ let larger = Rectangle { length: 8, width: 7 };
        let smaller = Rectangle { length: 5, width: 1 };

     ❹ assert!(larger.can_hold(&smaller));
    }
}
```

Listing 11-6: A test for can_hold that checks whether a larger rectangle can indeed hold a smaller rectangle

Note that we've added a new line inside the tests module: use super::*; ❶. The tests module is a regular module that follows the usual visibility rules we covered in "Privacy Rules" on page 121. Because the tests module is an inner module, we need to bring the code under test in the outer module into the scope of the inner module. We use a glob here so anything we define in the outer module is available to this tests module.

We've named our test larger_can_hold_smaller ❷, and we've created the two Rectangle instances that we need ❸. Then we called the assert! macro and passed it the result of calling larger.can_hold(&smaller) ❹. This expression is supposed to return true, so our test should pass. Let's find out!

```
running 1 test
test tests::larger_can_hold_smaller ... ok

test result: ok. 1 passed; 0 failed; 0 ignored; 0 measured; 0 filtered out
```

It does pass! Let's add another test, this time asserting that a smaller rectangle cannot hold a larger rectangle:

src/lib.rs

```
#[cfg(test)]
mod tests {
    use super::*;

    #[test]
    fn larger_can_hold_smaller() {
        // --snip--
    }

    #[test]
    fn smaller_cannot_hold_larger() {
        let larger = Rectangle { length: 8, width: 7 };
        let smaller = Rectangle { length: 5, width: 1 };

        assert!(!smaller.can_hold(&larger));
    }
}
```

Because the correct result of the can_hold function in this case is false, we need to negate that result before we pass it to the assert! macro. As a result, our test will pass if can_hold returns false:

```
running 2 tests
test tests::smaller_cannot_hold_larger ... ok
test tests::larger_can_hold_smaller ... ok

test result: ok. 2 passed; 0 failed; 0 ignored; 0 measured; 0 filtered out
```

Two tests that pass! Now let's see what happens to our test results when we introduce a bug in our code. Let's change the implementation of the can_hold method by replacing the greater than sign with a less than sign when it compares the lengths:

```
// --snip--

impl Rectangle {
    pub fn can_hold(&self, other: &Rectangle) -> bool {
        self.length < other.length && self.width > other.width
    }
}
```

Running the tests now produces the following:

```
running 2 tests
test tests::smaller_cannot_hold_larger ... ok
test tests::larger_can_hold_smaller ... FAILED

failures:

---- tests::larger_can_hold_smaller stdout ----
    thread 'tests::larger_can_hold_smaller' panicked at 'assertion failed:
    larger.can_hold(&smaller)', src/lib.rs:22:8
note: Run with `RUST_BACKTRACE=1` for a backtrace.

failures:
    tests::larger_can_hold_smaller

test result: FAILED. 1 passed; 1 failed; 0 ignored; 0 measured; 0 filtered out
```

Our tests caught the bug! Because larger.length is 8 and smaller.length is 5, the comparison of the lengths in can_hold now returns false: 8 is not less than 5.

Testing Equality with the assert_eq! and assert_ne! Macros

A common way to test functionality is to compare the result of the code under test to the value you expect the code to return to make sure they're equal. You could do this using the assert! macro and passing it an expression using the == operator. However, this is such a common test that the standard library provides a pair of macros—assert_eq! and assert_ne!—to perform this test more conveniently. These macros compare two arguments for equality or inequality, respectively. They'll also print the two values if the assertion fails, which makes it easier to see *why* the test failed; conversely, the assert! macro only indicates that it got a false value for the == expression, not the values that lead to the false value.

In Listing 11-7, we write a function named add_two that adds 2 to its parameter and returns the result. Then we test this function using the assert_eq! macro.

src/lib.rs

```
pub fn add_two(a: i32) -> i32 {
    a + 2
}

#[cfg(test)]
mod tests {
    use super::*;

    #[test]
    fn it_adds_two() {
        assert_eq!(4, add_two(2));
    }
}
```

Listing 11-7: Testing the function add_two using the assert_eq! macro

Let's check that it passes!

```
running 1 test
test tests::it_adds_two ... ok

test result: ok. 1 passed; 0 failed; 0 ignored; 0 measured; 0 filtered out
```

The first argument we gave to the assert_eq! macro, 4, is equal to the result of calling add_two(2). The line for this test is test tests::it_adds_two ... ok, and the ok text indicates that our test passed!

Let's introduce a bug into our code to see what it looks like when a test that uses assert_eq! fails. Change the implementation of the add_two function to instead add 3:

```
pub fn add_two(a: i32) -> i32 {
    a + 3
}
```

Run the tests again:

```
running 1 test
test tests::it_adds_two ... FAILED

failures:

---- tests::it_adds_two stdout ----
    ❶ thread 'tests::it_adds_two' panicked at 'assertion failed:
 `(left == right)`
❷ left: `4`,
❸ right: `5`', src/lib.rs:11:8
note: Run with `RUST_BACKTRACE=1` for a backtrace.

failures:
    tests::it_adds_two

test result: FAILED. 0 passed; 1 failed; 0 ignored; 0 measured; 0 filtered out
```

Our test caught the bug! The it_adds_two test failed, displaying the message assertion failed: `(left == right)` ❶ and showing that left was 4 ❷ and right was 5 ❸. This message is useful and helps us start debugging: it means the left argument to assert_eq! was 4 but the right argument, where we had add_two(2), was 5.

Note that in some languages and test frameworks, the parameters to the functions that assert two values are equal are called expected and actual, and the order in which we specify the arguments matters. However, in Rust, they're called left and right, and the order in which we specify the value we expect and the value that the code under test produces doesn't matter. We could write the assertion in this test as assert_eq!(add_two(2), 4), which would result in a failure message that displays assertion failed: `(left == right)` and that left was 5 and right was 4.

The assert_ne! macro will pass if the two values we give it are not equal and fail if they're equal. This macro is most useful for cases when we're not sure what a value *will* be, but we know what the value definitely *won't* be if our code is functioning as we intend. For example, if we're testing a function that is guaranteed to change its input in some way, but the way in which the input is changed depends on the day of the week that we run our tests, the best thing to assert might be that the output of the function is not equal to the input.

Under the surface, the assert_eq! and assert_ne! macros use the operators == and !=, respectively. When the assertions fail, these macros print their arguments using debug formatting, which means the values being compared must implement the PartialEq and Debug traits. All the primitive types and most of the standard library types implement these traits. For structs and enums that you define, you'll need to implement PartialEq to assert that values of those types are equal or not equal. You'll need to implement Debug to print the values when the assertion fails. Because both traits are derivable traits, as mentioned in Listing 5-12 on page 89, this is usually as straightforward as adding the #[derive(PartialEq, Debug)] annotation to your struct or enum definition. See Appendix C for more details about these and other derivable traits.

Adding Custom Failure Messages

You can also add a custom message to be printed with the failure message as optional arguments to the assert!, assert_eq!, and assert_ne! macros. Any arguments specified after the one required argument to assert! or the two required arguments to assert_eq! and assert_ne! are passed along to the format! macro (discussed in "Concatenation with the + Operator or the format! Macro" on page 137), so you can pass a format string that contains {} placeholders and values to go in those placeholders. Custom messages are useful to document what an assertion means; when a test fails, you'll have a better idea of what the problem is with the code.

For example, let's say we have a function that greets people by name and we want to test that the name we pass into the function appears in the output:

src/lib.rs

```
pub fn greeting(name: &str) -> String {
    format!("Hello {}!", name)
}

#[cfg(test)]
mod tests {
    use super::*;

    #[test]
    fn greeting_contains_name() {
        let result = greeting("Carol");
        assert!(result.contains("Carol"));
    }
}
```

The requirements for this program haven't been agreed upon yet, and we're pretty sure the Hello text at the beginning of the greeting will change.

We decided we don't want to have to update the test when the requirements change, so instead of checking for exact equality to the value returned from the greeting function, we'll just assert that the output contains the text of the input parameter.

Let's introduce a bug into this code by changing greeting to not include name to see what this test failure looks like:

```rust
pub fn greeting(name: &str) -> String {
    String::from("Hello!")
}
```

Running this test produces the following:

```
running 1 test
test tests::greeting_contains_name ... FAILED

failures:

---- tests::greeting_contains_name stdout ----
        thread 'tests::greeting_contains_name' panicked at 'assertion failed:
result.contains("Carol")', src/lib.rs:12:8
note: Run with `RUST_BACKTRACE=1` for a backtrace.

failures:
    tests::greeting_contains_name
```

This result just indicates that the assertion failed and which line the assertion is on. A more useful failure message in this case would print the value we got from the greeting function. Let's change the test function, giving it a custom failure message made from a format string with a placeholder filled in with the actual value we got from the greeting function:

```rust
#[test]
fn greeting_contains_name() {
    let result = greeting("Carol");
    assert!(
        result.contains("Carol"),
        "Greeting did not contain name, value was `{}`", result
    );
}
```

Now when we run the test, we'll get a more informative error message:

```
---- tests::greeting_contains_name stdout ----
        thread 'tests::greeting_contains_name' panicked at 'Greeting did not
contain name, value was `Hello!`', src/lib.rs:12:8
note: Run with `RUST_BACKTRACE=1` for a backtrace.
```

We can see the value we actually got in the test output, which would help us debug what happened instead of what we were expecting to happen.

Checking for Panics with should_panic

In addition to checking that our code returns the correct values we expect, it's also important to check that our code handles error conditions as we expect. For example, consider the Guess type that we created in Listing 9-9 on page 165. Other code that uses Guess depends on the guarantee that Guess instances will contain only values between 1 and 100. We can write a test that ensures that attempting to create a Guess instance with a value outside that range panics.

We do this by adding another attribute, should_panic, to our test function. This attribute makes a test pass if the code inside the function panics; the test will fail if the code inside the function doesn't panic.

Listing 11-8 shows a test that checks that the error conditions of Guess::new happen when we expect them to.

src/lib.rs

```rust
pub struct Guess {
    value: u32,
}

impl Guess {
    pub fn new(value: u32) -> Guess {
        if value < 1 || value > 100 {
            panic!("Guess value must be between 1 and 100, got {}.", value);
        }

        Guess {
            value
        }
    }
}

#[cfg(test)]
mod tests {
    use super::*;

    #[test]
    #[should_panic]
    fn greater_than_100() {
        Guess::new(200);
    }
}
```

Listing 11-8: Testing that a condition will cause a panic!

We place the #[should_panic] attribute after the #[test] attribute and before the test function it applies to. Let's look at the result when this test passes:

```
running 1 test
test tests::greater_than_100 ... ok

test result: ok. 1 passed; 0 failed; 0 ignored; 0 measured; 0 filtered out
```

Looks good! Now let's introduce a bug in our code by removing the condition that the new function will panic if the value is greater than 100:

```
// --snip--

impl Guess {
    pub fn new(value: u32) -> Guess {
        if value < 1 {
            panic!("Guess value must be between 1 and 100, got {}.", value);
        }

        Guess {
            value
        }
    }
}
```

When we run the test in Listing 11-8, it will fail:

```
running 1 test
test tests::greater_than_100 ... FAILED

failures:

failures:
    tests::greater_than_100

test result: FAILED. 0 passed; 1 failed; 0 ignored; 0 measured; 0 filtered out
```

We don't get a very helpful message in this case, but when we look at the test function, we see that it's annotated with #[should_panic]. The failure we got means that the code in the test function did not cause a panic.

Tests that use should_panic can be imprecise because they only indicate that the code has caused some panic. A should_panic test would pass even if the test panics for a different reason than the one we were expecting to happen. To make should_panic tests more precise, we can add an optional expected parameter to the should_panic attribute. The test harness will make sure that the failure message contains the provided text. For example, consider the modified code for Guess in Listing 11-9 where the new function panics with different messages depending on whether the value is too small or too large.

src/lib.rs

```
// --snip--

impl Guess {
    pub fn new(value: u32) -> Guess {
        if value < 1 {
            panic!("Guess value must be greater than or equal to 1, got {}.",
                value);
        } else if value > 100 {
            panic!("Guess value must be less than or equal to 100, got {}.",
                value);
        }
```

```
        Guess {
            value
        }
    }
}

#[cfg(test)]
mod tests {
    use super::*;

    #[test]
    #[should_panic(expected = "Guess value must be less than or equal to 100")]
    fn greater_than_100() {
        Guess::new(200);
    }
}
```

Listing 11-9: Testing that a condition will cause a panic! with a particular panic message

This test will pass because the value we put in the should_panic attribute's expected parameter is a substring of the message that the Guess::new function panics with. We could have specified the entire panic message that we expect, which in this case would be Guess value must be less than or equal to 100, got 200. What you choose to specify in the expected parameter for should_panic depends on how much of the panic message is unique or dynamic and how precise you want your test to be. In this case, a substring of the panic message is enough to ensure that the code in the test function executes the else if value > 100 case.

To see what happens when a should_panic test with an expected message fails, let's again introduce a bug into our code by swapping the bodies of the if value < 1 and the else if value > 100 blocks:

```
if value < 1 {
    panic!("Guess value must be less than or equal to 100, got {}.", value);
} else if value > 100 {
    panic!("Guess value must be greater than or equal to 1, got {}.", value);
}
```

This time when we run the should_panic test, it will fail:

```
running 1 test
test tests::greater_than_100 ... FAILED

failures:

---- tests::greater_than_100 stdout ----
        thread 'tests::greater_than_100' panicked at 'Guess value must be
greater than or equal to 1, got 200.', src/lib.rs:11:12
note: Run with `RUST_BACKTRACE=1` for a backtrace.
note: Panic did not include expected string 'Guess value must be less than or
equal to 100.'
```

```
failures:
    tests::greater_than_100

test result: FAILED. 0 passed; 1 failed; 0 ignored; 0 measured; 0 filtered out
```

The failure message indicates that this test did indeed panic as we expected, but the panic message did not include the expected string 'Guess value must be less than or equal to 100'. The panic message that we did get in this case was Guess value must be greater than or equal to 1, got 200. Now we can start figuring out where our bug is!

Now that you know several ways to write tests, let's look at what is happening when we run our tests and explore the different options we can use with cargo test.

Controlling How Tests Are Run

Just as cargo run compiles your code and then runs the resulting binary, cargo test compiles your code in test mode and runs the resulting test binary. You can specify command line options to change the default behavior of cargo test. For example, the default behavior of the binary produced by cargo test is to run all the tests in parallel and capture output generated during test runs, preventing the output from being displayed and making it easier to read the output related to the test results.

Some command line options go to cargo test, and some go to the resulting test binary. To separate these two types of arguments, you list the arguments that go to cargo test followed by the separator -- and then the ones that go to the test binary. Running cargo test --help displays the options you can use with cargo test, and running cargo test -- --help displays the options you can use after the separator --.

Running Tests in Parallel or Consecutively

When you run multiple tests, by default they run in parallel using threads. This means the tests will finish running faster so you can get feedback quicker on whether or not your code is working. Because the tests are running at the same time, make sure your tests don't depend on each other or on any shared state, including a shared environment, such as the current working directory or environment variables.

For example, say each of your tests runs some code that creates a file on disk named *test-output.txt* and writes some data to that file. Then each test reads the data in that file and asserts that the file contains a particular value, which is different in each test. Because the tests run at the same time, one test might overwrite the file between when another test writes and reads the file. The second test will then fail, not because the code is incorrect but because the tests have interfered with each other while running in parallel. One solution is to make sure each test writes to a different file; another solution is to run the tests one at a time.

If you don't want to run the tests in parallel or if you want more fine-grained control over the number of threads used, you can send the --test-threads flag and the number of threads you want to use to the test binary. Take a look at the following example:

```
$ cargo test -- --test-threads=1
```

We set the number of test threads to 1, telling the program not to use any parallelism. Running the tests using one thread will take longer than running them in parallel, but the tests won't interfere with each other if they share state.

Showing Function Output

By default, if a test passes, Rust's test library captures anything printed to standard output. For example, if we call println! in a test and the test passes, we won't see the println! output in the terminal; we'll see only the line that indicates the test passed. If a test fails, we'll see whatever was printed to standard output with the rest of the failure message.

As an example, Listing 11-10 has a silly function that prints the value of its parameter and returns 10, as well as a test that passes and a test that fails.

src/lib.rs

```
fn prints_and_returns_10(a: i32) -> i32 {
    println!("I got the value {}", a);
    10
}

#[cfg(test)]
mod tests {
    use super::*;

    #[test]
    fn this_test_will_pass() {
        let value = prints_and_returns_10(4);
        assert_eq!(10, value);
    }

    #[test]
    fn this_test_will_fail() {
        let value = prints_and_returns_10(8);
        assert_eq!(5, value);
    }
}
```

Listing 11-10: Tests for a function that calls println!

When we run these tests with cargo test, we'll see the following output:

```
running 2 tests
test tests::this_test_will_pass ... ok
test tests::this_test_will_fail ... FAILED
```

```
failures:

---- tests::this_test_will_fail stdout ----
    ❶ I got the value 8
thread 'tests::this_test_will_fail' panicked at 'assertion failed: `(left ==
right)`
  left: `5`,
 right: `10`', src/lib.rs:19:8
note: Run with `RUST_BACKTRACE=1` for a backtrace.

failures:
    tests::this_test_will_fail

test result: FAILED. 1 passed; 1 failed; 0 ignored; 0 measured; 0 filtered out
```

Note that nowhere in this output do we see I got the value 4, which is what is printed when the test that passes runs. That output has been captured. The output from the test that failed, I got the value 8 ❶, appears in the section of the test summary output, which also shows the cause of the test failure.

If we want to see printed values for passing tests as well, we can disable the output capture behavior by using the --nocapture flag:

```
$ cargo test -- --nocapture
```

When we run the tests in Listing 11-10 again with the --nocapture flag, we see the following output:

```
running 2 tests
I got the value 4
I got the value 8
test tests::this_test_will_pass ... ok
thread 'tests::this_test_will_fail' panicked at 'assertion failed: `(left ==
right)`
  left: `5`,
 right: `10`', src/lib.rs:19:8
note: Run with `RUST_BACKTRACE=1` for a backtrace.
test tests::this_test_will_fail ... FAILED

failures:

failures:
    tests::this_test_will_fail

test result: FAILED. 1 passed; 1 failed; 0 ignored; 0 measured; 0 filtered out
```

Note that the output for the tests and the test results are interleaved; the reason is that the tests are running in parallel, as we talked about in the previous section. Try using the --test-threads=1 option and the --nocapture flag and see what the output looks like then!

Running a Subset of Tests by Name

Sometimes, running a full test suite can take a long time. If you're working on code in a particular area, you might want to run only the tests pertaining to that code. You can choose which tests to run by passing cargo test the name or names of the test(s) you want to run as an argument.

To demonstrate how to run a subset of tests, we'll create three tests for our add_two function, as shown in Listing 11-11, and choose which ones to run.

src/lib.rs

```
pub fn add_two(a: i32) -> i32 {
    a + 2
}

#[cfg(test)]
mod tests {
    use super::*;

    #[test]
    fn add_two_and_two() {
        assert_eq!(4, add_two(2));
    }

    #[test]
    fn add_three_and_two() {
        assert_eq!(5, add_two(3));
    }

    #[test]
    fn one_hundred() {
        assert_eq!(102, add_two(100));
    }
}
```

Listing 11-11: Three tests with three different names

If we run the tests without passing any arguments, as we saw earlier, all the tests will run in parallel:

```
running 3 tests
test tests::add_two_and_two ... ok
test tests::add_three_and_two ... ok
test tests::one_hundred ... ok

test result: ok. 3 passed; 0 failed; 0 ignored; 0 measured; 0 filtered out
```

Running Single Tests

We can pass the name of any test function to cargo test to run only that test:

```
$ cargo test one_hundred
    Finished dev [unoptimized + debuginfo] target(s) in 0.0 secs
     Running target/debug/deps/adder-06a75b4a1f2515e9
```

```
running 1 test
test tests::one_hundred ... ok

test result: ok. 1 passed; 0 failed; 0 ignored; 0 measured; 2 filtered out
```

Only the test with the name one_hundred ran; the other two tests didn't match that name. The test output lets us know we had more tests than what this command ran by displaying 2 filtered out at the end of the summary line.

We can't specify the names of multiple tests in this way; only the first value given to cargo test will be used. But there is a way to run multiple tests.

Filtering to Run Multiple Tests

We can specify part of a test name, and any test whose name matches that value will be run. For example, because two of our tests' names contain add, we can run those two by running cargo test add:

```
$ cargo test add
    Finished dev [unoptimized + debuginfo] target(s) in 0.0 secs
     Running target/debug/deps/adder-06a75b4a1f2515e9

running 2 tests
test tests::add_two_and_two ... ok
test tests::add_three_and_two ... ok

test result: ok. 2 passed; 0 failed; 0 ignored; 0 measured; 1 filtered out
```

This command ran all tests with add in the name and filtered out the test named one_hundred. Also note that the module in which tests appear becomes part of the test's name, so we can run all the tests in a module by filtering on the module's name.

Ignoring Some Tests Unless Specifically Requested

Sometimes a few specific tests can be very time-consuming to execute, so you might want to exclude them during most runs of cargo test. Rather than listing as arguments all tests you do want to run, you can instead annotate the time-consuming tests using the ignore attribute to exclude them, as shown here:

src/lib.rs

```
#[test]
fn it_works() {
    assert_eq!(2 + 2, 4);
}

#[test]
#[ignore]
fn expensive_test() {
    // code that takes an hour to run
}
```

After #[test], we add the #[ignore] line to the test we want to exclude. Now when we run our tests, it_works runs, but expensive_test doesn't:

```
$ cargo test
   Compiling adder v0.1.0 (file:///projects/adder)
    Finished dev [unoptimized + debuginfo] target(s) in 0.24 secs
     Running target/debug/deps/adder-ce99bcc2479f4607

running 2 tests
test expensive_test ... ignored
test it_works ... ok

test result: ok. 1 passed; 0 failed; 1 ignored; 0 measured; 0 filtered out
```

The expensive_test function is listed as ignored. If we want to run only the ignored tests, we can use cargo test -- --ignored:

```
$ cargo test -- --ignored
    Finished dev [unoptimized + debuginfo] target(s) in 0.0 secs
     Running target/debug/deps/adder-ce99bcc2479f4607

running 1 test
test expensive_test ... ok

test result: ok. 1 passed; 0 failed; 0 ignored; 0 measured; 1 filtered out
```

By controlling which tests run, you can make sure your cargo test results will be fast. When you're at a point where it makes sense to check the results of the ignored tests and you have time to wait for the results, you can run cargo test -- --ignored instead.

Test Organization

As mentioned at the start of the chapter, testing is a complex discipline, and different people use different terminology and organization. The Rust community thinks about tests in terms of two main categories: *unit tests* and *integration tests*. Unit tests are small and more focused, testing one module in isolation at a time, and can test private interfaces. Integration tests are entirely external to your library and use your code in the same way any other external code would, using only the public interface and potentially exercising multiple modules per test.

Writing both kinds of tests is important to ensure that the pieces of your library are doing what you expect them to, separately and together.

Unit Tests

The purpose of unit tests is to test each unit of code in isolation from the rest of the code to quickly pinpoint where code is and isn't working as expected.

You'll put unit tests in the *src* directory in each file with the code that they're testing. The convention is to create a module named tests in each file to contain the test functions and to annotate the module with cfg(test).

The Tests Module and #[cfg(test)]

The #[cfg(test)] annotation on the tests module tells Rust to compile and run the test code only when you run cargo test, not when you run cargo build. This saves compile time when you only want to build the library and saves space in the resulting compiled artifact because the tests are not included. You'll see that because integration tests go in a different directory, they don't need the #[cfg(test)] annotation. However, because unit tests go in the same files as the code, you'll use #[cfg(test)] to specify that they shouldn't be included in the compiled result.

Recall that when we generated the new adder project in the first section of this chapter, Cargo generated this code for us:

src/lib.rs

```
#[cfg(test)]
mod tests {
    #[test]
    fn it_works() {
        assert_eq!(2 + 2, 4);
    }
}
```

This code is the automatically generated test module. The attribute cfg stands for *configuration* and tells Rust that the following item should only be included given a certain configuration option. In this case, the configuration option is test, which is provided by Rust for compiling and running tests. By using the cfg attribute, Cargo compiles our test code only if we actively run the tests with cargo test. This includes any helper functions that might be within this module, in addition to the functions annotated with #[test].

Testing Private Functions

There's debate within the testing community about whether or not private functions should be tested directly, and other languages make it difficult or impossible to test private functions. Regardless of which testing ideology you adhere to, Rust's privacy rules do allow you to test private functions. Consider the code in Listing 11-12 with the private function internal_adder.

src/lib.rs

```
pub fn add_two(a: i32) -> i32 {
    internal_adder(a, 2)
}

fn internal_adder(a: i32, b: i32) -> i32 {
    a + b
}
```

```
#[cfg(test)]
mod tests {
    use super::*;

    #[test]
    fn internal() {
        assert_eq!(4, internal_adder(2, 2));
    }
}
```

Listing 11-12: Testing a private function

Note that the `internal_adder` function is not marked as `pub`, but because tests are just Rust code and the tests module is just another module, you can import and call `internal_adder` in a test just fine. If you don't think private functions should be tested, nothing in Rust will compel you to do so.

Integration Tests

In Rust, integration tests are entirely external to your library. They use your library in the same way any other code would, which means they can only call functions that are part of your library's public API. Their purpose is to test whether many parts of your library work together correctly. Units of code that work correctly on their own could have problems when integrated, so test coverage of the integrated code is important as well. To create integration tests, you first need a *tests* directory.

The tests Directory

We create a *tests* directory at the top level of our project directory, next to *src*. Cargo knows to look for integration test files in this directory. We can then make as many test files as we want to in this directory, and Cargo will compile each of the files as an individual crate.

Let's create an integration test. With the code in Listing 11-12 still in the *src/lib.rs* file, make a *tests* directory, create a new file named *tests/integration _test.rs*, and enter the code in Listing 11-13.

tests/integration _test.rs

```
extern crate adder;

#[test]
fn it_adds_two() {
    assert_eq!(4, adder::add_two(2));
}
```

Listing 11-13: An integration test of a function in the adder crate

We've added `extern crate adder` at the top of the code, which we didn't need in the unit tests. The reason is that each test in the *tests* directory is a separate crate, so we need to import our library into each of them.

We don't need to annotate any code in *tests/integration_test.rs* with
#[cfg(test)]. Cargo treats the *tests* directory specially and compiles files
in this directory only when we run cargo test. Run cargo test now:

```
$ cargo test
   Compiling adder v0.1.0 (file:///projects/adder)
    Finished dev [unoptimized + debuginfo] target(s) in 0.31 secs
     Running target/debug/deps/adder-abcabcabc
```

❶ running 1 test
test tests::internal ... ok

test result: ok. 1 passed; 0 failed; 0 ignored; 0 measured; 0 filtered out

   ❷ Running target/debug/deps/integration_test-ce99bcc2479f4607

running 1 test
❸ test it_adds_two ... ok

❹ test result: ok. 1 passed; 0 failed; 0 ignored; 0 measured; 0 filtered out

    Doc-tests adder

running 0 tests

test result: ok. 0 passed; 0 failed; 0 ignored; 0 measured; 0 filtered out

The three sections of output include the unit tests, the integration test,
and the doc tests. The first section for the unit tests ❶ is the same as we've
been seeing: one line for each unit test (one named internal that we added
in Listing 11-12) and then a summary line for the unit tests.

The integration tests section starts with the line Running target/debug/
deps/integration-test-ce99bcc2479f4607 ❷ (the hash at the end of your output
will be different). Next, there is a line for each test function in that integration test ❸ and a summary line for the results of the integration test ❹ just
before the Doc-tests adder section starts.

Similarly to how adding more unit test functions adds more result lines
to the unit tests section, adding more test functions to the integration test file
adds more result lines to this integration test file's section. Each integration
test file has its own section, so if we add more files in the *tests* directory, there
will be more integration test sections.

We can still run a particular integration test function by specifying the
test function's name as an argument to cargo test. To run all the tests in a
particular integration test file, use the --test argument of cargo test followed
by the name of the file:

```
$ cargo test --test integration_test
    Finished dev [unoptimized + debuginfo] target(s) in 0.0 secs
     Running target/debug/integration_test-952a27e0126bb565

running 1 test
```

```
test it_adds_two ... ok

test result: ok. 1 passed; 0 failed; 0 ignored; 0 measured; 0 filtered out
```

This command runs only the tests in the *tests/integration_test.rs* file.

Submodules in Integration Tests

As you add more integration tests, you might want to make more than one file in the *tests* directory to help organize them; for example, you can group the test functions by the functionality they're testing. As mentioned earlier, each file in the *tests* directory is compiled as its own separate crate.

Treating each integration test file as its own crate is useful to create separate scopes that are more like the way end users will be using your crate. However, this means files in the *tests* directory don't share the same behavior as files in *src* do, as you learned in Chapter 7 regarding how to separate code into modules and files.

The different behavior of files in the *tests* directory is most noticeable when you have a set of helper functions that would be useful in multiple integration test files and you try to follow the steps in "Moving Modules to Other Files" on page 112 to extract them into a common module. For example, if we create *tests/common.rs* and place a function named setup in it, we can add some code to setup that we want to call from multiple test functions in multiple test files:

tests/common.rs
```
pub fn setup() {
    // setup code specific to your library's tests would go here
}
```

When we run the tests again, we'll see a new section in the test output for the *common.rs* file, even though this file doesn't contain any test functions nor did we call the setup function from anywhere:

```
running 1 test
test tests::internal ... ok

test result: ok. 1 passed; 0 failed; 0 ignored; 0 measured; 0 filtered out

     Running target/debug/deps/common-b8b07b6f1be2db70

running 0 tests

test result: ok. 0 passed; 0 failed; 0 ignored; 0 measured; 0 filtered out

     Running target/debug/deps/integration_test-d993c68b431d39df

running 1 test
test it_adds_two ... ok

test result: ok. 1 passed; 0 failed; 0 ignored; 0 measured; 0 filtered out
```

```
   Doc-tests adder

running 0 tests

test result: ok. 0 passed; 0 failed; 0 ignored; 0 measured; 0 filtered out
```

Having `common` appear in the test results with `running 0 tests` displayed for it is not what we wanted. We just wanted to share some code with the other integration test files.

To avoid having `common` appear in the test output, instead of creating *tests/common.rs*, we'll create *tests/common/mod.rs*. In "Rules of Module Filesystems" on page 117, we used the naming convention *module_name/mod.rs* for files of modules that have submodules. We don't have submodules for `common` here, but naming the file this way tells Rust not to treat the `common` module as an integration test file. When we move the `setup` function code into *tests/common/mod.rs* and delete the *tests/common.rs* file, the section in the test output will no longer appear. Files in subdirectories of the *tests* directory don't get compiled as separate crates or have sections in the test output.

After we've created *tests/common/mod.rs*, we can use it from any of the integration test files as a module. Here's an example of calling the `setup` function from the `it_adds_two` test in *tests/integration_test.rs*:

tests/integration_test.rs

```
extern crate adder;

mod common;

#[test]
fn it_adds_two() {
    common::setup();
    assert_eq!(4, adder::add_two(2));
}
```

Note that the `mod common;` declaration is the same as the module declarations we demonstrated in Listing 7-4 on page 113. Then in the test function, we can call the `common::setup()` function.

Integration Tests for Binary Crates

If our project is a binary crate that only contains a *src/main.rs* file and doesn't have a *src/lib.rs* file, we can't create integration tests in the *tests* directory and use `extern crate` to import functions defined in the *src/main.rs* file. Only library crates expose functions that other crates can call and use; binary crates are meant to be run on their own.

This is one of the reasons Rust projects that provide a binary have a straightforward *src/main.rs* file that calls logic that lives in the *src/lib.rs* file. Using that structure, integration tests *can* test the library crate by using `extern crate` to exercise the important functionality. If the important functionality works, the small amount of code in the *src/main.rs* file will work as well, and that small amount of code doesn't need to be tested.

Summary

Rust's testing features provide a way to specify how code should function to ensure it continues to work as you expect, even as you make changes. Unit tests exercise different parts of a library separately and can test private implementation details. Integration tests check that many parts of the library work together correctly, and they use the library's public API to test the code in the same way external code will use it. Even though Rust's type system and ownership rules help prevent some kinds of bugs, tests are still important to reduce logic bugs having to do with how your code is expected to behave.

Let's combine the knowledge you learned in this chapter and in previous chapters to work on a project!

12

AN I/O PROJECT: BUILDING A COMMAND LINE PROGRAM

This chapter is a recap of the many skills you've learned so far and an exploration of a few more standard library features. We'll build a command line tool that interacts with file and command line input/output to practice some of the Rust concepts you now have under your belt.

Rust's speed, safety, single binary output, and cross-platform support make it an ideal language for creating command line tools, so for our project, we'll make our own version of the classic command line tool grep (**g**lobally search a **r**egular **e**xpression and **p**rint). In the simplest use case, grep searches a specified file for a specified string. To do so, grep takes as its arguments a filename and a string. Then it reads the file, finds lines in that file that contain the string argument, and prints those lines.

Along the way, we'll show how to make our command line tool use features of the terminal that many command line tools use. We'll read the value of an environment variable to allow the user to configure the behavior of our tool. We'll also print to the standard error console stream (stderr) instead of standard output (stdout), so, for example, the user can redirect successful output to a file while still seeing error messages onscreen.

One Rust community member, Andrew Gallant, has already created a fully featured, very fast version of grep, called ripgrep. By comparison, our version of grep will be fairly simple, but this chapter will give you some of the background knowledge you need to understand a real-world project such as ripgrep.

Our grep project will combine a number of concepts you've learned so far:

- Organizing code (using what you learned in modules, Chapter 7)
- Using vectors and strings (collections, Chapter 8)
- Handling errors (Chapter 9)
- Using traits and lifetimes where appropriate (Chapter 10)
- Writing tests (Chapter 11)

We'll also briefly introduce closures, iterators, and trait objects, which Chapters 13 and 17 will cover in detail.

Accepting Command Line Arguments

Let's create a new project with, as always, cargo new. We'll call our project minigrep to distinguish it from the grep tool that you might already have on your system.

```
$ cargo new --bin minigrep
    Created binary (application) `minigrep` project
$ cd minigrep
```

The first task is to make minigrep accept its two command line arguments: the filename and a string to search for. That is, we want to be able to run our program with cargo run, a string to search for, and a path to a file to search in, like so:

```
$ cargo run searchstring example-filename.txt
```

Right now, the program generated by cargo new cannot process arguments we give it. Some existing libraries on *https://crates.io/* can help with writing a program that accepts command line arguments, but because you're just learning this concept, let's implement this capability ourselves.

Reading the Argument Values

To enable minigrep to read the values of command line arguments we pass to it, we'll need a function provided in Rust's standard library, which is std::env::args. This function returns an *iterator* of the command line arguments that were given to minigrep. We haven't discussed iterators yet (we'll cover them fully in Chapter 13), but for now, you only need to know two details about iterators: iterators produce a series of values, and we can call the `collect` method on an iterator to turn it into a collection, such as a vector, containing all the elements the iterator produces.

Use the code in Listing 12-1 to allow your minigrep program to read any command line arguments passed to it and then collect the values into a vector.

src/main.rs

```
use std::env;

fn main() {
    let args: Vec<String> = env::args().collect();
    println!("{:?}", args);
}
```

Listing 12-1: Collecting the command line arguments into a vector and printing them

First, we bring the `std::env` module into scope with a `use` statement so we can use its args function. Notice that the `std::env::args` function is nested in two levels of modules. As we discussed in Chapter 7, in cases where the desired function is nested in more than one module, it's conventional to bring the parent module into scope rather than the function. By doing so, we can easily use other functions from `std::env`. It's also less ambiguous than adding `use std::env::args` and then calling the function with just args, because args might easily be mistaken for a function that's defined in the current module.

THE ARGS FUNCTION AND INVALID UNICODE

Note that `std::env::args` will panic if any argument contains invalid Unicode. If your program needs to accept arguments containing invalid Unicode, use `std::env::args_os` instead. That function returns an iterator that produces `OsString` values instead of `String` values. We've chosen to use `std::env::args` here for simplicity, because `OsString` values differ per platform and are more complex to work with than `String` values.

On the first line of main, we call `env::args`, and we immediately use collect to turn the iterator into a vector containing all the values produced by the iterator. We can use the collect function to create many kinds of collections, so we explicitly annotate the type of args to specify that we want a vector of strings. Although we very rarely need to annotate types in Rust, collect is one function you often do need to annotate because Rust isn't able to infer the kind of collection you want.

Finally, we print the vector using the debug formatter, `:?`. Let's try running the code first with no arguments and then with two arguments:

```
$ cargo run
--snip--
```

```
["target/debug/minigrep"]
```

```
$ cargo run needle haystack
--snip--
["target/debug/minigrep", "needle", "haystack"]
```

Notice that the first value in the vector is "target/debug/minigrep", which is the name of our binary. This matches the behavior of the arguments list in C, letting programs use the name by which they were invoked in their execution. It's often convenient to have access to the program name in case you want to print it in messages or change behavior of the program based on what command line alias was used to invoke the program. But for the purposes of this chapter, we'll ignore it and save only the two arguments we need.

Saving the Argument Values in Variables

Printing the value of the vector of arguments illustrated that the program is able to access the values specified as command line arguments. Now we need to save the values of the two arguments in variables so we can use the values throughout the rest of the program. We do that in Listing 12-2.

src/main.rs

```
use std::env;

fn main() {
    let args: Vec<String> = env::args().collect();

    let query = &args[1];
    let filename = &args[2];

    println!("Searching for {}", query);
    println!("In file {}", filename);
}
```

Listing 12-2: Creating variables to hold the query argument and filename argument

As we saw when we printed the vector, the program's name takes up the first value in the vector at args[0], so we're starting at index 1. The first argument minigrep takes is the string we're searching for, so we put a reference to the first argument in the variable query. The second argument will be the filename, so we put a reference to the second argument in the variable filename.

We temporarily print the values of these variables to prove that the code is working as we intend. Let's run this program again with the arguments test and sample.txt:

```
$ cargo run test sample.txt
   Compiling minigrep v0.1.0 (file:///projects/minigrep)
    Finished dev [unoptimized + debuginfo] target(s) in 0.0 secs
     Running `target/debug/minigrep test sample.txt`
Searching for test
In file sample.txt
```

Great, the program is working! The values of the arguments we need are being saved into the right variables. Later we'll add some error handling to deal with certain potential erroneous situations, such as when the user provides no arguments; for now, we'll ignore that situation and work on adding file-reading capabilities instead.

Reading a File

Now we'll add functionality to read the file that is specified in the `filename` command line argument. First, we need a sample file to test it with: the best kind of file to use to make sure minigrep is working is one with a small amount of text over multiple lines with some repeated words. Listing 12-3 has an Emily Dickinson poem that will work well! Create a file called *poem.txt* at the root level of your project and enter the poem "I'm Nobody! Who are you?"

poem.txt

```
I'm nobody! Who are you?
Are you nobody, too?
Then there's a pair of us — don't tell!
They'd banish us, you know.

How dreary to be somebody!
How public, like a frog
To tell your name the livelong day
To an admiring bog!
```

Listing 12-3: A poem by Emily Dickinson makes a good test case.

With the text in place, edit *src/main.rs* and add code to open the file, as shown in Listing 12-4.

src/main.rs

```
use std::env;
❶ use std::fs::File;
❷ use std::io::prelude::*;

fn main() {
    // --snip--
    println!("In file {}", filename);

  ❸ let mut f = File::open(filename).expect("file not found");

  ❹ let mut contents = String::new();
  ❺ f.read_to_string(&mut contents)
        .expect("something went wrong reading the file");

  ❻ println!("With text:\n{}", contents);
}
```

Listing 12-4: Reading the contents of the file specified by the second argument

First, we add some more use statements to bring in relevant parts of the standard library: we need `std::fs::File` to handle files ❶, and `std::io::prelude::*` contains various useful traits for doing I/O, including file I/O ❷. In the same way that Rust has a general prelude that brings certain types and functions into scope automatically, the std::io module has its own prelude of common types and functions you'll need when working with I/O. Unlike with the default prelude, we must explicitly add a use statement for the prelude from std::io.

In main, we've added three statements: first, we get a mutable handle to the file by calling the File::open function and passing it the value of the filename variable ❸. Second, we create a variable called contents and set it to a mutable, empty String ❹. This will hold the content of the file after we read it in. Third, we call read_to_string on our file handle and pass a mutable reference to contents as an argument ❺.

After those lines, we've again added a temporary println! statement that prints the value of contents after the file is read, so we can check that the program is working so far ❻.

Let's run this code with any string as the first command line argument (because we haven't implemented the searching part yet) and the *poem.txt* file as the second argument:

```
$ cargo run the poem.txt
   Compiling minigrep v0.1.0 (file:///projects/minigrep)
   Finished dev [unoptimized + debuginfo] target(s) in 0.0 secs
    Running `target/debug/minigrep the poem.txt`
Searching for the
In file poem.txt
With text:
I'm nobody! Who are you?
Are you nobody, too?
Then there's a pair of us — don't tell!
They'd banish us, you know.

How dreary to be somebody!
How public, like a frog
To tell your name the livelong day
To an admiring bog!
```

Great! The code read and then printed the contents of the file. But the code has a few flaws. The main function has multiple responsibilities: generally, functions are clearer and easier to maintain if each function is responsible for only one idea. The other problem is that we're not handling errors as well as we could. The program is still small, so these flaws aren't a big problem, but as the program grows, it will be harder to fix them cleanly. It's good practice to begin refactoring early on when developing a program, because it's much easier to refactor smaller amounts of code. We'll do that next.

Refactoring to Improve Modularity and Error Handling

To improve our program, we'll fix four problems that have to do with the program's structure and how it's handling potential errors.

First, our main function now performs two tasks: it parses arguments and opens files. For such a small function, this isn't a major problem.

However, if we continue to grow our program inside main, the number of separate tasks the main function handles will increase. As a function gains responsibilities, it becomes more difficult to reason about, harder to test, and harder to change without breaking one of its parts. It's best to separate functionality so each function is responsible for one task.

This issue ties into the second problem: although query and filename are configuration variables to our program, variables like f and contents are used to perform the program's logic. The longer main becomes, the more variables we'll need to bring into scope; the more variables we have in scope, the harder it will be to keep track of the purpose of each. It's best to group the configuration variables into one structure to make their purpose clear.

The third problem is that we've used expect to print an error message when opening the file fails, but the error message just prints file not found. Opening a file can fail in a number of ways besides the file being missing: for example, the file might exist, but we might not have permission to open it. Right now, if we're in that situation, we'd print the file not found error message, which would give the user the wrong information!

Fourth, we use expect repeatedly to handle different errors, and if the user runs our program without specifying enough arguments, they'll get an index out of bounds error from Rust that doesn't clearly explain the problem. It would be best if all the error-handling code were in one place so future maintainers had only one place to consult in the code if the error-handling logic needed to change. Having all the error-handling code in one place will also ensure that we're printing messages that will be meaningful to our end users.

Let's address these four problems by refactoring our project.

Separation of Concerns for Binary Projects

The organizational problem of allocating responsibility for multiple tasks to the main function is common to many binary projects. As a result, the Rust community has developed a process to use as a guideline for splitting the separate concerns of a binary program when main starts getting large. The process has the following steps:

- Split your program into a *main.rs* and a *lib.rs* and move your program's logic to *lib.rs*.
- As long as your command line parsing logic is small, it can remain in *main.rs*.
- When the command line parsing logic starts getting complicated, extract it from *main.rs* and move it to *lib.rs*.

The responsibilities that remain in the main function after this process should be limited to the following:

- Calling the command line parsing logic with the argument values
- Setting up any other configuration
- Calling a run function in *lib.rs*
- Handling the error if run returns an error

This pattern is about separating concerns: *main.rs* handles running the program, and *lib.rs* handles all the logic of the task at hand. Because you can't test the main function directly, this structure lets you test all of your program's logic by moving it into functions in *lib.rs*. The only code that remains in *main.rs* will be small enough to verify its correctness by reading it. Let's rework our program by following this process.

Extracting the Argument Parser

We'll extract the functionality for parsing arguments into a function that main will call to prepare for moving the command line parsing logic to *src/lib.rs*. Listing 12-5 shows the new start of main that calls a new function parse_config, which we'll define in *src/main.rs* for the moment.

```
fn main() {
    let args: Vec<String> = env::args().collect();

    let (query, filename) = parse_config(&args);

    // --snip--
}

fn parse_config(args: &[String]) -> (&str, &str) {
    let query = &args[1];
    let filename = &args[2];

    (query, filename)
}
```

Listing 12-5: Extracting a parse_config function from main

We're still collecting the command line arguments into a vector, but instead of assigning the argument value at index 1 to the variable query and the argument value at index 2 to the variable filename within the main function, we pass the whole vector to the parse_config function. The parse_config function then holds the logic that determines which argument goes in which variable and passes the values back to main. We still create the query and filename variables in main, but main no longer has the responsibility of determining how the command line arguments and variables correspond.

This rework may seem like overkill for our small program, but we're refactoring in small, incremental steps. After making this change, run the program again to verify that the argument parsing still works. It's good to check your progress often to help identify the cause of problems when they occur.

Grouping Configuration Values

We can take another small step to improve the parse_config function further. At the moment, we're returning a tuple, but then we immediately break that tuple into individual parts again. This is a sign that perhaps we don't have the right abstraction yet.

Another indicator that shows there's room for improvement is the config part of parse_config, which implies that the two values we return are related and are both part of one configuration value. We're not currently conveying this meaning in the structure of the data other than by grouping the two values into a tuple; we could put the two values into one struct and give each of the struct fields a meaningful name. Doing so will make it easier for future maintainers of this code to understand how the different values relate to each other and what their purpose is.

NOTE   *Some people call this anti-pattern of using primitive values when a complex type would be more appropriate* primitive obsession.

Listing 12-6 shows the improvements to the parse_config function.

src/main.rs

```
fn main() {
    let args: Vec<String> = env::args().collect();

❶ let config = parse_config(&args);

    println!("Searching for {}", config.query❷);
    println!("In file {}", config.filename❸);

    let mut f = File::open(config.filename❹).expect("file not found");

    // --snip--
}

❺ struct Config {
    query: String,
    filename: String,
}

❻ fn parse_config(args: &[String]) -> Config {
    ❼ let query = args[1].clone();
    ❽ let filename = args[2].clone();

    Config { query, filename }
}
```

Listing 12-6: Refactoring parse_config to return an instance of a Config struct

We've added a struct named Config defined to have fields named query and filename ❺. The signature of parse_config now indicates that it returns a Config value ❻. In the body of parse_config, where we used to return string slices that reference String values in args, we now define Config to contain owned String values. The args variable in main is the owner of the argument values and is only letting the parse_config function borrow them, which means we'd violate Rust's borrowing rules if Config tried to take ownership of the values in args.

We could manage the String data in a number of different ways, but the easiest, though somewhat inefficient, route is to call the clone method on the values ❼❽. This will make a full copy of the data for the Config instance to own, which takes more time and memory than storing a reference to the string data. However, cloning the data also makes our code very straightforward because we don't have to manage the lifetimes of the references; in this circumstance, giving up a little performance to gain simplicity is a worthwhile trade-off.

> **THE TRADE-OFFS OF USING CLONE**
>
> There's a tendency among many Rustaceans to avoid using clone to fix ownership problems because of its runtime cost. In Chapter 13, you'll learn how to use more efficient methods in this type of situation. But for now, it's okay to copy a few strings to continue making progress because you'll make these copies only once and your filename and query string are very small. It's better to have a working program that's a bit inefficient than to try to hyperoptimize code on your first pass. As you become more experienced with Rust, it'll be easier to start with the most efficient solution, but for now, it's perfectly acceptable to call clone.

We've updated main so it places the instance of Config returned by parse_config into a variable named config ❶, and we updated the code that previously used the separate query and filename variables so it now uses the fields on the Config struct instead ❷❸❹.

Now our code more clearly conveys that query and filename are related and that their purpose is to configure how the program will work. Any code that uses these values knows to find them in the config instance in the fields named for their purpose.

Creating a Constructor for Config

So far, we've extracted the logic responsible for parsing the command line arguments from main and placed it in the parse_config function. Doing so helped us to see that the query and filename values were related and that relationship should be conveyed in our code. We then added a Config struct to name the related purpose of query and filename and to be able to return the values' names as struct field names from the parse_config function.

So now that the purpose of the parse_config function is to create a Config instance, we can change parse_config from a plain function to a function named new that is associated with the Config struct. Making this change will make the code more idiomatic. We can create instances of types in the standard library, such as String, by calling String::new. Similarly, by changing parse_config into a new function associated with Config, we'll be able to create instances of Config by calling Config::new. Listing 12-7 shows the changes we need to make.

```
fn main() {
    let args: Vec<String> = env::args().collect();

❶   let config = Config::new(&args);

    // --snip--
}

// --snip--

❷ impl Config {
❸   fn new(args: &[String]) -> Config {
        let query = args[1].clone();
        let filename = args[2].clone();

        Config { query, filename }
    }
}
```

Listing 12-7: Changing parse_config into Config::new

We've updated main where we were calling parse_config to instead call Config::new ❶. We've changed the name of parse_config to new ❸ and moved it within an impl block ❷, which associates the new function with Config. Try compiling this code again to make sure it works.

Fixing the Error Handling

Now we'll work on fixing our error handling. Recall that attempting to access the values in the args vector at index 1 or index 2 will cause the program to panic if the vector contains fewer than three items. Try running the program without any arguments; it will look like this:

```
$ cargo run
   Compiling minigrep v0.1.0 (file:///projects/minigrep)
    Finished dev [unoptimized + debuginfo] target(s) in 0.0 secs
     Running `target/debug/minigrep`
thread 'main' panicked at 'index out of bounds: the len is 1
but the index is 1', src/main.rs:29:21
note: Run with `RUST_BACKTRACE=1` for a backtrace.
```

The line index out of bounds: the len is 1 but the index is 1 is an error message intended for programmers. It won't help our end users understand what happened and what they should do instead. Let's fix that now.

Improving the Error Message

In Listing 12-8, we add a check in the new function that will verify that the slice is long enough before accessing index 1 and 2. If the slice isn't long enough, the program panics and displays a better error message than the index out of bounds message.

```
// --snip--
fn new(args: &[String]) -> Config {
    if args.len() < 3 {
        panic!("not enough arguments");
    }
    // --snip--
```

Listing 12-8: Adding a check for the number of arguments

This code is similar to the Guess::new function we wrote in Listing 9-9, where we called panic! when the value argument was out of the range of valid values. Instead of checking for a range of values here, we're checking that the length of args is at least 3 and the rest of the function can operate under the assumption that this condition has been met. If args has fewer than three items, this condition will be true, and we call the panic! macro to end the program immediately.

With these extra few lines of code in new, let's run the program without any arguments again to see what the error looks like now:

```
$ cargo run
   Compiling minigrep v0.1.0 (file:///projects/minigrep)
    Finished dev [unoptimized + debuginfo] target(s) in 0.0 secs
     Running `target/debug/minigrep`
thread 'main' panicked at 'not enough arguments', src/main.rs:30:12
note: Run with `RUST_BACKTRACE=1` for a backtrace.
```

This output is better: we now have a reasonable error message. However, we also have extraneous information we don't want to give to our users. Perhaps using the technique we used in Listing 9-9 isn't the best to use here: a call to panic! is more appropriate for a programming problem than a usage problem, as discussed in Chapter 9. Instead, we can use the other technique you learned about in Chapter 9—returning a Result that indicates either success or an error.

Returning a Result from new Instead of Calling panic!

We can instead return a Result value that will contain a Config instance in the successful case and will describe the problem in the error case. When Config::new is communicating to main, we can use the Result type to signal there was a problem. Then we can change main to convert an Err variant into a more practical error for our users without the surrounding text about thread 'main' and RUST_BACKTRACE that a call to panic! causes.

Listing 12-9 shows the changes we need to make to the return value of Config::new and the body of the function needed to return a Result. Note that this won't compile until we update main as well, which we'll do in the next listing.

```
impl Config {
    fn new(args: &[String]) -> Result<Config, &'static str> {
        if args.len() < 3 {
            return Err("not enough arguments");
        }
```

```
        let query = args[1].clone();
        let filename = args[2].clone();

        Ok(Config { query, filename })
    }
}
```

Listing 12-9: Returning a Result from Config::new

Our new function now returns a Result with a Config instance in the success case and a &'static str in the error case. Recall from "The Static Lifetime" on page 198 that &'static str is the type of string literals, which is our error message type for now.

We've made two changes in the body of the new function: instead of calling panic! when the user doesn't pass enough arguments, we now return an Err value, and we've wrapped the Config return value in an Ok. These changes make the function conform to its new type signature.

Returning an Err value from Config::new allows the main function to handle the Result value returned from the new function and exit the process more cleanly in the error case.

Calling Config::new and Handling Errors

To handle the error case and print a user-friendly message, we need to update main to handle the Result being returned by Config::new, as shown in Listing 12-10. We'll also take the responsibility of exiting the command line tool with a nonzero error code from panic! and implement it by hand. A nonzero exit status is a convention to signal to the process that called our program that the program exited with an error state.

src/main.rs

```
❶ use std::process;

fn main() {
    let args: Vec<String> = env::args().collect();

❷   let config = Config::new(&args).unwrap_or_else(❸|err❹| {
❺       println!("Problem parsing arguments: {}", err);
❻       process::exit(1);
    });

    // --snip--
```

Listing 12-10: Exiting with an error code if creating a new Config fails

In this listing, we've used a method we haven't covered before: unwrap_or_else, which is defined on Result<T, E> by the standard library ❷. Using unwrap_or_else allows us to define some custom, non-panic! error handling. If the Result is an Ok value, this method's behavior is similar to unwrap: it returns the inner value Ok is wrapping. However, if the value is an Err value, this method calls the code in the *closure*, which is an anonymous function we define and pass as an argument to unwrap_or_else ❸. We'll cover closures in more detail in Chapter 13. For now, you just need to know that unwrap_or_else will pass the inner value of the Err, which in this case is the static string not enough arguments that we added in Listing 12-9, to our closure in the argument err that appears between the vertical pipes ❹. The code in the closure can then use the err value when it runs.

We've added a new use line to import process from the standard library ❶. The code in the closure that will be run in the error case is only two lines: we print the err value ❺ and then call process::exit ❻. The process::exit function will stop the program immediately and return the number that was passed as the exit status code. This is similar to the panic!-based handling we used in Listing 12-8, but we no longer get all the extra output. Let's try it:

```
$ cargo run
   Compiling minigrep v0.1.0 (file:///projects/minigrep)
    Finished dev [unoptimized + debuginfo] target(s) in 0.48 secs
     Running `target/debug/minigrep`
Problem parsing arguments: not enough arguments
```

Great! This output is much friendlier for our users.

Extracting Logic from main

Now that we've finished refactoring the configuration parsing, let's turn to the program's logic. As we stated in "Separation of Concerns for Binary Projects" on page 233, we'll extract a function named run that will hold all the logic currently in the main function that isn't involved with setting up configuration or handling errors. When we're done, main will be concise and easy to verify by inspection, and we'll be able to write tests for all the other logic.

Listing 12-11 shows the extracted run function. For now, we're just making the small, incremental improvement of extracting the function. We're still defining the function in *src/main.rs*.

src/main.rs

```rust
fn main() {
    // --snip--

    println!("Searching for {}", config.query);
    println!("In file {}", config.filename);

    run(config);
}

fn run(config: Config) {
    let mut f = File::open(config.filename).expect("file not found");

    let mut contents = String::new();
    f.read_to_string(&mut contents)
        .expect("something went wrong reading the file");

    println!("With text:\n{}", contents);
}

// --snip--
```

Listing 12-11: Extracting a run function containing the rest of the program logic

The run function now contains all the remaining logic from main, starting from reading the file. The run function takes the Config instance as an argument.

Returning Errors from the run Function

With the remaining program logic separated into the run function, we can improve the error handling, as we did with Config::new in Listing 12-9. Instead of allowing the program to panic by calling expect, the run function will return a Result<T, E> when something goes wrong. This will let us further consolidate into main the logic around handling errors in a user-friendly way. Listing 12-12 shows the changes we need to make to the signature and body of run.

src/main.rs

```
❶ use std::error::Error;

// --snip--

❷ fn run(config: Config) -> Result<(), Box<Error>> {
       let mut f = File::open(config.filename)?❸;

       let mut contents = String::new();
       f.read_to_string(&mut contents)?❹;

       println!("With text:\n{}", contents);

    ❺ Ok(())
   }
```

Listing 12-12: Changing the run function to return Result

We've made three significant changes here. First, we changed the return type of the run function to Result<(), Box<Error>> ❷. This function previously returned the unit type, (), and we keep that as the value returned in the Ok case.

For the error type, we used the *trait object* Box<Error> (and we've brought std::error::Error into scope with a use statement at the top ❶). We'll cover trait objects in Chapter 17. For now, just know that Box<Error> means the function will return a type that implements the Error trait, but we don't have to specify what particular type the return value will be. This gives us flexibility to return error values that may be of different types in different error cases.

Second, we've removed the calls to expect in favor of the ? operator ❸❹, as we talked about in Chapter 9. Rather than panic! on an error, the ? operator will return the error value from the current function for the caller to handle.

Third, the run function now returns an Ok value in the success case ❺. We've declared the run function's success type as () in the signature, which means we need to wrap the unit type value in the Ok value. This Ok(()) syntax might look a bit strange at first, but using () like this is the idiomatic way to indicate that we're calling run for its side effects only; it doesn't return a value we need.

When you run this code, it will compile but will display a warning:

```
warning: unused `std::result::Result` which must be used
  --> src/main.rs:18:5
   |
18 |     run(config);
   |     ^^^^^^^^^^^^
= note: #[warn(unused_must_use)] on by default
```

Rust tells us that our code ignored the Result value and the Result value might indicate that an error occurred. But we're not checking to see whether or not there was an error, and the compiler reminds us that we probably meant to have some error-handling code here! Let's rectify that problem now.

Handling Errors Returned from run in main

We'll check for errors and handle them using a technique similar to the one we used with Config::new in Listing 12-10, but with a slight difference:

src/main.rs
```
fn main() {
    // --snip--

    println!("Searching for {}", config.query);
    println!("In file {}", config.filename);

    if let Err(e) = run(config) {
        println!("Application error: {}", e);

        process::exit(1);
    }
}
```

We use if let rather than unwrap_or_else to check whether run returns an Err value and call process::exit(1) if it does. The run function doesn't return a value that we want to unwrap in the same way that Config::new returns the Config instance. Because run returns () in the success case, we only care about detecting an error, so we don't need unwrap_or_else to return the unwrapped value because it would only be ().

The bodies of the if let and the unwrap_or_else functions are the same in both cases: we print the error and exit.

Splitting Code into a Library Crate

Our minigrep project is looking good so far! Now we'll split the *src/main.rs* file and put some code into the *src/lib.rs* file so we can test it and have a *src/main.rs* file with fewer responsibilities.

Let's move all the code that isn't the main function from *src/main.rs* to *src/lib.rs*:

- The run function definition
- The relevant use statements

- The definition of `Config`
- The `Config::new` function definition

The contents of *src/lib.rs* should have the signatures shown in Listing 12-13 (we've omitted the bodies of the functions for brevity). Note that this won't compile until we modify *src/main.rs* in Listing 12-14.

src/lib.rs

```
use std::error::Error;
use std::fs::File;
use std::io::prelude::*;

pub struct Config {
    pub query: String,
    pub filename: String,
}

impl Config {
    pub fn new(args: &[String]) -> Result<Config, &'static str> {
        // --snip--
    }
}

pub fn run(config: Config) -> Result<(), Box<Error>> {
    // --snip--
}
```

Listing 12-13: Moving Config and run into src/lib.rs

We've made liberal use of the `pub` keyword: on `Config`, on its fields and its new method, and on the run function. We now have a library crate that has a public API that we can test!

Now we need to bring the code we moved to *src/lib.rs* into the scope of the binary crate in *src/main.rs*, as shown in Listing 12-14.

src/main.rs

```
extern crate minigrep;

use std::env;
use std::process;

use minigrep::Config;

fn main() {
    // --snip--
    if let Err(e) = minigrep::run(config) {
        // --snip--
    }
}
```

Listing 12-14: Bringing the minigrep crate into the scope of src/main.rs

To bring the library crate into the binary crate, we use extern crate minigrep. Then we add a use minigrep::Config line to bring the Config type into scope, and we prefix the run function with our crate name. Now all the functionality should be connected and should work. Run the program with cargo run and make sure everything works correctly.

Whew! That was a lot of work, but we've set ourselves up for success in the future. Now it's much easier to handle errors, and we've made the code more modular. Almost all of our work will be done in *src/lib.rs* from here on out.

Let's take advantage of this newfound modularity by doing something that would have been difficult with the old code but is easy with the new code: we'll write some tests!

Developing the Library's Functionality with Test-Driven Development

Now that we've extracted the logic into *src/lib.rs* and left the argument collecting and error handling in *src/main.rs*, it's much easier to write tests for the core functionality of our code. We can call functions directly with various arguments and check return values without having to call our binary from the command line. Feel free to write some tests for the functionality in the Config::new and run functions on your own.

In this section, we'll add the searching logic to the minigrep program by using the test-driven development (TDD) process. This software development technique follows these steps:

1. Write a test that fails and run it to make sure it fails for the reason you expect.
2. Write or modify just enough code to make the new test pass.
3. Refactor the code you just added or changed and make sure the tests continue to pass.
4. Repeat from step 1!

This process is just one of many ways to write software, but TDD can help drive code design as well. Writing the test before you write the code that makes the test pass helps to maintain high test coverage throughout the process.

We'll test drive the implementation of the functionality that will actually do the searching for the query string in the file contents and produce a list of lines that match the query. We'll add this functionality in a function called search.

Writing a Failing Test

Because we don't need them anymore, let's remove the println! statements from *src/lib.rs* and *src/main.rs* that we used to check the program's behavior. Then, in *src/lib.rs*, we'll add a test module with a test function, as we did in Chapter 11. The test function specifies the behavior we want the search function to have: it will take a query and the text to search for the query in, and it will return only the lines from the text that contain the query. Listing 12-15 shows this test, which won't compile yet.

src/lib.rs

```
#[cfg(test)]
mod test {
    use super::*;

    #[test]
    fn one_result() {
        let query = "duct";
        let contents = "\
Rust:
safe, fast, productive.
Pick three.";

        assert_eq!(
            vec!["safe, fast, productive."],
            search(query, contents)
        );
    }
}
```

Listing 12-15: Creating a failing test for the search function we wish we had

This test searches for the string "duct". The text we're searching is three lines, only one of which contains "duct". We assert that the value returned from the search function contains only the line we expect.

We aren't able to run this test and watch it fail because the test doesn't even compile: the search function doesn't exist yet! So now we'll add just enough code to get the test to compile and run by adding a definition of the search function that always returns an empty vector, as shown in Listing 12-16. Then the test should compile and fail because an empty vector doesn't match a vector containing the line "safe, fast, productive."

src/lib.rs

```
pub fn search<'a>(query: &str, contents: &'a str) -> Vec<&'a str> {
    vec![]
}
```

Listing 12-16: Defining just enough of the search function so our test will compile

Notice that we need an explicit lifetime 'a defined in the signature of search and used with the contents argument and the return value. Recall in Chapter 10 that the lifetime parameters specify which argument lifetime is connected to the lifetime of the return value. In this case, we indicate that the returned vector should contain string slices that reference slices of the argument contents (rather than the argument query).

In other words, we tell Rust that the data returned by the search function will live as long as the data passed into the search function in the contents argument. This is important! The data referenced *by* a slice needs to be valid for the reference to be valid; if the compiler assumes we're making string slices of query rather than contents, it will do its safety checking incorrectly.

If we forget the lifetime annotations and try to compile this function, we'll get this error:

```
error[E0106]: missing lifetime specifier
 --> src/lib.rs:5:51
  |
5 | pub fn search(query: &str, contents: &str) -> Vec<&str> {
  |                                                   ^ expected lifetime
parameter
  |
  = help: this function's return type contains a borrowed value, but the
  signature does not say whether it is borrowed from `query` or `contents`
```

Rust can't possibly know which of the two arguments we need, so we need to tell it. Because contents is the argument that contains all of our text and we want to return the parts of that text that match, we know contents is the argument that should be connected to the return value using the lifetime syntax.

Other programming languages don't require you to connect arguments to return values in the signature. Although this might seem strange, it will get easier over time. You might want to compare this example with "Validating References with Lifetimes" on page 187.

Now let's run the test:

```
$ cargo test
   Compiling minigrep v0.1.0 (file:///projects/minigrep)
--warnings--
    Finished dev [unoptimized + debuginfo] target(s) in 0.43 secs
     Running target/debug/deps/minigrep-abcabcabc

running 1 test
test test::one_result ... FAILED

failures:

---- test::one_result stdout ----
        thread 'test::one_result' panicked at 'assertion failed: `(left ==
right)`
left: `["safe, fast, productive."]`,
right: `[]`)', src/lib.rs:48:8
note: Run with `RUST_BACKTRACE=1` for a backtrace.


failures:
    test::one_result

test result: FAILED. 0 passed; 1 failed; 0 ignored; 0 measured; 0 filtered out

error: test failed, to rerun pass '--lib'
```

Great, the test fails, exactly as we expected. Let's get the test to pass!

Writing Code to Pass the Test

Currently, our test is failing because we always return an empty vector. To fix that and implement search, our program needs to follow these steps:

1. Iterate through each line of the contents.
2. Check whether the line contains our query string.
3. If it does, add it to the list of values we're returning.
4. If it doesn't, do nothing.
5. Return the list of results that match.

Let's work through each step, starting with iterating through lines.

Iterating Through Lines with the lines Method

Rust has a helpful method to handle line-by-line iteration of strings, conveniently named lines, that works as shown in Listing 12-17. Note this won't compile yet.

src/lib.rs

```
pub fn search<'a>(query: &str, contents: &'a str) -> Vec<&'a str> {
    for line in contents.lines() {
        // do something with line
    }
}
```

Listing 12-17: Iterating through each line in contents

The lines method returns an iterator. We'll talk about iterators in depth in Chapter 13, but recall that you saw this way of using an iterator in Listing 3-5 on page 55, where we used a for loop with an iterator to run some code on each item in a collection.

Searching Each Line for the Query

Next, we'll check whether the current line contains our query string. Fortunately, strings have a helpful method named contains that does this for us! Add a call to the contains method in the search function, as shown in Listing 12-18. Note this still won't compile yet.

src/lib.rs

```
pub fn search<'a>(query: &str, contents: &'a str) -> Vec<&'a str> {
    for line in contents.lines() {
        if line.contains(query) {
            // do something with line
        }
    }
}
```

Listing 12-18: Adding functionality to see whether the line contains the string in query

Storing Matching Lines

We also need a way to store the lines that contain our query string. For that, we can make a mutable vector before the for loop and call the push method to store a line in the vector. After the for loop, we return the vector, as shown in Listing 12-19.

src/lib.rs

```
pub fn search<'a>(query: &str, contents: &'a str) -> Vec<&'a str> {
    let mut results = Vec::new();

    for line in contents.lines() {
        if line.contains(query) {
            results.push(line);
        }
    }

    results
}
```

Listing 12-19: Storing the lines that match so we can return them

Now the search function should return only the lines that contain query, and our test should pass. Let's run the test:

```
$ cargo test
--snip--
running 1 test
test test::one_result ... ok

test result: ok. 1 passed; 0 failed; 0 ignored; 0 measured; 0 filtered out
```

Our test passed, so we know it works!

At this point, we could consider opportunities for refactoring the implementation of the search function while keeping the tests passing to maintain the same functionality. The code in the search function isn't too bad, but it doesn't take advantage of some useful features of iterators. We'll return to this example in Chapter 13, where we'll explore iterators in detail, and look at how to improve it.

Using the search Function in the run Function

Now that the search function is working and tested, we need to call search from our run function. We need to pass the config.query value and the contents that run reads from the file to the search function. Then run will print each line returned from search:

src/lib.rs

```
pub fn run(config: Config) -> Result<(), Box<Error>> {
    let mut f = File::open(config.filename)?;

    let mut contents = String::new();
    f.read_to_string(&mut contents)?;
```

```
    for line in search(&config.query, &contents) {
        println!("{}", line);
    }

    Ok(())
}
```

We're still using a for loop to return each line from search and print it.

Now the entire program should work! Let's try it out, first with a word that should return exactly one line from the Emily Dickinson poem, "frog":

```
$ cargo run frog poem.txt
   Compiling minigrep v0.1.0 (file:///projects/minigrep)
    Finished dev [unoptimized + debuginfo] target(s) in 0.38 secs
     Running `target/debug/minigrep frog poem.txt`
How public, like a frog
```

Cool! Now let's try a word that will match multiple lines, like "body":

```
$ cargo run body poem.txt
    Finished dev [unoptimized + debuginfo] target(s) in 0.0 secs
     Running `target/debug/minigrep body poem.txt`
I'm nobody! Who are you?
Are you nobody, too?
How dreary to be somebody!
```

And finally, let's make sure that we don't get any lines when we search for a word that isn't anywhere in the poem, such as "monomorphization":

```
$ cargo run monomorphization poem.txt
    Finished dev [unoptimized + debuginfo] target(s) in 0.0 secs
     Running `target/debug/minigrep monomorphization poem.txt`
```

Excellent! We've built our own mini version of a classic tool and learned a lot about how to structure applications. We've also learned a bit about file input and output, lifetimes, testing, and command line parsing.

To round out this project, we'll briefly demonstrate how to work with environment variables and how to print to standard error, both of which are useful when you're writing command line programs.

Working with Environment Variables

We'll improve minigrep by adding an extra feature: an option for case-insensitive searching that the user can turn on via an environment variable. We could make this feature a command line option and require that users enter it each time they want it to apply, but instead we'll use an environment variable. Doing so allows our users to set the environment variable once and have all their searches be case insensitive in that terminal session.

Writing a Failing Test for the Case-Insensitive search Function

We want to add a new search_case_insensitive function that we'll call when the environment variable is on. We'll continue to follow the TDD process, so the first step is again to write a failing test. We'll add a new test for the new search_case_insensitive function and rename our old test from one_result to case_sensitive to clarify the differences between the two tests, as shown in Listing 12-20.

src/lib.rs

```
#[cfg(test)]
mod test {
    use super::*;

    #[test]
    fn case_sensitive() {
        let query = "duct";
        let contents = "\
Rust:
safe, fast, productive.
Pick three.
Duct tape.";

        assert_eq!(
            vec!["safe, fast, productive."],
            search(query, contents)
        );
    }

    #[test]
    fn case_insensitive() {
        let query = "rUsT";
        let contents = "\
Rust:
safe, fast, productive.
Pick three.
Trust me.";

        assert_eq!(
            vec!["Rust:", "Trust me."],
            search_case_insensitive(query, contents)
        );
    }
}
```

Listing 12-20: Adding a new failing test for the case-insensitive function we're about to add

Note that we've edited the old test's contents too. We've added a new line with the text "Duct tape." using a capital D that shouldn't match the query "duct" when we're searching in a case-sensitive manner. Changing the old test in this way helps ensure that we don't accidentally break the case-sensitive search functionality that we've already implemented. This test should pass now and should continue to pass as we work on the case-insensitive search.

The new test for the case-*insensitive* search uses "rUsT" as its query. In the search_case_insensitive function we're about to add, the query "rUsT" should match the line containing "Rust:" with a capital R and match the line "Trust me." even though both have different casing than the query. This is our failing test, and it will fail to compile because we haven't yet defined the search_case_insensitive function. Feel free to add a skeleton implementation that always returns an empty vector, similar to the way we did for the search function in Listing 12-16 to see the test compile and fail.

Implementing the search_case_insensitive Function

The search_case_insensitive function, shown in Listing 12-21, will be almost the same as the search function. The only difference is that we'll lowercase the query and each line so whatever the case of the input arguments, they'll be the same case when we check whether the line contains the query.

src/lib.rs

```
pub fn search_case_insensitive<'a>(query: &str, contents: &'a str) -> Vec<&'a
str> {
❶ let query = query.to_lowercase();
   let mut results = Vec::new();

   for line in contents.lines() {
       if line.to_lowercase()❷.contains(&query❸) {
           results.push(line);
       }
   }

   results
}
```

Listing 12-21: Defining the search_case_insensitive function to lowercase the query and the line before comparing them

First, we lowercase the query string and store it in a shadowed variable with the same name ❶. Calling to_lowercase on the query is necessary so no matter whether the user's query is "rust", "RUST", "Rust", or "rUsT", we'll treat the query as if it were "rust" and be insensitive to the case.

Note that query is now a String rather than a string slice, because calling to_lowercase creates new data rather than referencing existing data. Say the query is "rUsT", as an example: that string slice doesn't contain a lowercase u or t for us to use, so we have to allocate a new String containing "rust". When we pass query as an argument to the contains method now, we need to add an ampersand ❸ because the signature of contains is defined to take a string slice.

Next, we add a call to to_lowercase on each line before we check whether it contains query to lowercase all characters ❷. Now that we've converted line and query to lowercase, we'll find matches no matter what the case of the query is.

Let's see if this implementation passes the tests:

```
running 2 tests
test test::case_insensitive ... ok
test test::case_sensitive ... ok

test result: ok. 2 passed; 0 failed; 0 ignored; 0 measured; 0 filtered out
```

Great! They passed. Now, let's call the new search_case_insensitive function from the run function. First, we'll add a configuration option to the Config struct to switch between case-sensitive and case-insensitive search. Adding this field will cause compiler errors because we aren't initializing this field anywhere yet:

src/lib.rs

```
pub struct Config {
    pub query: String,
    pub filename: String,
    pub case_sensitive: bool,
}
```

Note that we added the case_sensitive field that holds a Boolean. Next, we need the run function to check the case_sensitive field's value and use that to decide whether to call the search function or the search_case_insensitive function, as shown in Listing 12-22. Note this still won't compile yet.

src/lib.rs

```
pub fn run(config: Config) -> Result<(), Box<Error>> {
    let mut f = File::open(config.filename)?;

    let mut contents = String::new();
    f.read_to_string(&mut contents)?;

    let results = if config.case_sensitive {
        search(&config.query, &contents)
    } else {
        search_case_insensitive(&config.query, &contents)
    };

    for line in results {
        println!("{}", line);
    }

    Ok(())
}
```

Listing 12-22: Calling either search or search_case_insensitive based on the value in config.case_sensitive

Finally, we need to check for the environment variable. The functions for working with environment variables are in the env module in the standard library, so we want to bring that module into scope with a use std::env;

line at the top of *src/lib.rs*. Then we'll use the var function from the env module to check for an environment variable named CASE_INSENSITIVE, as shown in Listing 12-23.

src/lib.rs

```
use std::env;

// --snip--

impl Config {
    pub fn new(args: &[String]) -> Result<Config, &'static str> {
        if args.len() < 3 {
            return Err("not enough arguments");
        }

        let query = args[1].clone();
        let filename = args[2].clone();

        let case_sensitive = env::var("CASE_INSENSITIVE").is_err();

        Ok(Config { query, filename, case_sensitive })
    }
}
```

Listing 12-23: Checking for an environment variable named CASE_INSENSITIVE

Here, we create a new variable case_sensitive. To set its value, we call the env::var function and pass it the name of the CASE_INSENSITIVE environment variable. The env::var function returns a Result that will be the successful Ok variant that contains the value of the environment variable if the environment variable is set. It will return the Err variant if the environment variable is not set.

We're using the is_err method on the Result to check whether it's an error and therefore unset, which means it *should* do a case-sensitive search. If the CASE_INSENSITIVE environment variable is set to anything, is_err will return false and the program will perform a case-insensitive search. We don't care about the *value* of the environment variable, just whether it's set or unset, so we're checking is_err rather than using unwrap, expect, or any of the other methods we've seen on Result.

We pass the value in the case_sensitive variable to the Config instance so the run function can read that value and decide whether to call search or search_case_insensitive, as we implemented in Listing 12-22.

Let's give it a try! First, we'll run our program without the environment variable set and with the query to, which should match any line that contains the word "to" in all lowercase:

```
$ cargo run to poem.txt
   Compiling minigrep v0.1.0 (file:///projects/minigrep)
    Finished dev [unoptimized + debuginfo] target(s) in 0.0 secs
     Running `target/debug/minigrep to poem.txt`
Are you nobody, too?
How dreary to be somebody!
```

Looks like that still works! Now, let's run the program with CASE
_INSENSITIVE set to 1 but with the same query to.

If you're using PowerShell, you will need to set the environment variable
and run the program in two commands rather than one:

```
$ $env:CASE_INSENSITIVE=1
$ cargo run to poem.txt
```

We should get lines that contain "to" that might have uppercase letters:

```
$ CASE_INSENSITIVE=1 cargo run to poem.txt
    Finished dev [unoptimized + debuginfo] target(s) in 0.0 secs
     Running `target/debug/minigrep to poem.txt`
Are you nobody, too?
How dreary to be somebody!
To tell your name the livelong day
To an admiring bog!
```

Excellent, we also got lines containing "To"! Our minigrep program can
now do case-insensitive searching controlled by an environment variable.
Now you know how to manage options set using either command line arguments or environment variables.

Some programs allow arguments *and* environment variables for the same
configuration. In those cases, the programs decide that one or the other
takes precedence. For another exercise on your own, try controlling case
insensitivity through either a command line argument or an environment
variable. Decide whether the command line argument or the environment
variable should take precedence if the program is run with one set to case
sensitive and one set to case insensitive.

The std::env module contains many more useful features for dealing with
environment variables: check out its documentation to see what is available.

Writing Error Messages to Standard Error Instead of Standard Output

At the moment, we're writing all of our output to the terminal using the
println! function. Most terminals provide two kinds of output: *standard
output* (stdout) for general information and *standard error* (stderr) for error
messages. This distinction enables users to choose to direct the successful
output of a program to a file but still print error messages to the screen.

The println! function is only capable of printing to standard output, so
we have to use something else to print to standard error.

Checking Where Errors Are Written

First, let's observe how the content printed by minigrep is currently being
written to standard output, including any error messages we want to write
to standard error instead. We'll do that by redirecting the standard output

stream to a file while also intentionally causing an error. We won't redirect the standard error stream, so any content sent to standard error will continue to display on the screen.

Command line programs are expected to send error messages to the standard error stream so we can still see error messages on the screen even if we redirect the standard output stream to a file. Our program is not currently well-behaved: we're about to see that it saves the error message output to a file instead!

The way to demonstrate this behavior is by running the program with > and the filename, *output.txt*, that we want to redirect the standard output stream to. We won't pass any arguments, which should cause an error:

```
$ cargo run > output.txt
```

The > syntax tells the shell to write the contents of standard output to *output.txt* instead of the screen. We didn't see the error message we were expecting printed to the screen, so that means it must have ended up in the file. This is what *output.txt* contains:

```
Problem parsing arguments: not enough arguments
```

Yup, our error message is being printed to standard output. It's much more useful for error messages like this to be printed to standard error so only data from a successful run ends up in the file. We'll change that.

Printing Errors to Standard Error

We'll use the code in Listing 12-24 to change how error messages are printed. Because of the refactoring we did earlier in this chapter, all the code that prints error messages is in one function, main. The standard library provides the eprintln! macro that prints to the standard error stream, so let's change the two places we were calling println! to print errors to use eprintln! instead.

src/main.rs
```
fn main() {
    let args: Vec<String> = env::args().collect();

    let config = Config::new(&args).unwrap_or_else(|err| {
        eprintln!("Problem parsing arguments: {}", err);
        process::exit(1);
    });

    if let Err(e) = minigrep::run(config) {
        eprintln!("Application error: {}", e);

        process::exit(1);
    }
}
```

Listing 12-24: Writing error messages to standard error instead of standard output using eprintln!

After changing println! to eprintln!, let's run the program again in the same way, without any arguments and redirecting standard output with >:

```
$ cargo run > output.txt
Problem parsing arguments: not enough arguments
```

Now we see the error onscreen and *output.txt* contains nothing, which is the behavior we expect of command line programs.

Let's run the program again with arguments that don't cause an error but still redirect standard output to a file, like so:

```
$ cargo run to poem.txt > output.txt
```

We won't see any output to the terminal, and *output.txt* will contain our results:

output.txt
```
Are you nobody, too?
How dreary to be somebody!
```

This demonstrates that we're now using standard output for successful output and standard error for error output as appropriate.

Summary

This chapter recapped some of the major concepts you've learned so far and covered how to perform common I/O operations in Rust. By using command line arguments, files, environment variables, and the eprintln! macro for printing errors, you're now prepared to write command line applications. By using the concepts in previous chapters, your code will be well organized, store data effectively in the appropriate data structures, handle errors nicely, and be well tested.

Next, we'll explore some Rust features that were influenced by functional languages: closures and iterators.

13

FUNCTIONAL LANGUAGE FEATURES: ITERATORS AND CLOSURES

Rust's design has taken inspiration from many existing languages and techniques, and one significant influence is *functional programming*. Programming in a functional style often includes using functions as values by passing them in arguments, returning them from other functions, assigning them to variables for later execution, and so forth.

In this chapter, we won't debate the issue of what functional programming is or isn't but will instead discuss some features of Rust that are similar to features in many languages often referred to as functional.

More specifically, we'll cover:

- *Closures*, a function-like construct you can store in a variable
- *Iterators*, a way of processing a series of elements

- How to use these two features to improve the I/O project in Chapter 12
- The performance of these two features (Spoiler alert: they're faster than you might think!)

Other Rust features, such as pattern matching and enums, which we've covered in other chapters, are influenced by the functional style as well. Mastering closures and iterators is an important part of writing idiomatic, fast Rust code, so we'll devote this entire chapter to them.

Closures: Anonymous Functions That Can Capture Their Environment

Rust's closures are anonymous functions you can save in a variable or pass as arguments to other functions. You can create the closure in one place and then call the closure to evaluate it in a different context. Unlike functions, closures can capture values from the scope in which they're called. We'll demonstrate how these closure features allow for code reuse and behavior customization.

Creating an Abstraction of Behavior with Closures

Let's work on an example of a situation in which it's useful to store a closure to be executed later. Along the way, we'll talk about the syntax of closures, type inference, and traits.

Consider this hypothetical situation: we work at a startup that's making an app to generate custom exercise workout plans. The backend is written in Rust, and the algorithm that generates the workout plan takes into account many factors, such as the app user's age, body mass index, exercise preferences, recent workouts, and an intensity number they specify. The actual algorithm used isn't important in this example; what's important is that this calculation takes a few seconds. We want to call this algorithm only when we need to and only call it once so we don't make the user wait more than necessary.

We'll simulate calling this hypothetical algorithm with the function simulated_expensive_calculation shown in Listing 13-1, which will print calculating slowly..., wait for 2 seconds, and then return whatever number we passed in.

src/main.rs

```
use std::thread;
use std::time::Duration;

fn simulated_expensive_calculation(intensity: u32) -> u32 {
    println!("calculating slowly...");
    thread::sleep(Duration::from_secs(2));
    intensity
}
```

Listing 13-1: A function to stand in for a hypothetical calculation that takes about 2 seconds to run

Next is the main function, which contains the parts of the workout app important for this example. This function represents the code that the app will call when a user asks for a workout plan. Because the interaction with the app's frontend isn't relevant to the use of closures, we'll hardcode values representing inputs to our program and print the outputs.

The required inputs are these:

- An intensity number from the user, which is specified when they request a workout to indicate whether they want a low-intensity workout or a high-intensity workout

- A random number that will generate some variety in the workout plans

The output will be the recommended workout plan. Listing 13-2 shows the main function we'll use.

src/main.rs

```
fn main() {
    let simulated_user_specified_value = 10;
    let simulated_random_number = 7;

    generate_workout(
        simulated_user_specified_value,
        simulated_random_number
    );
}
```

Listing 13-2: A main function with hardcoded values to simulate user input and random number generation

We've hardcoded the variable simulated_user_specified_value as 10 and the variable simulated_random_number as 7 for simplicity's sake; in an actual program, we'd get the intensity number from the app's frontend, and we'd use the rand crate to generate a random number, as we did in the Guessing Game example in Chapter 2. The main function calls a generate_workout function with the simulated input values.

Now that we have the context, let's get to the algorithm. The function generate_workout in Listing 13-3 contains the business logic of the app that we're most concerned with in this example. The rest of the code changes in this example will be made to this function.

src/main.rs

```
fn generate_workout(intensity: u32, random_number: u32) {
 ❶ if intensity < 25 {
        println!(
            "Today, do {} pushups!",
            simulated_expensive_calculation(intensity)
        );
        println!(
            "Next, do {} situps!",
            simulated_expensive_calculation(intensity)
        );
    } else {
     ❷ if random_number == 3 {
            println!("Take a break today! Remember to stay hydrated!");
```

```
❸ } else {
        println!(
            "Today, run for {} minutes!",
            simulated_expensive_calculation(intensity)
        );
    }
  }
}
```

Listing 13-3: The business logic that prints the workout plans based on the inputs and calls to the simulated_expensive_calculation function

The code in Listing 13-3 has multiple calls to the slow calculation function. The first if block ❶ calls simulated_expensive_calculation twice, the if inside the outer else ❷ doesn't call it at all, and the code inside the second else case ❸ calls it once.

The desired behavior of the generate_workout function is to first check whether the user wants a low-intensity workout (indicated by a number less than 25) or a high-intensity workout (a number of 25 or greater).

Low-intensity workout plans will recommend a number of push-ups and sit-ups based on the complex algorithm we're simulating.

If the user wants a high-intensity workout, there's some additional logic: if the value of the random number generated by the app happens to be 3, the app will recommend a break and hydration. If not, the user will get a number of minutes of running based on the complex algorithm.

This code works the way the business wants it to now, but let's say the data science team decides that we need to make some changes to the way we call the simulated_expensive_calculation function in the future. To simplify the update when those changes happen, we want to refactor this code so it calls the simulated_expensive_calculation function only once. We also want to cut the place where we're currently unnecessarily calling the function twice without adding any other calls to that function in the process. That is, we don't want to call it if the result isn't needed, and we still want to call it only once.

Refactoring Using Functions

We could restructure the workout program in many ways. First, we'll try extracting the duplicated call to the simulated_expensive_calculation function into a variable, as shown in Listing 13-4.

src/main.rs

```
fn generate_workout(intensity: u32, random_number: u32) {
    let expensive_result = simulated_expensive_calculation(intensity);

    if intensity < 25 {
        println!(
            "Today, do {} pushups!",
            expensive_result
        );
        println!(
            "Next, do {} situps!",
            expensive_result
```

```
        );
    } else {
        if random_number == 3 {
            println!("Take a break today! Remember to stay hydrated!");
        } else {
            println!(
                "Today, run for {} minutes!",
                expensive_result
            );
        }
    }
}
```

Listing 13-4: Extracting the calls to simulated_expensive_calculation *to one place and storing the result in the* expensive_result *variable*

This change unifies all the calls to simulated_expensive_calculation and solves the problem of the first if block unnecessarily calling the function twice. Unfortunately, we're now calling this function and waiting for the result in all cases, which includes the inner if block that doesn't use the result value at all.

We want to define code in one place in our program but only *execute* that code where we actually need the result. This is a use case for closures!

Refactoring with Closures to Store Code

Instead of always calling the simulated_expensive_calculation function before the if blocks, we can define a closure and store the *closure* in a variable rather than storing the result of the function call, as shown in Listing 13-5. We can actually move the whole body of simulated_expensive_calculation within the closure we're introducing here.

src/main.rs

```
let expensive_closure = |num| {
    println!("calculating slowly...");
    thread::sleep(Duration::from_secs(2));
    num
};
```

Listing 13-5: Defining a closure and storing it in the expensive_closure *variable*

The closure definition comes after the = to assign it to the variable expensive_closure. To define a closure, we start with a pair of vertical pipes (|), inside which we specify the parameters to the closure; this syntax was chosen because of its similarity to closure definitions in Smalltalk and Ruby. This closure has one parameter named num: if we had more than one parameter, we would separate them with commas, like |param1, param2|.

After the parameters, we place curly brackets that hold the body of the closure—these are optional if the closure body is a single expression. The end of the closure, after the curly brackets, needs a semicolon to complete the let statement. The value returned from the last line in the closure body (num) will be the value returned from the closure when it's called, because that line doesn't end in a semicolon, just as in function bodies.

Note that this let statement means expensive_closure contains the *definition* of an anonymous function, not the *resulting value* of calling the anonymous function. Recall that we're using a closure because we want to define the code to call at one point, store that code, and call it at a later point; the code we want to call is now stored in expensive_closure.

With the closure defined, we can change the code in the if blocks to call the closure to execute the code and get the resulting value. We call a closure like we do a function: we specify the variable name that holds the closure definition and follow it with parentheses containing the argument values we want to use, as shown in Listing 13-6.

src/main.rs

```
fn generate_workout(intensity: u32, random_number: u32) {
    let expensive_closure = |num| {
        println!("calculating slowly...");
        thread::sleep(Duration::from_secs(2));
        num
    };

    if intensity < 25 {
        println!(
            "Today, do {} pushups!",
            expensive_closure(intensity)
        );
        println!(
            "Next, do {} situps!",
            expensive_closure(intensity)
        );
    } else {
        if random_number == 3 {
            println!("Take a break today! Remember to stay hydrated!");
        } else {
            println!(
                "Today, run for {} minutes!",
                expensive_closure(intensity)
            );
        }
    }
}
```

Listing 13-6: Calling the expensive_closure we've defined

Now the expensive calculation is called in only one place, and we're only executing that code where we need the results.

However, we've reintroduced one of the problems from Listing 13-3: we're still calling the closure twice in the first if block, which will call the expensive code twice and make the user wait twice as long as they need to. We could fix this problem by creating a variable local to that if block to hold the result of calling the closure, but closures provide us with another solution. We'll talk about that solution in a bit. But first let's talk about why there aren't type annotations in the closure definition and the traits involved with closures.

Closure Type Inference and Annotation

Closures don't require you to annotate the types of the parameters or the return value like fn functions do. Type annotations are required on functions because they're part of an explicit interface exposed to your users. Defining this interface rigidly is important for ensuring that everyone agrees on what types of values a function uses and returns. But closures aren't used in an exposed interface like this: they're stored in variables and used without naming them and exposing them to users of our library.

Closures are usually short and relevant only within a narrow context rather than in any arbitrary scenario. Within these limited contexts, the compiler is reliably able to infer the types of the parameters and the return type, similar to how it's able to infer the types of most variables.

Making programmers annotate the types in these small, anonymous functions would be annoying and largely redundant with the information the compiler already has available.

As with variables, we can add type annotations if we want to increase explicitness and clarity at the cost of being more verbose than is strictly necessary. Annotating the types for the closure we defined in Listing 13-5 would look like the definition shown in Listing 13-7.

src/main.rs

```
let expensive_closure = |num: u32| -> u32 {
    println!("calculating slowly...");
    thread::sleep(Duration::from_secs(2));
    num
};
```

Listing 13-7: Adding optional type annotations of the parameter and return value types in the closure

With type annotations added, the syntax of closures looks more similar to the syntax of functions. The following is a vertical comparison of the syntax for the definition of a function that adds 1 to its parameter and a closure that has the same behavior. We've added some spaces to line up the relevant parts. This illustrates how closure syntax is similar to function syntax except for the use of pipes and the amount of syntax that is optional:

```
fn  add_one_v1   (x: u32) -> u32 { x + 1 }
let add_one_v2 = |x: u32| -> u32 { x + 1 };
let add_one_v3 = |x|             { x + 1 };
let add_one_v4 = |x|               x + 1  ;
```

The first line shows a function definition, and the second line shows a fully annotated closure definition. The third line removes the type annotations from the closure definition, and the fourth line removes the brackets, which are optional because the closure body has only one expression. These are all valid definitions that will produce the same behavior when they're called.

Closure definitions will have one concrete type inferred for each of their parameters and for their return value. For instance, Listing 13-8 shows the definition of a short closure that just returns the value it receives as a parameter. This closure isn't very useful except for the purposes of this example. Note that we haven't added any type annotations to the definition: if we then try to call the closure twice, using a String as an argument the first time and a u32 the second time, we'll get an error.

src/main.rs

```
let example_closure = |x| x;

let s = example_closure(String::from("hello"));
let n = example_closure(5);
```

Listing 13-8: Attempting to call a closure whose types are inferred with two different types

The compiler gives us this error:

```
error[E0308]: mismatched types
 --> src/main.rs
  |
  | let n = example_closure(5);
  |                         ^ expected struct `std::string::String`, found
integral variable
  |
  = note: expected type `std::string::String`
             found type `{integer}`
```

The first time we call example_closure with the String value, the compiler infers the type of x and the return type of the closure to be String. Those types are then locked into the closure in example_closure, and we get a type error if we try to use a different type with the same closure.

Storing Closures Using Generic Parameters and the Fn Traits

Let's return to our workout generation app. In Listing 13-6, our code was still calling the expensive calculation closure more times than it needed to. One option to solve this issue is to save the result of the expensive closure in a variable for reuse and use the variable in each place we need the result, instead of calling the closure again. However, this method could result in a lot of repeated code.

Fortunately, another solution is available to us. We can create a struct that will hold the closure and the resulting value of calling the closure. The struct will execute the closure only if we need the resulting value, and it will cache the resulting value so the rest of our code doesn't have to be responsible for saving and reusing the result. You may know this pattern as *memoization* or *lazy evaluation.*

To make a struct that holds a closure, we need to specify the type of the closure, because a struct definition needs to know the types of each of its fields. Each closure instance has its own unique anonymous type: that is, even if two closures have the same signature, their types are still considered different. To define structs, enums, or function parameters that use closures, we use generics and trait bounds, as we discussed in Chapter 10.

The Fn traits are provided by the standard library. All closures implement at least one of the traits: Fn, FnMut, or FnOnce. We'll discuss the difference between these traits in "Capturing the Environment with Closures" on page 268; in this example, we can use the Fn trait.

We add types to the Fn trait bound to represent the types of the parameters and return values the closures must have to match this trait bound. In this case, our closure has a parameter of type u32 and returns a u32, so the trait bound we specify is Fn(u32) -> u32.

Listing 13-9 shows the definition of the Cacher struct that holds a closure and an optional result value.

src/main.rs

```
struct Cacher<T>
    where T: Fn(u32) -> u32
{
    calculation: T,
    value: Option<u32>,
}
```

Listing 13-9: Defining a Cacher struct that holds a closure in calculation and an optional result in value

The Cacher struct has a calculation field of the generic type T. The trait bounds on T specify that it's a closure by using the Fn trait. Any closure we want to store in the calculation field must have one u32 parameter (specified within the parentheses after Fn) and must return a u32 (specified after the ->).

NOTE *Functions implement all three of the Fn traits, too. If what we want to do doesn't require capturing a value from the environment, we can use a function rather than a closure where we need something that implements an Fn trait.*

The value field is of type Option<u32>. Before we execute the closure, value will be None. When code using a Cacher asks for the *result* of the closure, the Cacher will execute the closure at that time and store the result within a Some variant in the value field. Then if the code asks for the result of the closure again, instead of executing the closure again, the Cacher will return the result held in the Some variant.

The logic around the value field we've just described is defined in Listing 13-10.

src/main.rs

```
impl<T> Cacher<T>
❶  where T: Fn(u32) -> u32
{
❷    fn new(calculation: T) -> Cacher<T> {
❸        Cacher {
            calculation,
            value: None,
        }
    }

❹    fn value(&mut self, arg: u32) -> u32 {
        match self.value {
```

```
        ❺ Some(v) => v,
        ❻ None => {
                let v = (self.calculation)(arg);
                self.value = Some(v);
                v
            },
        }
    }
}
```

Listing 13-10: The caching logic of Cacher

We want Cacher to manage the struct fields' values rather than letting the calling code potentially change the values in these fields directly, so these fields are private.

The Cacher::new function takes a generic parameter T ❷, which we've defined as having the same trait bound as the Cacher struct ❶. Then Cacher::new returns a Cacher instance ❸ that holds the closure specified in the calculation field and a None value in the value field, because we haven't executed the closure yet.

When the calling code needs the result of evaluating the closure, instead of calling the closure directly, it will call the value method ❹. This method checks whether we already have a resulting value in self.value in a Some; if we do, it returns the value within the Some without executing the closure again ❺.

If self.value is None, the code calls the closure stored in self.calculation, saves the result in self.value for future use, and returns the value as well ❻.

Listing 13-11 shows how we can use this Cacher struct in the function generate_workout from Listing 13-6.

src/main.rs

```
  fn generate_workout(intensity: u32, random_number: u32) {
❶ let mut expensive_result = Cacher::new(|num| {
        println!("calculating slowly...");
        thread::sleep(Duration::from_secs(2));
        num
    });

    if intensity < 25 {
        println!(
            "Today, do {} pushups!",
          ❷ expensive_result.value(intensity)
        );
        println!(
            "Next, do {} situps!",
          ❸ expensive_result.value(intensity)
        );
    } else {
        if random_number == 3 {
            println!("Take a break today! Remember to stay hydrated!");
        } else {
            println!(
                "Today, run for {} minutes!",
              ❹ expensive_result.value(intensity)
            );
```

```
        }
    }
}
```

Listing 13-11: Using Cacher in the generate_workout function to abstract away the caching logic

Instead of saving the closure in a variable directly, we save a new instance of Cacher that holds the closure ❶. Then, in each place we want the result ❷❸❹, we call the value method on the Cacher instance. We can call the value method as many times as we want, or not call it at all, and the expensive calculation will be run a maximum of once.

Try running this program with the main function from Listing 13-2. Change the values in the simulated_user_specified_value and simulated_random_number variables to verify that in all the cases in the various if and else blocks, calculating slowly... appears only once and only when needed. The Cacher takes care of the logic necessary to ensure we aren't calling the expensive calculation more than we need to so generate_workout can focus on the business logic.

Limitations of the Cacher Implementation

Caching values is a generally useful behavior that we might want to use in other parts of our code with different closures. However, there are two problems with the current implementation of Cacher that would make reusing it in different contexts difficult.

The first problem is that a Cacher instance assumes it will always get the same value for the parameter arg to the value method. That is, this test of Cacher will fail:

```
#[test]
fn call_with_different_values() {
    let mut c = Cacher::new(|a| a);

    let v1 = c.value(1);
    let v2 = c.value(2);

    assert_eq!(v2, 2);
}
```

This test creates a new Cacher instance with a closure that returns the value passed into it. We call the value method on this Cacher instance with an arg value of 1 and then an arg value of 2, and we expect the call to value with the arg value of 2 to return 2.

Run this test with the Cacher implementation in Listing 13-9 and Listing 13-10, and the test will fail on the assert_eq! with this message:

```
thread 'call_with_different_values' panicked at 'assertion failed: `(left ==
right)`
  left: `1`,
 right: `2`', src/main.rs
```

The problem is that the first time we called c.value with 1, the Cacher instance saved Some(1) in self.value. Thereafter, no matter what we pass in to the value method, it will always return 1.

Try modifying Cacher to hold a hash map rather than a single value. The keys of the hash map will be the arg values that are passed in, and the values of the hash map will be the result of calling the closure on that key. Instead of looking at whether self.value directly has a Some or a None value, the value function will look up the arg in the hash map and return the value if it's present. If it's not present, the Cacher will call the closure and save the resulting value in the hash map associated with its arg value.

The second problem with the current Cacher implementation is that it only accepts closures that take one parameter of type u32 and return a u32. We might want to cache the results of closures that take a string slice and return usize values, for example. To fix this issue, try introducing more generic parameters to increase the flexibility of the Cacher functionality.

Capturing the Environment with Closures

In the workout generator example, we only used closures as inline anonymous functions. However, closures have an additional capability that functions don't have: they can capture their environment and access variables from the scope in which they're defined.

Listing 13-12 has an example of a closure stored in the equal_to_x variable that uses the x variable from the closure's surrounding environment.

src/main.rs

```
fn main() {
    let x = 4;

    let equal_to_x = |z| z == x;

    let y = 4;

    assert!(equal_to_x(y));
}
```

Listing 13-12: Example of a closure that refers to a variable in its enclosing scope

Here, even though x is not one of the parameters of equal_to_x, the equal_to_x closure is allowed to use the x variable that's defined in the same scope that equal_to_x is defined in.

We can't do the same with functions; if we try with the following example, our code won't compile:

src/main.rs

```
fn main() {
    let x = 4;

    fn equal_to_x(z: i32) -> bool { z == x }

    let y = 4;
```

```
        assert!(equal_to_x(y));
}
```

We get an error:

```
error[E0434]: can't capture dynamic environment in a fn item; use the || { ...
} closure form instead
 --> src/main.rs
  |
4 |     fn equal_to_x(z: i32) -> bool { z == x }
  |                                          ^
```

The compiler even reminds us that this only works with closures!

When a closure captures a value from its environment, it uses memory to store the values for use in the closure body. This use of memory is overhead that we don't want to pay in more common cases where we want to execute code that doesn't capture its environment. Because functions are never allowed to capture their environment, defining and using functions will never incur this overhead.

Closures can capture values from their environment in three ways, which directly map to the three ways a function can take a parameter: taking ownership, borrowing mutably, and borrowing immutably. These are encoded in the three Fn traits as follows:

- FnOnce consumes the variables it captures from its enclosing scope, known as the closure's *environment*. To consume the captured variables, the closure must take ownership of these variables and move them into the closure when it is defined. The Once part of the name represents the fact that the closure can't take ownership of the same variables more than once, so it can be called only once.

- FnMut can change the environment because it mutably borrows values.

- Fn borrows values from the environment immutably.

When you create a closure, Rust infers which trait to use based on how the closure uses the values from the environment. All closures implement FnOnce because they can all be called at least once. Closures that don't move the captured variables also implement FnMut, and closures that don't need mutable access to the captured variables also implement Fn. In Listing 13-12, the equal_to_x closure borrows x immutably (so equal_to_x has the Fn trait) because the body of the closure only needs to read the value in x.

If you want to force the closure to take ownership of the values it uses in the environment, you can use the move keyword before the parameter list. This technique is mostly useful when passing a closure to a new thread to move the data so it's owned by the new thread.

We'll have more examples of move closures in Chapter 16 when we talk about concurrency. For now, here's the code from Listing 13-12 with the move keyword added to the closure definition and using vectors instead of integers, because integers can be copied rather than moved; note that this code will not yet compile.

```rust
fn main() {
    let x = vec![1, 2, 3];

    let equal_to_x = move |z| z == x;

    println!("can't use x here: {:?}", x);

    let y = vec![1, 2, 3];

    assert!(equal_to_x(y));
}
```

We receive the following error:

```
error[E0382]: use of moved value: `x`
 --> src/main.rs:6:40
  |
4 |     let equal_to_x = move |z| z == x;
  |                               -------- value moved (into closure) here
5 |
6 |     println!("can't use x here: {:?}", x);
  |                                        ^ value used here after move
  |
  = note: move occurs because `x` has type `std::vec::Vec<i32>`, which does
not implement the `Copy` trait
```

The x value is moved into the closure when the closure is defined, because we added the move keyword. The closure then has ownership of x, and main isn't allowed to use x anymore in the println! statement. Removing println! will fix this example.

Most of the time when specifying one of the Fn trait bounds, you can start with Fn and the compiler will tell you if you need FnMut or FnOnce based on what happens in the closure body.

To illustrate situations where closures that can capture their environment are useful as function parameters, let's move on to our next topic: iterators.

Processing a Series of Items with Iterators

The iterator pattern allows you to perform some task on a sequence of items in turn. An iterator is responsible for the logic of iterating over each item and determining when the sequence has finished. When you use iterators, you don't have to reimplement that logic yourself.

In Rust, iterators are *lazy*, meaning they have no effect until you call methods that consume the iterator to use it up. For example, the code in Listing 13-13 creates an iterator over the items in the vector v1 by calling the iter method defined on Vec<T>. This code by itself doesn't do anything useful.

```
let v1 = vec![1, 2, 3];

let v1_iter = v1.iter();
```

Listing 13-13: Creating an iterator

Once we've created an iterator, we can use it in a variety of ways. In Listing 3-5, we used iterators with for loops to execute some code on each item, although we glossed over what the call to iter did until now.

The example in Listing 13-14 separates the creation of the iterator from the use of the iterator in the for loop. The iterator is stored in the v1_iter variable, and no iteration takes place at that time. When the for loop is called using the iterator in v1_iter, each element in the iterator is used in one iteration of the loop, which prints each value.

```
let v1 = vec![1, 2, 3];

let v1_iter = v1.iter();

for val in v1_iter {
    println!("Got: {}", val);
}
```

Listing 13-14: Using an iterator in a for loop

In languages that don't have iterators provided by their standard libraries, you would likely write this same functionality by starting a variable at index 0, using that variable to index into the vector to get a value, and incrementing the variable value in a loop until it reached the total number of items in the vector.

Iterators handle all that logic for you, cutting down on repetitive code you could potentially mess up. Iterators give you more flexibility to use the same logic with many different kinds of sequences, not just data structures you can index into, like vectors. Let's examine how iterators do that.

The Iterator Trait and the next Method

All iterators implement a trait named Iterator that is defined in the standard library. The definition of the trait looks like this:

```
pub trait Iterator {
    type Item;

    fn next(&mut self) -> Option<Self::Item>;

    // methods with default implementations elided
}
```

Notice this definition uses some new syntax: type Item and Self::Item, which are defining an *associated type* with this trait. We'll talk about associated types in depth in Chapter 19. For now, all you need to know is that this code says implementing the Iterator trait requires that you also define an Item type, and this Item type is used in the return type of the next method. In other words, the Item type will be the type returned from the iterator.

The Iterator trait only requires implementors to define one method: the next method, which returns one item of the iterator at a time wrapped in Some and, when iteration is over, returns None.

We can call the next method on iterators directly; Listing 13-15 demonstrates what values are returned from repeated calls to next on the iterator created from the vector.

```
#[test]
fn iterator_demonstration() {
    let v1 = vec![1, 2, 3];

    let mut v1_iter = v1.iter();

    assert_eq!(v1_iter.next(), Some(&1));
    assert_eq!(v1_iter.next(), Some(&2));
    assert_eq!(v1_iter.next(), Some(&3));
    assert_eq!(v1_iter.next(), None);
}
```

Listing 13-15: Calling the next method on an iterator

Note that we needed to make v1_iter mutable: calling the next method on an iterator changes internal state that the iterator uses to keep track of where it is in the sequence. In other words, this code *consumes*, or uses up, the iterator. Each call to next eats up an item from the iterator. We didn't need to make v1_iter mutable when we used a for loop because the loop took ownership of v1_iter and made it mutable behind the scenes.

Also note that the values we get from the calls to next are immutable references to the values in the vector. The iter method produces an iterator over immutable references. If we want to create an iterator that takes ownership of v1 and returns owned values, we can call into_iter instead of iter. Similarly, if we want to iterate over mutable references, we can call iter_mut instead of iter.

Methods That Consume the Iterator

The Iterator trait has a number of different methods with default implementations provided by the standard library; you can find out about these methods by looking in the standard library API documentation for the Iterator trait. Some of these methods call the next method in their definition, which is why you're required to implement the next method when implementing the Iterator trait.

Methods that call next are referred to as *consuming adaptors*, because calling them uses up the iterator. One example is the sum method, which takes ownership of the iterator and iterates through the items by repeatedly calling next, thus consuming the iterator. As it iterates through, it adds each item to a running total and returns the total when iteration is complete. Listing 13-16 has a test illustrating a use of the sum method.

```
#[test]
fn iterator_sum() {
    let v1 = vec![1, 2, 3];

    let v1_iter = v1.iter();

    let total: i32 = v1_iter.sum();

    assert_eq!(total, 6);
}
```

Listing 13-16: Calling the sum method to get the total of all items in the iterator

We aren't allowed to use v1_iter after the call to sum because sum takes ownership of the iterator we call it on.

Methods That Produce Other Iterators

Other methods defined on the Iterator trait, known as *iterator adaptors*, allow you to change iterators into different kinds of iterators. You can chain multiple calls to iterator adaptors to perform complex actions in a readable way. But because all iterators are lazy, you have to call one of the consuming adaptor methods to get results from calls to iterator adaptors.

Listing 13-17 shows an example of calling the iterator adaptor method map, which takes a closure to call on each item to produce a new iterator. The closure here creates a new iterator in which each item from the vector has been incremented by 1. However, this code produces a warning.

```
let v1: Vec<i32> = vec![1, 2, 3];

v1.iter().map(|x| x + 1);
```

Listing 13-17: Calling the iterator adaptor map to create a new iterator

The warning we get is this:

```
warning: unused `std::iter::Map` which must be used: iterator adaptors are
lazy and do nothing unless consumed
  --> src/main.rs:4:5
   |
4  |     v1.iter().map(|x| x + 1);
   |     ^^^^^^^^^^^^^^^^^^^^^^^^^
   |
   = note: #[warn(unused_must_use)] on by default
```

The code in Listing 13-17 doesn't do anything; the closure we've specified never gets called. The warning reminds us why: iterator adaptors are lazy, and we need to consume the iterator here.

To fix this and consume the iterator, we'll use the collect method, which we used with env:args in Listing 12-1. This method consumes the iterator and collects the resulting values into a collection data type.

In Listing 13-18, we collect the results of iterating over the iterator that's returned from the call to map into a vector. This vector will end up containing each item from the original vector incremented by 1.

src/main.rs

```
let v1: Vec<i32> = vec![1, 2, 3];

let v2: Vec<_> = v1.iter().map(|x| x + 1).collect();

assert_eq!(v2, vec![2, 3, 4]);
```

Listing 13-18: Calling the map method to create a new iterator and then calling the collect method to consume the new iterator and create a vector

Because map takes a closure, we can specify any operation we want to perform on each item. This is a great example of how closures let you customize some behavior while reusing the iteration behavior that the Iterator trait provides.

Using Closures That Capture Their Environment

Now that we've introduced iterators, we can demonstrate a common use of closures that capture their environment by using the filter iterator adaptor. The filter method on an iterator takes a closure that takes each item from the iterator and returns a Boolean. If the closure returns true, the value will be included in the iterator produced by filter. If the closure returns false, the value won't be included in the resulting iterator.

In Listing 13-19, we use filter with a closure that captures the shoe_size variable from its environment to iterate over a collection of Shoe struct instances. It will return only shoes that are the specified size.

src/lib.rs

```
#[derive(PartialEq, Debug)]
struct Shoe {
    size: u32,
    style: String,
}

❶ fn shoes_in_my_size(shoes: Vec<Shoe>, shoe_size: u32) -> Vec<Shoe> {
  ❷ shoes.into_iter()
      ❸ .filter(|s| s.size == shoe_size)
      ❹ .collect()
}

#[test]
fn filters_by_size() {
    let shoes = vec![
        Shoe { size: 10, style: String::from("sneaker") },
        Shoe { size: 13, style: String::from("sandal") },
        Shoe { size: 10, style: String::from("boot") },
    ];

    let in_my_size = shoes_in_my_size(shoes, 10);
```

```
        assert_eq!(
            in_my_size,
            vec![
                Shoe { size: 10, style: String::from("sneaker") },
                Shoe { size: 10, style: String::from("boot") },
            ]
        );
    }
```

Listing 13-19: Using the `filter` method with a closure that captures `shoe_size`

The `shoes_in_my_size` function takes ownership of a vector of shoes and a shoe size as parameters ❶. It returns a vector containing only shoes of the specified size.

In the body of `shoes_in_my_size`, we call `into_iter` to create an iterator that takes ownership of the vector ❷. Then we call `filter` to adapt that iterator into a new iterator that only contains elements for which the closure returns true ❸.

The closure captures the `shoe_size` parameter from the environment and compares the value with each shoe's size, keeping only shoes of the size specified. Finally, calling `collect` gathers the values returned by the adapted iterator into a vector that's returned by the function ❹.

The test shows that when we call `shoes_in_my_size`, we get back only shoes that have the same size as the value we specified.

Creating Our Own Iterators with the Iterator Trait

We've shown that you can create an iterator by calling `iter`, `into_iter`, or `iter_mut` on a vector. You can create iterators from the other collection types in the standard library, such as hash map. You can also create iterators that do anything you want by implementing the `Iterator` trait on your own types. As previously mentioned, the only method you're required to provide a definition for is the `next` method. Once you've done that, you can use all other methods that have default implementations provided by the `Iterator` trait!

To demonstrate, let's create an iterator that will only ever count from 1 to 5. First, we'll create a struct to hold some values. Then we'll make this struct into an iterator by implementing the `Iterator` trait and using the values in that implementation.

Listing 13-20 has the definition of the `Counter` struct and an associated new function to create instances of `Counter`.

src/lib.rs
```
struct Counter {
    count: u32,
}

impl Counter {
    fn new() -> Counter {
        Counter { count: 0 }
```

```
        }
    }
```

Listing 13-20: Defining the Counter *struct and a* new *function that creates instances of* Counter *with an initial value of 0 for* count

The Counter struct has one field named count. This field holds a u32 value that will keep track of where we are in the process of iterating from 1 to 5. The count field is private because we want the implementation of Counter to manage its value. The new function enforces the behavior of always starting new instances with a value of 0 in the count field.

Next, we'll implement the Iterator trait for our Counter type by defining the body of the next method to specify what we want to happen when this iterator is used, as shown in Listing 13-21.

src/lib.rs

```rust
impl Iterator for Counter {
    type Item = u32;

    fn next(&mut self) -> Option<Self::Item> {
        self.count += 1;

        if self.count < 6 {
            Some(self.count)
        } else {
            None
        }
    }
}
```

Listing 13-21: Implementing the Iterator *trait on our* Counter *struct*

We set the associated Item type for our iterator to u32, meaning the iterator will return u32 values. Again, don't worry about associated types yet, we'll cover them in Chapter 19.

We want our iterator to add 1 to the current state, so we initialized count to 0 so it would return 1 first. If the value of count is less than 6, next will return the current value wrapped in Some, but if count is 6 or higher, our iterator will return None.

Using Our Counter Iterator's next Method

Once we've implemented the Iterator trait, we have an iterator! Listing 13-22 shows a test demonstrating that we can use the iterator functionality of our Counter struct by calling the next method on it directly, just as we did with the iterator created from a vector in Listing 13-15.

src/lib.rs

```rust
#[test]
fn calling_next_directly() {
    let mut counter = Counter::new();
```

```
        assert_eq!(counter.next(), Some(1));
        assert_eq!(counter.next(), Some(2));
        assert_eq!(counter.next(), Some(3));
        assert_eq!(counter.next(), Some(4));
        assert_eq!(counter.next(), Some(5));
        assert_eq!(counter.next(), None);
    }
```

Listing 13-22: Testing the functionality of the next method implementation

This test creates a new Counter instance in the counter variable and then calls next repeatedly, verifying that we have implemented the behavior we want this iterator to have: returning the values from 1 to 5.

Using Other Iterator Trait Methods

We implemented the Iterator trait by defining the next method, so we can now use any Iterator trait method's default implementations as defined in the standard library, because they all use the next method's functionality.

For example, if for some reason we wanted to take the values produced by an instance of Counter, pair them with values produced by another Counter instance after skipping the first value, multiply each pair together, keep only those results that are divisible by 3, and add all the resulting values together, we could do so, as shown in the test in Listing 13-23.

src/lib.rs
```
#[test]
fn using_other_iterator_trait_methods() {
    let sum: u32 = Counter::new().zip(Counter::new().skip(1))
                                 .map(|(a, b)| a * b)
                                 .filter(|x| x % 3 == 0)
                                 .sum();
    assert_eq!(18, sum);
}
```

Listing 13-23: Using a variety of Iterator trait methods on our Counter iterator

Note that zip produces only four pairs; the theoretical fifth pair (5, None) is never produced because zip returns None when either of its input iterators returns None.

All of these method calls are possible because we specified how the next method works, and the standard library provides default implementations for other methods that call next.

Improving Our I/O Project

With this new knowledge about iterators, we can improve the I/O project in Chapter 12 by using iterators to make places in the code clearer and more concise. Let's look at how iterators can improve our implementation of the Config::new function and the search function.

Removing a clone Using an Iterator

In Listing 12-6, we added code that took a slice of String values and created an instance of the Config struct by indexing into the slice and cloning the values, allowing the Config struct to own those values. In Listing 13-24, we've reproduced the implementation of the Config::new function as it was in Listing 12-23.

src/lib.rs

```
impl Config {
    pub fn new(args: &[String]) -> Result<Config, &'static str> {
        if args.len() < 3 {
            return Err("not enough arguments");
        }

        let query = args[1].clone();
        let filename = args[2].clone();

        let case_sensitive = env::var("CASE_INSENSITIVE").is_err();

        Ok(Config { query, filename, case_sensitive })
    }
}
```

Listing 13-24: Reproduction of the Config::new function from Listing 12-23

At the time, we said not to worry about the inefficient clone calls because we would remove them in the future. Well, that time is now!

We needed clone here because we have a slice with String elements in the parameter args, but the new function doesn't own args. To return ownership of a Config instance, we had to clone the values from the query and filename fields of Config so the Config instance can own its values.

With our new knowledge about iterators, we can change the new function to take ownership of an iterator as its argument instead of borrowing a slice. We'll use the iterator functionality instead of the code that checks the length of the slice and indexes into specific locations. This will clarify what the Config::new function is doing because the iterator will access the values.

Once Config::new takes ownership of the iterator and stops using indexing operations that borrow, we can move the String values from the iterator into Config rather than calling clone and making a new allocation.

Using the Returned Iterator Directly

Open your I/O project's *src/main.rs* file, which should look like this:

src/main.rs

```
fn main() {
    let args: Vec<String> = env::args().collect();

    let config = Config::new(&args).unwrap_or_else(|err| {
        eprintln!("Problem parsing arguments: {}", err);
        process::exit(1);
    });

    // --snip--
}
```

We'll change the start of the main function that we had in Listing 12-24 to the code in Listing 13-25. This won't compile until we update Config::new as well.

src/main.rs

```
fn main() {
    let config = Config::new(env::args()).unwrap_or_else(|err| {
        eprintln!("Problem parsing arguments: {}", err);
        process::exit(1);
    });

    // --snip--
}
```

Listing 13-25: Passing the return value of env::args to Config::new

The env::args function returns an iterator! Rather than collecting the iterator values into a vector and then passing a slice to Config::new, now we're passing ownership of the iterator returned from env::args to Config::new directly.

Next, we need to update the definition of Config::new. In your I/O project's *src/lib.rs* file, let's change the signature of Config::new to look like Listing 13-26. This still won't compile because we need to update the function body.

src/lib.rs

```
impl Config {
    pub fn new(mut args: std::env::Args) -> Result<Config, &'static str> {
        // --snip--
```

Listing 13-26: Updating the signature of Config::new to expect an iterator

The standard library documentation for the env::args function shows that the type of the iterator it returns is std::env::Args. We've updated the signature of the Config::new function so the parameter args has the type std::env::Args instead of &[String]. Because we're taking ownership of args and we'll be mutating args by iterating over it, we can add the mut keyword into the specification of the args parameter to make it mutable.

Using Iterator Trait Methods Instead of Indexing

Next, we'll fix the body of Config::new. The standard library documentation also mentions that std::env::Args implements the Iterator trait, so we know we can call the next method on it! Listing 13-27 updates the code from Listing 12-23 to use the next method.

src/lib.rs

```
impl Config {
    pub fn new(mut args: std::env::Args) -> Result<Config, &'static str> {
        args.next();

        let query = match args.next() {
            Some(arg) => arg,
            None => return Err("Didn't get a query string"),
        };
```

```
        let filename = match args.next() {
            Some(arg) => arg,
            None => return Err("Didn't get a file name"),
        };

        let case_sensitive = env::var("CASE_INSENSITIVE").is_err();

        Ok(Config { query, filename, case_sensitive })
    }
}
```

Listing 13-27: Changing the body of Config::new to use iterator methods

Remember that the first value in the return value of env::args is the name of the program. We want to ignore that and get to the next value, so first we call next and do nothing with the return value. Second, we call next to get the value we want to put in the query field of Config. If next returns a Some, we use a match to extract the value. If it returns None, it means not enough arguments were given and we return early with an Err value. We do the same thing for the filename value.

Making Code Clearer with Iterator Adaptors

We can also take advantage of iterators in the search function in our I/O project, which is reproduced in Listing 13-28 as it was in Listing 12-19.

src/lib.rs

```
pub fn search<'a>(query: &str, contents: &'a str) -> Vec<&'a str> {
    let mut results = Vec::new();

    for line in contents.lines() {
        if line.contains(query) {
            results.push(line);
        }
    }

    results
}
```

Listing 13-28: The implementation of the search function from Listing 12-19

We can write this code in a more concise way using iterator adaptor methods. Doing so also lets us avoid having a mutable intermediate results vector. The functional programming style prefers to minimize the amount of mutable state to make code clearer. Removing the mutable state might enable a future enhancement to make searching happen in parallel, because we wouldn't have to manage concurrent access to the results vector. Listing 13-29 shows this change.

```
pub fn search<'a>(query: &str, contents: &'a str) -> Vec<&'a str> {
    contents.lines()
        .filter(|line| line.contains(query))
        .collect()
}
```

Listing 13-29: Using iterator adaptor methods in the implementation of the search function

Recall that the search function's purpose is to return all lines in contents that contain the query. Similar to the filter example in Listing 13-19, this code uses the filter adaptor to keep only the lines that line.contains(query) returns true for. We then collect the matching lines into another vector with collect. Much simpler! Feel free to make the same change to use iterator methods in the search_case_insensitive function as well.

The next logical question is which style you should choose in your own code and why: the original implementation in Listing 13-28 or the version using iterators in Listing 13-29. Most Rust programmers prefer to use the iterator style. It's a bit tougher to get the hang of at first, but once you get a feel for the various iterator adaptors and what they do, iterators can be easier to understand. Instead of fiddling with the various bits of looping and building new vectors, the code focuses on the high-level objective of the loop. This abstracts away some of the commonplace code so it's easier to see the concepts that are unique to this code, such as the filtering condition each element in the iterator must pass.

But are the two implementations truly equivalent? The intuitive assumption might be that the more low-level loop will be faster. Let's talk about performance.

Comparing Performance: Loops vs. Iterators

To determine whether to use loops or iterators, you need to know which version of the search function is faster: the version with an explicit for loop or the version with iterators.

We ran a benchmark by loading the entire contents of *The Adventures of Sherlock Holmes* by Sir Arthur Conan Doyle into a String and looking for the word *the* in the contents. Here are the results of the benchmark on the version of search using the for loop and the version using iterators:

```
test bench_search_for  ... bench:  19,620,300 ns/iter (+/- 915,700)
test bench_search_iter ... bench:  19,234,900 ns/iter (+/- 657,200)
```

The iterator version was slightly faster! We won't explain the benchmark code here, because the point is not to prove that the two versions are equivalent but to get a general sense of how these two implementations compare performance-wise.

For a more comprehensive benchmark, you should check using various texts of various sizes as the contents, different words, words of different lengths as the query, and all kinds of other variations. The point is this: iterators, although a high-level abstraction, get compiled down to roughly the same code as if you'd written the lower-level code yourself. Iterators are one of Rust's *zero-cost abstractions*, by which we mean using the abstraction imposes no additional runtime overhead. This is analogous to how Bjarne Stroustrup, the original designer and implementor of C++, defines *zero-overhead* in "Foundations of C++" (2012):

> In general, C++ implementations obey the zero-overhead principle: What you don't use, you don't pay for. And further: What you do use, you couldn't hand code any better.

As another example, the following code is taken from an audio decoder. The decoding algorithm uses the linear prediction mathematical operation to estimate future values based on a linear function of the previous samples. This code uses an iterator chain to do some math on three variables in scope: a buffer slice of data, an array of 12 coefficients, and an amount by which to shift data in qlp_shift. We've declared the variables within this example but not given them any values; although this code doesn't have much meaning outside of its context, it's still a concise, real-world example of how Rust translates high-level ideas to low-level code.

```
let buffer: &mut [i32];
let coefficients: [i64; 12];
let qlp_shift: i16;

for i in 12..buffer.len() {
    let prediction = coefficients.iter()
                                 .zip(&buffer[i - 12..i])
                                 .map(|(&c, &s)| c * s as i64)
                                 .sum::<i64>() >> qlp_shift;
    let delta = buffer[i];
    buffer[i] = prediction as i32 + delta;
}
```

To calculate the value of prediction, this code iterates through each of the 12 values in coefficients and uses the zip method to pair the coefficient values with the previous 12 values in buffer. Then, for each pair, we multiply the values together, sum all the results, and shift the bits in the sum qlp_shift bits to the right.

Calculations in applications like audio decoders often prioritize performance most highly. Here, we're creating an iterator, using two adaptors, and then consuming the value. What assembly code would this Rust code compile to? Well, as of this writing, it compiles down to the same assembly you'd write by hand. There's no loop at all corresponding to the iteration over the values in coefficients: Rust knows that there are 12 iterations, so it "unrolls" the loop. *Unrolling* is an optimization that removes the overhead of the loop-controlling code and instead generates repetitive code for each iteration of the loop.

All of the coefficients get stored in registers, which means accessing the values is very fast. There are no bounds checks on the array access at runtime. All these optimizations that Rust is able to apply make the resulting code extremely efficient. Now that you know this, you can use iterators and closures without fear! They make code seem like it's higher level but don't impose a runtime performance penalty for doing so.

Summary

Closures and iterators are Rust features inspired by functional programming language ideas. They contribute to Rust's capability to clearly express high-level ideas at low-level performance. The implementations of closures and iterators are such that runtime performance is not affected. This is part of Rust's goal to strive to provide zero-cost abstractions.

Now that we've improved the expressiveness of our I/O project, let's look at some more features of cargo that will help us share the project with the world.

14

MORE ABOUT CARGO AND CRATES.IO

So far we've used only the most basic features of Cargo to build, run, and test our code, but it can do a lot more. In this chapter, we'll discuss some of its other, more advanced features to show you how to do the following:

- Customize your build through release profiles
- Publish libraries on *https://crates.io/*
- Organize large projects with workspaces
- Install binaries from *https://crates.io/*
- Extend Cargo using custom commands

Cargo can do even more than what we cover in this chapter, so for a full explanation of all its features, see its documentation at *https://doc.rust-lang .org/cargo/*.

Customizing Builds with Release Profiles

In Rust, *release profiles* are predefined and customizable profiles with different configurations that allow a programmer to have more control over various options for compiling code. Each profile is configured independently of the others.

Cargo has two main profiles: the dev profile Cargo uses when you run cargo build and the release profile Cargo uses when you run cargo build --release. The dev profile is defined with good defaults for development, and the release profile has good defaults for release builds.

These profile names might be familiar from the output of your builds:

```
$ cargo build
    Finished dev [unoptimized + debuginfo] target(s) in 0.0 secs
$ cargo build --release
    Finished release [optimized] target(s) in 0.0 secs
```

The dev and release shown in this build output indicate that the compiler is using different profiles.

Cargo has default settings for each of the profiles that apply when there aren't any [profile.*] sections in the project's *Cargo.toml* file. By adding [profile.*] sections for any profile you want to customize, you can override any subset of the default settings. For example, here are the default values for the opt-level setting for the dev and release profiles:

Cargo.toml
```
[profile.dev]
opt-level = 0

[profile.release]
opt-level = 3
```

The opt-level setting controls the number of optimizations Rust will apply to your code, with a range of 0 to 3. Applying more optimizations extends compiling time, so if you're in development and compiling your code often, you'll want faster compiling even if the resulting code runs slower. That is the reason the default opt-level for dev is 0. When you're ready to release your code, it's best to spend more time compiling. You'll only compile in release mode once, but you'll run the compiled program many times, so release mode trades longer compile time for code that runs faster. That's why the default opt-level for the release profile is 3.

You can override any default setting by adding a different value for it in *Cargo.toml*. For example, if we want to use optimization level 1 in the development profile, we can add these two lines to our project's *Cargo.toml* file:

Cargo.toml
```
[profile.dev]
opt-level = 1
```

This code overrides the default setting of 0. Now when we run cargo build, Cargo will use the defaults for the dev profile plus our customization to opt-level. Because we set `opt-level` to 1, Cargo will apply more optimizations than with the default settings, but not as many as in a release build.

For the full list of configuration options and defaults for each profile, see Cargo's documentation at *https://doc.rust-lang.org/cargo/*.

Publishing a Crate to Crates.io

We've used packages from *https://crates.io/* as dependencies of our project, but you can also share your code with other people by publishing your own packages. The crate registry at *https://crates.io/* distributes the source code of your packages, so it primarily hosts code that is open source.

Rust and Cargo have features that help make your published package easier for people to use and to find in the first place. We'll talk about some of these features next and then explain how to publish a package.

Making Useful Documentation Comments

Accurately documenting your packages will help other users know how and when to use them, so it's worth investing the time to write documentation. In Chapter 3, we discussed how to comment Rust code using two slashes, //. Rust also has a particular kind of comment for documentation, known conveniently as a *documentation comment*, that will generate HTML documentation. The HTML displays the contents of documentation comments for public API items intended for programmers interested in knowing how to *use* your crate as opposed to how your crate is *implemented*.

Documentation comments use three slashes, ///, instead of two and support Markdown notation for formatting the text. Place documentation comments just before the item they're documenting. Listing 14-1 shows documentation comments for an `add_one` function in a crate named `my_crate`.

src/lib.rs

```
/// Adds one to the number given.
///
/// # Examples
///
/// ```
/// let five = 5;
///
/// assert_eq!(6, my_crate::add_one(5));
/// ```
pub fn add_one(x: i32) -> i32 {
    x + 1
}
```

Listing 14-1: A documentation comment for a function

Here, we give a description of what the `add_one` function does, start a section with the heading `Examples`, and then provide code that demonstrates how to use the `add_one` function. We can generate the HTML documentation from this documentation comment by running `cargo doc`. This command runs the `rustdoc` tool distributed with Rust and puts the generated HTML documentation in the *target/doc* directory.

For convenience, running `cargo doc --open` will build the HTML for your current crate's documentation (as well as the documentation for all of your crate's dependencies) and open the result in a web browser. Navigate to the add_one function and you'll see how the text in the documentation comments is rendered, as shown in Figure 14-1.

Figure 14-1: HTML documentation for the add_one *function*

Commonly Used Sections

We used the `# Examples` Markdown heading in Listing 14-1 to create a section in the HTML with the title "Examples." Here are some other sections that crate authors commonly use in their documentation:

Panics   The scenarios in which the function being documented could panic. Callers of the function who don't want their programs to panic should make sure they don't call the function in these situations.

Errors   If the function returns a `Result`, describing the kinds of errors that might occur and what conditions might cause those errors to be returned can be helpful to callers so they can write code to handle the different kinds of errors in different ways.

Safety   If the function is `unsafe` to call (we discuss unsafety in Chapter 19), there should be a section explaining why the function is unsafe and covering the invariants that the function expects callers to uphold.

Most documentation comments don't need all of these sections, but this is a good checklist to remind you of the aspects of your code that people calling your code will be interested in knowing about.

Documentation Comments as Tests

Adding example code blocks to your documentation comments can help demonstrate how to use your library, and doing so has an additional bonus: running cargo test will run the code examples in your documentation as tests! Nothing is better than documentation with examples. But nothing is worse than examples that don't work because the code has changed since the documentation was written. If we run cargo test with the documentation for the add_one function from Listing 14-1, we will see a section in the test results like this:

```
   Doc-tests my_crate

running 1 test
test src/lib.rs - add_one (line 5) ... ok

test result: ok. 1 passed; 0 failed; 0 ignored; 0 measured; 0 filtered out
```

Now if we change either the function or the example so the assert_eq! in the example panics and run cargo test again, we'll see that the doc tests catch that the example and the code are out of sync with each other!

Commenting Contained Items

Another style of doc comment, //!, adds documentation to the item that contains the comments rather than adding documentation to the items following the comments. We typically use these doc comments inside the crate root file (*src/lib.rs* by convention) or inside a module to document the crate or the module as a whole.

For example, if we want to add documentation that describes the purpose of the my_crate crate that contains the add_one function, we can add documentation comments that start with //! to the beginning of the *src/lib.rs* file, as shown in Listing 14-2.

src/lib.rs
```
//! # My Crate
//!
//! `my_crate` is a collection of utilities to make performing certain
//! calculations more convenient.

/// Adds one to the number given.
// --snip--
```

Listing 14-2: Documentation for the my_crate crate as a whole

Notice there isn't any code after the last line that begins with //!. Because we started the comments with //! instead of ///, we're documenting the item that contains this comment rather than an item that follows this comment. In this case, the item that contains this comment is the *src/lib.rs* file, which is the crate root. These comments describe the entire crate.

When we run cargo doc --open, these comments will display on the front page of the documentation for my_crate above the list of public items in the crate, as shown in Figure 14-2.

Figure 14-2: Rendered documentation for my_crate, including the comment describing the crate as a whole

Documentation comments within items are useful for describing crates and modules especially. Use them to explain the overall purpose of the container to help your users understand the crate's organization.

Exporting a Convenient Public API with pub use

In Chapter 7, we covered how to organize our code into modules using the mod keyword, how to make items public using the pub keyword, and how to bring items into a scope using the use keyword. However, the structure that makes sense to you while you're developing a crate might not be very convenient for your users. You might want to organize your structs in a hierarchy containing multiple levels, but then people who want to use a type you've defined deep in the hierarchy could have trouble finding out that type exists. They might also be annoyed at having to enter use my_crate::some _module::another_module::UsefulType; rather than use my_crate::UsefulType;.

The structure of your public API is a major consideration when publishing a crate. People who use your crate are less familiar with the structure than you are and might have difficulty finding the pieces they want to use if your crate has a large module hierarchy.

The good news is that if the structure *isn't* convenient for others to use from another library, you don't have to rearrange your internal organization: instead, you can re-export items to make a public structure that's different from your private structure by using pub use. Re-exporting takes a public item in one location and makes it public in another location, as if it were defined in the other location instead.

For example, say we made a library named art for modeling artistic concepts. Within this library are two modules: a kinds module containing two enums named PrimaryColor and SecondaryColor and a utils module containing a function named mix, as shown in Listing 14-3.

src/lib.rs

```
//! # Art
//!
//! A library for modeling artistic concepts.

pub mod kinds {
    /// The primary colors according to the RYB color model.
    pub enum PrimaryColor {
        Red,
        Yellow,
        Blue,
    }

    /// The secondary colors according to the RYB color model.
    pub enum SecondaryColor {
        Orange,
        Green,
        Purple,
    }
}

pub mod utils {
    use kinds::*;

    /// Combines two primary colors in equal amounts to create
    /// a secondary color.
    pub fn mix(c1: PrimaryColor, c2: PrimaryColor) -> SecondaryColor {
        // --snip--
    }
}
```

Listing 14-3: An art library with items organized into kinds and utils modules

Figure 14-3 shows what the front page of the documentation for this crate generated by cargo doc would look like.

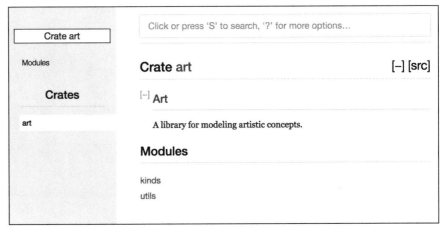

Figure 14-3: Front page of the documentation for art that lists the kinds and utils modules

Note that the `PrimaryColor` and `SecondaryColor` types aren't listed on the front page, nor is the `mix` function. We have to click kinds and utils to see them.

Another crate that depends on this library would need use statements that import the items from art, specifying the module structure that's currently defined. Listing 14-4 shows an example of a crate that uses the `PrimaryColor` and `mix` items from the art crate.

src/main.rs

```
extern crate art;

use art::kinds::PrimaryColor;
use art::utils::mix;

fn main() {
    let red = PrimaryColor::Red;
    let yellow = PrimaryColor::Yellow;
    mix(red, yellow);
}
```

Listing 14-4: A crate using the art crate's items with its internal structure exported

The author of the code in Listing 14-4, which uses the art crate, had to figure out that `PrimaryColor` is in the kinds module and `mix` is in the utils module. The module structure of the art crate is more relevant to developers working on the art crate than to developers using the art crate. The internal structure that organizes parts of the crate into the kinds module and the utils module doesn't contain any useful information for someone trying to understand how to use the art crate. Instead, the art crate's module structure causes confusion because developers have to figure out where to look, and the structure is inconvenient because developers must specify the module names in the use statements.

To remove the internal organization from the public API, we can modify the art crate code in Listing 14-3 to add `pub use` statements to re-export the items at the top level, as shown in Listing 14-5.

src/lib.rs

```
//! # Art
//!
//! A library for modeling artistic concepts.

pub use kinds::PrimaryColor;
pub use kinds::SecondaryColor;
pub use utils::mix;

pub mod kinds {
    // --snip--
}

pub mod utils {
    // --snip--
}
```

Listing 14-5: Adding pub use statements to re-export items

The API documentation that cargo doc generates for this crate will now list and link re-exports on the front page, as shown in Figure 14-4, making the PrimaryColor and SecondaryColor types and the mix function easier to find.

Figure 14-4: The front page of the documentation for art *that lists the re-exports*

The art crate users can still see and use the internal structure from Listing 14-3 as demonstrated in Listing 14-4, or they can use the more convenient structure in Listing 14-5, as shown in Listing 14-6.

src/main.rs

```
extern crate art;

use art::PrimaryColor;
use art::mix;

fn main() {
    // --snip--
}
```

Listing 14-6: A program using the re-exported items from the art *crate*

In cases where there are many nested modules, re-exporting the types at the top level with pub use can make a significant difference in the experience of people who use the crate.

Creating a useful public API structure is more of an art than a science, and you can iterate to find the API that works best for your users. Choosing pub use gives you flexibility in how you structure your crate internally and decouples that internal structure from what you present to your users. Look at some of the code of crates you've installed to see if their internal structure differs from their public API.

Setting Up a Crates.io Account

Before you can publish any crates, you need to create an account on *https://crates.io/* and get an API token. To do so, visit the home page at *https://crates.io/* and log in via a GitHub account. (The GitHub account is currently a requirement, but the site might support other ways of creating an account in the future.) Once you're logged in, visit your account settings at *https://crates.io/me/* and retrieve your API key. Then run the cargo login command with your API key, like this:

```
$ cargo login abcdefghijklmnopqrstuvwxyz012345
```

This command will inform Cargo of your API token and store it locally in *~/.cargo/credentials*. Note that this token is a *secret*: do not share it with anyone else. If you do share it with anyone for any reason, you should revoke it and generate a new token on *https://crates.io/*.

Adding Metadata to a New Crate

Now that you have an account, let's say you have a crate you want to publish. Before publishing, you'll need to add some metadata to your crate by adding it to the [package] section of the crate's *Cargo.toml* file.

Your crate will need a unique name. While you're working on a crate locally, you can name a crate whatever you'd like. However, crate names on *https://crates.io/* are allocated on a first-come, first-served basis. Once a crate name is taken, no one else can publish a crate with that name. Search for the name you want to use on the site to find out whether it has been used. If it hasn't, edit the name in the *Cargo.toml* file under [package] to use the name for publishing, like so:

Cargo.toml
```
[package]
name = "guessing_game"
```

Even if you've chosen a unique name, when you run cargo publish to publish the crate at this point, you'll get a warning and then an error:

```
$ cargo publish
    Updating registry `https://github.com/rust-lang/crates.io-index`
warning: manifest has no description, license, license-file, documentation,
homepage or repository.
--snip--
error: api errors: missing or empty metadata fields: description, license.
```

The reason is that you're missing some crucial information: a description and license are required so people will know what your crate does and under what terms they can use it. To rectify this error, you need to include this information in the *Cargo.toml* file.

Add a description that is just a sentence or two, because it will appear with your crate in search results. For the license field, you need to give a *license identifier value*. The Linux Foundation's Software Package Data Exchange (SPDX) at *http://spdx.org/licenses/* lists the identifiers you can use for this value. For example, to specify that you've licensed your crate using the MIT License, add the MIT identifier:

Cargo.toml

```
[package]
name = "guessing_game"
license = "MIT"
```

If you want to use a license that doesn't appear in the SPDX, you need to place the text of that license in a file, include the file in your project, and then use license-file to specify the name of that file instead of using the license key.

Guidance on which license is appropriate for your project is beyond the scope of this book. Many people in the Rust community license their projects in the same way as Rust by using a dual license of MIT OR Apache-2.0. This practice demonstrates that you can specify multiple license identifiers separated by OR to have multiple licenses for your project.

With a unique name, the version, the author details that cargo new added when you created the crate, your description, and a license added, the *Cargo.toml* file for a project that is ready to publish might look like this:

Cargo.toml

```
[package]
name = "guessing_game"
version = "0.1.0"
authors = ["Your Name <you@example.com>"]
description = "A fun game where you guess what number the computer has
chosen."
license = "MIT OR Apache-2.0"

[dependencies]
```

Cargo's documentation at *https://doc.rust-lang.org/cargo/* describes other metadata you can specify to ensure others can discover and use your crate more easily.

Publishing to Crates.io

Now that you've created an account, saved your API token, chosen a name for your crate, and specified the required metadata, you're ready to publish! Publishing a crate uploads a specific version to *https://crates.io/* for others to use.

Be careful when publishing a crate because a publish is *permanent*. The version can never be overwritten, and the code cannot be deleted. One major goal of *https://crates.io/* is to act as a permanent archive of code so that builds of all projects that depend on crates from *https://crates.io/* will continue to work. Allowing version deletions would make fulfilling that goal impossible. However, there is no limit to the number of crate versions you can publish.

Run the cargo publish command again. It should succeed now:

```
$ cargo publish
 Updating registry `https://github.com/rust-lang/crates.io-index`
Packaging guessing_game v0.1.0 (file:///projects/guessing_game)
Verifying guessing_game v0.1.0 (file:///projects/guessing_game)
Compiling guessing_game v0.1.0
(file:///projects/guessing_game/target/package/guessing_game-0.1.0)
 Finished dev [unoptimized + debuginfo] target(s) in 0.19 secs
Uploading guessing_game v0.1.0 (file:///projects/guessing_game)
```

Congratulations! You've now shared your code with the Rust community, and anyone can easily add your crate as a dependency of their project.

Publishing a New Version of an Existing Crate

When you've made changes to your crate and are ready to release a new version, you change the version value specified in your *Cargo.toml* file and republish. Use the Semantic Versioning rules at *http://semver.org/* to decide what an appropriate next version number is based on the kinds of changes you've made. Then run cargo publish to upload the new version.

Removing Versions from Crates.io with cargo yank

Although you can't remove previous versions of a crate, you can prevent any future projects from adding them as a new dependency. This is useful when a crate version is broken for one reason or another. In such situations, Cargo supports *yanking* a crate version.

Yanking a version prevents new projects from starting to depend on that version while allowing all existing projects that depend on it to continue to download and depend on that version. Essentially, a yank means that all projects with a *Cargo.lock* will not break, and any future *Cargo.lock* files generated will not use the yanked version.

To yank a version of a crate, run cargo yank and specify which version you want to yank:

```
$ cargo yank --vers 1.0.1
```

By adding --undo to the command, you can also undo a yank and allow projects to start depending on a version again:

```
$ cargo yank --vers 1.0.1 --undo
```

A yank *does not* delete any code. For example, the yank feature is not intended for deleting accidentally uploaded secrets. If that happens, you must reset those secrets immediately.

Cargo Workspaces

In Chapter 12, we built a package that included a binary crate and a library crate. As your project develops, you might find that the library crate continues to get bigger and you want to split up your package further into multiple library crates. In this situation, Cargo offers a feature called *workspaces* that can help manage multiple related packages that are developed in tandem.

Creating a Workspace

A workspace is a set of packages that share the same *Cargo.lock* and output directory. Let's make a project using a workspace—we'll use trivial code so we can concentrate on the structure of the workspace. There are multiple ways to structure a workspace; we're going to show one common way. We'll have a workspace containing a binary and two libraries. The binary, which will provide the main functionality, will depend on the two libraries. One library will provide an add_one function, and a second library an add_two function. These three crates will be part of the same workspace. We'll start by creating a new directory for the workspace:

```
$ mkdir add
$ cd add
```

Next, in the *add* directory, we create the *Cargo.toml* file that will configure the entire workspace. This file won't have a [package] section or the metadata we've seen in other *Cargo.toml* files. Instead, it will start with a [workspace] section that will allow us to add members to the workspace by specifying the path to our binary crate; in this case, that path is *adder*:

Cargo.toml
```
[workspace]

members = [
    "adder",
]
```

Next, we'll create the adder binary crate by running cargo new within the *add* directory:

```
$ cargo new --bin adder
    Created binary (application) `adder` project
```

At this point, we can build the workspace by running cargo build. The files in your *add* directory should look like this:

```
├── Cargo.lock
├── Cargo.toml
├── adder
│   ├── Cargo.toml
│   └── src
│       └── main.rs
└── target
```

The workspace has one *target* directory at the top level for the compiled artifacts to be placed into; the adder crate doesn't have its own *target* directory. Even if we were to run cargo build from inside the *adder* directory, the compiled artifacts would still end up in *add/target* rather than *add/adder/target*. Cargo structures the target directory in a workspace like this because the crates in a workspace are meant to depend on each other. If each crate had its own *target* directory, each crate would have to recompile each of the other crates in the workspace to have the artifacts in its own *target* directory. By sharing one *target* directory, the crates can avoid unnecessary rebuilding.

Creating the Second Crate in the Workspace

Next, let's create another member crate in the workspace and call it add-one. Change the top-level *Cargo.toml* to specify the *add-one* path in the members list:

Cargo.toml

```
[workspace]

members = [
    "adder",
    "add-one",
]
```

Then generate a new library crate named add-one:

```
$ cargo new add-one --lib
    Created library `add-one` project
```

Your *add* directory should now have these directories and files:

```
├── Cargo.lock
├── Cargo.toml
├── add-one
│   ├── Cargo.toml
│   └── src
│       └── lib.rs
├── adder
│   ├── Cargo.toml
│   └── src
│       └── main.rs
└── target
```

In the *add-one/src/lib.rs* file, let's add an add_one function:

add-one/src/lib.rs

```
pub fn add_one(x: i32) -> i32 {
    x + 1
}
```

Now that we have a library crate in the workspace, we can have the binary crate adder depend on the library crate add-one. First, we'll need to add a path dependency on add-one to *adder/Cargo.toml*.

```
[dependencies]

add-one = { path = "../add-one" }
```

Cargo doesn't assume that crates in a workspace will depend on each other, so we need to be explicit about the dependency relationships between the crates.

Next, let's use the `add_one` function from the add-one crate in the adder crate. Open the *adder/src/main.rs* file and add an extern crate line at the top to bring the new add-one library crate into scope. Then change the main function to call the add_one function, as in Listing 14-7.

```
extern crate add_one;

fn main() {
    let num = 10;
    println!("Hello, world! {} plus one is {}!", num, add_one::add_one(num));
}
```

Listing 14-7: Using the add-one library crate from the adder crate

Let's build the workspace by running `cargo build` in the top-level *add* directory!

```
$ cargo build
   Compiling add-one v0.1.0 (file:///projects/add/add-one)
   Compiling adder v0.1.0 (file:///projects/add/adder)
    Finished dev [unoptimized + debuginfo] target(s) in 0.68 secs
```

To run the binary crate from the *add* directory, we need to specify which package in the workspace we want to use by including the -p argument and the package name with `cargo run`:

```
$ cargo run -p adder
    Finished dev [unoptimized + debuginfo] target(s) in 0.0 secs
     Running `target/debug/adder`
Hello, world! 10 plus one is 11!
```

This runs the code in *adder/src/main.rs*, which depends on the add-one crate.

Depending on an External Crate in a Workspace

Notice that the workspace has only one *Cargo.lock* file at the top level of the workspace rather than having a *Cargo.lock* in each crate's directory. This ensures that all crates are using the same version of all dependencies. If we add the rand crate to the *adder/Cargo.toml* and *add-one/Cargo.toml* files, Cargo will resolve both of those to one version of rand and record that in the one *Cargo.lock*. Making all crates in the workspace use the same dependencies means the crates in the workspace will always be compatible with each other. Let's add the rand crate to the [dependencies] section in the *add-one/Cargo.toml* file to be able to use the rand crate in the add-one crate:

add-one/Cargo.toml
```
[dependencies]

rand = "0.3.14"
```

We can now add extern crate rand; to the *add-one/src/lib.rs* file, and building the whole workspace by running cargo build in the *add* directory will bring in and compile the rand crate:

```
$ cargo build
    Updating registry `https://github.com/rust-lang/crates.io-index`
 Downloading rand v0.3.14
   --snip--
   Compiling rand v0.3.14
   Compiling add-one v0.1.0 (file:///projects/add/add-one)
   Compiling adder v0.1.0 (file:///projects/add/adder)
   Finished dev [unoptimized + debuginfo] target(s) in 10.18 secs
```

The top-level *Cargo.lock* now contains information about the dependency of add-one on rand. However, even though rand is used somewhere in the workspace, we can't use it in other crates in the workspace unless we add rand to their *Cargo.toml* files as well. For example, if we add extern crate rand; to the *adder/src/main.rs* file for the adder crate, we'll get an error:

```
$ cargo build
   Compiling adder v0.1.0 (file:///projects/add/adder)
error: use of unstable library feature 'rand': use `rand` from crates.io (see
issue #27703)
 --> adder/src/main.rs:1:1
  |
1 | extern crate rand;
```

To fix this, edit the *Cargo.toml* file for the adder crate and indicate that rand is a dependency for that crate as well. Building the adder crate will add rand to the list of dependencies for adder in *Cargo.lock*, but no additional copies of rand will be downloaded. Cargo has ensured that every crate in the workspace using the rand crate will be using the same version. Using the same version of rand across the workspace saves space because we won't have multiple copies and ensures that the crates in the workspace will be compatible with each other.

Adding a Test to a Workspace

For another enhancement, let's add a test of the add_one::add_one function within the add_one crate:

add-one/src/lib.rs
```
pub fn add_one(x: i32) -> i32 {
    x + 1
}
```

```
#[cfg(test)]
mod tests {
    use super::*;

    #[test]
    fn it_works() {
        assert_eq!(3, add_one(2));
    }
}
```

Now run cargo test in the top-level *add* directory:

```
$ cargo test
   Compiling add-one v0.1.0 (file:///projects/add/add-one)
   Compiling adder v0.1.0 (file:///projects/add/adder)
    Finished dev [unoptimized + debuginfo] target(s) in 0.27 secs
     Running target/debug/deps/add_one-f0253159197f7841

running 1 test
test tests::it_works ... ok

test result: ok. 1 passed; 0 failed; 0 ignored; 0 measured; 0 filtered out

     Running target/debug/deps/adder-f88af9d2cc175a5e

running 0 tests

test result: ok. 0 passed; 0 failed; 0 ignored; 0 measured; 0 filtered out

   Doc-tests add-one

running 0 tests

test result: ok. 0 passed; 0 failed; 0 ignored; 0 measured; 0 filtered out
```

The first section of the output shows that the it_works test in the add-one crate passed. The next section shows that zero tests were found in the adder crate, and then the last section shows zero documentation tests were found in the add-one crate. Running cargo test in a workspace structured like this one will run the tests for all the crates in the workspace.

We can also run tests for one particular crate in a workspace from the top-level directory by using the -p flag and specifying the name of the crate we want to test:

```
$ cargo test -p add-one
    Finished dev [unoptimized + debuginfo] target(s) in 0.0 secs
     Running target/debug/deps/add_one-b3235fea9a156f74

running 1 test
test tests::it_works ... ok

test result: ok. 1 passed; 0 failed; 0 ignored; 0 measured; 0 filtered out
```

```
    Doc-tests add-one

running 0 tests

test result: ok. 0 passed; 0 failed; 0 ignored; 0 measured; 0 filtered out
```

This output shows cargo test only ran the tests for the add-one crate and didn't run the adder crate tests.

If you publish the crates in the workspace to *https://crates.io/*, each crate in the workspace will need to be published separately. The cargo publish command does not have an --all flag or a -p flag, so you must change to each crate's directory and run cargo publish on each crate in the workspace to publish the crates.

For additional practice, add an add-two crate to this workspace in a similar way as the add-one crate!

As your project grows, consider using a workspace: it's easier to understand smaller, individual components than one big blob of code. Furthermore, keeping the crates in a workspace can make coordination between them easier if they are often changed at the same time.

Installing Binaries from Crates.io with cargo install

The cargo install command allows you to install and use binary crates locally. This isn't intended to replace system packages; it's meant to be a convenient way for Rust developers to install tools that others have shared on *https://crates.io/*. Note that you can only install packages that have binary targets. A *binary target* is the runnable program that is created if the crate has a *src/main.rs* file or another file specified as a binary, as opposed to a library target that isn't runnable on its own but is suitable for including within other programs. Usually, crates have information in the *README* file about whether a crate is a library, has a binary target, or both.

All binaries installed with cargo install are stored in the installation root's *bin* folder. If you installed Rust using rustup and don't have any custom configurations, this directory will be *$HOME/.cargo/bin*. Ensure that directory is in your $PATH to be able to run programs you've installed with cargo install.

For example, in Chapter 12 we mentioned that there's a Rust implementation of the grep tool called ripgrep for searching files. If we want to install ripgrep, we can run the following:

```
$ cargo install ripgrep
Updating registry `https://github.com/rust-lang/crates.io-index`
 Downloading ripgrep v0.3.2
 --snip--
   Compiling ripgrep v0.3.2
    Finished release [optimized + debuginfo] target(s) in 97.91 secs
  Installing ~/.cargo/bin/rg
```

The last line of the output shows the location and the name of the installed binary, which in the case of ripgrep is rg. As long as the installation directory is in your $PATH, as mentioned previously, you can then run rg --help and start using a faster, rustier tool for searching files!

Extending Cargo with Custom Commands

Cargo is designed so you can extend it with new subcommands without having to modify Cargo. If a binary in your $PATH is named cargo-something, you can run it as if it were a Cargo subcommand by running cargo something. Custom commands like this are also listed when you run cargo --list. Being able to use cargo install to install extensions and then run them just like the built-in Cargo tools is a super convenient benefit of Cargo's design!

Summary

Sharing code with Cargo and *https://crates.io/* is part of what makes the Rust ecosystem useful for many different tasks. Rust's standard library is small and stable, but crates are easy to share, use, and improve on a timeline different from that of the language. Don't be shy about sharing code that's useful to you on *https://crates.io/*; it's likely that it will be useful to someone else as well!

15

SMART POINTERS

A *pointer* is a general concept for a variable that contains an address in memory. This address refers to, or "points at," some other data. The most common kind of pointer in Rust is a reference, which you learned about in Chapter 4. References are indicated by the & symbol and borrow the value they point to. They don't have any special capabilities other than referring to data. Also, they don't have any overhead and are the kind of pointer we use most often.

Smart pointers, on the other hand, are data structures that not only act like a pointer but also have additional metadata and capabilities. The concept of smart pointers isn't unique to Rust: smart pointers originated in C++ and exist in other languages as well. In Rust, the different smart pointers defined in the standard library provide functionality beyond that provided by references. One example that we'll explore in this chapter is the *reference counting* smart pointer type. This pointer enables you to have multiple owners of data by keeping track of the number of owners and, when no owners remain, cleaning up the data.

In Rust, which uses the concept of ownership and borrowing, an additional difference between references and smart pointers is that references are pointers that only borrow data; in contrast, in many cases, smart pointers *own* the data they point to.

We've already encountered a few smart pointers in this book, such as String and Vec<T> in Chapter 8, although we didn't call them smart pointers at the time. Both these types count as smart pointers because they own some memory and allow you to manipulate it. They also have metadata (such as their capacity) and extra capabilities or guarantees (such as with String ensuring its data will always be valid UTF-8).

Smart pointers are usually implemented using structs. The characteristic that distinguishes a smart pointer from an ordinary struct is that smart pointers implement the Deref and Drop traits. The Deref trait allows an instance of the smart pointer struct to behave like a reference so you can write code that works with either references or smart pointers. The Drop trait allows you to customize the code that is run when an instance of the smart pointer goes out of scope. In this chapter, we'll discuss both traits and demonstrate why they're important to smart pointers.

Given that the smart pointer pattern is a general design pattern used frequently in Rust, this chapter won't cover every existing smart pointer. Many libraries have their own smart pointers, and you can even write your own. We'll cover the most common smart pointers in the standard library:

- Box<T> for allocating values on the heap
- Rc<T>, a reference counting type that enables multiple ownership
- Ref<T> and RefMut<T>, accessed through RefCell<T>, a type that enforces the borrowing rules at runtime instead of compile time

In addition, we'll cover the *interior mutability* pattern where an immutable type exposes an API for mutating an interior value. We'll also discuss *reference cycles*: how they can leak memory and how to prevent them.

Let's dive in!

Using Box<T> to Point to Data on the Heap

The most straightforward smart pointer is a *box*, whose type is written Box<T>. Boxes allow you to store data on the heap rather than the stack. What remains on the stack is the pointer to the heap data. Refer to Chapter 4 to review the difference between the stack and the heap.

Boxes don't have performance overhead, other than storing their data on the heap instead of on the stack. But they don't have many extra capabilities either. You'll use them most often in these situations:

- When you have a type whose size can't be known at compile time and you want to use a value of that type in a context that requires an exact size
- When you have a large amount of data and you want to transfer ownership but ensure the data won't be copied when you do so
- When you want to own a value and you care only that it's a type that implements a particular trait rather than being of a specific type

We'll demonstrate the first situation in "Enabling Recursive Types with Boxes" on page 308. In the second case, transferring ownership of a large amount of data can take a long time because the data is copied around on the stack. To improve performance in this situation, we can store the large amount of data on the heap in a box. Then, only the small amount of pointer data is copied around on the stack, while the data it references stays in one place on the heap. The third case is known as a *trait object*, and Chapter 17 devotes an entire section ("Using Trait Objects That Allow for Values of Different Types" on page 369) just to that topic. So what you learn here you'll apply again in Chapter 17!

Using a Box<T> to Store Data on the Heap

Before we discuss this use case for Box<T>, we'll cover the syntax and how to interact with values stored within a Box<T>.

Listing 15-1 shows how to use a box to store an i32 value on the heap.

src/main.rs

```
fn main() {
    let b = Box::new(5);
    println!("b = {}", b);
}
```

Listing 15-1: Storing an i32 value on the heap using a box

We define the variable b to have the value of a Box that points to the value 5, which is allocated on the heap. This program will print b = 5; in this case, we can access the data in the box similar to how we would if this data were on the stack. Just like any owned value, when a box goes out of scope, as b does at the end of main, it will be deallocated. The deallocation happens for the box (stored on the stack) and the data it points to (stored on the heap).

Putting a single value on the heap isn't very useful, so you won't use boxes by themselves in this way very often. Having values like a single i32 on the stack, where they're stored by default, is more appropriate in the majority of situations. Let's look at a case where boxes allow us to define types that we wouldn't be allowed to if we didn't have boxes.

Enabling Recursive Types with Boxes

At compile time, Rust needs to know how much space a type takes up. One type whose size can't be known at compile time is a *recursive type*, where a value can have as part of itself another value of the same type. Because this nesting of values could theoretically continue infinitely, Rust doesn't know how much space a value of a recursive type needs. However, boxes have a known size, so by inserting a box in a recursive type definition, you can have recursive types.

Let's explore the *cons list*, which is a data type common in functional programming languages, as an example of a recursive type. The cons list type we'll define is straightforward except for the recursion; therefore, the concepts in the example we'll work with will be useful any time you get into more complex situations involving recursive types.

More Information About the Cons List

A *cons list* is a data structure that comes from the Lisp programming language and its dialects. In Lisp, the cons function (short for "construct function") constructs a new pair from its two arguments, which usually are a single value and another pair. These pairs containing pairs form a list.

The cons function concept has made its way into more general functional programming jargon: "to cons *x* onto *y*" informally means to construct a new container instance by putting the element *x* at the start of this new container, followed by the container *y*.

Each item in a cons list contains two elements: the value of the current item and the next item. The last item in the list contains only a value called Nil without a next item. A cons list is produced by recursively calling the cons function. The canonical name to denote the base case of the recursion is Nil. Note that this is not the same as the "null" concept in Chapter 6, which is an invalid or absent value.

Although functional programming languages use cons lists frequently, the cons list isn't a commonly used data structure in Rust. Most of the time when you have a list of items in Rust, Vec<T> is a better choice. Other, more complex recursive data types *are* useful in various situations, but by starting with the cons list, we can explore how boxes let us define a recursive data type without much distraction.

Listing 15-2 contains an enum definition for a cons list. Note that this code won't compile yet because the List type doesn't have a known size, which we'll demonstrate.

src/main.rs

```
enum List {
    Cons(i32, List),
    Nil,
}
```

Listing 15-2: The first attempt at defining an enum to represent a cons list data structure of i32 values

We're implementing a cons list that holds only i32 values for the purposes of this example. We could have implemented it using generics, as we discussed in Chapter 10, to define a cons list type that could store values of any type.

Using the List type to store the list 1, 2, 3 would look like the code in Listing 15-3.

src/main.rs

```
use List::{Cons, Nil};

fn main() {
    let list = Cons(1, Cons(2, Cons(3, Nil)));
}
```

Listing 15-3: Using the List enum to store the list 1, 2, 3

The first Cons value holds 1 and another List value. This List value is another Cons value that holds 2 and another List value. This List value is one more Cons value that holds 3 and a List value, which is finally Nil, the non-recursive variant that signals the end of the list.

If we try to compile the code in Listing 15-3, we get the error shown in Listing 15-4.

```
error[E0072]: recursive type `List` has infinite size
 --> src/main.rs:1:1
  |
1 | enum List {
  | ^^^^^^^^^ recursive type has infinite size
2 |     Cons(i32, List),
  |               ----- recursive without indirection
  |
  = help: insert indirection (e.g., a `Box`, `Rc`, or `&`) at some point to
  make `List` representable
```

Listing 15-4: The error we get when attempting to define a recursive enum

The error shows this type "has infinite size." The reason is that we've defined List with a variant that is recursive: it holds another value of itself directly. As a result, Rust can't figure out how much space it needs to store a List value. Let's break down why we get this error a bit. First, let's look at how Rust decides how much space it needs to store a value of a non-recursive type.

Computing the Size of a Non-Recursive Type

Recall the Message enum we defined in Listing 6-2 when we discussed enum definitions in Chapter 6:

```
enum Message {
    Quit,
    Move { x: i32, y: i32 },
    Write(String),
    ChangeColor(i32, i32, i32),
}
```

To determine how much space to allocate for a Message value, Rust goes through each of the variants to see which variant needs the most space. Rust sees that Message::Quit doesn't need any space, Message::Move needs enough space to store two i32 values, and so forth. Because only one variant will be used, the most space a Message value will need is the space it would take to store the largest of its variants.

Contrast this with what happens when Rust tries to determine how much space a recursive type like the List enum in Listing 15-2 needs. The compiler starts by looking at the Cons variant, which holds a value of type i32 and a value of type List. Therefore, Cons needs an amount of space equal to the size of an i32 plus the size of a List. To figure out how much memory the List type needs, the compiler looks at the variants, starting with the Cons variant. The Cons variant holds a value of type i32 and a value of type List, and this process continues infinitely, as shown in Figure 15-1.

Figure 15-1: An infinite List consisting of infinite Cons variants

Using Box<T> to Get a Recursive Type with a Known Size

Rust can't figure out how much space to allocate for recursively defined types, so the compiler gives the error in Listing 15-4. But the error does include this helpful suggestion:

```
= help: insert indirection (e.g., a `Box`, `Rc`, or `&`) at some point to
make `List` representable
```

In this suggestion, *indirection* means that instead of storing a value directly, we'll change the data structure to store the value indirectly by storing a pointer to the value instead.

Because a Box<T> is a pointer, Rust always knows how much space a Box<T> needs: a pointer's size doesn't change based on the amount of data it's pointing to. This means we can put a Box<T> inside the Cons variant instead of another List value directly. The Box<T> will point to the next List value that will be on the heap rather than inside the Cons variant. Conceptually, we still have a list, created with lists "holding" other lists, but this implementation is now more like placing the items next to one another rather than inside one another.

We can change the definition of the List enum in Listing 15-2 and the usage of the List in Listing 15-3 to the code in Listing 15-5, which will compile.

src/main.rs

```
enum List {
    Cons(i32, Box<List>),
    Nil,
}
```

```
use List::{Cons, Nil};

fn main() {
    let list = Cons(1,
        Box::new(Cons(2,
            Box::new(Cons(3,
                Box::new(Nil))))));
}
```

Listing 15-5: Definition of `List` that uses `Box<T>` in order to have a known size

The `Cons` variant will need the size of an `i32` plus the space to store the box's pointer data. The `Nil` variant stores no values, so it needs less space than the `Cons` variant. We now know that any `List` value will take up the size of an `i32` plus the size of a box's pointer data. By using a box, we've broken the infinite, recursive chain, so the compiler can figure out the size it needs to store a `List` value. Figure 15-2 shows what the `Cons` variant looks like now.

Figure 15-2: A `List` that is not infinitely sized because `Cons` holds a `Box`

Boxes provide only the indirection and heap allocation; they don't have any other special capabilities, like those we'll see with the other smart pointer types. They also don't have any performance overhead that these special capabilities incur, so they can be useful in cases like the cons list where the indirection is the only feature we need. We'll look at more use cases for boxes in Chapter 17, too.

The `Box<T>` type is a smart pointer because it implements the `Deref` trait, which allows `Box<T>` values to be treated like references. When a `Box<T>` value goes out of scope, the heap data that the box is pointing to is cleaned up as well because of the `Drop` trait implementation. Let's explore these two traits in more detail. These two traits will be even more important to the functionality provided by the other smart pointer types we'll discuss in the rest of this chapter.

Treating Smart Pointers Like Regular References with the Deref Trait

Implementing the `Deref` trait allows you to customize the behavior of the *dereference operator,* * (as opposed to the multiplication or glob operator). By implementing `Deref` in such a way that a smart pointer can be treated like a regular reference, you can write code that operates on references and use that code with smart pointers too.

Let's first look at how the dereference operator works with regular references. Then we'll try to define a custom type that behaves like `Box<T>`, and see why the dereference operator doesn't work like a reference on our newly defined type. We'll explore how implementing the `Deref` trait makes it possible for smart pointers to work in a similar way as references. Then we'll look at Rust's *deref coercion* feature and how it lets us work with either references or smart pointers.

Following the Pointer to the Value with the Dereference Operator

A regular reference is a type of pointer, and one way to think of a pointer is as an arrow to a value stored somewhere else. In Listing 15-6, we create a reference to an i32 value and then use the dereference operator to follow the reference to the data.

```
fn main() {
❶ let x = 5;
❷ let y = &x;

❸ assert_eq!(5, x);
❹ assert_eq!(5, *y);
}
```

Listing 15-6: Using the dereference operator to follow a reference to an i32 value

The variable x holds an i32 value, 5 ❶. We set y equal to a reference to x ❷. We can assert that x is equal to 5 ❸. However, if we want to make an assertion about the value in y, we have to use *y to follow the reference to the value it's pointing to (hence *dereference*) ❹. Once we dereference y, we have access to the integer value y is pointing to, which we can compare with 5.

If we tried to write assert_eq!(5, y); instead, we would get this compilation error:

```
error[E0277]: the trait bound `{integer}: std::cmp::PartialEq<&{integer}>` is
not satisfied
  --> src/main.rs:6:5
   |
6  |     assert_eq!(5, y);
   |     ^^^^^^^^^^^^^^^^^ can't compare `{integer}` with `&{integer}`
   |
   = help: the trait `std::cmp::PartialEq<&{integer}>` is not implemented for
`{integer}`
```

Comparing a number and a reference to a number isn't allowed because they're different types. We must use the dereference operator to follow the reference to the value it's pointing to.

Using Box<T> Like a Reference

We can rewrite the code in Listing 15-6 to use a Box<T> instead of a reference; the dereference operator will work as shown in Listing 15-7.

```
fn main() {
    let x = 5;
❶ let y = Box::new(x);

    assert_eq!(5, x);
❷ assert_eq!(5, *y);
}
```

Listing 15-7: Using the dereference operator on a Box<i32>

The only difference between Listing 15-7 and Listing 15-6 is that here we set y to be an instance of a box pointing to the value in x rather than a reference pointing to the value of x ❶. In the last assertion ❷, we can use the dereference operator to follow the box's pointer in the same way that we did when y was a reference. Next, we'll explore what is special about Box<T> that enables us to use the dereference operator by defining our own box type.

Defining Our Own Smart Pointer

Let's build a smart pointer similar to the Box<T> type provided by the standard library to experience how smart pointers behave differently than references by default. Then we'll look at how to add the ability to use the dereference operator.

The Box<T> type is ultimately defined as a tuple struct with one element, so Listing 15-8 defines a MyBox<T> type in the same way. We'll also define a new function to match the new function defined on Box<T>.

src/main.rs

```
❶ struct MyBox<T>(T);

impl<T> MyBox<T> {
❷ fn new(x: T) -> MyBox<T> {
    ❸ MyBox(x)
    }
}
```

Listing 15-8: Defining a MyBox<T> type

We define a struct named MyBox and declare a generic parameter T ❶, because we want our type to hold values of any type. The MyBox type is a tuple struct with one element of type T. The MyBox::new function takes one parameter of type T ❷ and returns a MyBox instance that holds the value passed in ❸.

Let's try adding the main function in Listing 15-7 to Listing 15-8 and changing it to use the MyBox<T> type we've defined instead of Box<T>. The code in Listing 15-9 won't compile because Rust doesn't know how to dereference MyBox.

src/main.rs

```
fn main() {
    let x = 5;
    let y = MyBox::new(x);

    assert_eq!(5, x);
    assert_eq!(5, *y);
}
```

Listing 15-9: Attempting to use MyBox<T> in the same way we used references and Box<T>

Here's the resulting compilation error:

```
error[E0614]: type `MyBox<{integer}>` cannot be dereferenced
  --> src/main.rs:14:19
   |
```

```
14 |    assert_eq!(5, *y);
   |                  ^^
```

Our MyBox<T> type can't be dereferenced because we haven't implemented
that ability on our type. To enable dereferencing with the * operator, we
implement the Deref trait.

Treating a Type Like a Reference by Implementing the Deref Trait

As discussed in Chapter 10, to implement a trait, we need to provide implementations for the trait's required methods. The Deref trait, provided by the
standard library, requires us to implement one method named deref that
borrows self and returns a reference to the inner data. Listing 15-10 contains an implementation of Deref to add to the definition of MyBox.

src/main.rs

```
use std::ops::Deref;

impl<T> Deref for MyBox<T> {
❶ type Target = T;

    fn deref(&self) -> &T {
    ❷ &self.0
    }
}
```

Listing 15-10: Implementing Deref on MyBox<T>

The type Target = T; syntax ❶ defines an associated type for the Deref
trait to use. Associated types are a slightly different way of declaring a
generic parameter, but you don't need to worry about them for now; we'll
cover them in more detail in Chapter 19.

We fill in the body of the deref method with &self.0 so deref returns a
reference to the value we want to access with the * operator ❷. The main
function in Listing 15-9 that calls * on the MyBox<T> value now compiles,
and the assertions pass!

Without the Deref trait, the compiler can dereference only & references.
The deref method gives the compiler the ability to take a value of any type
that implements Deref and call the deref method to get a & reference that it
knows how to dereference.

When we entered *y in Listing 15-9, behind the scenes Rust actually ran
this code:

```
*(y.deref())
```

Rust substitutes the * operator with a call to the deref method and then a
plain dereference so we don't have to think about whether or not we need to
call the deref method. This Rust feature lets us write code that functions iden-
tically whether we have a regular reference or a type that implements Deref.

The reason the deref method returns a reference to a value and that the
plain dereference outside the parentheses in *(y.deref()) is still necessary

is the ownership system. If the `deref` method returned the value directly instead of a reference to the value, the value would be moved out of `self`. We don't want to take ownership of the inner value inside `MyBox<T>` in this case or in most cases where we use the dereference operator.

Note that the `*` operator is replaced with a call to the `deref` method and then a call to the `*` operator just once, each time we use a `*` in our code. Because the substitution of the `*` operator does not recurse infinitely, we end up with data of type `i32`, which matches the 5 in `assert_eq!` in Listing 15-9.

Implicit Deref Coercions with Functions and Methods

Deref coercion is a convenience that Rust performs on arguments to functions and methods. Deref coercion converts a reference to a type that implements `Deref` into a reference to a type that `Deref` can convert the original type into. Deref coercion happens automatically when we pass a reference to a particular type's value as an argument to a function or method that doesn't match the parameter type in the function or method definition. A sequence of calls to the `deref` method converts the type we provided into the type the parameter needs.

Deref coercion was added to Rust so that programmers writing function and method calls don't need to add as many explicit references and dereferences with `&` and `*`. The deref coercion feature also lets us write more code that can work for either references or smart pointers.

To see deref coercion in action, let's use the `MyBox<T>` type we defined in Listing 15-8 as well as the implementation of `Deref` that we added in Listing 15-10. Listing 15-11 shows the definition of a function that has a string slice parameter.

src/main.rs

```
fn hello(name: &str) {
    println!("Hello, {}!", name);
}
```

Listing 15-11: A hello function that has the parameter name of type &str

We can call the `hello` function with a string slice as an argument, such as `hello("Rust")`; for example. Deref coercion makes it possible to call `hello` with a reference to a value of type `MyBox<String>`, as shown in Listing 15-12.

src/main.rs

```
fn main() {
    let m = MyBox::new(String::from("Rust"));
    hello(&m);
}
```

Listing 15-12: Calling hello with a reference to a MyBox<String> value, which works because of deref coercion

Here we're calling the `hello` function with the argument `&m`, which is a reference to a `MyBox<String>` value. Because we implemented the `Deref` trait on `MyBox<T>` in Listing 15-10, Rust can turn `&MyBox<String>` into `&String` by calling deref. The standard library provides an implementation of `Deref` on

String that returns a string slice, and this is in the API documentation for Deref. Rust calls deref again to turn the &String into &str, which matches the hello function's definition.

If Rust didn't implement deref coercion, we would have to write the code in Listing 15-13 instead of the code in Listing 15-12 to call hello with a value of type &MyBox<String>.

src/main.rs

```
fn main() {
    let m = MyBox::new(String::from("Rust"));
    hello(&(*m)[..]);
}
```

Listing 15-13: The code we would have to write if Rust didn't have deref coercion

The (*m) dereferences the MyBox<String> into a String. Then the & and [..] take a string slice of the String that is equal to the whole string to match the signature of hello. The code without deref coercions is harder to read, write, and understand with all of these symbols involved. Deref coercion allows Rust to handle these conversions for us automatically.

When the Deref trait is defined for the types involved, Rust will analyze the types and use Deref::deref as many times as necessary to get a reference to match the parameter's type. The number of times that Deref::deref needs to be inserted is resolved at compile time, so there is no runtime penalty for taking advantage of deref coercion!

How Deref Coercion Interacts with Mutability

Similar to how you use the Deref trait to override the * operator on immutable references, you can use the DerefMut trait to override the * operator on mutable references.

Rust does deref coercion when it finds types and trait implementations in three cases:

- From &T to &U when T: Deref<Target=U>
- From &mut T to &mut U when T: DerefMut<Target=U>
- From &mut T to &U when T: Deref<Target=U>

The first two cases are the same except for mutability. The first case states that if you have a &T, and T implements Deref to some type U, you can get a &U transparently. The second case states that the same deref coercion happens for mutable references.

The third case is trickier: Rust will also coerce a mutable reference to an immutable one. But the reverse is *not* possible: immutable references will never coerce to mutable references. Because of the borrowing rules, if you have a mutable reference, that mutable reference must be the only reference to that data (otherwise, the program wouldn't compile). Converting one mutable reference to one immutable reference will never break the borrowing rules. Converting an immutable reference to a mutable reference would require that there is only one immutable reference to that data, and the borrowing rules don't guarantee that. Therefore, Rust can't make the assumption that converting an immutable reference to a mutable reference is possible.

Running Code on Cleanup with the Drop Trait

The second trait important to the smart pointer pattern is Drop, which lets you customize what happens when a value is about to go out of scope. You can provide an implementation for the Drop trait on any type, and the code you specify can be used to release resources like files or network connections. We're introducing Drop in the context of smart pointers because the functionality of the Drop trait is almost always used when implementing a smart pointer. For example, Box<T> customizes Drop to deallocate the space on the heap that the box points to.

In some languages, the programmer must call code to free memory or resources every time they finish using an instance of a smart pointer. If they forget, the system might become overloaded and crash. In Rust, you can specify that a particular bit of code be run whenever a value goes out of scope, and the compiler will insert this code automatically. As a result, you don't need to be careful about placing cleanup code everywhere in a program that an instance of a particular type is finished with—you still won't leak resources!

Specify the code to run when a value goes out of scope by implementing the Drop trait. The Drop trait requires you to implement one method named drop that takes a mutable reference to self. To see when Rust calls drop, let's implement drop with println! statements for now.

Listing 15-14 shows a CustomSmartPointer struct whose only custom functionality is that it will print Dropping CustomSmartPointer! when the instance goes out of scope. This example demonstrates when Rust runs the drop function.

src/main.rs

```
struct CustomSmartPointer {
    data: String,
}

❶ impl Drop for CustomSmartPointer {
    fn drop(&mut self) {
      ❷ println!("Dropping CustomSmartPointer with data `{}`!", self.data);
    }
}

fn main() {
  ❸ let c = CustomSmartPointer { data: String::from("my stuff") };
  ❹ let d = CustomSmartPointer { data: String::from("other stuff") };
  ❺ println!("CustomSmartPointers created.");
❻ }
```

Listing 15-14: A CustomSmartPointer struct that implements the Drop trait where we would put our cleanup code

The Drop trait is included in the prelude, so we don't need to import it. We implement the Drop trait on CustomSmartPointer ❶ and provide an implementation for the drop method that calls println! ❷. The body of the drop function is where you would place any logic that you wanted to run when an instance of your type goes out of scope. We're printing some text here to demonstrate when Rust will call drop.

In main, we create two instances of CustomSmartPointer ❸❹ and then print CustomSmartPointers created. ❺. At the end of main ❻, our instances of CustomSmartPointer will go out of scope, and Rust will call the code we put in the drop method ❷, printing our final message. Note that we didn't need to call the drop method explicitly.

When we run this program, we'll see the following output:

```
CustomSmartPointers created.
Dropping CustomSmartPointer with data `other stuff`!
Dropping CustomSmartPointer with data `my stuff`!
```

Rust automatically called drop for us when our instances went out of scope, calling the code we specified. Variables are dropped in the reverse order of their creation, so d was dropped before c. This example gives you a visual guide to how the drop method works; usually you would specify the cleanup code that your type needs to run rather than a print message.

Dropping a Value Early with std::mem::drop

Unfortunately, it's not straightforward to disable the automatic drop functionality. Disabling drop isn't usually necessary; the whole point of the Drop trait is that it's taken care of automatically. Occasionally, however, you might want to clean up a value early. One example is when using smart pointers that manage locks: you might want to force the drop method that releases the lock to run so other code in the same scope can acquire the lock. Rust doesn't let you call the Drop trait's drop method manually; instead you have to call the std::mem::drop function provided by the standard library if you want to force a value to be dropped before the end of its scope.

If we try to call the Drop trait's drop method manually by modifying the main function in Listing 15-14, as shown in Listing 15-15, we'll get a compiler error.

src/main.rs

```
fn main() {
    let c = CustomSmartPointer { data: String::from("some data") };
    println!("CustomSmartPointer created.");
    c.drop();
    println!("CustomSmartPointer dropped before the end of main.");
}
```

Listing 15-15: Attempting to call the drop method from the Drop trait manually to clean up early

When we try to compile this code, we'll get this error:

```
error[E0040]: explicit use of destructor method
  --> src/main.rs:14:7
   |
14 |     c.drop();
   |       ^^^^ explicit destructor calls not allowed
```

This error message states that we're not allowed to explicitly call drop. The error message uses the term *destructor*, which is the general programming term for a function that cleans up an instance. A destructor is analogous to a *constructor*, which creates an instance. The drop function in Rust is one particular destructor.

Rust doesn't let us call drop explicitly because Rust would still automatically call drop on the value at the end of main. This would be a *double free* error because Rust would be trying to clean up the same value twice.

We can't disable the automatic insertion of drop when a value goes out of scope, and we can't call the drop method explicitly. So, if we need to force a value to be cleaned up early, we can use the std::mem::drop function.

The std::mem::drop function is different from the drop method in the Drop trait. We call it by passing the value we want to force to be dropped early as an argument. The function is in the prelude, so we can modify main in Listing 15-15 to call the drop function, as shown in Listing 15-16.

src/main.rs
```
fn main() {
    let c = CustomSmartPointer { data: String::from("some data") };
    println!("CustomSmartPointer created.");
    drop(c);
    println!("CustomSmartPointer dropped before the end of main.");
}
```

Listing 15-16: Calling *std::mem::drop* to explicitly drop a value before it goes out of scope

Running this code will print the following:

```
CustomSmartPointer created.
Dropping CustomSmartPointer with data `some data`!
CustomSmartPointer dropped before the end of main.
```

The text Dropping CustomSmartPointer with data `some data`! is printed between the CustomSmartPointer created. and CustomSmartPointer dropped before the end of main. text, showing that the drop method code is called to drop c at that point.

You can use code specified in a Drop trait implementation in many ways to make cleanup convenient and safe: for instance, you could use it to create your own memory allocator! With the Drop trait and Rust's ownership system, you don't have to remember to clean up because Rust does it automatically.

You also don't have to worry about problems resulting from accidentally cleaning up values still in use: the ownership system that makes sure references are always valid also ensures that drop gets called only once when the value is no longer being used.

Now that we've examined Box<T> and some of the characteristics of smart pointers, let's look at a few other smart pointers defined in the standard library.

Rc<T>, the Reference Counted Smart Pointer

In the majority of cases, ownership is clear: you know exactly which variable owns a given value. However, there are cases when a single value might have multiple owners. For example, in graph data structures, multiple edges might point to the same node, and that node is conceptually owned by all of the edges that point to it. A node shouldn't be cleaned up unless it doesn't have any edges pointing to it.

To enable multiple ownership, Rust has a type called Rc<T>, which is an abbreviation for *reference counting*. The Rc<T> type keeps track of the number of references to a value, which determines whether or not a value is still in use. If there are zero references to a value, the value can be cleaned up without any references becoming invalid.

Imagine Rc<T> as a TV in a family room. When one person enters to watch TV, they turn it on. Others can come into the room and watch the TV. When the last person leaves the room, they turn off the TV because it's no longer being used. If someone turns off the TV while others are still watching it, there would be uproar from the remaining TV watchers!

We use the Rc<T> type when we want to allocate some data on the heap for multiple parts of our program to read and we can't determine at compile time which part will finish using the data last. If we knew which part would finish last, we could just make that part the data's owner, and the normal ownership rules enforced at compile time would take effect.

Note that Rc<T> is only for use in single-threaded scenarios. When we discuss concurrency in Chapter 16, we'll cover how to do reference counting in multithreaded programs.

Using Rc<T> to Share Data

Let's return to our cons list example in Listing 15-5. Recall that we defined it using Box<T>. This time, we'll create two lists that share ownership of a third list. Conceptually, this looks similar to Figure 15-3.

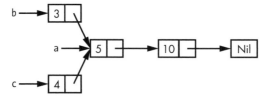

Figure 15-3: Two lists, b and c, sharing ownership of a third list, a

We'll create list a that contains 5 and then 10. Then we'll make two more lists: b that starts with 3 and c that starts with 4. Both b and c lists will then continue on to the first a list containing 5 and 10. In other words, both lists will share the first list containing 5 and 10.

Trying to implement this scenario using our definition of List with Box<T> won't work, as shown in Listing 15-17.

src/main.rs

```
enum List {
    Cons(i32, Box<List>),
    Nil,
}

use List::{Cons, Nil};

fn main() {
    let a = Cons(5,
        Box::new(Cons(10,
            Box::new(Nil))));
❶ let b = Cons(3, Box::new(a));
❷ let c = Cons(4, Box::new(a));
}
```

Listing 15-17: Demonstrating we're not allowed to have two lists using Box<T> that try to share ownership of a third list

When we compile this code, we get this error:

```
error[E0382]: use of moved value: `a`
  --> src/main.rs:13:30
   |
12 |     let b = Cons(3, Box::new(a));
   |                              - value moved here
13 |     let c = Cons(4, Box::new(a));
   |                              ^ value used here after move
   |
   = note: move occurs because `a` has type `List`, which does not implement
   the `Copy` trait
```

The Cons variants own the data they hold, so when we create the b list ❶, a is moved into b and b owns a. Then, when we try to use a again when creating c ❷, we're not allowed to because a has been moved.

We could change the definition of Cons to hold references instead, but then we would have to specify lifetime parameters. By specifying lifetime parameters, we would be specifying that every element in the list will live at least as long as the entire list. The borrow checker wouldn't let us compile let a = Cons(10, &Nil); for example, because the temporary Nil value would be dropped before a could take a reference to it.

Instead, we'll change our definition of List to use Rc<T> in place of Box<T>, as shown in Listing 15-18. Each Cons variant will now hold a value and an Rc<T> pointing to a List. When we create b, instead of taking ownership of a, we'll clone the Rc<List> that a is holding, thereby increasing the number of references from one to two and letting a and b share ownership of the data in that

`Rc<List>`. We'll also clone a when creating c, increasing the number of references from two to three. Every time we call Rc::clone, the reference count to the data within the `Rc<List>` will increase, and the data won't be cleaned up unless there are zero references to it.

src/main.rs

```
enum List {
    Cons(i32, Rc<List>),
    Nil,
}

use List::{Cons, Nil};
❶ use std::rc::Rc;

fn main() {
  ❷ let a = Rc::new(Cons(5, Rc::new(Cons(10, Rc::new(Nil)))));
  ❸ let b = Cons(3, Rc::clone(&a));
  ❹ let c = Cons(4, Rc::clone(&a));
}
```

Listing 15-18: A definition of List that uses Rc<T>

We need to add a use statement to bring `Rc<T>` into scope ❶ because it's not in the prelude. In main, we create the list holding 5 and 10 and store it in a new `Rc<List>` in a ❷. Then when we create b ❸ and c ❹, we call the Rc::clone function and pass a reference to the `Rc<List>` in a as an argument.

We could have called a.clone() rather than Rc::clone(&a), but Rust's convention is to use Rc::clone in this case. The implementation of Rc::clone doesn't make a deep copy of all the data as most types' implementations of clone do. The call to Rc::clone only increments the reference count, which doesn't take much time. Deep copies of data can take a lot of time. By using Rc::clone for reference counting, we can visually distinguish between the deep-copy kinds of clones and the kinds of clones that increase the reference count. When looking for performance problems in the code, we only need to consider the deep-copy clones and can disregard calls to Rc::clone.

Cloning an Rc<T> Increases the Reference Count

Let's change our working example in Listing 15-18 so we can see the reference counts changing as we create and drop references to the `Rc<List>` in a.

In Listing 15-19, we'll change main so it has an inner scope around list c; then we can see how the reference count changes when c goes out of scope.

src/main.rs

```
fn main() {
    let a = Rc::new(Cons(5, Rc::new(Cons(10, Rc::new(Nil)))));
    println!("count after creating a = {}", Rc::strong_count(&a));
    let b = Cons(3, Rc::clone(&a));
    println!("count after creating b = {}", Rc::strong_count(&a));
    {
        let c = Cons(4, Rc::clone(&a));
        println!("count after creating c = {}", Rc::strong_count(&a));
    }
```

```
    println!("count after c goes out of scope = {}", Rc::strong_count(&a));
}
```

Listing 15-19: Printing the reference count

At each point in the program where the reference count changes, we print the reference count, which we can get by calling the Rc::strong_count function. This function is named strong_count rather than count because the Rc<T> type also has a weak_count; we'll see what weak_count is used for in "Preventing Reference Cycles: Turning an Rc<T> into a Weak<T>" on page 334.

This code prints the following:

```
count after creating a = 1
count after creating b = 2
count after creating c = 3
count after c goes out of scope = 2
```

We can see that the Rc<List> in a has an initial reference count of 1; then each time we call clone, the count goes up by 1. When c goes out of scope, the count goes down by 1. We don't have to call a function to decrease the reference count like we have to call Rc::clone to increase the reference count: the implementation of the Drop trait decreases the reference count automatically when an Rc<T> value goes out of scope.

What we can't see in this example is that when b and then a go out of scope at the end of main, the count is then 0, and the Rc<List> is cleaned up completely at that point. Using Rc<T> allows a single value to have multiple owners, and the count ensures that the value remains valid as long as any of the owners still exist.

Via immutable references, Rc<T> allows you to share data between multiple parts of your program for reading only. If Rc<T> allowed you to have multiple mutable references too, you might violate one of the borrowing rules discussed in Chapter 4: multiple mutable borrows to the same place can cause data races and inconsistencies. But being able to mutate data is very useful! In the next section, we'll discuss the interior mutability pattern and the RefCell<T> type that you can use in conjunction with an Rc<T> to work with this immutability restriction.

RefCell<T> and the Interior Mutability Pattern

Interior mutability is a design pattern in Rust that allows you to mutate data even when there are immutable references to that data; normally, this action is disallowed by the borrowing rules. To mutate data, the pattern uses unsafe code inside a data structure to bend Rust's usual rules that govern mutation and borrowing. We haven't yet covered unsafe code; we will in Chapter 19. We can use types that use the interior mutability pattern when we can ensure that the borrowing rules will be followed at runtime, even though the compiler can't guarantee that. The unsafe code involved is then wrapped in a safe API, and the outer type is still immutable.

Let's explore this concept by looking at the RefCell<T> type that follows the interior mutability pattern.

Enforcing Borrowing Rules at Runtime with RefCell<T>

Unlike Rc<T>, the RefCell<T> type represents single ownership over the data it holds. So, what makes RefCell<T> different from a type like Box<T>? Recall the borrowing rules you learned in Chapter 4:

- At any given time, you can have *either* but not both of the following: one mutable reference or any number of immutable references.
- References must always be valid.

With references and Box<T>, the borrowing rules' invariants are enforced at compile time. With RefCell<T>, these invariants are enforced *at runtime.* With references, if you break these rules, you'll get a compiler error. With RefCell<T>, if you break these rules, your program will panic and exit.

The advantages of checking the borrowing rules at compile time are that errors will be caught sooner in the development process, and there is no impact on runtime performance because all the analysis is completed beforehand. For those reasons, checking the borrowing rules at compile time is the best choice in the majority of cases, which is why this is Rust's default.

The advantage of checking the borrowing rules at runtime instead is that certain memory-safe scenarios are then allowed, whereas they are disallowed by the compile-time checks. Static analysis, like the Rust compiler, is inherently conservative. Some properties of code are impossible to detect by analyzing the code: the most famous example is the Halting Problem, which is beyond the scope of this book but is an interesting topic to research.

Because some analysis is impossible, if the Rust compiler can't be sure the code complies with the ownership rules, it might reject a correct program; in this way, it's conservative. If Rust accepted an incorrect program, users wouldn't be able to trust in the guarantees Rust makes. However, if Rust rejects a correct program, the programmer will be inconvenienced, but nothing catastrophic can occur. The RefCell<T> type is useful when you're sure your code follows the borrowing rules but the compiler is unable to understand and guarantee that.

Similar to Rc<T>, RefCell<T> is only for use in single-threaded scenarios and will give you a compile-time error if you try using it in a multithreaded context. We'll talk about how to get the functionality of RefCell<T> in a multithreaded program in Chapter 16.

Here is a recap of the reasons to choose Box<T>, Rc<T>, or RefCell<T>:

- Rc<T> enables multiple owners of the same data; Box<T> and RefCell<T> have single owners.
- Box<T> allows immutable or mutable borrows checked at compile time; Rc<T> allows only immutable borrows checked at compile time; RefCell<T> allows immutable or mutable borrows checked at runtime.

- Because RefCell<T> allows mutable borrows checked at runtime, you can mutate the value inside the RefCell<T> even when the RefCell<T> is immutable.

Mutating the value inside an immutable value is the *interior mutability* pattern. Let's look at a situation in which interior mutability is useful and examine how it's possible.

Interior Mutability: A Mutable Borrow to an Immutable Value

A consequence of the borrowing rules is that when you have an immutable value, you can't borrow it mutably. For example, this code won't compile:

```
fn main() {
    let x = 5;
    let y = &mut x;
}
```

If you tried to compile this code, you'd get the following error:

```
error[E0596]: cannot borrow immutable local variable 'x' as mutable
 --> src/main.rs:3:18
  |
2 |     let x = 5;
  |         - consider changing this to 'mut x'
3 |     let y = &mut x;
  |                  ^ cannot borrow mutably
```

However, there are situations in which it would be useful for a value to mutate itself in its methods but appear immutable to other code. Code outside the value's methods would not be able to mutate the value. Using RefCell<T> is one way to get the ability to have interior mutability. But RefCell<T> doesn't get around the borrowing rules completely: the borrow checker in the compiler allows this interior mutability, and the borrowing rules are checked at runtime instead. If you violate the rules, you'll get a panic! instead of a compiler error.

Let's work through a practical example where we can use RefCell<T> to mutate an immutable value and see why that is useful.

A Use Case for Interior Mutability: Mock Objects

A *test double* is the general programming concept for a type used in place of another type during testing. *Mock objects* are specific types of test doubles that record what happens during a test so you can assert that the correct actions took place.

Rust doesn't have objects in the same sense as other languages have objects, and Rust doesn't have mock object functionality built into the standard library as some other languages do. However, you can definitely create a struct that will serve the same purposes as a mock object.

Here's the scenario we'll test: we'll create a library that tracks a value against a maximum value and sends messages based on how close to the maximum value the current value is. This library could be used to keep track of a user's quota for the number of API calls they're allowed to make, for example.

Our library will only provide the functionality of tracking how close to the maximum a value is and what the messages should be at what times. Applications that use our library will be expected to provide the mechanism for sending the messages: the application could put a message in the application, send an email, send a text message, or something else. The library doesn't need to know that detail. All it needs is something that implements a trait we'll provide called Messenger. Listing 15-20 shows the library code.

src/lib.rs

```
pub trait Messenger {
❶ fn send(&self, msg: &str);
}

pub struct LimitTracker<'a, T: 'a + Messenger> {
    messenger: &'a T,
    value: usize,
    max: usize,
}

impl<'a, T> LimitTracker<'a, T>
    where T: Messenger {
    pub fn new(messenger: &T, max: usize) -> LimitTracker<T> {
        LimitTracker {
            messenger,
            value: 0,
            max,
        }
    }

❷ pub fn set_value(&mut self, value: usize) {
        self.value = value;

        let percentage_of_max = self.value as f64 / self.max as f64;

        if percentage_of_max >= 0.75 && percentage_of_max < 0.9 {
            self.messenger.send("Warning: You've used up over 75% of your
quota!");
        } else if percentage_of_max >= 0.9 && percentage_of_max < 1.0 {
            self.messenger.send("Urgent warning: You've used up over 90% of
your quota!");
        } else if percentage_of_max >= 1.0 {
            self.messenger.send("Error: You are over your quota!");
        }
    }
}
```

Listing 15-20: A library to keep track of how close a value is to a maximum value and warn when the value is at certain levels

One important part of this code is that the Messenger trait has one method called send that takes an immutable reference to self and the text of the message ❶. This is the interface our mock object needs to have. The other important part is that we want to test the behavior of the set_value method on the LimitTracker ❷. We can change what we pass in for the value parameter, but set_value doesn't return anything for us to make assertions on. We want to be able to say that if we create a LimitTracker with something that implements the Messenger trait and a particular value for max, when we pass different numbers for value, the messenger is told to send the appropriate messages.

We need a mock object that, instead of sending an email or text message when we call send, will only keep track of the messages it's told to send. We can create a new instance of the mock object, create a LimitTracker that uses the mock object, call the set_value method on LimitTracker, and then check that the mock object has the messages we expect. Listing 15-21 shows an attempt to implement a mock object to do just that, but the borrow checker won't allow it.

src/lib.rs

```
#[cfg(test)]
mod tests {
    use super::*;

❶  struct MockMessenger {
     ❷  sent_messages: Vec<String>,
    }

    impl MockMessenger {
     ❸  fn new() -> MockMessenger {
            MockMessenger { sent_messages: vec![] }
        }
    }

❹  impl Messenger for MockMessenger {
        fn send(&self, message: &str) {
         ❺  self.sent_messages.push(String::from(message));
        }
    }

    #[test]
❻  fn it_sends_an_over_75_percent_warning_message() {
        let mock_messenger = MockMessenger::new();
        let mut limit_tracker = LimitTracker::new(&mock_messenger, 100);

        limit_tracker.set_value(80);

        assert_eq!(mock_messenger.sent_messages.len(), 1);
    }
}
```

Listing 15-21: An attempt to implement a MockMessenger that isn't allowed by the borrow checker

This test code defines a MockMessenger struct ❶ that has a sent_messages field with a Vec of String values ❷ to keep track of the messages it's told to send. We also define an associated function new ❸ to make it convenient to create new MockMessenger values that start with an empty list of messages. We then implement the Messenger trait for MockMessenger ❹ so we can give a MockMessenger to a LimitTracker. In the definition of the send method ❺, we take the message passed in as a parameter and store it in the MockMessenger list of sent_messages.

In the test, we're testing what happens when the LimitTracker is told to set value to something that is more than 75 percent of the max value ❻. First, we create a new MockMessenger, which will start with an empty list of messages. Then we create a new LimitTracker and give it a reference to the new MockMessenger and a max value of 100. We call the set_value method on the LimitTracker with a value of 80, which is more than 75 percent of 100. Then we assert that the list of messages the MockMessenger is keeping track of should now have one message in it.

However, there's one problem with this test, as shown here:

```
error[E0596]: cannot borrow immutable field 'self.sent_messages' as mutable
  --> src/lib.rs:52:13
   |
51 |         fn send(&self, message: &str) {
   |                 ----- use '&mut self' here to make mutable
52 |             self.sent_messages.push(String::from(message));
   |             ^^^^^^^^^^^^^^^^^^ cannot mutably borrow immutable field
```

We can't modify the MockMessenger to keep track of the messages, because the send method takes an immutable reference to self. We also can't take the suggestion from the error text to use &mut self instead, because then the signature of send wouldn't match the signature in the Messenger trait definition (feel free to try it out and see what error message you get).

This is a situation in which interior mutability can help! We'll store the sent_messages within a RefCell<T>, and then the send message will be able to modify sent_messages to store the messages we've seen. Listing 15-22 shows what that looks like.

src/lib.rs

```
#[cfg(test)]
mod tests {
    use super::*;
    use std::cell::RefCell;

    struct MockMessenger {
    ❶   sent_messages: RefCell<Vec<String>>,
    }

    impl MockMessenger {
        fn new() -> MockMessenger {
        ❷   MockMessenger { sent_messages: RefCell::new(vec![]) }
        }
    }
}
```

```
impl Messenger for MockMessenger {
    fn send(&self, message: &str) {
      ❸ self.sent_messages.borrow_mut().push(String::from(message));
    }
}

#[test]
fn it_sends_an_over_75_percent_warning_message() {
    // --snip--

  ❹ assert_eq!(mock_messenger.sent_messages.borrow().len(), 1);
    }
}
```

Listing 15-22: Using RefCell<T> to mutate an inner value while the outer value is considered immutable

The sent_messages field is now of type RefCell<Vec<String>> ❶ instead of Vec<String>. In the new function, we create a new RefCell<Vec<String>> instance around the empty vector ❷.

For the implementation of the send method, the first parameter is still an immutable borrow of self, which matches the trait definition. We call borrow_mut on the RefCell<Vec<String>> in self.sent_messages ❸ to get a mutable reference to the value inside the RefCell<Vec<String>>, which is the vector. Then we can call push on the mutable reference to the vector to keep track of the messages sent during the test.

The last change we have to make is in the assertion: to see how many items are in the inner vector, we call borrow on the RefCell<Vec<String>> to get an immutable reference to the vector ❹.

Now that you've seen how to use RefCell<T>, let's dig into how it works!

Keeping Track of Borrows at Runtime with RefCell<T>

When creating immutable and mutable references, we use the & and &mut syntax, respectively. With RefCell<T>, we use the borrow and borrow_mut methods, which are part of the safe API that belongs to RefCell<T>. The borrow method returns the smart pointer type Ref<T>, and borrow_mut returns the smart pointer type RefMut<T>. Both types implement Deref, so we can treat them like regular references.

The RefCell<T> keeps track of how many Ref<T> and RefMut<T> smart pointers are currently active. Every time we call borrow, the RefCell<T> increases its count of how many immutable borrows are active. When a Ref<T> value goes out of scope, the count of immutable borrows goes down by one. Just like the compile-time borrowing rules, RefCell<T> lets us have many immutable borrows or one mutable borrow at any point in time.

If we try to violate these rules, rather than getting a compiler error as we would with references, the implementation of RefCell<T> will panic at runtime. Listing 15-23 shows a modification of the implementation of send in Listing 15-22. We're deliberately trying to create two mutable borrows active for the same scope to illustrate that RefCell<T> prevents us from doing this at runtime.

```
impl Messenger for MockMessenger {
    fn send(&self, message: &str) {
        let mut one_borrow = self.sent_messages.borrow_mut();
        let mut two_borrow = self.sent_messages.borrow_mut();

        one_borrow.push(String::from(message));
        two_borrow.push(String::from(message));
    }
}
```

Listing 15-23: Creating two mutable references in the same scope to see that RefCell<T> will panic

We create a variable one_borrow for the RefMut<T> smart pointer returned from borrow_mut. Then we create another mutable borrow in the same way in the variable two_borrow. This makes two mutable references in the same scope, which isn't allowed. When we run the tests for our library, the code in Listing 15-23 will compile without any errors, but the test will fail:

```
---- tests::it_sends_an_over_75_percent_warning_message stdout ----
        thread 'tests::it_sends_an_over_75_percent_warning_message' panicked
at 'already borrowed: BorrowMutError', src/libcore/result.rs:906:4
note: Run with 'RUST_BACKTRACE=1' for a backtrace.
```

Notice that the code panicked with the message already borrowed: BorrowMutError. This is how RefCell<T> handles violations of the borrowing rules at runtime.

Catching borrowing errors at runtime rather than compile time means that you would find a mistake in your code later in the development process and possibly not until your code was deployed to production. Also, your code would incur a small runtime performance penalty as a result of keeping track of the borrows at runtime rather than compile time. However, using RefCell<T> makes it possible to write a mock object that can modify itself to keep track of the messages it has seen while you're using it in a context where only immutable values are allowed. You can use RefCell<T> despite its trade-offs to get more functionality than regular references provide.

Having Multiple Owners of Mutable Data by Combining Rc<T> and RefCell<T>

A common way to use RefCell<T> is in combination with Rc<T>. Recall that Rc<T> lets you have multiple owners of some data, but it only gives immutable access to that data. If you have an Rc<T> that holds a RefCell<T>, you can get a value that can have multiple owners *and* that you can mutate!

For example, recall the cons list example in Listing 15-18 where we used Rc<T> to allow multiple lists to share ownership of another list. Because Rc<T> holds only immutable values, we can't change any of the values in the list once we've created them. Let's add in RefCell<T> to gain the ability to change the values in the lists. Listing 15-24 shows that by using a RefCell<T> in the Cons definition, we can modify the value stored in all the lists.

```rust
#[derive(Debug)]
enum List {
    Cons(Rc<RefCell<i32>>, Rc<List>),
    Nil,
}

use List::{Cons, Nil};
use std::rc::Rc;
use std::cell::RefCell;

fn main() {
  ❶ let value = Rc::new(RefCell::new(5));

  ❷ let a = Rc::new(Cons(Rc::clone(&value), Rc::new(Nil)));

    let b = Cons(Rc::new(RefCell::new(6)), Rc::clone(&a));
    let c = Cons(Rc::new(RefCell::new(10)), Rc::clone(&a));

  ❸ *value.borrow_mut() += 10;

    println!("a after = {:?}", a);
    println!("b after = {:?}", b);
    println!("c after = {:?}", c);
}
```

Listing 15-24: Using Rc<RefCell<i32>> to create a List that we can mutate

We create a value that is an instance of Rc<RefCell<i32>> and store it in a variable named value ❶ so we can access it directly later. Then we create a List in a with a Cons variant that holds value ❷. We need to clone value so both a and value have ownership of the inner 5 value rather than transferring ownership from value to a or having a borrow from value.

We wrap the list a in an Rc<T> so when we create lists b and c, they can both refer to a, which is what we did in Listing 15-18.

After we've created the lists in a, b, and c, we add 10 to the value in value ❸. We do this by calling borrow_mut on value, which uses the automatic dereferencing feature we discussed in Chapter 5 (see "Where's the -> Operator?" on page 92) to dereference the Rc<T> to the inner RefCell<T> value. The borrow_mut method returns a RefMut<T> smart pointer, and we use the dereference operator on it and change the inner value.

When we print a, b, and c, we can see that they all have the modified value of 15 rather than 5:

```
a after = Cons(RefCell { value: 15 }, Nil)
b after = Cons(RefCell { value: 6 }, Cons(RefCell { value: 15 }, Nil))
c after = Cons(RefCell { value: 10 }, Cons(RefCell { value: 15 }, Nil))
```

This technique is pretty neat! By using RefCell<T>, we have an outwardly immutable List value. But we can use the methods on RefCell<T> that provide access to its interior mutability so we can modify our data when we need to. The runtime checks of the borrowing rules protect us from data races, and it's sometimes worth trading a bit of speed for this flexibility in our data structures.

The standard library has other types that provide interior mutability, such as Cell<T>, which is similar except that instead of giving references to the inner value, the value is copied in and out of the Cell<T>. There's also Mutex<T>, which offers interior mutability that's safe to use across threads; we'll discuss its use in Chapter 16. Check out the standard library docs for more details on the differences between these types.

Reference Cycles Can Leak Memory

Rust's memory safety guarantees make it difficult, but not impossible, to accidentally create memory that is never cleaned up (known as a *memory leak*). Preventing memory leaks entirely is not one of Rust's guarantees in the same way that disallowing data races at compile time is, meaning memory leaks are memory safe in Rust. We can see that Rust allows memory leaks by using Rc<T> and RefCell<T>: it's possible to create references where items refer to each other in a cycle. This creates memory leaks because the reference count of each item in the cycle will never reach 0, and the values will never be dropped.

Creating a Reference Cycle

Let's look at how a reference cycle might happen and how to prevent it, starting with the definition of the List enum and a tail method in Listing 15-25.

src/main.rs

```
use std::rc::Rc;
use std::cell::RefCell;
use List::{Cons, Nil};

#[derive(Debug)]
enum List {
❶ Cons(i32, RefCell<Rc<List>>),
    Nil,
}

impl List {
❷ fn tail(&self) -> Option<&RefCell<Rc<List>>> {
        match *self {
            Cons(_, ref item) => Some(item),
            Nil => None,
        }
    }
}
```

Listing 15-25: A cons list definition that holds a RefCell<T> so we can modify what a Cons variant is referring to

We're using another variation of the List definition in Listing 15-5. The second element in the Cons variant is now RefCell<Rc<List>> ❶, meaning that instead of having the ability to modify the i32 value as we did in Listing 15-24, we want to modify which List value a Cons variant is pointing to. We're also adding a tail method ❷ to make it convenient for us to access the second item if we have a Cons variant.

In Listing 15-26, we're adding a main function that uses the definitions in Listing 15-25. This code creates a list in a and a list in b that points to the list in a. Then it modifies the list in a to point to b, creating a reference cycle. There are println! statements along the way to show what the reference counts are at various points in this process.

src/main.rs

```
fn main() {
❶   let a = Rc::new(Cons(5, RefCell::new(Rc::new(Nil))));

    println!("a initial rc count = {}", Rc::strong_count(&a));
    println!("a next item = {:?}", a.tail());

❷   let b = Rc::new(Cons(10, RefCell::new(Rc::clone(&a))));

    println!("a rc count after b creation = {}", Rc::strong_count(&a));
    println!("b initial rc count = {}", Rc::strong_count(&b));
    println!("b next item = {:?}", b.tail());

❸   if let Some(link) = a.tail() {
❹       *link.borrow_mut() = Rc::clone(&b);
    }

    println!("b rc count after changing a = {}", Rc::strong_count(&b));
    println!("a rc count after changing a = {}", Rc::strong_count(&a));

    // Uncomment the next line to see that we have a cycle;
    // it will overflow the stack.
    // println!("a next item = {:?}", a.tail());
}
```

Listing 15-26: Creating a reference cycle of two List values pointing to each other

We create an Rc<List> instance holding a List value in the variable a with an initial list of 5, Nil ❶. We then create an Rc<List> instance holding another List value in the variable b that contains the value 10 and points to the list in a ❷.

We modify a so it points to b instead of Nil, creating a cycle. We do that by using the tail method to get a reference to the RefCell<Rc<List>> in a, which we put in the variable link ❸. Then we use the borrow_mut method on the RefCell<Rc<List>> to change the value inside from an Rc<List> that holds a Nil value to the Rc<List> in b ❹.

When we run this code, keeping the last println! commented out for the moment, we'll get this output:

```
a initial rc count = 1
a next item = Some(RefCell { value: Nil })
a rc count after b creation = 2
b initial rc count = 1
```

```
b next item = Some(RefCell { value: Cons(5, RefCell { value: Nil }) })
b rc count after changing a = 2
a rc count after changing a = 2
```

The reference count of the Rc<List> instances in both a and b are 2 after we change the list in a to point to b. At the end of main, Rust will try to drop b first, which will decrease the count in each of the Rc<List> instances in a and b by 1.

However, because a is still referencing the Rc<List> that was in b, that Rc<List> has a count of 1 rather than 0, so the memory the Rc<List> has on the heap won't be dropped. The memory will just sit there with a count of 1, forever. To visualize this reference cycle, we've created the diagram in Figure 15-4.

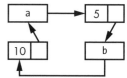

Figure 15-4: A reference cycle of lists a and b pointing to each other

If you uncomment the last println! and run the program, Rust will try to print this cycle with a pointing to b pointing to a and so forth until it overflows the stack.

In this case, right after we create the reference cycle, the program ends. The consequences of this cycle aren't very dire. However, if a more complex program allocated lots of memory in a cycle and held onto it for a long time, the program would use more memory than it needed and might overwhelm the system, causing it to run out of available memory.

Creating reference cycles is not easily done, but it's not impossible either. If you have RefCell<T> values that contain Rc<T> values or similar nested combinations of types with interior mutability and reference counting, you must ensure that you don't create cycles; you can't rely on Rust to catch them. Creating a reference cycle would be a logic bug in your program that you should use automated tests, code reviews, and other software development practices to minimize.

Another solution for avoiding reference cycles is reorganizing your data structures so that some references express ownership and some references don't. As a result, you can have cycles made up of some ownership relationships and some non-ownership relationships, and only the ownership relationships affect whether or not a value can be dropped. In Listing 15-25, we always want Cons variants to own their list, so reorganizing the data structure isn't possible. Let's look at an example using graphs made up of parent nodes and child nodes to see when non-ownership relationships are an appropriate way to prevent reference cycles.

Preventing Reference Cycles: Turning an Rc<T> into a Weak<T>

So far, we've demonstrated that calling Rc::clone increases the strong_count of an Rc<T> instance, and an Rc<T> instance is only cleaned up if its strong_count is 0. You can also create a *weak reference* to the value within an Rc<T> instance by calling Rc::downgrade and passing a reference to the Rc<T>. When you call Rc::downgrade, you get a smart pointer of type Weak<T>. Instead of increasing the strong_count in the Rc<T> instance by 1, calling Rc::downgrade increases the weak_count by 1. The Rc<T> type uses weak_count to keep track of how many Weak<T> references exist, similar to strong_count. The difference is the weak_count doesn't need to be 0 for the Rc<T> instance to be cleaned up.

Strong references are how you can share ownership of an Rc<T> instance. Weak references don't express an ownership relationship. They won't cause a reference cycle because any cycle involving some weak references will be broken once the strong reference count of values involved is 0.

Because the value that Weak<T> references might have been dropped, to do anything with the value that a Weak<T> is pointing to, you must make sure the value still exists. Do this by calling the upgrade method on a Weak<T> instance, which will return an Option<Rc<T>>. You'll get a result of Some if the Rc<T> value has not been dropped yet and a result of None if the Rc<T> value has been dropped. Because upgrade returns an Option<T>, Rust will ensure that the Some case and the None case are handled, and there won't be an invalid pointer.

As an example, rather than using a list whose items know only about the next item, we'll create a tree whose items know about their children items *and* their parent items.

Creating a Tree Data Structure: a Node with Child Nodes

To start, we'll build a tree with nodes that know about their child nodes. We'll create a struct named Node that holds its own i32 value as well as references to its children Node values:

src/main.rs

```
use std::rc::Rc;
use std::cell::RefCell;

#[derive(Debug)]
struct Node {
    value: i32,
    children: RefCell<Vec<Rc<Node>>>,
}
```

We want a Node to own its children, and we want to share that ownership with variables so we can access each Node in the tree directly. To do this, we define the Vec<T> items to be values of type Rc<Node>. We also want to modify which nodes are children of another node, so we have a RefCell<T> in children around the Vec<Rc<Node>>.

Next, we'll use our struct definition and create one Node instance named leaf with the value 3 and no children, and another instance named branch with the value 5 and leaf as one of its children, as shown in Listing 15-27.

src/main.rs

```
fn main() {
    let leaf = Rc::new(Node {
        value: 3,
        children: RefCell::new(vec![]),
    });

    let branch = Rc::new(Node {
        value: 5,
```

```
        children: RefCell::new(vec![Rc::clone(&leaf)]),
    });
}
```

Listing 15-27: Creating a leaf node with no children and a branch node with leaf as one of its children

We clone the Rc<Node> in leaf and store that in branch, meaning the Node in leaf now has two owners: leaf and branch. We can get from branch to leaf through branch.children, but there's no way to get from leaf to branch. The reason is that leaf has no reference to branch and doesn't know they're related. We want leaf to know that branch is its parent. We'll do that next.

Adding a Reference from a Child to Its Parent

To make the child node aware of its parent, we need to add a parent field to our Node struct definition. The trouble is in deciding what the type of parent should be. We know it can't contain an Rc<T>, because that would create a reference cycle with leaf.parent pointing to branch and branch.children pointing to leaf, which would cause their strong_count values to never be 0.

Thinking about the relationships another way, a parent node should own its children: if a parent node is dropped, its child nodes should be dropped as well. However, a child should not own its parent: if we drop a child node, the parent should still exist. This is a case for weak references!

So instead of Rc<T>, we'll make the type of parent use Weak<T>, specifically a RefCell<Weak<Node>>. Now our Node struct definition looks like this:

src/main.rs
```
use std::rc::{Rc, Weak};
use std::cell::RefCell;

#[derive(Debug)]
struct Node {
    value: i32,
    parent: RefCell<Weak<Node>>,
    children: RefCell<Vec<Rc<Node>>>,
}
```

A node will be able to refer to its parent node but doesn't own its parent. In Listing 15-28, we update main to use this new definition so the leaf node will have a way to refer to its parent, branch.

src/main.rs
```
fn main() {
    let leaf = Rc::new(Node {
        value: 3,
❶       parent: RefCell::new(Weak::new()),
        children: RefCell::new(vec![]),
    });

❷   println!("leaf parent = {:?}", leaf.parent.borrow().upgrade());

    let branch = Rc::new(Node {
        value: 5,
```

```
❸ parent: RefCell::new(Weak::new()),
    children: RefCell::new(vec![Rc::clone(&leaf)]),
});

❹ *leaf.parent.borrow_mut() = Rc::downgrade(&branch);

❺ println!("leaf parent = {:?}", leaf.parent.borrow().upgrade());
}
```

Listing 15-28: A leaf *node with a weak reference to its parent node* branch

Creating the leaf node looks similar to how creating the leaf node looked in Listing 15-27 with the exception of the parent field: leaf starts out without a parent, so we create a new, empty Weak<Node> reference instance ❶.

At this point, when we try to get a reference to the parent of leaf by using the upgrade method, we get a None value. We see this in the output from the first println! statement ❷:

```
leaf parent = None
```

When we create the branch node, it will also have a new Weak<Node> reference in the parent field ❸, because branch doesn't have a parent node. We still have leaf as one of the children of branch. Once we have the Node instance in branch, we can modify leaf to give it a Weak<Node> reference to its parent ❹. We use the borrow_mut method on the RefCell<Weak<Node>> in the parent field of leaf, and then we use the Rc::downgrade function to create a Weak<Node> reference to branch from the Rc<Node> in branch.

When we print the parent of leaf again ❺, this time we'll get a Some variant holding branch: now leaf can access its parent! When we print leaf, we also avoid the cycle that eventually ended in a stack overflow like we had in Listing 15-26; the Weak<Node> references are printed as (Weak):

```
leaf parent = Some(Node { value: 5, parent: RefCell { value: (Weak) },
children: RefCell { value: [Node { value: 3, parent: RefCell { value: (Weak)
}, children: RefCell { value: [] } }] } })
```

The lack of infinite output indicates that this code didn't create a reference cycle. We can also tell this by looking at the values we get from calling Rc::strong_count and Rc::weak_count.

Visualizing Changes to strong_count and weak_count

Let's look at how the strong_count and weak_count values of the Rc<Node> instances change by creating a new inner scope and moving the creation of branch into that scope. By doing so, we can see what happens when branch is created and then dropped when it goes out of scope. The modifications are shown in Listing 15-29.

src/main.rs
```
fn main() {
    let leaf = Rc::new(Node {
        value: 3,
```

```
            parent: RefCell::new(Weak::new()),
            children: RefCell::new(vec![]),
        });

❶    println!(
            "leaf strong = {}, weak = {}",
            Rc::strong_count(&leaf),
            Rc::weak_count(&leaf),
        );

❷    {
            let branch = Rc::new(Node {
                value: 5,
                parent: RefCell::new(Weak::new()),
                children: RefCell::new(vec![Rc::clone(&leaf)]),
            });

            *leaf.parent.borrow_mut() = Rc::downgrade(&branch);

❸        println!(
                "branch strong = {}, weak = {}",
                Rc::strong_count(&branch),
                Rc::weak_count(&branch),
            );

❹        println!(
                "leaf strong = {}, weak = {}",
                Rc::strong_count(&leaf),
                Rc::weak_count(&leaf),
            );
❺    }

❻    println!("leaf parent = {:?}", leaf.parent.borrow().upgrade());
❼    println!(
            "leaf strong = {}, weak = {}",
            Rc::strong_count(&leaf),
            Rc::weak_count(&leaf),
        );
    }
```

Listing 15-29: Creating branch in an inner scope and examining strong and weak reference counts

After leaf is created, its Rc<Node> has a strong count of 1 and a weak count of 0 ❶. In the inner scope ❷, we create branch and associate it with leaf, at which point when we print the counts ❸, the Rc<Node> in branch will have a strong count of 1 and a weak count of 1 (for leaf.parent pointing to branch with a Weak<Node>). When we print the counts in leaf ❹, we'll see it will have a strong count of 2, because branch now has a clone of the Rc<Node> of leaf stored in branch.children, but will still have a weak count of 0.

When the inner scope ends ❺, branch goes out of scope and the strong count of the Rc<Node> decreases to 0, so its Node is dropped. The weak count of 1 from leaf.parent has no bearing on whether or not Node is dropped, so we don't get any memory leaks!

If we try to access the parent of leaf after the end of the scope, we'll get None again ❻. At the end of the program ❼, the Rc<Node> in leaf has a strong count of 1 and a weak count of 0, because the variable leaf is now the only reference to the Rc<Node> again.

All of the logic that manages the counts and value dropping is built into Rc<T> and Weak<T> and their implementations of the Drop trait. By specifying that the relationship from a child to its parent should be a Weak<T> reference in the definition of Node, you're able to have parent nodes point to child nodes and vice versa without creating a reference cycle and memory leaks.

Summary

This chapter covered how to use smart pointers to make different guarantees and trade-offs than those Rust makes by default with regular references. The Box<T> type has a known size and points to data allocated on the heap. The Rc<T> type keeps track of the number of references to data on the heap so that data can have multiple owners. The RefCell<T> type with its interior mutability gives us a type that we can use when we need an immutable type but need to change an inner value of that type; it also enforces the borrowing rules at runtime instead of at compile time.

Also discussed were the Deref and Drop traits, which enable a lot of the functionality of smart pointers. We explored reference cycles that can cause memory leaks and how to prevent them using Weak<T>.

If this chapter has piqued your interest and you want to implement your own smart pointers, check out "The Rustonomicon" at *https://doc.rust-lang.org/stable/nomicon/* for more information.

Next, we'll talk about concurrency in Rust. You'll even learn about a few new smart pointers.

16

FEARLESS CONCURRENCY

Handling concurrent programming safely and efficiently is another of Rust's major goals. *Concurrent programming*, where different parts of a program execute independently, and *parallel programming*, where different parts of a program execute at the same time, are becoming increasingly important as more computers take advantage of their multiple processors. Historically, programming in these contexts has been difficult and error prone: Rust hopes to change that.

Initially, the Rust team thought that ensuring memory safety and preventing concurrency problems were two separate challenges to be solved with different methods. Over time, the team discovered that the ownership and type systems are a powerful set of tools to help manage memory safety *and* concurrency problems! By leveraging ownership and type checking, many concurrency errors are compile-time errors in Rust rather than runtime errors. Therefore, rather than making you spend lots of time trying to reproduce the exact circumstances under which a runtime concurrency bug occurs, incorrect code will refuse to compile and present an error explaining the problem. As a result, you can fix your code while you're working on it rather than potentially after it has been shipped to production. We've nicknamed this aspect of Rust *fearless concurrency*. Fearless concurrency allows you to write code that is free of subtle bugs and is easy to refactor without introducing new bugs.

NOTE *For simplicity's sake, we'll refer to many of the problems as* concurrent *rather than being more precise by saying* concurrent and/or parallel. *If this book were about concurrency and/or parallelism, we'd be more specific. For this chapter, please mentally substitute* concurrent and/or parallel *whenever we use* concurrent.

Many languages are dogmatic about the solutions they offer for handling concurrent problems. For example, Erlang has elegant functionality for message-passing concurrency but has only obscure ways to share state between threads. Supporting only a subset of possible solutions is a reasonable strategy for higher-level languages, because a higher-level language promises benefits from giving up some control to gain abstractions. However, lower-level languages are expected to provide the solution with the best performance in any given situation and have fewer abstractions over the hardware. Therefore, Rust offers a variety of tools for modeling problems in whatever way is appropriate for your situation and requirements.

Here are the topics we'll cover in this chapter:

- How to create threads to run multiple pieces of code at the same time
- *Message-passing* concurrency, where channels send messages between threads
- *Shared-state* concurrency, where multiple threads have access to some piece of data
- The Sync and Send traits, which extend Rust's concurrency guarantees to user-defined types as well as types provided by the standard library

Using Threads to Run Code Simultaneously

In most current operating systems, an executed program's code is run in a *process*, and the operating system manages multiple processes at once. Within your program, you can also have independent parts that run simultaneously. The features that run these independent parts are called *threads*.

Splitting the computation in your program into multiple threads can improve performance because the program does multiple tasks at the same time, but it also adds complexity. Because threads can run simultaneously, there's no inherent guarantee about the order in which parts of your code on different threads will run. This can lead to problems, such as:

- Race conditions, where threads are accessing data or resources in an inconsistent order
- Deadlocks, where two threads are waiting for each other to finish using a resource the other thread has, preventing both threads from continuing
- Bugs that happen only in certain situations and are hard to reproduce and fix reliably

Rust attempts to mitigate the negative effects of using threads, but programming in a multithreaded context still takes careful thought and requires a code structure that is different from that in programs running in a single thread.

Programming languages implement threads in a few different ways. Many operating systems provide an API for creating new threads. This model where a language calls the operating system APIs to create threads is sometimes called *1:1*, meaning one operating system thread per one language thread.

Many programming languages provide their own special implementation of threads. Programming language–provided threads are known as *green* threads, and languages that use these green threads will execute them in the context of a different number of operating system threads. For this reason, the green-threaded model is called the *M:N* model: there are *M* green threads per *N* operating system threads, where *M* and *N* are not necessarily the same number.

Each model has its own advantages and trade-offs, and the trade-off most important to Rust is runtime support. *Runtime* is a confusing term and can have different meanings in different contexts.

In this context, by *runtime* we mean code that is included by the language in every binary. This code can be large or small depending on the language, but every non-assembly language will have some amount of runtime code. For that reason, colloquially when people say a language has "no runtime," they often mean "small runtime." Smaller runtimes have fewer features but have the advantage of resulting in smaller binaries, which make it easier to combine the language with other languages in more contexts. Although many languages are okay with increasing the runtime size in exchange for more features, Rust needs to have nearly no runtime and cannot compromise on being able to call into C to maintain performance.

The green-threading M:N model requires a larger language runtime to manage threads. As such, the Rust standard library only provides an implementation of 1:1 threading. Because Rust is such a low-level language, there are crates that implement M:N threading if you would rather trade overhead for aspects such as more control over which threads run when and lower costs of context switching, for example.

Now that we've defined threads in Rust, let's explore how to use the thread-related API provided by the standard library.

Creating a New Thread with spawn

To create a new thread, we call the thread::spawn function and pass it a closure (we talked about closures in Chapter 13) containing the code we want to run in the new thread. The example in Listing 16-1 prints some text from a main thread and other text from a new thread.

src/main.rs

```rust
use std::thread;
use std::time::Duration;

fn main() {
    thread::spawn(|| {
        for i in 1..10 {
            println!("hi number {} from the spawned thread!", i);
            thread::sleep(Duration::from_millis(1));
        }
    });

    for i in 1..5 {
        println!("hi number {} from the main thread!", i);
        thread::sleep(Duration::from_millis(1));
    }
}
```

Listing 16-1: Creating a new thread to print one thing while the main thread prints something else

Note that with this function, the new thread will be stopped when the main thread ends, whether or not it has finished running. The output from this program might be a little different every time, but it will look similar to the following:

```
hi number 1 from the main thread!
hi number 1 from the spawned thread!
hi number 2 from the main thread!
hi number 2 from the spawned thread!
hi number 3 from the main thread!
hi number 3 from the spawned thread!
hi number 4 from the main thread!
hi number 4 from the spawned thread!
hi number 5 from the spawned thread!
```

The calls to thread::sleep force a thread to stop its execution for a short duration, allowing a different thread to run. The threads will probably take turns, but that isn't guaranteed: it depends on how your operating system schedules the threads. In this run, the main thread printed first, even though the print statement from the spawned thread appears first in the code. And even though we told the spawned thread to print until i is 9, it only got to 5 before the main thread shut down.

If you run this code and only see output from the main thread, or don't see any overlap, try increasing the numbers in the ranges to create more opportunities for the operating system to switch between the threads.

Waiting for All Threads to Finish Using join Handles

The code in Listing 16-1 not only stops the spawned thread prematurely most of the time due to the main thread ending, but also can't guarantee that the spawned thread will get to run at all. The reason is that there is no guarantee on the order in which threads run!

We can fix the problem of the spawned thread not getting to run, or not getting to run completely, by saving the return value of thread::spawn in a variable. The return type of thread::spawn is JoinHandle. A JoinHandle is an owned value that, when we call the join method on it, will wait for its thread to finish. Listing 16-2 shows how to use the JoinHandle of the thread we created in Listing 16-1 and call join to make sure the spawned thread finishes before main exits.

src/main.rs

```rust
use std::thread;
use std::time::Duration;

fn main() {
    let handle = thread::spawn(|| {
        for i in 1..10 {
            println!("hi number {} from the spawned thread!", i);
            thread::sleep(Duration::from_millis(1));
        }
    });

    for i in 1..5 {
        println!("hi number {} from the main thread!", i);
        thread::sleep(Duration::from_millis(1));
    }

    handle.join().unwrap();
}
```

Listing 16-2: Saving a JoinHandle from thread::spawn to guarantee the thread is run to completion

Calling join on the handle blocks the thread currently running until the thread represented by the handle terminates. *Blocking* a thread means that thread is prevented from performing work or exiting. Because we've put the call to join after the main thread's for loop, running Listing 16-2 should produce output similar to this:

```
hi number 1 from the main thread!
hi number 2 from the main thread!
hi number 1 from the spawned thread!
hi number 3 from the main thread!
hi number 2 from the spawned thread!
hi number 4 from the main thread!
hi number 3 from the spawned thread!
hi number 4 from the spawned thread!
hi number 5 from the spawned thread!
```

```
hi number 6 from the spawned thread!
hi number 7 from the spawned thread!
hi number 8 from the spawned thread!
hi number 9 from the spawned thread!
```

The two threads continue alternating, but the main thread waits because of the call to handle.join() and does not end until the spawned thread is finished.

But let's see what happens when we instead move handle.join() before the for loop in main, like this:

src/main.rs

```rust
use std::thread;
use std::time::Duration;

fn main() {
    let handle = thread::spawn(|| {
        for i in 1..10 {
            println!("hi number {} from the spawned thread!", i);
            thread::sleep(Duration::from_millis(1));
        }
    });

    handle.join().unwrap();

    for i in 1..5 {
        println!("hi number {} from the main thread!", i);
        thread::sleep(Duration::from_millis(1));
    }
}
```

The main thread will wait for the spawned thread to finish and then run its for loop, so the output won't be interleaved anymore, as shown here:

```
hi number 1 from the spawned thread!
hi number 2 from the spawned thread!
hi number 3 from the spawned thread!
hi number 4 from the spawned thread!
hi number 5 from the spawned thread!
hi number 6 from the spawned thread!
hi number 7 from the spawned thread!
hi number 8 from the spawned thread!
hi number 9 from the spawned thread!
hi number 1 from the main thread!
hi number 2 from the main thread!
hi number 3 from the main thread!
hi number 4 from the main thread!
```

Small details, such as where join is called, can affect whether or not your threads run at the same time.

Using move Closures with Threads

The move closure is often used alongside thread::spawn because it allows you to use data from one thread in another thread.

In Chapter 13, we mentioned we can use the move keyword before the parameter list of a closure to force the closure to take ownership of the values it uses in the environment. This technique is especially useful when creating new threads in order to transfer ownership of values from one thread to another.

Notice in Listing 16-1 that the closure we pass to thread::spawn takes no arguments: we're not using any data from the main thread in the spawned thread's code. To use data from the main thread in the spawned thread, the spawned thread's closure must capture the values it needs. Listing 16-3 shows an attempt to create a vector in the main thread and use it in the spawned thread. However, this won't yet work, as you'll see in a moment.

src/main.rs

```
use std::thread;

fn main() {
    let v = vec![1, 2, 3];

    let handle = thread::spawn(|| {
        println!("Here's a vector: {:?}", v);
    });

    handle.join().unwrap();
}
```

Listing 16-3: Attempting to use a vector created by the main thread in another thread

The closure uses v, so it will capture v and make it part of the closure's environment. Because thread::spawn runs this closure in a new thread, we should be able to access v inside that new thread. But when we compile this example, we get the following error:

```
error[E0373]: closure may outlive the current function, but it borrows `v`,
which is owned by the current function
  --> src/main.rs:6:32
   |
6  |     let handle = thread::spawn(|| {
   |                                ^^ may outlive borrowed value `v`
7  |         println!("Here's a vector: {:?}", v);
   |                                           - `v` is borrowed here
   |
help: to force the closure to take ownership of `v` (and any other referenced
variables), use the `move` keyword
   |
6  |     let handle = thread::spawn(move || {
   |                                ^^^^^^^
```

Rust *infers* how to capture v, and because println! only needs a reference to v, the closure tries to borrow v. However, there's a problem: Rust can't tell how long the spawned thread will run, so it doesn't know whether the reference to v will always be valid.

Listing 16-4 provides a scenario that's more likely to have a reference to v that won't be valid.

src/main.rs

```
use std::thread;

fn main() {
    let v = vec![1, 2, 3];

    let handle = thread::spawn(|| {
        println!("Here's a vector: {:?}", v);
    });

    drop(v); // oh no!

    handle.join().unwrap();
}
```

Listing 16-4: A thread with a closure that attempts to capture a reference to v from a main thread that drops v

If we were allowed to run this code, there's a possibility the spawned thread would be immediately put in the background without running at all. The spawned thread has a reference to v inside, but the main thread immediately drops v, using the drop function we discussed in Chapter 15. Then, when the spawned thread starts to execute, v is no longer valid, so a reference to it is also invalid. Oh no!

To fix the compiler error in Listing 16-3, we can use the error message's advice:

```
help: to force the closure to take ownership of `v` (and any other referenced
variables), use the `move` keyword
  |
6 |     let handle = thread::spawn(move || {
  |                                ^^^^^^^
```

By adding the move keyword before the closure, we force the closure to take ownership of the values it's using rather than allowing Rust to infer that it should borrow the values. The modification to Listing 16-3 shown in Listing 16-5 will compile and run as we intend.

src/main.rs

```
use std::thread;

fn main() {
    let v = vec![1, 2, 3];

    let handle = thread::spawn(move || {
        println!("Here's a vector: {:?}", v);
    });
```

```
        handle.join().unwrap();
}
```

Listing 16-5: Using the move keyword to force a closure to take ownership of the values it uses

What would happen to the code in Listing 16-4 where the main thread called drop if we used a move closure? Would move fix that case? Unfortunately, no; we would get a different error because what Listing 16-4 is trying to do isn't allowed for a different reason. If we added move to the closure, we would move v into the closure's environment, and we could no longer call drop on it in the main thread. We would get this compiler error instead:

```
error[E0382]: use of moved value: `v`
  --> src/main.rs:10:10
   |
6  |      let handle = thread::spawn(move || {
   |                                  ------- value moved (into closure) here
...
10 |      drop(v); // oh no!
   |           ^ value used here after move
   |
   = note: move occurs because `v` has type `std::vec::Vec<i32>`, which does
   not implement the `Copy` trait
```

Rust's ownership rules have saved us again! We got an error from the code in Listing 16-3 because Rust was being conservative and only borrowing v for the thread, which meant the main thread could theoretically invalidate the spawned thread's reference. By telling Rust to move ownership of v to the spawned thread, we're guaranteeing Rust that the main thread won't use v anymore. If we change Listing 16-4 in the same way, we're then violating the ownership rules when we try to use v in the main thread. The move keyword overrides Rust's conservative default of borrowing; it doesn't let us violate the ownership rules.

With a basic understanding of threads and the thread API, let's look at what we can *do* with threads.

Using Message Passing to Transfer Data Between Threads

One increasingly popular approach to ensuring safe concurrency is *message passing*, where threads or actors communicate by sending each other messages containing data. Here's the idea in a slogan from the Go language documentation (*http://golang.org/doc/effective_go.html*): "Do not communicate by sharing memory; instead, share memory by communicating."

One major tool Rust has for accomplishing message-sending concurrency is the *channel*, a programming concept that Rust's standard library provides an implementation of. You can imagine a channel in programming as being like a channel of water, such as a stream or river. If you put something like a rubber duck or boat into a stream, it will travel downstream to the end of the waterway.

A channel in programming has two halves: a transmitter and a receiver. The transmitter half is the upstream location where you put rubber ducks into the river, and the receiver half is where the rubber duck ends up downstream. One part of your code calls methods on the transmitter with the data you want to send, and another part checks the receiving end for arriving messages. A channel is said to be *closed* if either the transmitter or receiver half is dropped.

Here, we'll work up to a program that has one thread to generate values and send them down a channel, and another thread that will receive the values and print them. We'll be sending simple values between threads using a channel to illustrate the feature. Once you're familiar with the technique, you could use channels to implement a chat system or a system where many threads perform parts of a calculation and send the parts to one thread that aggregates the results.

First, in Listing 16-6, we'll create a channel but not do anything with it. Note that this won't compile yet because Rust can't tell what type of values we want to send over the channel.

<table>
<tr><td>src/main.rs</td><td>

```
use std::sync::mpsc;

fn main() {
    let (tx, rx) = mpsc::channel();
}
```
</td></tr>
</table>

Listing 16-6: Creating a channel and assigning the two halves to tx and rx

We create a new channel using the `mpsc::channel` function; `mpsc` stands for *multiple producer, single consumer*. In short, the way Rust's standard library implements channels means a channel can have multiple *sending* ends that produce values but only one *receiving* end that consumes those values. Imagine multiple streams flowing together into one big river: everything sent down any of the streams will end up in one river at the end. We'll start with a single producer for now, but we'll add multiple producers when we get this example working.

The `mpsc::channel` function returns a tuple, the first element of which is the sending end and the second element the receiving end. The abbreviations tx and rx are traditionally used in many fields for *transmitter* and *receiver*, respectively, so we name our variables as such to indicate each end. We're using a let statement with a pattern that destructures the tuples; we'll discuss the use of patterns in let statements and destructuring in Chapter 18. Using a let statement this way is a convenient approach to extract the pieces of the tuple returned by `mpsc::channel`.

Let's move the transmitting end into a spawned thread and have it send one string so the spawned thread is communicating with the main thread, as shown in Listing 16-7. This is like putting a rubber duck in the river upstream or sending a chat message from one thread to another.

```
use std::thread;
use std::sync::mpsc;

fn main() {
    let (tx, rx) = mpsc::channel();

    thread::spawn(move || {
        let val = String::from("hi");
        tx.send(val).unwrap();
    });
}
```

Listing 16-7: Moving tx to a spawned thread and sending "hi"

Again, we're using thread::spawn to create a new thread and then using move to move tx into the closure so the spawned thread owns tx. The spawned thread needs to own the transmitting end of the channel to be able to send messages through the channel.

The transmitting end has a send method that takes the value we want to send. The send method returns a Result<T, E> type, so if the receiving end has already been dropped and there's nowhere to send a value, the send operation will return an error. In this example, we're calling unwrap to panic in case of an error. But in a real application, we would handle it properly: return to Chapter 9 to review strategies for proper error handling.

In Listing 16-8, we'll get the value from the receiving end of the channel in the main thread. This is like retrieving the rubber duck from the water at the end of the river or like getting a chat message.

```
use std::thread;
use std::sync::mpsc;

fn main() {
    let (tx, rx) = mpsc::channel();

    thread::spawn(move || {
        let val = String::from("hi");
        tx.send(val).unwrap();
    });

    let received = rx.recv().unwrap();
    println!("Got: {}", received);
}
```

Listing 16-8: Receiving the value "hi" in the main thread and printing it

The receiving end of a channel has two useful methods: recv and try_recv. We're using recv, short for *receive*, which will block the main thread's execution and wait until a value is sent down the channel. Once a value is sent, recv will return it in a Result<T, E>. When the sending end of the channel closes, recv will return an error to signal that no more values will be coming.

The try_recv method doesn't block, but will instead return a Result<T, E> immediately: an Ok value holding a message if one is available and an Err value if there aren't any messages this time. Using try_recv is useful if this thread has other work to do while waiting for messages: we could write a loop that calls try_recv every so often, handles a message if one is available, and otherwise does other work for a little while until checking again.

We've used recv in this example for simplicity; we don't have any other work for the main thread to do other than wait for messages, so blocking the main thread is appropriate.

When we run the code in Listing 16-8, we'll see the value printed from the main thread:

Got: hi

Perfect!

Channels and Ownership Transference

The ownership rules play a vital role in message sending because they help you write safe, concurrent code. Preventing errors in concurrent programming is the advantage of thinking about ownership throughout your Rust programs. Let's do an experiment to show how channels and ownership work together to prevent problems: we'll try to use a val value in the spawned thread *after* we've sent it down the channel. Try compiling the code in Listing 16-9 to see why this code isn't allowed.

src/main.rs

```
use std::thread;
use std::sync::mpsc;

fn main() {
    let (tx, rx) = mpsc::channel();

    thread::spawn(move || {
        let val = String::from("hi");
        tx.send(val).unwrap();
        println!("val is {}", val);
    });

    let received = rx.recv().unwrap();
    println!("Got: {}", received);
}
```

Listing 16-9: Attempting to use val after we've sent it down the channel

Here, we try to print val after we've sent it down the channel via tx.send. Allowing this would be a bad idea: once the value has been sent to another thread, that thread could modify or drop it before we try to use the value again. Potentially, the other thread's modifications could cause errors or unexpected results due to inconsistent or nonexistent data. However, Rust gives us an error if we try to compile the code in Listing 16-9.

```
error[E0382]: use of moved value: `val`
  --> src/main.rs:10:31
```

```
 9 |             tx.send(val).unwrap();
   |                 --- value moved here
10 |             println!("val is {}", val);
   |                                   ^^^ value used here after move
   |
   = note: move occurs because `val` has type `std::string::String`, which
does not implement the `Copy` trait
```

Our concurrency mistake has caused a compile-time error. The send function takes ownership of its parameter, and when the value is moved, the receiver takes ownership of it. This stops us from accidentally using the value again after sending it; the ownership system checks that everything is okay.

Sending Multiple Values and Seeing the Receiver Waiting

The code in Listing 16-8 compiled and ran, but it didn't clearly show us that two separate threads were talking to each other over the channel. In Listing 16-10, we've made some modifications that will prove the code in Listing 16-8 is running concurrently: the spawned thread will now send multiple messages and pause for a second between each message.

src/main.rs

```rust
use std::thread;
use std::sync::mpsc;
use std::time::Duration;

fn main() {
    let (tx, rx) = mpsc::channel();

    thread::spawn(move || {
        let vals = vec![
            String::from("hi"),
            String::from("from"),
            String::from("the"),
            String::from("thread"),
        ];

        for val in vals {
            tx.send(val).unwrap();
            thread::sleep(Duration::from_secs(1));
        }
    });

    for received in rx {
        println!("Got: {}", received);
    }
}
```

Listing 16-10: Sending multiple messages and pausing between each

This time, the spawned thread has a vector of strings that we want to send to the main thread. We iterate over them, sending each individually, and pause between each by calling the thread::sleep function with a Duration value of 1 second.

In the main thread, we're not calling the recv function explicitly anymore: instead, we're treating rx as an iterator. For each value received, we're printing it. When the channel is closed, iteration will end.

When running the code in Listing 16-10, you should see the following output with a 1-second pause between each line:

```
Got: hi
Got: from
Got: the
Got: thread
```

Because we don't have any code that pauses or delays in the for loop in the main thread, we can tell that the main thread is waiting to receive values from the spawned thread.

Creating Multiple Producers by Cloning the Transmitter

Earlier we mentioned that mpsc was an acronym for *multiple producer, single consumer*. Let's put mpsc to use and expand the code in Listing 16-10 to create multiple threads that all send values to the same receiver. We can do so by cloning the transmitting half of the channel, as shown in Listing 16-11.

src/main.rs

```
// --snip--

let (tx, rx) = mpsc::channel();

let tx1 = mpsc::Sender::clone(&tx);
thread::spawn(move || {
    let vals = vec![
        String::from("hi"),
        String::from("from"),
        String::from("the"),
        String::from("thread"),
    ];

    for val in vals {
        tx1.send(val).unwrap();
        thread::sleep(Duration::from_secs(1));
    }
});

thread::spawn(move || {
    let vals = vec![
        String::from("more"),
        String::from("messages"),
        String::from("for"),
        String::from("you"),
    ];
```

```
    for val in vals {
        tx.send(val).unwrap();
        thread::sleep(Duration::from_secs(1));
    }
});

for received in rx {
    println!("Got: {}", received);
}

// --snip--
```

Listing 16-11: Sending multiple messages from multiple producers

This time, before we create the first spawned thread, we call clone on the sending end of the channel. This will give us a new sending handle we can pass to the first spawned thread. We pass the original sending end of the channel to a second spawned thread. This gives us two threads, each sending different messages to the receiving end of the channel.

When you run the code, your output should look something like this:

```
Got: hi
Got: more
Got: from
Got: messages
Got: for
Got: the
Got: thread
Got: you
```

You might see the values in another order; it depends on your system. This is what makes concurrency interesting as well as difficult. If you experiment with thread::sleep, giving it various values in the different threads, each run will be more nondeterministic and create different output each time.

Now that we've looked at how channels work, let's look at a different method of concurrency.

Shared-State Concurrency

Message passing is a fine way of handling concurrency, but it's not the only one. Consider this part of the slogan from the Go language documentation again: "communicate by sharing memory."

What would communicating by sharing memory look like? In addition, why would message-passing enthusiasts not use it and do the opposite instead?

In a way, channels in any programming language are similar to single ownership, because once you transfer a value down a channel, you should no longer use that value. Shared memory concurrency is like multiple ownership: multiple threads can access the same memory location at the same time. As you saw in Chapter 15, where smart pointers made multiple ownership possible, multiple ownership can add complexity because these different owners need managing. Rust's type system and ownership rules greatly assist in getting this management correct. For an example, let's look at mutexes, one of the more common concurrency primitives for shared memory.

Using Mutexes to Allow Access to Data from One Thread at a Time

Mutex is an abbreviation for *mutual exclusion*, as in, a mutex allows only one thread to access some data at any given time. To access the data in a mutex, a thread must first signal that it wants access by asking to acquire the mutex's *lock*. The lock is a data structure that is part of the mutex that keeps track of who currently has exclusive access to the data. Therefore, the mutex is described as *guarding* the data it holds via the locking system.

Mutexes have a reputation for being difficult to use because you have to remember two rules:

- You must attempt to acquire the lock before using the data.
- When you're done with the data that the mutex guards, you must unlock the data so other threads can acquire the lock.

For a real-world metaphor for a mutex, imagine a panel discussion at a conference with only one microphone. Before a panelist can speak, they have to ask or signal that they want to use the microphone. When they get the microphone, they can talk for as long as they want and then hand the microphone to the next panelist who requests to speak. If a panelist forgets to hand the microphone off when they're finished with it, no one else is able to speak. If management of the shared microphone goes wrong, the panel won't work as planned!

Management of mutexes can be incredibly tricky to get right, which is why so many people are enthusiastic about channels. However, thanks to Rust's type system and ownership rules, you can't get locking and unlocking wrong.

The API of Mutex<T>

As an example of how to use a mutex, let's start by using a mutex in a single-threaded context, as shown in Listing 16-12.

src/main.rs
```
use std::sync::Mutex;

fn main() {
❶ let m = Mutex::new(5);

    {
    ❷ let mut num = m.lock().unwrap();
    ❸ *num = 6;
❹ }

❺ println!("m = {:?}", m);
}
```

Listing 16-12: Exploring the API of Mutex<T> in a single-threaded context for simplicity

As with many types, we create a `Mutex<T>` using the associated function new ❶. To access the data inside the mutex, we use the `lock` method to acquire the lock ❷. This call will block the current thread so it can't do any work until it's our turn to have the lock.

The call to `lock` would fail if another thread holding the lock panicked. In that case, no one would ever be able to get the lock, so we've chosen to use `unwrap` and have this thread panic if we're in that situation.

After we've acquired the lock, we can treat the return value, named `num` in this case, as a mutable reference to the data inside ❸. The type system ensures that we acquire a lock before using the value in `m: Mutex<i32>` is not an `i32`, so we *must* acquire the lock to be able to use the `i32` value. We can't forget; the type system won't let us access the inner `i32` otherwise.

As you might suspect, `Mutex<T>` is a smart pointer. More accurately, the call to `lock` *returns* a smart pointer called `MutexGuard`. This smart pointer implements `Deref` to point at our inner data; the smart pointer also has a `Drop` implementation that releases the lock automatically when a `MutexGuard` goes out of scope, which happens at the end of the inner scope ❹. As a result, we don't risk forgetting to release the lock and blocking the mutex from being used by other threads because the lock release happens automatically.

After dropping the lock, we can print the mutex value and see that we were able to change the inner `i32` to 6 ❺.

Sharing a Mutex<T> Between Multiple Threads

Now, let's try to share a value between multiple threads using `Mutex<T>`. We'll spin up 10 threads and have them each increment a counter value by 1, so the counter goes from 0 to 10. Note that the next few examples will have compiler errors, and we'll use those errors to learn more about `Mutex<T>` and how Rust helps us implement it correctly. Listing 16-13 has our starting example.

src/main.rs

```
use std::sync::Mutex;
use std::thread;

fn main() {
❶  let counter = Mutex::new(0);
    let mut handles = vec![];

❷  for _ in 0..10 {
❸      let handle = thread::spawn(move || {
❹          let mut num = counter.lock().unwrap();

❺          *num += 1;
        });
❻      handles.push(handle);
    }

    for handle in handles {
❼      handle.join().unwrap();
    }
}
```

```
❽ println!("Result: {}", *counter.lock().unwrap());
}
```

Listing 16-13: Ten threads each increment a counter guarded by a Mutex<T>

We create a counter variable to hold an i32 inside a Mutex<T> ❶, as we did in Listing 16-12. Next, we create 10 threads by iterating over a range of numbers ❷. We use thread::spawn and give all the threads the same closure, one that moves the counter into the thread ❸, acquires a lock on the Mutex<T> by calling the lock method ❹, and then adds 1 to the value in the mutex ❺. When a thread finishes running its closure, num will go out of scope and release the lock so another thread can acquire it.

In the main thread, we collect all the join handles ❻. Then, as we did in Listing 16-2, we call join on each handle to make sure all the threads finish ❼. At that point, the main thread will acquire the lock and print the result of this program ❽.

We hinted that this example wouldn't compile. Now let's find out why!

```
error[E0382]: capture of moved value: `counter`
  --> src/main.rs:10:27
   |
9  |          let handle = thread::spawn(move || {
   |                                     ------- value moved (into closure) here
10 |              let mut num = counter.lock().unwrap();
   |                            ^^^^^^^ value captured here after move
   |
   = note: move occurs because `counter` has type `std::sync::Mutex<i32>`,
   which does not implement the `Copy` trait

error[E0382]: use of moved value: `counter`
  --> src/main.rs:21:29
   |
9  |          let handle = thread::spawn(move || {
   |                                     ------- value moved (into closure) here
...
21 |      println!("Result: {}", *counter.lock().unwrap());
   |                              ^^^^^^^ value used here after move
   |
   = note: move occurs because `counter` has type `std::sync::Mutex<i32>`,
   which does not implement the `Copy` trait

error: aborting due to 2 previous errors
```

The error message states that the counter value is moved into the closure and then captured when we call lock. That description sounds like what we wanted, but it's not allowed!

Let's figure this out by simplifying the program. Instead of making 10 threads in a for loop, let's just make 2 threads without a loop and see what happens. Replace the first for loop in Listing 16-13 with the following code instead.

```
let handle = thread::spawn(move || {
    let mut num = counter.lock().unwrap();

    *num += 1;
});
handles.push(handle);

let handle2 = thread::spawn(move || {
    let mut num2 = counter.lock().unwrap();

    *num2 += 1;
});
handles.push(handle2);
```

We make two threads and change the variable names used with the second thread to handle2 and num2. When we run the code this time, compiling gives us the following:

```
error[E0382]: capture of moved value: `counter`
  --> src/main.rs:16:24
   |
8  |      let handle = thread::spawn(move || {
   |                                 ------- value moved (into closure) here
...
16 |          let mut num2 = counter.lock().unwrap();
   |                         ^^^^^^^ value captured here after move
   |
   = note: move occurs because `counter` has type `std::sync::Mutex<i32>`,
   which does not implement the `Copy` trait

error[E0382]: use of moved value: `counter`
  --> src/main.rs:26:29
   |
8  |      let handle = thread::spawn(move || {
   |                                 ------- value moved (into closure) here
...
26 |      println!("Result: {}", *counter.lock().unwrap());
   |                              ^^^^^^^ value used here after move
   |
   = note: move occurs because `counter` has type `std::sync::Mutex<i32>`,
   which does not implement the `Copy` trait

error: aborting due to 2 previous errors
```

Aha! The first error message indicates that counter is moved into the closure for the thread associated with handle. That move is preventing us from capturing counter when we try to call lock on it and store the result in num2 in the second thread! So Rust is telling us that we can't move ownership of counter into multiple threads. This was hard to see earlier because our threads were in a loop, and Rust can't point to different threads in different iterations of the loop. Let's fix the compiler error with a multiple-ownership method.

Multiple Ownership with Multiple Threads

In Chapter 15, we gave a value multiple owners by using the smart pointer `Rc<T>` to create a reference counted value. Let's do the same here and see what happens. We'll wrap the `Mutex<T>` in `Rc<T>` in Listing 16-14 and clone the `Rc<T>` before moving ownership to the thread. Now that we've seen the errors, we'll also switch back to using the for loop, and we'll keep the `move` keyword with the closure.

src/main.rs

```
use std::rc::Rc;
use std::sync::Mutex;
use std::thread;

fn main() {
    let counter = Rc::new(Mutex::new(0));
    let mut handles = vec![];

    for _ in 0..10 {
        let counter = Rc::clone(&counter);
        let handle = thread::spawn(move || {
            let mut num = counter.lock().unwrap();

            *num += 1;
        });
        handles.push(handle);
    }

    for handle in handles {
        handle.join().unwrap();
    }

    println!("Result: {}", *counter.lock().unwrap());
}
```

Listing 16-14: Attempting to use `Rc<T>` to allow multiple threads to own the `Mutex<T>`

Once again, we compile and get . . . different errors! The compiler is teaching us a lot.

❶ error[E0277]: the trait bound `std::rc::Rc<std::sync::Mutex<i32>>:
std::marker::Send` is not satisfied in `[closure@src/main.rs:11:36: 15:10
counter:std::rc::Rc<std::sync::Mutex<i32>>]`
  --> src/main.rs:11:22
   |
11 | let handle = thread::spawn(move || {
❷ | ^^^^^^^^^^^^^ `std::rc::Rc<std::sync::Mutex<i32>>`
cannot be sent between threads safely
   |
   = help: within `[closure@src/main.rs:11:36: 15:10 counter:std::rc::Rc<std::
sync::Mutex<i32>>]`, the trait `std::marker::Send` is not implemented for `std
::rc::Rc<std::sync::Mutex<i32>>`
   = note: required because it appears within the type `[closure@src/main.
rs:11:36: 15:10 counter:std::rc::Rc<std::sync::Mutex<i32>>]`
   = note: required by `std::thread::spawn`

Wow, that error message is very wordy! Here are some important parts to focus on: the first inline error says `std::rc::Rc<std::sync::Mutex<i32>>` cannot be sent between threads safely ❷. The reason for this is in the next important part to focus on, the error message. The distilled error message says the trait bound `Send` is not satisfied ❶. We'll talk about Send in the next section: it's one of the traits that ensures the types we use with threads are meant for use in concurrent situations.

Unfortunately, Rc<T> is not safe to share across threads. When Rc<T> manages the reference count, it adds to the count for each call to clone and subtracts from the count when each clone is dropped. But it doesn't use any concurrency primitives to make sure that changes to the count can't be interrupted by another thread. This could lead to wrong counts—subtle bugs that could in turn lead to memory leaks or a value being dropped before we're done with it. What we need is a type exactly like Rc<T> but one that makes changes to the reference count in a thread-safe way.

Atomic Reference Counting with Arc<T>

Fortunately, Arc<T> *is* a type like Rc<T> that is safe to use in concurrent situations. The *a* stands for *atomic*, meaning it's an *atomically reference counted* type. Atomics are an additional kind of concurrency primitive that we won't cover in detail here: see the standard library documentation for std::sync::atomic for more details. At this point, you just need to know that atomics work like primitive types but are safe to share across threads.

You might then wonder why all primitive types aren't atomic and why standard library types aren't implemented to use Arc<T> by default. The reason is that thread safety comes with a performance penalty that you only want to pay when you really need to. If you're just performing operations on values within a single thread, your code can run faster if it doesn't have to enforce the guarantees atomics provide.

Let's return to our example: Arc<T> and Rc<T> have the same API, so we fix our program by changing the use line, the call to new, and the call to clone. The code in Listing 16-15 will finally compile and run.

src/main.rs
```
use std::sync::{Mutex, Arc};
use std::thread;

fn main() {
    let counter = Arc::new(Mutex::new(0));
    let mut handles = vec![];

    for _ in 0..10 {
        let counter = Arc::clone(&counter);
        let handle = thread::spawn(move || {
            let mut num = counter.lock().unwrap();

            *num += 1;
        });
        handles.push(handle);
    }
```

```
    for handle in handles {
        handle.join().unwrap();
    }

    println!("Result: {}", *counter.lock().unwrap());
}
```

Listing 16-15: Using an Arc<T> to wrap the Mutex<T> to be able to share ownership across multiple threads

This code will print the following:

```
Result: 10
```

We did it! We counted from 0 to 10, which may not seem very impressive, but it did teach us a lot about Mutex<T> and thread safety. You could also use this program's structure to do more complicated operations than just incrementing a counter. Using this strategy, you can divide a calculation into independent parts, split those parts across threads, and then use a Mutex<T> to have each thread update the final result with its part.

Similarities Between RefCell<T>/Rc<T> and Mutex<T>/Arc<T>

You might have noticed that counter is immutable but we could get a mutable reference to the value inside it; this means Mutex<T> provides interior mutability, as the Cell family does. In the same way we used RefCell<T> in Chapter 15 to allow us to mutate contents inside an Rc<T>, we use Mutex<T> to mutate contents inside an Arc<T>.

Another detail to note is that Rust can't protect you from all kinds of logic errors when you use Mutex<T>. Recall in Chapter 15 that using Rc<T> came with the risk of creating reference cycles, where two Rc<T> values refer to each other, causing memory leaks. Similarly, Mutex<T> comes with the risk of creating *deadlocks*. These occur when an operation needs to lock two resources and two threads have each acquired one of the locks, causing them to wait for each other forever. If you're interested in deadlocks, try creating a Rust program that has a deadlock; then research deadlock mitigation strategies for mutexes in any language and have a go at implementing them in Rust. The standard library API documentation for Mutex<T> and MutexGuard offers useful information.

We'll round out this chapter by talking about the Send and Sync traits and how we can use them with custom types.

Extensible Concurrency with the Sync and Send Traits

Interestingly, the Rust language has *very* few concurrency features. Almost every concurrency feature we've talked about so far in this chapter has been part of the standard library, not the language. Your options for handling concurrency are not limited to the language or the standard library; you can write your own concurrency features or use those written by others.

However, two concurrency concepts are embedded in the language: the std::marker traits Sync and Send.

Allowing Transference of Ownership Between Threads with Send

The Send marker trait indicates that ownership of the type implementing Send can be transferred between threads. Almost every Rust type is Send, but there are some exceptions, including Rc<T>: this cannot be Send because if you cloned an Rc<T> value and tried to transfer ownership of the clone to another thread, both threads might update the reference count at the same time. For this reason, Rc<T> is implemented for use in single-threaded situations where you don't want to pay the thread-safe performance penalty.

Therefore, Rust's type system and trait bounds ensure that you can never accidentally send an Rc<T> value across threads unsafely. When we tried to do this in Listing 16-14, we got the error the trait Send is not implemented for Rc<Mutex<i32>>. When we switched to Arc<T>, which is Send, the code compiled.

Any type composed entirely of Send types is automatically marked as Send as well. Almost all primitive types are Send, aside from raw pointers, which we'll discuss in Chapter 19.

Allowing Access from Multiple Threads with Sync

The Sync marker trait indicates that it is safe for the type implementing Sync to be referenced from multiple threads. In other words, any type T is Sync if &T (a reference to T) is Send, meaning the reference can be sent safely to another thread. Similar to Send, primitive types are Sync, and types composed entirely of types that are Sync are also Sync.

The smart pointer Rc<T> is also not Sync for the same reasons that it's not Send. The RefCell<T> type (which we talked about in Chapter 15) and the family of related Cell<T> types are not Sync. The implementation of borrow checking that RefCell<T> does at runtime is not thread-safe. The smart pointer Mutex<T> is Sync and can be used to share access with multiple threads, as you saw in "Sharing a Mutex<T> Between Multiple Threads" on page 357.

Implementing Send and Sync Manually Is Unsafe

Because types that are made up of Send and Sync traits are automatically also Send and Sync, we don't have to implement those traits manually. As marker traits, they don't even have any methods to implement. They're just useful for enforcing invariants related to concurrency.

Manually implementing these traits involves implementing unsafe Rust code. We'll talk about using unsafe Rust code in Chapter 19; for now, the important information is that building new concurrent types not made up of Send and Sync parts requires careful thought to uphold the safety guarantees. The Rustonomicon at *https://doc.rust-lang.org/stable/nomicon/* has more information about these guarantees and how to uphold them.

Summary

This isn't the last you'll see of concurrency in this book: the project in Chapter 20 will use the concepts in this chapter in a more realistic situation than the smaller examples discussed here.

As mentioned earlier, because very little of how Rust handles concurrency is part of the language, many concurrency solutions are implemented as crates. These evolve more quickly than the standard library, so be sure to search online for the current, state-of-the-art crates to use in multithreaded situations.

The Rust standard library provides channels for message passing and smart pointer types, such as `Mutex<T>` and `Arc<T>`, that are safe to use in concurrent contexts. The type system and the borrow checker ensure that the code using these solutions won't end up with data races or invalid references. Once you get your code to compile, you can rest assured that it will happily run on multiple threads without the kinds of hard-to-track-down bugs common in other languages. Concurrent programming is no longer a concept to be afraid of: go forth and make your programs concurrent, fearlessly!

Next, we'll talk about idiomatic ways to model problems and structure solutions as your Rust programs get bigger. In addition, we'll discuss how Rust's idioms relate to those you might be familiar with from object-oriented programming.

17

OBJECT-ORIENTED PROGRAMMING FEATURES OF RUST

Object-oriented programming (OOP) is a way of modeling programs. Objects came from Simula in the 1960s. Those objects influenced Alan Kay's programming architecture in which objects pass messages to each other. He coined the term *object-oriented programming* in 1967 to describe this architecture. Many competing definitions describe what OOP is; some definitions would classify Rust as object oriented, but other definitions would not. In this chapter, we'll explore certain characteristics that are commonly considered object oriented and how those characteristics translate to idiomatic Rust. We'll then show you how to implement an object-oriented design pattern in Rust and discuss the trade-offs of doing so versus implementing a solution using some of Rust's strengths instead.

Characteristics of Object-Oriented Languages

There is no consensus in the programming community about what features a language must have to be considered object oriented. Rust is influenced by many programming paradigms, including OOP; for example, we explored the features that came from functional programming in Chapter 13. Arguably, OOP languages share certain common characteristics, namely objects, encapsulation, and inheritance. Let's look at what each of those characteristics means and whether Rust supports it.

Objects Contain Data and Behavior

The book *Design Patterns: Elements of Reusable Object-Oriented Software* by Erich Gamma, Richard Helm, Ralph Johnson, and John Vlissides (Addison-Wesley Professional, 1994) colloquially referred to as *The Gang of Four* book, is a catalog of object-oriented design patterns. It defines OOP this way:

> Object-oriented programs are made up of objects. An *object* packages both data and the procedures that operate on that data. The procedures are typically called *methods* or *operations*.

Using this definition, Rust is object oriented: structs and enums have data, and impl blocks provide methods on structs and enums. Even though structs and enums with methods aren't *called* objects, they provide the same functionality, according to the Gang of Four's definition of objects.

Encapsulation That Hides Implementation Details

Another aspect commonly associated with OOP is the idea of *encapsulation*, which means that the implementation details of an object aren't accessible to code using that object. Therefore, the only way to interact with an object is through its public API; code using the object shouldn't be able to reach into the object's internals and change data or behavior directly. This enables the programmer to change and refactor an object's internals without needing to change the code that uses the object.

We discussed how to control encapsulation in Chapter 7: we can use the pub keyword to decide which modules, types, functions, and methods in our code should be public, and by default everything else is private. For example, we can define a struct AveragedCollection that has a field containing a vector of i32 values. The struct can also have a field that contains the average of the values in the vector, meaning the average doesn't have to be computed on demand whenever anyone needs it. In other words, AveragedCollection will cache the calculated average for us. Listing 17-1 has the definition of the AveragedCollection struct.

src/lib.rs

```
pub struct AveragedCollection {
    list: Vec<i32>,
    average: f64,
}
```

Listing 17-1: An AveragedCollection struct that maintains a list of integers and the average of the items in the collection

The struct is marked pub so that other code can use it, but the fields within the struct remain private. This is important in this case because we want to ensure that whenever a value is added or removed from the list, the average is also updated. We do this by implementing add, remove, and average methods on the struct, as shown in Listing 17-2.

src/lib.rs

```rust
impl AveragedCollection {
    pub fn add(&mut self, value: i32) {
        self.list.push(value);
        self.update_average();
    }

    pub fn remove(&mut self) -> Option<i32> {
        let result = self.list.pop();
        match result {
            Some(value) => {
                self.update_average();
                Some(value)
            },
            None => None,
        }
    }

    pub fn average(&self) -> f64 {
        self.average
    }

    fn update_average(&mut self) {
        let total: i32 = self.list.iter().sum();
        self.average = total as f64 / self.list.len() as f64;
    }
}
```

Listing 17-2: Implementations of the public methods add, remove, and average on AveragedCollection

The public methods add, remove, and average are the only ways to modify an instance of AveragedCollection. When an item is added to list using the add method or removed using the remove method, the implementations of each call the private update_average method that handles updating the average field as well.

We leave the list and average fields private so there is no way for external code to add or remove items to the list field directly; otherwise, the average field might become out of sync when the list changes. The average method returns the value in the average field, allowing external code to read the average but not modify it.

Because we've encapsulated the implementation details of the struct AveragedCollection, we can easily change aspects, such as the data structure, in the future. For instance, we could use a HashSet<i32> instead of a Vec<i32> for the list field. As long as the signatures of the add, remove, and average public methods stay the same, code using AveragedCollection wouldn't need to change. If we made list public instead, this wouldn't necessarily be the case: HashSet<i32> and Vec<i32> have different methods for adding and removing items, so the external code would likely have to change if it were modifying list directly.

If encapsulation is a required aspect for a language to be considered object oriented, then Rust meets that requirement. The option to use `pub` or not for different parts of code enables encapsulation of implementation details.

Inheritance as a Type System and as Code Sharing

Inheritance is a mechanism whereby an object can inherit from another object's definition, thus gaining the parent object's data and behavior without you having to define them again.

If a language must have inheritance to be an object-oriented language, then Rust is not one. There is no way to define a struct that inherits the parent struct's fields and method implementations. However, if you're used to having inheritance in your programming toolbox, you can use other solutions in Rust, depending on your reason for reaching for inheritance in the first place.

You choose inheritance for two main reasons. One is for reuse of code: you can implement a particular behavior for one type, and inheritance enables you to reuse that implementation for a different type. You can share Rust code using default trait method implementations instead, which you saw in Listing 10-14 when we added a default implementation of the `summarize` method on the `Summary` trait. Any type implementing the `Summary` trait would have the `summarize` method available on it without any further code. This is similar to a parent class having an implementation of a method and an inheriting child class also having the implementation of the method. We can also override the default implementation of the `summarize` method when we implement the `Summary` trait, which is similar to a child class overriding the implementation of a method inherited from a parent class.

The other reason to use inheritance relates to the type system: to enable a child type to be used in the same places as the parent type. This is also called *polymorphism*, which means that you can substitute multiple objects for each other at runtime if they share certain characteristics.

POLYMORPHISM

To many people, polymorphism is synonymous with inheritance. But it's actually a more general concept that refers to code that can work with data of multiple types. For inheritance, those types are generally subclasses.

Rust instead uses generics to abstract over different possible types and trait bounds to impose constraints on what those types must provide. This is sometimes called *bounded parametric polymorphism*.

Inheritance has recently fallen out of favor as a programming design solution in many programming languages because it's often at risk of sharing more code than necessary. Subclasses shouldn't always share all characteristics of their parent class but will do so with inheritance. This can make a program's design less flexible. It also introduces the possibility of calling methods on subclasses that don't make sense or that cause errors because the methods don't apply to the subclass. In addition, some languages will only allow a subclass to inherit from one class, further restricting the flexibility of a program's design.

For these reasons, Rust takes a different approach, using trait objects instead of inheritance. Let's look at how trait objects enable polymorphism in Rust.

Using Trait Objects That Allow for Values of Different Types

In Chapter 8, we mentioned that one limitation of vectors is that they can store elements of only one type. We created a workaround in Listing 8-10 where we defined a SpreadsheetCell enum that had variants to hold integers, floats, and text. This meant we could store different types of data in each cell and still have a vector that represented a row of cells. This is a perfectly good solution when our interchangeable items are a fixed set of types that we know when our code is compiled.

However, sometimes we want our library user to be able to extend the set of types that are valid in a particular situation. To show how we might achieve this, we'll create an example graphical user interface (GUI) tool that iterates through a list of items, calling a draw method on each one to draw it to the screen—a common technique for GUI tools. We'll create a library crate called gui that contains the structure of a GUI library. This crate might include some types for people to use, such as Button or TextField. In addition, gui users will want to create their own types that can be drawn: for instance, one programmer might add an Image and another might add a SelectBox.

We won't implement a fully fledged GUI library for this example but will show how the pieces would fit together. At the time of writing the library, we can't know and define all the types other programmers might want to create. But we do know that gui needs to keep track of many values of different types, and it needs to call a draw method on each of these differently typed values. It doesn't need to know exactly what will happen when we call the draw method, just that the value will have that method available for us to call.

To do this in a language with inheritance, we might define a class named Component that has a method named draw on it. The other classes, such as Button, Image, and SelectBox, would inherit from Component and thus inherit the draw method. They could each override the draw method to define their custom behavior, but the framework could treat all of the types as if they were Component instances and call draw on them. But because Rust doesn't have inheritance, we need another way to structure the gui library to allow users to extend it with new types.

Defining a Trait for Common Behavior

To implement the behavior we want gui to have, we'll define a trait named Draw that will have one method named draw. Then we can define a vector that takes a *trait object*. A trait object points to an instance of a type that implements the trait we specify. We create a trait object by specifying some sort of pointer, such as a & reference or a Box<T> smart pointer, and then specifying the relevant trait. (We'll talk about the reason trait objects must use a pointer in "Dynamically Sized Types and the Sized Trait" on page 445.) We can use trait objects in place of a generic or concrete type. Wherever we use a trait object, Rust's type system will ensure at compile time that any value used in that context will implement the trait object's trait. Consequently, we don't need to know all the possible types at compile time.

We've mentioned that in Rust, we refrain from calling structs and enums "objects" to distinguish them from other languages' objects. In a struct or enum, the data in the struct fields and the behavior in impl blocks are separated, whereas in other languages, the data and behavior combined into one concept is often labeled an object. However, trait objects *are* more like objects in other languages in the sense that they combine data and behavior. But trait objects differ from traditional objects in that we can't add data to a trait object. Trait objects aren't as generally useful as objects in other languages: their specific purpose is to allow abstraction across common behavior.

Listing 17-3 shows how to define a trait named Draw with one method named draw.

src/lib.rs

```
pub trait Draw {
    fn draw(&self);
}
```

Listing 17-3: Definition of the Draw trait

This syntax should look familiar from our discussions on how to define traits in Chapter 10. Next comes some new syntax: Listing 17-4 defines a struct named Screen that holds a vector named components. This vector is of type Box<Draw>, which is a trait object; it's a stand-in for any type inside a Box that implements the Draw trait.

src/lib.rs

```
pub struct Screen {
    pub components: Vec<Box<Draw>>,
}
```

Listing 17-4: Definition of the Screen struct with a components field holding a vector of trait objects that implement the Draw trait

On the Screen struct, we'll define a method named run that will call the draw method on each of its components, as shown in Listing 17-5.

src/lib.rs

```
impl Screen {
    pub fn run(&self) {
        for component in self.components.iter() {
            component.draw();
        }
    }
}
```

Listing 17-5: A run method on Screen that calls the draw method on each component

This works differently than defining a struct that uses a generic type parameter with trait bounds. A generic type parameter can only be substituted with one concrete type at a time, whereas trait objects allow for multiple concrete types to fill in for the trait object at runtime. For example, we could have defined the Screen struct using a generic type and a trait bound, as in Listing 17-6.

src/lib.rs

```
pub struct Screen<T: Draw> {
    pub components: Vec<T>,
}

impl<T> Screen<T>
    where T: Draw {
    pub fn run(&self) {
        for component in self.components.iter() {
            component.draw();
        }
    }
}
```

Listing 17-6: An alternate implementation of the Screen struct and its run method using generics and trait bounds

This restricts us to a Screen instance that has a list of components all of type Button or all of type TextField. If you'll only ever have homogeneous collections, using generics and trait bounds is preferable because the definitions will be monomorphized at compile time to use the concrete types.

On the other hand, with the method using trait objects, one Screen instance can hold a Vec<T> that contains a Box<Button> as well as a Box<TextField>. Let's look at how this works, and then we'll talk about the runtime performance implications.

Implementing the Trait

Now we'll add some types that implement the Draw trait. We'll provide the Button type. Again, actually implementing a GUI library is beyond the scope of this book, so the draw method won't have any useful implementation in its body. To imagine what the implementation might look like, a Button struct might have fields for width, height, and label, as shown in Listing 17-7.

src/lib.rs

```
pub struct Button {
    pub width: u32,
    pub height: u32,
    pub label: String,
}

impl Draw for Button {
    fn draw(&self) {
        // code to actually draw a button
    }
}
```

Listing 17-7: A Button struct that implements the Draw trait

The width, height, and label fields on Button will differ from the fields on other components, such as a TextField type, that might have those fields plus a placeholder field instead. Each of the types we want to draw on the screen will implement the Draw trait but will use different code in the draw method to define how to draw that particular type, as Button has here (without the actual GUI code, which is beyond the scope of this chapter). The Button type, for instance, might have an additional impl block containing methods related to what happens when a user clicks the button. These kinds of methods won't apply to types like TextField.

If someone using our library decides to implement a SelectBox struct that has width, height, and options fields, they implement the Draw trait on the SelectBox type as well, as shown in Listing 17-8.

src/main.rs

```
extern crate gui;
use gui::Draw;

struct SelectBox {
    width: u32,
    height: u32,
    options: Vec<String>,
}

impl Draw for SelectBox {
    fn draw(&self) {
        // code to actually draw a select box
    }
}
```

Listing 17-8: Another crate using gui and implementing the Draw trait on a SelectBox struct

Our library's user can now write their main function to create a Screen instance. To the Screen instance, they can add a SelectBox and a Button by putting each in a Box<T> to become a trait object. They can then call the run method on the Screen instance, which will call draw on each of the components. Listing 17-9 shows this implementation.

src/main.rs

```
use gui::{Screen, Button};

fn main() {
    let screen = Screen {
        components: vec![
            Box::new(SelectBox {
                width: 75,
                height: 10,
                options: vec![
                    String::from("Yes"),
                    String::from("Maybe"),
                    String::from("No")
                ],
            }),
```

```
            Box::new(Button {
                width: 50,
                height: 10,
                label: String::from("OK"),
            }),
        ],
    };

    screen.run();
}
```

Listing 17-9: Using trait objects to store values of different types that implement the same trait

When we wrote the library, we didn't know that someone might add the SelectBox type, but our Screen implementation was able to operate on the new type and draw it because SelectBox implements the Draw type, which means it implements the draw method.

This concept—of being concerned only with the messages a value responds to rather than the value's concrete type—is similar to the concept *duck typing* in dynamically typed languages: if it walks like a duck and quacks like a duck, then it must be a duck! In the implementation of run on Screen in Listing 17-5, run doesn't need to know what the concrete type of each component is. It doesn't check whether a component is an instance of a Button or a SelectBox; it just calls the draw method on the component. By specifying Box<Draw> as the type of the values in the components vector, we've defined Screen to need values that we can call the draw method on.

The advantage of using trait objects and Rust's type system to write code similar to code using duck typing is that we never have to check whether a value implements a particular method at runtime or worry about getting errors if a value doesn't implement a method but we call it anyway. Rust won't compile our code if the values don't implement the traits that the trait objects need.

For example, Listing 17-10 shows what happens if we try to create a Screen with a String as a component.

src/main.rs

```
extern crate gui;
use gui::Screen;

fn main() {
    let screen = Screen {
        components: vec![
            Box::new(String::from("Hi")),
        ],
    };

    screen.run();
}
```

Listing 17-10: Attempting to use a type that doesn't implement the trait object's trait

We'll get this error because String doesn't implement the Draw trait:

```
error[E0277]: the trait bound `std::string::String: gui::Draw` is not
satisfied
  --> src/main.rs:7:13
   |
 7 |             Box::new(String::from("Hi")),
   |             ^^^^^^^^^^^^^^^^^^^^^^^^^^^^ the trait gui::Draw is not
   implemented for `std::string::String`
   |
   = note: required for the cast to the object type `gui::Draw`
```

This error lets us know that either we're passing something to Screen we didn't mean to pass and we should pass a different type or we should implement Draw on String so that Screen is able to call draw on it.

Trait Objects Perform Dynamic Dispatch

Recall in "Performance of Code Using Generics" on page 177 our discussion on the monomorphization process performed by the compiler when we use trait bounds on generics: the compiler generates nongeneric implementations of functions and methods for each concrete type that we use in place of a generic type parameter. The code that results from monomorphization is doing *static dispatch*, which is when the compiler knows what method you're calling at compile time. This is opposed to *dynamic dispatch*, which is when the compiler can't tell at compile time which method you're calling. In dynamic dispatch cases, the compiler emits code that at runtime will figure out which method to call.

When we use trait objects, Rust must use dynamic dispatch. The compiler doesn't know all the types that might be used with the code that is using trait objects, so it doesn't know which method implemented on which type to call. Instead, at runtime, Rust uses the pointers inside the trait object to know which method to call. There is a runtime cost when this lookup happens that doesn't occur with static dispatch. Dynamic dispatch also prevents the compiler from choosing to inline a method's code, which in turn prevents some optimizations. However, we did get extra flexibility in the code that we wrote in Listing 17-5 and were able to support in Listing 17-9, so it's a trade-off to consider.

Object Safety Is Required for Trait Objects

You can only make *object-safe* traits into trait objects. Some complex rules govern all the properties that make a trait object safe, but in practice, only two rules are relevant. A trait is object safe if all the methods defined in the trait have the following properties:

- The return type isn't Self.
- There are no generic type parameters.

The Self keyword is an alias for the type we're implementing the traits or methods on. Trait objects must be object safe because once you've used a trait object, Rust no longer knows the concrete type that's implementing that trait. If a trait method returns the concrete Self type, but a trait object forgets the exact type that Self is, there is no way the method can use the original concrete type. The same is true of generic type parameters that are filled in with concrete type parameters when the trait is used: the concrete types become part of the type that implements the trait. When the type is forgotten through the use of a trait object, there is no way to know what types to fill in the generic type parameters with.

An example of a trait whose methods are not object safe is the standard library's Clone trait. The signature for the clone method in the Clone trait looks like this:

```
pub trait Clone {
    fn clone(&self) -> Self;
}
```

The String type implements the Clone trait, and when we call the clone method on an instance of String, we get back an instance of String. Similarly, if we call clone on an instance of Vec<T>, we get back an instance of Vec<T>. The signature of clone needs to know what type will stand in for Self, because that's the return type.

The compiler will indicate when you're trying to do something that violates the rules of object safety in regard to trait objects. For example, let's say we tried to implement the Screen struct in Listing 17-4 to hold types that implement the Clone trait instead of the Draw trait, like this:

```
pub struct Screen {
    pub components: Vec<Box<Clone>>,
}
```

We would get this error:

```
error[E0038]: the trait `std::clone::Clone` cannot be made into an object
 --> src/lib.rs:2:5
  |
2 |     pub components: Vec<Box<Clone>>,
  |     ^^^^^^^^^^^^^^^^^^^^^^^^^^^^^^^^ the trait `std::clone::Clone` cannot
be made into an object
  |
  = note: the trait cannot require that `Self : Sized`
```

This error means you can't use this trait as a trait object in this way. If you're interested in more details on object safety, see Rust RFC 255 at *https://github.com/rust-lang/rfcs/blob/master/text/0255-object-safety.md/*.

Implementing an Object-Oriented Design Pattern

The *state pattern* is an object-oriented design pattern. The crux of the pattern is that a value has some internal state, which is represented by a set of *state objects*, and the value's behavior changes based on the internal state. The state objects share functionality: in Rust, of course, we use structs and traits rather than objects and inheritance. Each state object is responsible for its own behavior and for governing when it should change into another state. The value that holds a state object knows nothing about the different behavior of the states or when to transition between states.

Using the state pattern means when the business requirements of the program change, we won't need to change the code of the value holding the state or the code that uses the value. We'll only need to update the code inside one of the state objects to change its rules or perhaps add more state objects. Let's look at an example of the state design pattern and how to use it in Rust.

We'll implement a blog post workflow in an incremental way. The blog's final functionality will look like this:

1. A blog post starts as an empty draft.
2. When the draft is done, a review of the post is requested.
3. When the post is approved, it gets published.
4. Only published blog posts return content to print, so unapproved posts can't accidentally be published.

Any other changes attempted on a post should have no effect. For example, if we try to approve a draft blog post before we've requested a review, the post should remain an unpublished draft.

Listing 17-11 shows this workflow in code form: this is an example usage of the API we'll implement in a library crate named blog. This won't compile yet because we haven't implemented the blog crate yet.

src/main.rs

```
extern crate blog;
use blog::Post;

fn main() {
❶ let mut post = Post::new();

❷ post.add_text("I ate a salad for lunch today");
❸ assert_eq!("", post.content());

❹ post.request_review();
❺ assert_eq!("", post.content());

❻ post.approve();
❼ assert_eq!("I ate a salad for lunch today", post.content());
}
```

Listing 17-11: Code that demonstrates the desired behavior we want our blog crate to have

We want to allow the user to create a new draft blog post with `Post::new` ❶.
Then we want to allow text to be added to the blog post while it's in the draft
state ❷. If we try to get the post's content immediately, before approval, nothing should happen because the post is still a draft. We've added `assert_eq!` in
the code for demonstration purposes ❸. An excellent unit test for this would
be to assert that a draft blog post returns an empty string from the `content`
method, but we're not going to write tests for this example.

Next, we want to enable a request for a review of the post ❹, and we want
`content` to return an empty string while waiting for the review ❺. When the
post receives approval ❻, it should get published, meaning the text of the post
will be returned when `content` is called ❼.

Notice that the only type we're interacting with from the crate is the `Post`
type. This type will use the state pattern and will hold a value that will be one
of three state objects representing the various states a post can be in—draft,
waiting for review, or published. Changing from one state to another will be
managed internally within the `Post` type. The states change in response to the
methods called by our library's users on the `Post` instance, but they don't have
to manage the state changes directly. Also, users can't make a mistake with
the states, like publishing a post before it's reviewed.

Defining Post and Creating a New Instance in the Draft State

Let's get started on the implementation of the library! We know we need a
public `Post` struct that holds some content, so we'll start with the definition of
the struct and an associated public `new` function to create an instance of `Post`,
as shown in Listing 17-12. We'll also make a private `State` trait. Then `Post` will
hold a trait object of `Box<State>` inside an `Option` in a private field named `state`.
You'll see why the `Option` is necessary in a bit.

src/lib.rs

```
pub struct Post {
    state: Option<Box<State>>,
    content: String,
}

impl Post {
    pub fn new() -> Post {
        Post {
          ❶ state: Some(Box::new(Draft {})),
          ❷ content: String::new(),
        }
    }
}

trait State {}

struct Draft {}

impl State for Draft {}
```

Listing 17-12: Definition of a Post struct and a new function that creates a new Post
instance, a State trait, and a Draft struct

The State trait defines the behavior shared by different post states, and the Draft, PendingReview, and Published states will all implement the State trait. For now, the trait doesn't have any methods, and we'll start by defining just the Draft state because that is the state we want a post to start in.

When we create a new Post, we set its state field to a Some value that holds a Box ❶. This Box points to a new instance of the Draft struct. This ensures whenever we create a new instance of Post, it will start out as a draft. Because the state field of Post is private, there is no way to create a Post in any other state! In the Post::new function, we set the content field to a new, empty String ❷.

Storing the Text of the Post Content

Listing 17-11 showed that we want to be able to call a method named add_text and pass it a &str that is then added to the text content of the blog post. We implement this as a method rather than exposing the content field as pub. This means we can implement a method later that will control how the content field's data is read. The add_text method is pretty straightforward, so let's add the implementation in Listing 17-13 to the impl Post block.

src/lib.rs

```
impl Post {
    // --snip--
    pub fn add_text(&mut self, text: &str) {
        self.content.push_str(text);
    }
}
```

Listing 17-13: Implementing the add_text method to add text to a post's content

The add_text method takes a mutable reference to self, because we're changing the Post instance that we're calling add_text on. We then call push_str on the String in content and pass the text argument to add to the saved content. This behavior doesn't depend on the state the post is in, so it's not part of the state pattern. The add_text method doesn't interact with the state field at all, but it is part of the behavior we want to support.

Ensuring the Content of a Draft Post Is Empty

Even after we've called add_text and added some content to our post, we still want the content method to return an empty string slice because the post is still in the draft state, as shown at ❸ in Listing 17-11. For now, let's implement the content method with the simplest thing that will fulfill this requirement: always returning an empty string slice. We'll change this later once we implement the ability to change a post's state so it can be published. So far, posts can only be in the draft state, so the post content should always be empty. Listing 17-14 shows this placeholder implementation.

src/lib.rs

```
impl Post {
    // --snip--
```

```
    pub fn content(&self) -> &str {
        ""
    }
}
```

Listing 17-14: Adding a placeholder implementation for the content method on Post that always returns an empty string slice

With this added content method, everything in Listing 17-11 up to the line at ❸ works as intended.

Requesting a Review of the Post Changes Its State

Next, we need to add functionality to request a review of a post, which should change its state from Draft to PendingReview. Listing 17-15 shows this code.

src/lib.rs

```
impl Post {
    // --snip--
❶   pub fn request_review(&mut self) {
❷       if let Some(s) = self.state.take() {
❸           self.state = Some(s.request_review())
        }
    }
}

trait State {
❹   fn request_review(self: Box<Self>) -> Box<State>;
}

struct Draft {}

impl State for Draft {
    fn request_review(self: Box<Self>) -> Box<State> {
❺       Box::new(PendingReview {})
    }
}

struct PendingReview {}

impl State for PendingReview {
    fn request_review(self: Box<Self>) -> Box<State> {
❻       self
    }
}
```

Listing 17-15: Implementing request_review methods on Post and the State trait

We give Post a public method named request_review that will take a mutable reference to self ❶. Then we call an internal request_review method on the current state of Post ❸, and this second request_review method consumes the current state and returns a new state.

We've added the request_review method to the State trait ❹; all types that implement the trait will now need to implement the request_review method. Note that rather than having self, &self, or &mut self as the first parameter of the method, we have self: Box<Self>. This syntax means the method is valid only when called on a Box holding the type. This syntax takes ownership of Box<Self>, invalidating the old state so the state value of the Post can transform into a new state.

To consume the old state, the request_review method needs to take ownership of the state value. This is where the Option in the state field of Post comes in: we call the take method to take the Some value out of the state field and leave a None in its place, because Rust doesn't let us have unpopulated fields in structs ❷. This lets us move the state value out of Post rather than borrowing it. Then we'll set the post's state value to the result of this operation.

We need to set state to None temporarily rather than setting it directly with code like self.state = self.state.request_review(); to get ownership of the state value. This ensures Post can't use the old state value after we've transformed it into a new state.

The request_review method on Draft needs to return a new, boxed instance of a new PendingReview struct ❺, which represents the state when a post is waiting for a review. The PendingReview struct also implements the request_review method but doesn't do any transformations. Rather, it returns itself ❻, because when we request a review on a post already in the PendingReview state, it should stay in the PendingReview state.

Now we can start seeing the advantages of the state pattern: the request_review method on Post is the same no matter its state value. Each state is responsible for its own rules.

We'll leave the content method on Post as is, returning an empty string slice. We can now have a Post in the PendingReview state as well as in the Draft state, but we want the same behavior in the PendingReview state. Listing 17-11 now works up to the line at ❺!

Adding the approve Method that Changes the Behavior of content

The approve method will be similar to the request_review method: it will set state to the value that the current state says it should have when that state is approved, as shown in Listing 17-16.

src/lib.rs

```
impl Post {
    // --snip--
    pub fn approve(&mut self) {
        if let Some(s) = self.state.take() {
            self.state = Some(s.approve())
        }
    }
}

trait State {
    fn request_review(self: Box<Self>) -> Box<State>;
    fn approve(self: Box<Self>) -> Box<State>;
}

struct Draft {}
```

```
impl State for Draft {
    // --snip--
    fn approve(self: Box<Self>) -> Box<State> {
     ❶ self
    }
}

struct PendingReview {}

impl State for PendingReview {
    // --snip--
    fn approve(self: Box<Self>) -> Box<State> {
     ❷ Box::new(Published {})
    }
}

struct Published {}

impl State for Published {
    fn request_review(self: Box<Self>) -> Box<State> {
        self
    }

    fn approve(self: Box<Self>) -> Box<State> {
        self
    }
}
```

Listing 17-16: Implementing the approve method on Post and the State trait

We add the approve method to the State trait and add a new struct that implements State, the Published state.

Similar to request_review, if we call the approve method on a Draft, it will have no effect because it will return self ❶. When we call approve on PendingReview, it returns a new, boxed instance of the Published struct ❷. The Published struct implements the State trait, and for both the request_review method and the approve method, it returns itself, because the post should stay in the Published state in those cases.

Now we need to update the content method on Post: if the state is Published, we want to return the value in the post's content field; otherwise, we want to return an empty string slice, as shown in Listing 17-17.

src/lib.rs

```
impl Post {
    // --snip--
    pub fn content(&self) -> &str {
        self.state.as_ref().unwrap().content(&self)
    }
    // --snip--
}
```

Listing 17-17: Updating the content method on Post to delegate to a content method on State

Because the goal is to keep all these rules inside the structs that implement State, we call a content method on the value in state and pass the post instance (that is, self) as an argument. Then we return the value that is returned from using the content method on the state value.

We call the as_ref method on the Option because we want a reference to the value inside the Option rather than ownership of the value. Because state is an Option<Box<State>>, when we call as_ref, an Option<&Box<State>> is returned. If we didn't call as_ref, we would get an error because we can't move state out of the borrowed &self of the function parameter.

We then call the unwrap method, which we know will never panic, because we know the methods on Post ensure that state will always contain a Some value when those methods are done. This is one of the cases we talked about in "Cases in Which You Have More Information Than the Compiler" on page 162 when we know that a None value is never possible, even though the compiler isn't able to understand that.

At this point, when we call content on the &Box<State>, deref coercion will take effect on the & and the Box so the content method will ultimately be called on the type that implements the State trait. That means we need to add content to the State trait definition, and that is where we'll put the logic for what content to return depending on which state we have, as shown in Listing 17-18.

src/lib.rs

```
trait State {
    // --snip--
    fn content<'a>(&self, post: &'a Post) -> &'a str {
    ❶ ""
    }
}

// --snip--

struct Published {}

impl State for Published {
    // --snip--
    fn content<'a>(&self, post: &'a Post) -> &'a str {
    ❷ &post.content
    }
}
```

Listing 17-18: Adding the content method to the State trait

We add a default implementation for the content method that returns an empty string slice ❶. That means we don't need to implement content on the Draft and PendingReview structs. The Published struct will override the content method and return the value in post.content ❷.

Note that we need lifetime annotations on this method, as we discussed in Chapter 10. We're taking a reference to a post as an argument and returning a reference to part of that post, so the lifetime of the returned reference is related to the lifetime of the post argument.

And we're done—all of Listing 17-11 now works! We've implemented the state pattern with the rules of the blog post workflow. The logic related to the rules lives in the state objects rather than being scattered throughout Post.

Trade-offs of the State Pattern

We've shown that Rust is capable of implementing the object-oriented state pattern to encapsulate the different kinds of behavior a post should have in each state. The methods on Post know nothing about the various behaviors. The way we organized the code, we have to look in only one place to know the different ways a published post can behave: the implementation of the State trait on the Published struct.

If we were to create an alternative implementation that didn't use the state pattern, we might instead use match expressions in the methods on Post or even in the main code that checks the state of the post and changes behavior in those places. That would mean we would have to look in several places to understand all the implications of a post being in the published state! This would only increase the more states we added: each of those match expressions would need another arm.

With the state pattern, the Post methods and the places we use Post don't need match expressions, and to add a new state, we would only need to add a new struct and implement the trait methods on that one struct.

The implementation using the state pattern is easy to extend to add more functionality. To see the simplicity of maintaining code that uses the state pattern, try a few of these suggestions:

- Add a reject method that changes the post's state from PendingReview back to Draft.
- Require two calls to approve before the state can be changed to Published.
- Allow users to add text content only when a post is in the Draft state. Hint: have the state object be responsible for what might change about the content but not responsible for modifying the Post.

One downside of the state pattern is that, because the states implement the transitions between states, some of the states are coupled to each other. If we added another state between PendingReview and Published, such as Scheduled, we would have to change the code in PendingReview to transition to Scheduled instead. It would be less work if PendingReview didn't need to change with the addition of a new state, but that would mean switching to another design pattern.

Another downside is that we've duplicated some logic. To eliminate some of the duplication, we might try to make default implementations for the request_review and approve methods on the State trait that return self; however, this would violate object safety, because the trait doesn't know what the concrete self will be exactly. We want to be able to use State as a trait object, so we need its methods to be object safe.

Other duplication includes the similar implementations of the request_review and approve methods on Post. Both methods delegate to the implementation of the same method on the value in the state field of Option and set the new value of the state field to the result. If we had a lot of methods on Post that followed this pattern, we might consider defining a macro to eliminate the repetition (see Appendix D for more on macros).

By implementing the state pattern exactly as it's defined for object-oriented languages, we're not taking as full advantage of Rust's strengths as we could. Let's look at some changes we can make to the blog crate that can make invalid states and transitions into compile time errors.

Encoding States and Behavior as Types

We'll show you how to rethink the state pattern to get a different set of trade-offs. Rather than encapsulating the states and transitions completely so outside code has no knowledge of them, we'll encode the states into different types. Consequently, Rust's type-checking system will prevent attempts to use draft posts where only published posts are allowed by issuing a compiler error.

Let's consider the first part of main in Listing 17-11:

src/main.rs

```
fn main() {
    let mut post = Post::new();

    post.add_text("I ate a salad for lunch today");
    assert_eq!("", post.content());
}
```

We still enable the creation of new posts in the draft state using Post::new and the ability to add text to the post's content. But instead of having a content method on a draft post that returns an empty string, we'll make it so draft posts don't have the content method at all. That way, if we try to get a draft post's content, we'll get a compiler error telling us the method doesn't exist. As a result, it will be impossible for us to accidentally display draft post content in production, because that code won't even compile. Listing 17-19 shows the definition of a Post struct and a DraftPost struct, as well as methods on each.

src/lib.rs

```
pub struct Post {
    content: String,
}

pub struct DraftPost {
    content: String,
}

impl Post {
  ❶ pub fn new() -> DraftPost {
        DraftPost {
            content: String::new(),
        }
    }
```

```
❷ pub fn content(&self) -> &str {
      &self.content
  }
}

impl DraftPost {
❸ pub fn add_text(&mut self, text: &str) {
      self.content.push_str(text);
  }
}
```

Listing 17-19: A Post *with a* content *method and a* DraftPost *without a* content *method*

Both the Post and DraftPost structs have a private content field that stores the blog post text. The structs no longer have the state field because we're moving the encoding of the state to the types of the structs. The Post struct will represent a published post, and it has a content method that returns the content ❷.

We still have a Post::new function, but instead of returning an instance of Post, it returns an instance of DraftPost ❶. Because content is private and there aren't any functions that return Post, it's not possible to create an instance of Post right now.

The DraftPost struct has an add_text method, so we can add text to content as before ❸, but note that DraftPost does not have a content method defined! So now the program ensures all posts start as draft posts, and draft posts don't have their content available for display. Any attempt to get around these constraints will result in a compiler error.

Implementing Transitions as Transformations into Different Types

So how do we get a published post? We want to enforce the rule that a draft post has to be reviewed and approved before it can be published. A post in the pending review state should still not display any content. Let's implement these constraints by adding another struct, PendingReviewPost, defining the request_review method on DraftPost to return a PendingReviewPost, and defining an approve method on PendingReviewPost to return a Post, as shown in Listing 17-20.

src/lib.rs

```
impl DraftPost {
    // --snip--

    pub fn request_review(self) -> PendingReviewPost {
        PendingReviewPost {
            content: self.content,
        }
    }
}

pub struct PendingReviewPost {
    content: String,
}
```

```
impl PendingReviewPost {
    pub fn approve(self) -> Post {
        Post {
            content: self.content,
        }
    }
}
```

Listing 17-20: A *PendingReviewPost* that gets created by calling *request_review* on *DraftPost* and an *approve* method that turns a *PendingReviewPost* into a published *Post*

The request_review and approve methods take ownership of self, thus consuming the DraftPost and PendingReviewPost instances and transforming them into a PendingReviewPost and a published Post, respectively. This way, we won't have any lingering DraftPost instances after we've called request _review on them, and so forth. The PendingReviewPost struct doesn't have a content method defined on it, so attempting to read its content results in a compiler error, as with DraftPost. Because the only way to get a published Post instance that does have a content method defined is to call the approve method on a PendingReviewPost, and the only way to get a PendingReviewPost is to call the request_review method on a DraftPost, we've now encoded the blog post workflow into the type system.

But we also have to make some small changes to main. The request_review and approve methods return new instances rather than modifying the struct they're called on, so we need to add more let post = shadowing assignments to save the returned instances. We also can't have the assertions about the draft and pending review post's contents be empty strings, nor do we need them: we can't compile code that tries to use the content of posts in those states any longer. The updated code in main is shown in Listing 17-21.

src/main.rs

```
extern crate blog;
use blog::Post;

fn main() {
    let mut post = Post::new();

    post.add_text("I ate a salad for lunch today");

    let post = post.request_review();

    let post = post.approve();

    assert_eq!("I ate a salad for lunch today", post.content());
}
```

Listing 17-21: Modifications to *main* to use the new implementation of the blog post workflow

The changes we needed to make to main to reassign post mean that this implementation doesn't quite follow the object-oriented state pattern any-more: the transformations between the states are no longer encapsulated entirely within the Post implementation. However, our gain is that invalid states are now impossible because of the type system and the type checking that happens at compile time! This ensures that certain bugs, such as display of the content of an unpublished post, will be discovered before they make it to production.

Try the tasks suggested for additional requirements that we mentioned at the start of this section on the blog crate as it is after Listing 17-20 to see what you think about the design of this version of the code. Note that some of the tasks might be completed already in this design.

We've seen that even though Rust is capable of implementing object-oriented design patterns, other patterns, such as encoding state into the type system, are also available in Rust. These patterns have different trade-offs. Although you might be very familiar with object-oriented patterns, rethinking the problem to take advantage of Rust's features can provide benefits, such as preventing some bugs at compile time. Object-oriented patterns won't always be the best solution in Rust due to certain features, like ownership, that object-oriented languages don't have.

Summary

No matter whether or not you think Rust is an object-oriented language after reading this chapter, you now know that you can use trait objects to get some object-oriented features in Rust. Dynamic dispatch can give your code some flexibility in exchange for a bit of runtime performance. You can use this flexibility to implement object-oriented patterns that can help your code's maintainability. Rust also has other features, like ownership, that object-oriented languages don't have. An object-oriented pattern won't always be the best way to take advantage of Rust's strengths, but it is an available option.

Next, we'll look at patterns, which are another of Rust's features that enable lots of flexibility. We've looked at them briefly throughout the book but haven't seen their full capability yet. Let's go!

18

PATTERNS AND MATCHING

Patterns are a special syntax in Rust for matching against the structure of types, both complex and simple. Using patterns in conjunction with match expressions and other constructs gives you more control over a program's control flow. A pattern consists of some combination of the following:

- Literals
- Destructured arrays, enums, structs, or tuples
- Variables
- Wildcards
- Placeholders

These components describe the shape of the data we're working with, which we then match against values to determine whether our program has the correct data to continue running a particular piece of code.

To use a pattern, we compare it to some value. If the pattern matches the value, we use the value parts in our code. Recall the match expressions in Chapter 6 that used patterns, such as the coin-sorting machine example. If the value fits the shape of the pattern, we can use the named pieces. If it doesn't, the code associated with the pattern won't run.

This chapter is a reference on all things related to patterns. We'll cover the valid places to use patterns, the difference between refutable and irrefutable patterns, and the different kinds of pattern syntax that you might see. By the end of the chapter, you'll know how to use patterns to express many concepts in a clear way.

All the Places Patterns Can Be Used

Patterns pop up in a number of places in Rust, and you've been using them a lot without realizing it! This section discusses all the places where patterns are valid.

match Arms

As discussed in Chapter 6, we use patterns in the arms of match expressions. Formally, match expressions are defined as the keyword match, a value to match on, and one or more match arms that consist of a pattern and an expression to run if the value matches that arm's pattern, like this:

```
match VALUE {
    PATTERN => EXPRESSION,
    PATTERN => EXPRESSION,
    PATTERN => EXPRESSION,
}
```

One requirement for match expressions is that they need to be *exhaustive* in the sense that all possibilities for the value in the match expression must be accounted for. One way to ensure you've covered every possibility is to have a catchall pattern for the last arm: for example, a variable name matching any value can never fail and thus covers every remaining case.

A particular pattern _ will match anything, but it never binds to a variable, so it's often used in the last match arm. The _ pattern can be useful when you want to ignore any value not specified, for example. We'll cover the _ pattern in more detail in "Ignoring Values in a Pattern" on page 403.

Conditional if let Expressions

In Chapter 6, we discussed how to use if let expressions mainly as a shorter way to write the equivalent of a match that only matches one case. Optionally, if let can have a corresponding else containing code to run if the pattern in the if let doesn't match.

Listing 18-1 shows that it's also possible to mix and match if let, else if, and else if let expressions. Doing so gives us more flexibility than a match expression, in which we can express only one value to compare with the patterns. Also, the conditions in a series of if let, else if, and else if let arms aren't required to relate to each other.

The code in Listing 18-1 shows a series of checks for several conditions that decide what the background color should be. For this example, we've created variables with hardcoded values that a real program might receive from user input.

src/main.rs

```
fn main() {
    let favorite_color: Option<&str> = None;
    let is_tuesday = false;
    let age: Result<u8, _> = "34".parse();

❶  if let Some(color) = favorite_color {
❷      println!("Using your favorite color, {}, as the background", color);
❸  } else if is_tuesday {
❹      println!("Tuesday is green day!");
❺  } else if let Ok(age) = age {
❻      if age > 30 {
❼          println!("Using purple as the background color");
        } else {
❽          println!("Using orange as the background color");
        }
❾  } else {
❿      println!("Using blue as the background color");
    }
}
```

Listing 18-1: Mixing if let, else if, else if let, and else

If the user specifies a favorite color ❶, that color is the background color ❷. If today is Tuesday ❸, the background color is green ❹. If the user specifies their age as a string and we can parse it as a number successfully ❺, the color is either purple ❼ or orange ❽ depending on the value of the number ❻. If none of these conditions apply ❾, the background color is blue ❿.

This conditional structure lets us support complex requirements. With the hardcoded values we have here, this example will print Using purple as the background color.

You can see that if let can also introduce shadowed variables in the same way that match arms can: the line if let Ok(age) = age ❺ introduces a new shadowed age variable that contains the value inside the Ok variant. This means we need to place the if age > 30 condition ❻ within that block: we can't combine these two conditions into if let Ok(age) = age && age > 30. The shadowed age we want to compare to 30 isn't valid until the new scope starts with the curly bracket.

The downside of using if let expressions is that the compiler doesn't check exhaustiveness, whereas with match expressions it does. If we omitted the last else block ❾ and therefore missed handling some cases, the compiler would not alert us to the possible logic bug.

while let Conditional Loops

Similar in construction to if let, the while let conditional loop allows a while loop to run for as long as a pattern continues to match. The example in Listing 18-2 shows a while let loop that uses a vector as a stack and prints the values in the vector in the opposite order in which they were pushed.

```
let mut stack = Vec::new();

stack.push(1);
stack.push(2);
stack.push(3);

while let Some(top) = stack.pop() {
    println!("{}", top);
}
```

Listing 18-2: Using a while let loop to print values for as long as stack.pop() returns Some

This example prints 3, 2, and then 1. The pop method takes the last element out of the vector and returns Some(value). If the vector is empty, pop returns None. The while loop continues running the code in its block as long as pop returns Some. When pop returns None, the loop stops. We can use while let to pop every element off our stack.

for Loops

In Chapter 3, we mentioned that the for loop is the most common loop construction in Rust code, but we haven't yet discussed the pattern that for takes. In a for loop, the pattern is the value that directly follows the keyword for, so in for x in y the x is the pattern.

Listing 18-3 demonstrates how to use a pattern in a for loop to destructure, or break apart, a tuple as part of the for loop.

```
let v = vec!['a', 'b', 'c'];

for (index, value) in v.iter().enumerate() {
    println!("{} is at index {}", value, index);
}
```

Listing 18-3: Using a pattern in a for loop to destructure a tuple

The code in Listing 18-3 will print the following:

```
a is at index 0
b is at index 1
c is at index 2
```

We use the enumerate method to adapt an iterator to produce a value and that value's index in the iterator, placed into a tuple. The first call to enumerate produces the tuple (0, 'a'). When this value is matched to the pattern (index, value), index will be 0 and value will be 'a', printing the first line of the output.

let Statements

Prior to this chapter, we had only explicitly discussed using patterns with match and if let, but in fact, we've used patterns in other places as well, including in let statements. For example, consider this straightforward variable assignment with let:

```
let x = 5;
```

Throughout this book, we've used let like this hundreds of times, and although you might not have realized it, you were using patterns! More formally, a let statement looks like this:

```
let PATTERN = EXPRESSION;
```

In statements like let x = 5; with a variable name in the PATTERN slot, the variable name is just a particularly simple form of a pattern. Rust compares the expression against the pattern and assigns any names it finds. So in the let x = 5; example, x is a pattern that means "bind what matches here to the variable x." Because the name x is the whole pattern, this pattern effectively means "bind everything to the variable x, whatever the value is."

To see the pattern-matching aspect of let more clearly, consider Listing 18-4, which uses a pattern with let to destructure a tuple.

```
let (x, y, z) = (1, 2, 3);
```

Listing 18-4: Using a pattern to destructure a tuple and create three variables at once

Here, we match a tuple against a pattern. Rust compares the value (1, 2, 3) to the pattern (x, y, z) and sees that the value matches the pattern, so Rust binds 1 to x, 2 to y, and 3 to z. You can think of this tuple pattern as nesting three individual variable patterns inside it.

If the number of elements in the pattern doesn't match the number of elements in the tuple, the overall type won't match and we'll get a compiler error. For example, Listing 18-5 shows an attempt to destructure a tuple with three elements into two variables, which won't work.

```
let (x, y) = (1, 2, 3);
```

Listing 18-5: Incorrectly constructing a pattern whose variables don't match the number of elements in the tuple

Attempting to compile this code results in this type error:

```
error[E0308]: mismatched types
 --> src/main.rs:2:9
```

```
2 |      let (x, y) = (1, 2, 3);
  |          ^^^^^^ expected a tuple with 3 elements, found one with 2 elements
  |
  = note: expected type `({integer}, {integer}, {integer})`
             found type `(_, _)`
```

If we wanted to ignore one or more of the values in the tuple, we could use _ or .., as you'll see in "Ignoring Values in a Pattern" on page 403. If the problem is that we have too many variables in the pattern, the solution is to make the types match by removing variables so the number of variables equals the number of elements in the tuple.

Function Parameters

Function parameters can also be patterns. The code in Listing 18-6, which declares a function named foo that takes one parameter named x of type i32, should by now look familiar.

```
fn foo(x: i32) {
    // code goes here
}
```

Listing 18-6: A function signature uses patterns in the parameters

The x part is a pattern! As we did with let, we could match a tuple in a function's arguments to the pattern. Listing 18-7 splits the values in a tuple as we pass it to a function.

src/main.rs

```
fn print_coordinates(&(x, y): &(i32, i32)) {
    println!("Current location: ({}, {})", x, y);
}

fn main() {
    let point = (3, 5);
    print_coordinates(&point);
}
```

Listing 18-7: A function with parameters that destructure a tuple

This code prints Current location: (3, 5). The values &(3, 5) match the pattern &(x, y), so x is the value 3 and y is the value 5.

We can also use patterns in closure parameter lists in the same way as in function parameter lists, because closures are similar to functions, as discussed in Chapter 13.

At this point, you've seen several ways of using patterns, but patterns don't work the same in every place we can use them. In some places, the patterns must be irrefutable; in other circumstances, they can be refutable. We'll discuss these two concepts next.

Refutability: Whether a Pattern Might Fail to Match

Patterns come in two forms: refutable and irrefutable. Patterns that will match for any possible value passed are *irrefutable*. An example would be x in the statement let x = 5; because x matches anything and therefore cannot fail to match. Patterns that can fail to match for some possible value are *refutable*. An example would be Some(x) in the expression if let Some(x) = a_value because if the value in the a_value variable is None rather than Some, the Some(x) pattern will not match.

Function parameters, let statements, and for loops can only accept irrefutable patterns, because the program cannot do anything meaningful when values don't match. The if let and while let expressions only accept refutable patterns, because by definition they're intended to handle possible failure: the functionality of a conditional is in its ability to perform differently depending on success or failure.

In general, you shouldn't have to worry about the distinction between refutable and irrefutable patterns; however, you do need to be familiar with the concept of refutability so you can respond when you see it in an error message. In those cases, you'll need to change either the pattern or the construct you're using the pattern with, depending on the intended behavior of the code.

Let's look at an example of what happens when we try to use a refutable pattern where Rust requires an irrefutable pattern and vice versa. Listing 18-8 shows a let statement, but for the pattern we've specified Some(x), a refutable pattern. As you might expect, this code will not compile.

```
let Some(x) = some_option_value;
```

Listing 18-8: Attempting to use a refutable pattern with let

If some_option_value were a None value, it would fail to match the pattern Some(x), meaning the pattern is refutable. However, the let statement can only accept an irrefutable pattern because there is nothing valid the code can do with a None value. At compile time, Rust will complain that we've tried to use a refutable pattern where an irrefutable pattern is required:

```
error[E0005]: refutable pattern in local binding: `None` not covered
  -->
   |
3  | let Some(x) = some_option_value;
   |     ^^^^^^^ pattern `None` not covered
```

Because we didn't cover (and couldn't cover!) every valid value with the pattern Some(x), Rust rightfully produces a compiler error.

To fix the problem where we have a refutable pattern when an irrefutable pattern is needed, we can change the code that uses the pattern: instead of using let, we can use if let. Then if the pattern doesn't match, the code will just skip the code in the curly brackets, giving it a way to continue validly. Listing 18-9 shows how to fix the code in Listing 18-8.

```
if let Some(x) = some_option_value {
    println!("{}", x);
}
```

Listing 18-9: Using if let and a block with refutable patterns instead of let

We've given the code an out! This code is perfectly valid, although it means we cannot use an irrefutable pattern without receiving an error. If we give if let a pattern that will always match, such as x, as shown in Listing 18-10, it will not compile.

```
if let x = 5 {
    println!("{}", x);
};
```

Listing 18-10: Attempting to use an irrefutable pattern with if let

Rust complains that it doesn't make sense to use if let with an irrefutable pattern:

```
error[E0162]: irrefutable if-let pattern
 --> <anon>:2:8
  |
2 | if let x = 5 {
  |        ^ irrefutable pattern
```

For this reason, match arms must use refutable patterns, except for the last arm, which should match any remaining values with an irrefutable pattern. Rust allows us to use an irrefutable pattern in a match with only one arm, but this syntax isn't particularly useful and could be replaced with a simpler let statement.

Now that you know where to use patterns and the difference between refutable and irrefutable patterns, let's cover all the syntax we can use to create patterns.

Pattern Syntax

Throughout the book, you've seen examples of many kinds of patterns. In this section, we gather all the syntax valid in patterns and discuss why you might want to use each one.

Matching Literals

As you saw in Chapter 6, you can match patterns against literals directly. The following code gives some examples:

```
let x = 1;

match x {
    1 => println!("one"),
    2 => println!("two"),
```

```
        3 => println!("three"),
        _ => println!("anything"),
}
```

This code prints one because the value in x is 1. This syntax is useful when you want your code to take an action if it gets a particular concrete value.

Matching Named Variables

Named variables are irrefutable patterns that match any value, and we've used them many times in the book. However, there is a complication when you use named variables in match expressions. Because match starts a new scope, variables declared as part of a pattern inside the match expression will shadow those with the same name outside the match construct, as is the case with all variables. In Listing 18-11, we declare a variable named x with the value Some(5) and a variable y with the value 10. We then create a match expression on the value x. Look at the patterns in the match arms and println! at the end and try to figure out what the code will print before running this code or reading further.

src/main.rs

```
fn main() {
❶  let x = Some(5);
❷  let y = 10;

    match x {
❸      Some(50) => println!("Got 50"),
❹      Some(y) => println!("Matched, y = {:?}", y),
❺      _ => println!("Default case, x = {:?}", x),
    }

❻  println!("at the end: x = {:?}, y = {:?}", x, y);
}
```

Listing 18-11: A match expression with an arm that introduces a shadowed variable y

Let's walk through what happens when the match expression runs. The pattern in the first match arm ❸ doesn't match the defined value of x ❶, so the code continues.

The pattern in the second match arm ❹ introduces a new variable named y that will match any value inside a Some value. Because we're in a new scope inside the match expression, this is a new y variable, not the y we declared at the beginning with the value 10 ❷. This new y binding will match any value inside a Some, which is what we have in x. Therefore, this new y binds to the inner value of the Some in x. That value is 5, so the expression for that arm executes and prints Matched, y = 5.

If x had been a None value instead of Some(5), the patterns in the first two arms wouldn't have matched, so the value would have matched to the underscore ❺. We didn't introduce the x variable in the pattern of the underscore arm, so the x in the expression is still the outer x that hasn't been shadowed. In this hypothetical case, the match would print Default case, x = None.

When the match expression is done, its scope ends, and so does the scope of the inner y. The last println! ❻ produces at the end: x = Some(5), y = 10.

To create a match expression that compares the values of the outer x and y, rather than introducing a shadowed variable, we would need to use a match guard conditional instead. We'll talk about match guards later in "Extra Conditionals with Match Guards" on page 408.

Multiple Patterns

In match expressions, you can match multiple patterns using the | syntax, which means *or*. For example, the following code matches the value of x against the match arms, the first of which has an *or* option, meaning if the value of x matches either of the values in that arm, that arm's code will run:

```
let x = 1;

match x {
    1 | 2 => println!("one or two"),
    3 => println!("three"),
    _ => println!("anything"),
}
```

This code prints one or two.

Matching Ranges of Values with the ... Syntax

The ... syntax allows us to match to an inclusive range of values. In the following code, when a pattern matches any of the values within the range, that arm will execute:

```
let x = 5;

match x {
    1 ... 5 => println!("one through five"),
    _ => println!("something else"),
}
```

If x is 1, 2, 3, 4, or 5, the first arm will match. This syntax is more convenient than using the | operator to express the same idea; instead of 1 ... 5, we would have to specify 1 | 2 | 3 | 4 | 5 if we used |. Specifying a range is much shorter, especially if we want to match, say, any number between 1 and 1,000!

Ranges are only allowed with numeric values or char values, because the compiler checks that the range isn't empty at compile time. The only types for which Rust can tell whether a range is empty or not are char and numeric values.

Here is an example using ranges of char values:

```
let x = 'c';

match x {
```

```
        'a' ... 'j' => println!("early ASCII letter"),
        'k' ... 'z' => println!("late ASCII letter"),
        _ => println!("something else"),
    }
}
```

Rust can tell that c is within the first pattern's range and prints early ASCII letter.

Destructuring to Break Apart Values

We can also use patterns to destructure structs, enums, tuples, and references to use different parts of these values. Let's walk through each value.

Destructuring Structs

Listing 18-12 shows a Point struct with two fields, x and y, that we can break apart using a pattern with a let statement.

src/main.rs
```
struct Point {
    x: i32,
    y: i32,
}

fn main() {
    let p = Point { x: 0, y: 7 };

    let Point { x: a, y: b } = p;
    assert_eq!(0, a);
    assert_eq!(7, b);
}
```

Listing 18-12: Destructuring a struct's fields into separate variables

This code creates the variables a and b that match the values of the x and y fields of the p variable. This example shows that the names of the variables in the pattern don't have to match the field names of the struct. But it's common to want the variable names to match the field names to make it easier to remember which variables came from which fields.

Because having variable names match the fields is common and because writing let Point { x: x, y: y } = p; contains a lot of duplication, there is a shorthand for patterns that match struct fields: you only need to list the name of the struct field, and the variables created from the pattern will have the same names. Listing 18-13 shows code that behaves in the same way as the code in Listing 18-12, but the variables created in the let pattern are x and y instead of a and b.

src/main.rs
```
struct Point {
    x: i32,
    y: i32,
}
```

```
fn main() {
    let p = Point { x: 0, y: 7 };

    let Point { x, y } = p;
    assert_eq!(0, x);
    assert_eq!(7, y);
}
```

Listing 18-13: Destructuring struct fields using struct field shorthand

This code creates the variables x and y that match the x and y fields of the p variable. The outcome is that the variables x and y contain the values from the p struct.

We can also destructure with literal values as part of the struct pattern rather than creating variables for all the fields. Doing so allows us to test some of the fields for particular values while creating variables to destructure the other fields.

Listing 18-14 shows a match expression that separates Point values into three cases: points that lie directly on the x axis (which is true when y = 0), on the y axis (x = 0), or neither.

src/main.rs

```
fn main() {
    let p = Point { x: 0, y: 7 };

    match p {
        Point { x, y: 0 } => println!("On the x axis at {}", x),
        Point { x: 0, y } => println!("On the y axis at {}", y),
        Point { x, y } => println!("On neither axis: ({}, {})", x, y),
    }
}
```

Listing 18-14: Destructuring and matching literal values in one pattern

The first arm will match any point that lies on the x axis by specifying that the y field matches if its value matches the literal 0. The pattern still creates an x variable that we can use in the code for this arm.

Similarly, the second arm matches any point on the y axis by specifying that the x field matches if its value is 0 and creates a variable y for the value of the y field. The third arm doesn't specify any literals, so it matches any other Point and creates variables for both the x and y fields.

In this example, the value p matches the second arm by virtue of x containing a 0, so this code will print On the y axis at 7.

Destructuring Enums

We've destructured enums earlier in this book, for example, when we destructured Option<i32> in Listing 6-5 on page 105. One detail we haven't mentioned explicitly is that the pattern to destructure an enum should correspond to the way the data stored within the enum is defined. As an example, in Listing 18-15 we use the Message enum from Listing 6-2 on page 98 and write a match with patterns that will destructure each inner value.

```rust
enum Message {
    Quit,
    Move { x: i32, y: i32 },
    Write(String),
    ChangeColor(i32, i32, i32),
}

fn main() {
❶   let msg = Message::ChangeColor(0, 160, 255);

    match msg {
❷       Message::Quit => {
            println!("The Quit variant has no data to destructure.")
        },
❸       Message::Move { x, y } => {
            println!(
                "Move in the x direction {} and in the y direction {}",
                x,
                y
            );
        }
❹       Message::Write(text) => println!("Text message: {}", text),
❺       Message::ChangeColor(r, g, b) => {
            println!(
                "Change the color to red {}, green {}, and blue {}",
                r,
                g,
                b
            )
        }
    }
}
```

Listing 18-15: Destructuring enum variants that hold different kinds of values

This code will print Change the color to red 0, green 160, and blue 255. Try changing the value of msg ❶ to see the code from the other arms run.

For enum variants without any data, like Message::Quit ❷, we can't destructure the value any further. We can only match on the literal Message::Quit value, and no variables are in that pattern.

For struct-like enum variants, such as Message::Move ❸, we can use a pattern similar to the pattern we specify to match structs. After the variant name, we place curly brackets and then list the fields with variables so we break apart the pieces to use in the code for this arm. Here we use the short-hand form as we did in Listing 18-13.

For tuple-like enum variants, like Message::Write that holds a tuple with one element ❹ and Message::ChangeColor that holds a tuple with three elements ❺, the pattern is similar to the pattern we specify to match tuples. The number of variables in the pattern must match the number of elements in the variant we're matching.

Destructuring References

When the value we're matching to our pattern contains a reference, we need to destructure the reference from the value, which we can do by specifying a & in the pattern. Doing so lets us get a variable holding the value that the reference points to rather than getting a variable that holds the reference. This technique is especially useful in closures where we have iterators that iterate over references, but we want to use the values in the closure rather than the references.

The example in Listing 18-16 iterates over references to Point instances in a vector, destructuring the reference and the struct so we can perform calculations on the x and y values easily.

```
let points = vec![
    Point { x: 0, y: 0 },
    Point { x: 1, y: 5 },
    Point { x: 10, y: -3 },
];

let sum_of_squares: i32 = points
    .iter()
    .map(|&Point { x, y }| x * x + y * y)
    .sum();
```

Listing 18-16: Destructuring a reference to a struct into the struct field values

This code gives us the variable sum_of_squares holding the value 135, which is the result of squaring the x value and the y value, adding those together, and then adding the result for each Point in the points vector to get one number.

If we had not included the & in &Point { x, y }, we'd get a type mismatch error, because iter would then iterate over references to the items in the vector rather than the actual values. The error would look like this:

```
error[E0308]: mismatched types
  -->
   |
14 |         .map(|Point { x, y }| x * x + y * y)
   |               ^^^^^^^^^^^^ expected &Point, found struct `Point`
   |
   = note: expected type `&Point`
              found type `Point`
```

This error indicates that Rust was expecting our closure to match &Point but we tried to match directly to a Point value, not a reference to a Point.

Destructuring Structs and Tuples

We can mix, match, and nest destructuring patterns in even more complex ways. The following example shows a complicated destructure where we nest structs and tuples inside a tuple and destructure all the primitive values out:

```
let ((feet, inches), Point {x, y}) = ((3, 10), Point { x: 3, y: -10 });
```

This code lets us break complex types into their component parts so we can use the values we're interested in separately.

Destructuring with patterns is a convenient way to use pieces of values, such as the value from each field in a struct, separately from each other.

Ignoring Values in a Pattern

You've seen that it's sometimes useful to ignore values in a pattern, such as in the last arm of a match, to get a catchall that doesn't actually do anything but does account for all remaining possible values. There are a few ways to ignore entire values or parts of values in a pattern: using the _ pattern (which you've seen), using the _ pattern within another pattern, using a name that starts with an underscore, or using .. to ignore remaining parts of a value. Let's explore how and why to use each of these patterns.

Ignoring an Entire Value with _

We've used the underscore (_) as a wildcard pattern that will match any value but not bind to the value. Although the _ pattern is especially useful as the last arm in a match expression, we can use it in any pattern, including function parameters, as shown in Listing 18-17.

src/main.rs

```
fn foo(_: i32, y: i32) {
    println!("This code only uses the y parameter: {}", y);
}

fn main() {
    foo(3, 4);
}
```

Listing 18-17: Using _ in a function signature

This code will completely ignore the value passed as the first argument, 3, and will print This code only uses the y parameter: 4.

In most cases when you no longer need a particular function parameter, you would change the signature so it doesn't include the unused parameter. Ignoring a function parameter can be especially useful in some cases, for example, when implementing a trait when you need a certain type signature but the function body in your implementation doesn't need one of the parameters. The compiler will then not warn about unused function parameters, as it would if you used a name instead.

Ignoring Parts of a Value with a Nested _

We can also use _ inside another pattern to ignore just part of a value, for example, when we want to test for only part of a value but have no use for the other parts in the corresponding code we want to run. Listing 18-18 shows code responsible for managing a setting's value. The business requirements are that the user should not be allowed to overwrite an existing customization of a setting but can unset the setting and can give the setting a value if it is currently unset.

```
let mut setting_value = Some(5);
let new_setting_value = Some(10);

match (setting_value, new_setting_value) {
    (Some(_), Some(_)) => {
        println!("Can't overwrite an existing customized value");
    }
    _ => {
        setting_value = new_setting_value;
    }
}

println!("setting is {:?}", setting_value);
```

Listing 18-18: Using an underscore within patterns that match Some variants when we don't need to use the value inside the Some

This code will print Can't overwrite an existing customized value and then setting is Some(5). In the first match arm, we don't need to match on or use the values inside either Some variant, but we do need to test for the case when setting_value and new_setting_value are the Some variant. In that case, we print why we're not changing setting_value, and it doesn't get changed.

In all other cases (if either setting_value or new_setting_value are None) expressed by the _ pattern in the second arm, we want to allow new_setting_value to become setting_value.

We can also use underscores in multiple places within one pattern to ignore particular values. Listing 18-19 shows an example of ignoring the second and fourth values in a tuple of five items.

```
let numbers = (2, 4, 8, 16, 32);

match numbers {
    (first, _, third, _, fifth) => {
        println!("Some numbers: {}, {}, {}", first, third, fifth)
    },
}
```

Listing 18-19: Ignoring multiple parts of a tuple

This code will print Some numbers: 2, 8, 32, and the values 4 and 16 will be ignored.

Ignoring an Unused Variable by Starting Its Name with _

If you create a variable but don't use it anywhere, Rust will usually issue a warning because that could be a bug. But sometimes it's useful to create a variable you won't use yet, such as when you're prototyping or just starting a project. In this situation, you can tell Rust not to warn you about the unused variable by starting the name of the variable with an underscore. In Listing 18-20, we create two unused variables, but when we run this code, we should get a warning about only one of them.

```
fn main() {
    let _x = 5;
    let y = 10;
}
```

Listing 18-20: Starting a variable name with an underscore to avoid getting unused variable warnings

Here we get a warning about not using the variable y, but we don't get a warning about not using the variable preceded by the underscore.

Note that there is a subtle difference between using only _ and using a name that starts with an underscore. The syntax _x still binds the value to the variable, whereas _ doesn't bind at all. To show a case where this distinction matters, Listing 18-21 will provide us with an error.

```
let s = Some(String::from("Hello!"));

if let Some(_s) = s {
    println!("found a string");
}

println!("{:?}", s);
```

Listing 18-21: An unused variable starting with an underscore still binds the value, which might take ownership of the value

We'll receive an error because the s value will still be moved into _s, which prevents us from using s again. However, using the underscore by itself doesn't ever bind to the value. Listing 18-22 will compile without any errors because s doesn't get moved into _.

```
let s = Some(String::from("Hello!"));

if let Some(_) = s {
    println!("found a string");
}

println!("{:?}", s);
```

Listing 18-22: Using an underscore does not bind the value

This code works just fine because we never bind s to anything; it isn't moved.

Ignoring Remaining Parts of a Value with ..

With values that have many parts, we can use the .. syntax to use only a few parts and ignore the rest, avoiding the need to list underscores for each ignored value. The .. pattern ignores any parts of a value that we haven't explicitly matched in the rest of the pattern. In Listing 18-23, we have a Point struct that holds a coordinate in three-dimensional space.

In the match expression, we want to operate only on the x coordinate and ignore the values in the y and z fields.

```
struct Point {
    x: i32,
    y: i32,
    z: i32,
}

let origin = Point { x: 0, y: 0, z: 0 };

match origin {
    Point { x, .. } => println!("x is {}", x),
}
```

Listing 18-23: Ignoring all fields of a Point except for x by using ..

We list the x value and then just include the .. pattern. This is quicker than having to list y: _ and z: _, particularly when we're working with structs that have lots of fields in situations where only one or two fields are relevant.

The syntax .. will expand to as many values as it needs to. Listing 18-24 shows how to use .. with a tuple.

src/main.rs

```
fn main() {
    let numbers = (2, 4, 8, 16, 32);

    match numbers {
        (first, .., last) => {
            println!("Some numbers: {}, {}", first, last);
        },
    }
}
```

Listing 18-24: Matching only the first and last values in a tuple and ignoring all other values

In this code, the first and last value are matched with first and last. The .. will match and ignore everything in the middle.

However, using .. must be unambiguous. If it is unclear which values are intended for matching and which should be ignored, Rust will give us an error. Listing 18-25 shows an example of using .. ambiguously, so it will not compile.

src/main.rs

```
fn main() {
    let numbers = (2, 4, 8, 16, 32);

    match numbers {
        (.., second, ..) => {
            println!("Some numbers: {}", second)
        },
    }
}
```

Listing 18-25: An attempt to use .. in an ambiguous way

When we compile this example, we get this error:

```
error: `..` can only be used once per tuple or tuple struct pattern
 --> src/main.rs:5:22
  |
5 |          (.., second, ..) => {
  |                       ^^
```

It's impossible for Rust to determine how many values in the tuple to ignore before matching a value with second and then how many further values to ignore thereafter. This code could mean that we want to ignore 2, bind second to 4, and then ignore 8, 16, and 32; or that we want to ignore 2 and 4, bind second to 8, and then ignore 16 and 32; and so forth. The variable name second doesn't mean anything special to Rust, so we get a compiler error because using .. in two places like this is ambiguous.

Creating References in Patterns with ref and ref mut

Let's look at using ref to make references so ownership of the values isn't moved to variables in the pattern. Usually, when you match against a pattern, the variables introduced by the pattern are bound to a value. Rust's ownership rules mean the value will be moved into the match or wherever you're using the pattern. Listing 18-26 shows an example of a match that has a pattern with a variable and then usage of the entire value in the println! statement later, after the match. This code will fail to compile because ownership of part of the robot_name value is transferred to the name variable in the pattern of the first match arm.

```
let robot_name = Some(String::from("Bors"));

match robot_name {
    Some(name) => println!("Found a name: {}", name),
    None => (),
}

println!("robot_name is: {:?}", robot_name);
```

Listing 18-26: Creating a variable in a match arm pattern takes ownership of the value

Because ownership of part of robot_name has been moved to name, we can no longer use robot_name in the println! after the match because robot_name no longer has ownership.

To fix this code, we want to make the Some(name) pattern *borrow* that part of robot_name rather than taking ownership. You've already seen that, outside of patterns, the way to borrow a value is to create a reference using &, so you might think the solution is changing Some(name) to Some(&name).

However, as you saw in "Destructuring to Break Apart Values" on page 399, the syntax & in patterns does not *create* a reference but *matches* an existing reference in the value. Because & already has that meaning in patterns, we can't use & to create a reference in a pattern.

Instead, to create a reference in a pattern, we use the ref keyword before the new variable, as shown in Listing 18-27.

```
let robot_name = Some(String::from("Bors"));

match robot_name {
    Some(ref name) => println!("Found a name: {}", name),
    None => (),
}

println!("robot_name is: {:?}", robot_name);
```

Listing 18-27: Creating a reference so a pattern variable does not take ownership of a value

This example will compile because the value in the Some variant in robot_name is not moved into the match; the match only took a reference to the data in robot_name rather than moving it.

To create a mutable reference so we're able to mutate a value matched in a pattern, we use ref mut instead of &mut. The reason is, again, that in patterns, the latter is for matching existing mutable references, not creating new ones. Listing 18-28 shows an example of a pattern creating a mutable reference.

```
let mut robot_name = Some(String::from("Bors"));

match robot_name {
    Some(ref mut name) => *name = String::from("Another name"),
    None => (),
}

println!("robot_name is: {:?}", robot_name);
```

Listing 18-28: Creating a mutable reference to a value as part of a pattern using ref mut

This example will compile and print robot_name is: Some("Another name"). Because name is a mutable reference, we need to dereference within the match arm code using the * operator to mutate the value.

Extra Conditionals with Match Guards

A *match guard* is an additional if condition specified after the pattern in a match arm that must also match, along with the pattern matching, for that arm to be chosen. Match guards are useful for expressing more complex ideas than a pattern alone allows.

The condition can use variables created in the pattern. Listing 18-29 shows a match where the first arm has the pattern Some(x) and also has a match guard of if x < 5.

```
let num = Some(4);

match num {
    Some(x) if x < 5 => println!("less than five: {}", x),
    Some(x) => println!("{}", x),
```

```
        None => (),
    }
```

Listing 18-29: Adding a match guard to a pattern

This example will print less than five: 4. When num is compared to the pattern in the first arm, it matches, because Some(4) matches Some(x). Then the match guard checks whether the value in x is less than 5, and because it is, the first arm is selected.

If num had been Some(10) instead, the match guard in the first arm would have been false because 10 is not less than 5. Rust would then go to the second arm, which would match because the second arm doesn't have a match guard and therefore matches any Some variant.

There is no way to express the if x < 5 condition within a pattern, so the match guard gives us the ability to express this logic.

In the discussion of Listing 18-11, we mentioned that we could use match guards to solve our pattern-shadowing problem. Recall that a new variable was created inside the pattern in the match expression instead of using the variable outside the match. That new variable meant we couldn't test against the value of the outer variable. Listing 18-30 shows how we can use a match guard to fix this problem.

src/main.rs

```
fn main() {
    let x = Some(5);
    let y = 10;

    match x {
        Some(50) => println!("Got 50"),
        Some(n) if n == y => println!("Matched, n = {:?}", n),
        _ => println!("Default case, x = {:?}", x),
    }

    println!("at the end: x = {:?}, y = {:?}", x, y);
}
```

Listing 18-30: Using a match guard to test for equality with an outer variable

This code will now print Default case, x = Some(5). The pattern in the second match arm doesn't introduce a new variable y that would shadow the outer y, meaning we can use the outer y in the match guard. Instead of specifying the pattern as Some(y), which would have shadowed the outer y, we specify Some(n). This creates a new variable n that doesn't shadow anything because there is no n variable outside the match.

The match guard if n == y is not a pattern and therefore doesn't introduce new variables. This y *is* the outer y rather than a new shadowed y, and we can look for a value that has the same value as the outer y by comparing n to y.

You can also use the *or* operator | in a match guard to specify multiple patterns; the match guard condition will apply to all the patterns. Listing 18-31 shows the precedence of combining a match guard with a pattern that uses |. The important part of this example is that the if y match guard applies to 4, 5, *and* 6, even though it might look like if y only applies to 6.

```
let x = 4;
let y = false;

match x {
    4 | 5 | 6 if y => println!("yes"),
    _ => println!("no"),
}
```

Listing 18-31: Combining multiple patterns with a match guard

The match condition states that the arm matches only if the value of x is equal to 4, 5, or 6 *and* if y is true. When this code runs, the pattern of the first arm matches because x is 4, but the match guard if y is false, so the first arm is not chosen. The code moves on to the second arm, which does match, and this program prints no. The reason is that the if condition applies to the whole pattern 4 | 5 | 6, not only to the last value 6. In other words, the precedence of a match guard in relation to a pattern behaves like this:

```
(4 | 5 | 6) if y => ...
```

rather than this:

```
4 | 5 | (6 if y) => ...
```

After running the code, the precedence behavior is evident: if the match guard were applied only to the final value in the list of values specified using the | operator, the arm would have matched and the program would have printed yes.

@ Bindings

The *at* operator (@) lets us create a variable that holds a value at the same time we're testing that value to see whether it matches a pattern. Listing 18-32 shows an example where we want to test whether a Message::Hello id field is within the range 3...7. But we also want to bind the value to the variable id_variable so we can use it in the code associated with the arm. We could name this variable id, the same as the field, but for this example, we'll use a different name.

```
enum Message {
    Hello { id: i32 },
}

let msg = Message::Hello { id: 5 };

match msg {
    Message::Hello { id: id_variable @ 3...7 } => {
```

```
        println!("Found an id in range: {}", id_variable)
    },
    Message::Hello { id: 10...12 } => {
        println!("Found an id in another range")
    },
    Message::Hello { id } => {
        println!("Found some other id: {}", id)
    },
}
```

Listing 18-32: Using @ to bind to a value in a pattern while also testing it

This example will print Found an id in range: 5. By specifying id_variable @ before the range 3...7, we're capturing whatever value matched the range while also testing that the value matched the range pattern.

In the second arm, where we only have a range specified in the pattern, the code associated with the arm doesn't have a variable that contains the actual value of the id field. The id field's value could have been 10, 11, or 12, but the code that goes with that pattern doesn't know which it is. The pattern code isn't able to use the value from the id field, because we haven't saved the id value in a variable.

In the last arm, where we've specified a variable without a range, we do have the value available to use in the arm's code in a variable named id. The reason is that we've used the struct field shorthand syntax. But we haven't applied any test to the value in the id field in this arm, as we did with the first two arms: any value would match this pattern.

Using @ lets us test a value and save it in a variable within one pattern.

Summary

Rust's patterns are very useful in that they help distinguish between different kinds of data. When used in match expressions, Rust ensures your patterns cover every possible value, or your program won't compile. Patterns in let statements and function parameters make those constructs more useful, enabling the destructuring of values into smaller parts at the same time as assigning to variables. We can create simple or complex patterns to suit our needs.

Next, for the penultimate chapter of the book, we'll look at some advanced aspects of a variety of Rust's features.

19

ADVANCED FEATURES

By now, you've learned the most commonly used parts of the Rust programming language. Before we do one more project in Chapter 20, we'll look at a few aspects of the language you might run into every once in a while. You can use this chapter as a reference for when you encounter any unknowns when using Rust. The features you'll learn to use in this chapter are useful in very specific situations. Although you might not reach for them often, we want to make sure you have a grasp of all the features Rust has to offer.

In this chapter, we'll cover:

Unsafe Rust   How to opt out of some of Rust's guarantees and take responsibility for manually upholding those guarantees

Advanced lifetimes   Syntax for complex lifetime situations

Advanced traits   Associated types, default type parameters, fully qualified syntax, supertraits, and the newtype pattern in relation to traits

Advanced types   More about the newtype pattern, type aliases, the never type, and dynamically sized types

Advanced functions and closures   Function pointers and returning closures

It's a panoply of Rust features with something for everyone! Let's dive in!

Unsafe Rust

All the code we've discussed so far has had Rust's memory safety guarantees enforced at compile time. However, Rust has a second language hidden inside it that doesn't enforce these memory safety guarantees: it's called *unsafe Rust* and works just like regular Rust, but gives us extra superpowers.

Unsafe Rust exists because, by nature, static analysis is conservative. When the compiler tries to determine whether or not code upholds the guarantees, it's better for it to reject some valid programs rather than accept some invalid programs. Although the code might be okay, as far as Rust is able to tell, it's not! In these cases, you can use unsafe code to tell the compiler, "Trust me, I know what I'm doing." The downside is that you use it at your own risk: if you use unsafe code incorrectly, problems due to memory unsafety, such as null pointer dereferencing, can occur.

Another reason Rust has an unsafe alter ego is that the underlying computer hardware is inherently unsafe. If Rust didn't let you do unsafe operations, you couldn't do certain tasks. Rust needs to allow you to do low-level systems programming, such as directly interacting with the operating system or even writing your own operating system. Indeed, working with low-level systems programming is one of the goals of the language. Let's explore what we can do with unsafe Rust and how to do it.

Unsafe Superpowers

To switch to unsafe Rust, use the unsafe keyword and then start a new block that holds the unsafe code. You can take four actions in unsafe Rust, called *unsafe superpowers*, that you can't in safe Rust. Those superpowers include the ability to:

- Dereference a raw pointer
- Call an unsafe function or method
- Access or modify a mutable static variable
- Implement an unsafe trait

It's important to understand that unsafe doesn't turn off the borrow checker or disable any other of Rust's safety checks: if you use a reference in unsafe code, it will still be checked. The unsafe keyword only gives you access to these four features that are then not checked by the compiler for memory safety. You'll still get some degree of safety inside of an unsafe block.

In addition, unsafe does not mean the code inside the block is necessarily dangerous or that it will definitely have memory safety problems: the intent is that as the programmer, you'll ensure the code inside an unsafe block will access memory in a valid way.

People are fallible, and mistakes will happen, but by requiring these four unsafe operations to be inside blocks annotated with unsafe you'll know that any errors related to memory safety must be within an unsafe block. Keep unsafe blocks small; you'll be thankful later when you investigate memory bugs.

To isolate unsafe code as much as possible, it's best to enclose unsafe code within a safe abstraction and provide a safe API, which we'll discuss later in the chapter when we examine unsafe functions and methods. Parts of the standard library are implemented as safe abstractions over unsafe code that has been audited. Wrapping unsafe code in a safe abstraction prevents uses of unsafe from leaking out into all the places that you or your users might want to use the functionality implemented with unsafe code, because using a safe abstraction is safe.

Let's look at each of the four unsafe superpowers in turn. We'll also look at some abstractions that provide a safe interface to unsafe code.

Dereferencing a Raw Pointer

In "Dangling References" on page 72, we mentioned that the compiler ensures references are always valid. Unsafe Rust has two new types called *raw pointers* that are similar to references. As with references, raw pointers can be immutable or mutable and are written as *const T and *mut T, respectively. The asterisk isn't the dereference operator; it's part of the type name. In the context of raw pointers, *immutable* means that the pointer can't be directly assigned to after being dereferenced.

Different from references and smart pointers, raw pointers:

- Are allowed to ignore the borrowing rules by having both immutable and mutable pointers or multiple mutable pointers to the same location
- Aren't guaranteed to point to valid memory
- Are allowed to be null
- Don't implement any automatic cleanup

By opting out of having Rust enforce these guarantees, you can give up guaranteed safety in exchange for greater performance or the ability to interface with another language or hardware where Rust's guarantees don't apply.

Listing 19-1 shows how to create an immutable and a mutable raw pointer from references.

```
let mut num = 5;

let r1 = &num as *const i32;
let r2 = &mut num as *mut i32;
```

Listing 19-1: Creating raw pointers from references

Notice that we don't include the unsafe keyword in this code. We can create raw pointers in safe code; we just can't dereference raw pointers outside an unsafe block, as you'll see in a bit.

We've created raw pointers by using as to cast an immutable and a mutable reference into their corresponding raw pointer types. Because we created them directly from references guaranteed to be valid, we know these particular raw pointers are valid, but we can't make that assumption about just any raw pointer.

Next, we'll create a raw pointer whose validity we can't be so certain of. Listing 19-2 shows how to create a raw pointer to an arbitrary location in memory. Trying to use arbitrary memory is undefined: there might be data at that address or there might not, the compiler might optimize the code so there is no memory access, or the program might error with a segmentation fault. Usually, there is no good reason to write code like this, but it is possible.

```
let address = 0x012345usize;
let r = address as *const i32;
```

Listing 19-2: Creating a raw pointer to an arbitrary memory address

Recall that we can create raw pointers in safe code, but we can't *dereference* raw pointers and read the data being pointed to. In Listing 19-3, we use the dereference operator * on a raw pointer that requires an unsafe block.

```
let mut num = 5;

let r1 = &num as *const i32;
let r2 = &mut num as *mut i32;

unsafe {
    println!("r1 is: {}", *r1);
    println!("r2 is: {}", *r2);
}
```

Listing 19-3: Dereferencing raw pointers within an unsafe block

Creating a pointer does no harm; it's only when we try to access the value that it points at that we might end up dealing with an invalid value.

Note also that in Listings 19-1 and 19-3, we created *const i32 and *mut i32 raw pointers that both pointed to the same memory location, where num is stored. If we instead tried to create an immutable and a mutable reference to num, the code would not have compiled because Rust's ownership rules don't allow a mutable reference at the same time as any immutable references. With raw pointers, we can create a mutable pointer and an immutable pointer to the same location and change data through the mutable pointer, potentially creating a data race. Be careful!

With all of these dangers, why would you ever use raw pointers? One major use case is when interfacing with C code, as you'll see in the next section. Another case is when building up safe abstractions that the borrow checker doesn't understand. We'll introduce unsafe functions and then look at an example of a safe abstraction that uses unsafe code.

Calling an Unsafe Function or Method

The second type of operation that requires an unsafe block is calls to unsafe functions. Unsafe functions and methods look exactly like regular functions and methods, but they have an extra unsafe before the rest of the definition. The unsafe keyword in this context indicates the function has requirements we need to uphold when we call this function, because Rust can't guarantee we've met these requirements. By calling an unsafe function within an unsafe block, we're saying that we've read this function's documentation and take responsibility for upholding the function's contracts.

Here is an unsafe function named dangerous that doesn't do anything in its body:

```
unsafe fn dangerous() {}

unsafe {
    dangerous();
}
```

We must call the dangerous function within a separate unsafe block. If we try to call dangerous without the unsafe block, we'll get an error:

```
error[E0133]: call to unsafe function requires unsafe function or block
  -->
   |
4  |     dangerous();
   |     ^^^^^^^^^^^ call to unsafe function
```

By inserting the unsafe block around our call to dangerous, we're asserting to Rust that we've read the function's documentation, we understand how to use it properly, and we've verified that we're fulfilling the contract of the function.

Bodies of unsafe functions are effectively unsafe blocks, so to perform other unsafe operations within an unsafe function, we don't need to add another unsafe block.

Creating a Safe Abstraction over Unsafe Code

Just because a function contains unsafe code doesn't mean we need to mark the entire function as unsafe. In fact, wrapping unsafe code in a safe function is a common abstraction. As an example, let's study a function from the standard library, split_at_mut, that requires some unsafe code and explore how we might implement it. This safe method is defined on mutable slices: it takes one slice and makes it two by splitting the slice at the index given as an argument. Listing 19-4 shows how to use split_at_mut.

```
let mut v = vec![1, 2, 3, 4, 5, 6];

let r = &mut v[..];

let (a, b) = r.split_at_mut(3);

assert_eq!(a, &mut [1, 2, 3]);
assert_eq!(b, &mut [4, 5, 6]);
```

Listing 19-4: Using the safe `split_at_mut` function

We can't implement this function using only safe Rust. An attempt might look something like Listing 19-5, which won't compile. For simplicity, we'll implement split_at_mut as a function rather than a method and only for slices of i32 values rather than for a generic type T.

```
fn split_at_mut(slice: &mut [i32], mid: usize) -> (&mut [i32], &mut [i32]) {
    let len = slice.len();

    assert!(mid <= len);

    (&mut slice[..mid],
     &mut slice[mid..])
}
```

Listing 19-5: An attempted implementation of `split_at_mut` using only safe Rust

This function first gets the total length of the slice. Then it asserts that the index given as a parameter is within the slice by checking whether it's less than or equal to the length. The assertion means that if we pass an index that is greater than the index to split the slice at, the function will panic before it attempts to use that index.

Then we return two mutable slices in a tuple: one from the start of the original slice to the mid index and another from mid to the end of the slice.

When we try to compile the code in Listing 19-5, we'll get an error:

```
error[E0499]: cannot borrow `*slice` as mutable more than once at a time
  -->
   |
6  |      (&mut slice[..mid],
   |            ----- first mutable borrow occurs here
7  |       &mut slice[mid..])
   |            ^^^^^ second mutable borrow occurs here
8  | }
   | - first borrow ends here
```

Rust's borrow checker can't understand that we're borrowing different parts of the slice; it only knows that we're borrowing from the same slice twice. Borrowing different parts of a slice is fundamentally okay because the two slices aren't overlapping, but Rust isn't smart enough to know this. When we know code is okay, but Rust doesn't, it's time to reach for unsafe code.

Listing 19-6 shows how to use an unsafe block, a raw pointer, and some calls to unsafe functions to make the implementation of split_at_mut work.

```
use std::slice;

fn split_at_mut(slice: &mut [i32], mid: usize) -> (&mut [i32], &mut [i32]) {
❶ let len = slice.len();
❷ let ptr = slice.as_mut_ptr();

❸ assert!(mid <= len);

❹ unsafe {
    ❺ (slice::from_raw_parts_mut(ptr, mid),
    ❻ slice::from_raw_parts_mut(ptr.offset(mid as isize), len - mid))
    }
}
```

Listing 19-6: Using unsafe code in the implementation of the split_at_mut function

Recall from "The Slice Type" on page 73 that slices are a pointer to some data and the length of the slice. We use the len method to get the length of a slice ❶ and the as_mut_ptr method to access the raw pointer of a slice ❷. In this case, because we have a mutable slice to i32 values, as_mut_ptr returns a raw pointer with the type *mut i32, which we've stored in the variable ptr.

We keep the assertion that the mid index is within the slice ❸. Then we get to the unsafe code ❹: the slice::from_raw_parts_mut function takes a raw pointer and a length, and it creates a slice. We use this function to create a slice that starts from ptr and is mid items long ❺. Then we call the offset method on ptr with mid as an argument to get a raw pointer that starts at mid, and we create a slice using that pointer and the remaining number of items after mid as the length ❻.

The function slice::from_raw_parts_mut is unsafe because it takes a raw pointer and must trust that this pointer is valid. The offset method on raw pointers is also unsafe, because it must trust that the offset location is also a valid pointer. Therefore, we had to put an unsafe block around our calls to slice::from_raw_parts_mut and offset so we could call them. By looking at the code and by adding the assertion that mid must be less than or equal to len, we can tell that all the raw pointers used within the unsafe block will be valid pointers to data within the slice. This is an acceptable and appropriate use of unsafe.

Note that we don't need to mark the resulting split_at_mut function as unsafe, and we can call this function from safe Rust. We've created a safe abstraction to the unsafe code with an implementation of the function that uses unsafe code in a safe way, because it creates only valid pointers from the data this function has access to.

In contrast, the use of slice::from_raw_parts_mut in Listing 19-7 would likely crash when the slice is used. This code takes an arbitrary memory location and creates a slice 10,000 items long.

```
use std::slice;

let address = 0x012345usize;
let r = address as *mut i32;

let slice = unsafe {
    slice::from_raw_parts_mut(r, 10000)
};
```

Listing 19-7: Creating a slice from an arbitrary memory location

We don't own the memory at this arbitrary location, and there is no guarantee that the slice this code creates contains valid i32 values. Attempting to use slice as though it's a valid slice results in undefined behavior.

Using extern Functions to Call External Code

Sometimes, your Rust code might need to interact with code written in another language. For this, Rust has a keyword, extern, that facilitates the creation and use of a *Foreign Function Interface (FFI)*. An FFI is a way for a programming language to define functions and enable a different (foreign) programming language to call those functions.

Listing 19-8 demonstrates how to set up an integration with the abs function from the C standard library. Functions declared within extern blocks are always unsafe to call from Rust code. The reason is that other languages don't enforce Rust's rules and guarantees, and Rust can't check them, so responsibility falls on the programmer to ensure safety.

src/main.rs

```
extern "C" {
    fn abs(input: i32) -> i32;
}

fn main() {
    unsafe {
        println!("Absolute value of -3 according to C: {}", abs(-3));
    }
}
```

Listing 19-8: Declaring and calling an extern function defined in another language

Within the extern "C" block, we list the names and signatures of external functions from another language we want to call. The "C" part defines which *application binary interface (ABI)* the external function uses: the ABI defines how to call the function at the assembly level. The "C" ABI is the most common and follows the C programming language's ABI.

Accessing or Modifying a Mutable Static Variable

Until now, we've not talked about *global variables*, which Rust does support but can be problematic with Rust's ownership rules. If two threads are accessing the same mutable global variable, a data race can result.

In Rust, global variables are called *static* variables. Listing 19-9 shows an example declaration and use of a static variable with a string slice as a value.

src/main.rs

```
static HELLO_WORLD: &str = "Hello, world!";

fn main() {
    println!("name is: {}", HELLO_WORLD);
}
```

Listing 19-9: Defining and using an immutable static variable

Static variables are similar to constants, which we discussed in "Differences Between Variables and Constants" on page 34. The names of static variables are in SCREAMING_SNAKE_CASE by convention, and we *must* annotate the variable's type, which is &'static str in this example. Static variables can only store references with the 'static lifetime, which means the Rust compiler can figure out the lifetime; we don't need to annotate it explicitly. Accessing an immutable static variable is safe.

Constants and immutable static variables might seem similar, but a subtle difference is that values in a static variable have a fixed address in memory. Using the value will always access the same data. Constants, on the other hand, are allowed to duplicate their data whenever they are used.

Another difference between constants and static variables is that static variables can be mutable. Accessing and modifying mutable static variables is *unsafe*. Listing 19-10 shows how to declare, access, and modify a mutable static variable named COUNTER.

src/main.rs

```
static mut COUNTER: u32 = 0;

fn add_to_count(inc: u32) {
    unsafe {
        COUNTER += inc;
    }
}

fn main() {
    add_to_count(3);

    unsafe {
        println!("COUNTER: {}", COUNTER);
    }
}
```

Listing 19-10: Reading from or writing to a mutable static variable is unsafe.

As with regular variables, we specify mutability using the mut keyword. Any code that reads or writes from COUNTER must be within an unsafe block. This code compiles and prints COUNTER: 3 as we would expect because it's single threaded. Having multiple threads access COUNTER would likely result in data races.

With mutable data that is globally accessible, it's difficult to ensure there are no data races, which is why Rust considers mutable static variables to be unsafe. Where possible, it's preferable to use the concurrency techniques and thread-safe smart pointers we discussed in Chapter 16 so the compiler checks that data accessed from different threads is done safely.

Implementing an Unsafe Trait

The final action that works only with unsafe is implementing an unsafe trait. A trait is unsafe when at least one of its methods has some invariant that the compiler can't verify. We can declare that a trait is unsafe by adding the unsafe keyword before trait and marking the implementation of the trait as unsafe too, as shown in Listing 19-11.

```
unsafe trait Foo {
    // methods go here
}

unsafe impl Foo for i32 {
    // method implementations go here
}
```

Listing 19-11: Defining and implementing an unsafe trait

By using `unsafe impl`, we're promising that we'll uphold the invariants that the compiler can't verify.

As an example, recall the `Sync` and `Send` marker traits we discussed in "Extensible Concurrency with the Sync and Send Traits" on page 362: the compiler implements these traits automatically if our types are composed entirely of `Send` and `Sync` types. If we implement a type that contains a type that is not `Send` or `Sync`, such as raw pointers, and we want to mark that type as `Send` or `Sync`, we must use `unsafe`. Rust can't verify that our type upholds the guarantees that it can be safely sent across threads or accessed from multiple threads; therefore, we need to do those checks manually and indicate as such with `unsafe`.

When to Use Unsafe Code

Using `unsafe` to take one of the four actions (superpowers) just discussed isn't wrong or even frowned upon. But it is trickier to get `unsafe` code correct because the compiler can't help uphold memory safety. When you have a reason to use `unsafe` code, you can do so, and having the explicit `unsafe` annotation makes it easier to track down the source of problems if they occur.

Advanced Lifetimes

In "Validating References with Lifetimes" on page 187, you learned how to annotate references with lifetime parameters to tell Rust how lifetimes of different references relate. You saw how every reference has a lifetime, but most of the time, Rust will let you elide lifetimes. Now we'll look at three advanced features of lifetimes that we haven't covered yet:

Lifetime subtyping Ensures that one lifetime outlives another lifetime

Lifetime bounds Specifies a lifetime for a reference to a generic type

Inference of trait object lifetimes Allows the compiler to infer trait object lifetimes and when they need to be specified

Ensuring One Lifetime Outlives Another with Lifetime Subtyping

Lifetime subtyping specifies that one lifetime should outlive another lifetime. To explore lifetime subtyping, imagine we want to write a parser. We'll use a structure called `Context` that holds a reference to the string we're parsing. We'll write a parser that will parse this string and return success or failure. The parser will need to borrow the `Context` to do the parsing. Listing 19-12 implements this parser code, except the code doesn't have the required lifetime annotations, so it won't compile.

src/lib.rs

```rust
struct Context(&str);

struct Parser {
    context: &Context,
}
```

```
impl Parser {
    fn parse(&self) -> Result<(), &str> {
        Err(&self.context.0[1..])
    }
}
```

Listing 19-12: Defining a parser without lifetime annotations

Compiling the code results in errors because Rust expects lifetime parameters on the string slice in Context and the reference to a Context in Parser.

For simplicity's sake, the parse function returns Result<(), &str>. That is, the function will do nothing on success and, on failure, will return the part of the string slice that didn't parse correctly. A real implementation would provide more error information and would return a structured data type when parsing succeeds. We won't be discussing those details because they aren't relevant to the lifetimes part of this example.

To keep this code simple, we won't write any parsing logic. However, it's very likely that somewhere in the parsing logic we would handle invalid input by returning an error that references the part of the input that is invalid; this reference is what makes the code example interesting in regard to lifetimes. Let's pretend that the logic of our parser is that the input is invalid after the first byte. Note that this code might panic if the first byte is not on a valid character boundary; again, we're simplifying the example to focus on the lifetimes involved.

To get this code to compile, we need to fill in the lifetime parameters for the string slice in Context and the reference to the Context in Parser. The most straightforward way to do this is to use the same lifetime name everywhere, as shown in Listing 19-13. Recall from "Lifetime Annotations in Struct Definitions" on page 194 that each of struct Context<'a>, struct Parser<'a>, and impl<'a> is declaring a new lifetime parameter. While their names happen to all be the same, the three lifetime parameters declared in this example aren't related.

src/lib.rs

```
struct Context<'a>(&'a str);

struct Parser<'a> {
    context: &'a Context<'a>,
}

impl<'a> Parser<'a> {
    fn parse(&self) -> Result<(), &str> {
        Err(&self.context.0[1..])
    }
}
```

Listing 19-13: Annotating all references in Context and Parser with lifetime parameters

This code compiles just fine. It tells Rust that a Parser holds a reference to a Context with lifetime 'a and that Context holds a string slice that also lives as long as the reference to the Context in Parser. Rust's compiler error message stated that lifetime parameters were required for these references, and we've now added lifetime parameters.

Next, in Listing 19-14, we'll add a function that takes an instance of Context, uses a Parser to parse that context, and returns what parse returns. This code doesn't quite work.

src/lib.rs

```
fn parse_context(context: Context) -> Result<(), &str> {
    Parser { context: &context }.parse()
}
```

Listing 19-14: An attempt to add a parse_context function that takes a Context and uses a Parser

We get two verbose errors when we try to compile the code with the addition of the parse_context function:

```
error[E0597]: borrowed value does not live long enough
  --> src/lib.rs:14:5
   |
14 |     Parser { context: &context }.parse()
   |     ^^^^^^^^^^^^^^^^^^^^^^^^^^^^^^ does not live long enough
15 | }
   | - temporary value only lives until here
   |
note: borrowed value must be valid for the anonymous lifetime #1 defined on
the function body at 13:1...
  --> src/lib.rs:13:1
   |
13 | / fn parse_context(context: Context) -> Result<(), &str> {
14 | |     Parser { context: &context }.parse()
15 | | }
   | |_^

error[E0597]: `context` does not live long enough
  --> src/lib.rs:14:24
   |
14 |     Parser { context: &context }.parse()
   |                        ^^^^^^^ does not live long enough
15 | }
   | - borrowed value only lives until here
   |
note: borrowed value must be valid for the anonymous lifetime #1 defined on
the function body at 13:1...
  --> src/lib.rs:13:1
   |
13 | / fn parse_context(context: Context) -> Result<(), &str> {
14 | |     Parser { context: &context }.parse()
15 | | }
   | |_^
```

These errors state that the `Parser` instance that is created and the `context` parameter live only until the end of the `parse_context` function. But they both need to live for the entire lifetime of the function.

In other words, `Parser` and `context` need to *outlive* the entire function and be valid before the function starts as well as after it ends for all the references in this code to always be valid. The `Parser` we're creating and the `context` parameter go out of scope at the end of the function, because `parse_context` takes ownership of `context`.

To figure out why these errors occur, let's look at the definitions in Listing 19-13 again, specifically the references in the signature of the `parse` method:

```
fn parse(&self) -> Result<(), &str> {
```

Remember the elision rules? If we annotate the lifetimes of the references rather than eliding, the signature would be as follows:

```
fn parse<'a>(&'a self) -> Result<(), &'a str> {
```

That is, the error part of the return value of parse has a lifetime that is tied to the lifetime of the `Parser` instance (that of `&self` in the parse method signature). That makes sense: the returned string slice references the string slice in the `Context` instance held by the `Parser`, and the definition of the `Parser` struct specifies that the lifetime of the reference to `Context` and the lifetime of the string slice that `Context` holds should be the same.

The problem is that the `parse_context` function returns the value returned from parse, so the lifetime of the return value of `parse_context` is tied to the lifetime of the `Parser` as well. But the `Parser` instance created in the `parse_context` function won't live past the end of the function (it's temporary), and `context` will go out of scope at the end of the function (`parse_context` takes ownership of it).

Rust thinks we're trying to return a reference to a value that goes out of scope at the end of the function, because we annotated all the lifetimes with the same lifetime parameter. The annotations told Rust the lifetime of the string slice that `Context` holds is the same as that of the lifetime of the reference to `Context` that `Parser` holds.

The `parse_context` function can't see that within the parse function, the string slice returned will outlive `Context` and `Parser` and that the reference `parse_context` returns refers to the string slice, not to `Context` or `Parser`.

By knowing what the implementation of parse does, we know that the only reason the return value of parse is tied to the `Parser` instance is that it's referencing the `Parser` instance's `Context`, which is referencing the string slice. So, it's really the lifetime of the string slice that `parse_context` needs to care about. We need a way to tell Rust that the string slice in `Context` and the reference to the `Context` in `Parser` have different lifetimes and that the return value of `parse_context` is tied to the lifetime of the string slice in `Context`.

First, we'll try giving `Parser` and `Context` different lifetime parameters, as shown in Listing 19-15. We'll use `'s` and `'c` as lifetime parameter names to clarify which lifetime goes with the string slice in Context and which goes with the reference to Context in Parser. Note that this solution won't completely fix the problem, but it's a start. We'll look at why this fix isn't sufficient when we try to compile.

src/lib.rs

```
struct Context<'s>(&'s str);

struct Parser<'c, 's> {
    context: &'c Context<'s>,
}

impl<'c, 's> Parser<'c, 's> {
    fn parse(&self) -> Result<(), &'s str> {
        Err(&self.context.0[1..])
    }
}

fn parse_context(context: Context) -> Result<(), &str> {
    Parser { context: &context }.parse()
}
```

Listing 19-15: Specifying different lifetime parameters for the references to the string slice and to Context

We've annotated the lifetimes of the references in all the same places that we annotated them in Listing 19-13. But this time we used different parameters depending on whether the reference goes with the string slice or with Context. We've also added an annotation to the string slice part of the return value of parse to indicate that it goes with the lifetime of the string slice in Context.

When we try to compile now, we get the following error:

```
error[E0491]: in type `&'c Context<'s>`, reference has a longer lifetime than
the data it references
 --> src/lib.rs:4:5
  |
4 |     context: &'c Context<'s>,
  |     ^^^^^^^^^^^^^^^^^^^^^^^^^
  |
note: the pointer is valid for the lifetime 'c as defined on the struct at 3:1
 --> src/lib.rs:3:1
  |
3 | / struct Parser<'c, 's> {
4 | |     context: &'c Context<'s>,
5 | | }
  | |_^
note: but the referenced data is only valid for the lifetime 's as defined on
the struct at 3:1
 --> src/lib.rs:3:1
  |
3 | / struct Parser<'c, 's> {
4 | |     context: &'c Context<'s>,
5 | | }
  | |_^
```

Rust doesn't know of any relationship between 'c and 's. To be valid, the referenced data in Context with lifetime 's needs to be constrained to guarantee that it lives longer than the reference with lifetime 'c. If 's is not longer than 'c, the reference to Context might not be valid.

Now we get to the point of this section: the Rust feature *lifetime subtyping* specifies that one lifetime parameter lives at least as long as another one. In the angle brackets where we declare lifetime parameters, we can declare a lifetime 'a as usual and declare a lifetime 'b that lives at least as long as 'a by declaring 'b using the syntax 'b: 'a.

In our definition of Parser, to say that 's (the lifetime of the string slice) is guaranteed to live at least as long as 'c (the lifetime of the reference to Context), we change the lifetime declarations to look like this:

src/lib.rs

```
struct Parser<'c, 's: 'c> {
    context: &'c Context<'s>,
}
```

Now the reference to Context in the Parser and the reference to the string slice in the Context have different lifetimes; we've ensured that the lifetime of the string slice is longer than the reference to the Context.

That was a very long-winded example, but as we mentioned at the start of this chapter, Rust's advanced features are very specific. You won't often need the syntax we described in this example, but in such situations, you'll know how to refer to something and give it the necessary lifetime.

Lifetime Bounds on References to Generic Types

In "Trait Bounds" on page 182, we discussed using trait bounds on generic types. We can also add lifetime parameters as constraints on generic types; these are called *lifetime bounds*. Lifetime bounds help Rust verify that references in generic types won't outlive the data they're referencing.

As an example, consider a type that is a wrapper over references. Recall the RefCell<T> type from "RefCell<T> and the Interior Mutability Pattern" on page 323: its borrow and borrow_mut methods return the types Ref and RefMut, respectively. These types are wrappers over references that keep track of the borrowing rules at runtime. The definition of the Ref struct is shown in Listing 19-16, without lifetime bounds for now.

src/lib.rs

```
struct Ref<'a, T>(&'a T);
```

Listing 19-16: Defining a struct to wrap a reference to a generic type, without lifetime bounds

Without explicitly constraining the lifetime 'a in relation to the generic parameter T, Rust will error because it doesn't know how long the generic type T will live:

```
error[E0309]: the parameter type `T` may not live long enough
 --> src/lib.rs:1:19
  |
```

```
1 | struct Ref<'a, T>(&'a T);
  |                    ^^^^^^
  |
  |
  = help: consider adding an explicit lifetime bound `T: 'a`...
note: ...so that the reference type `&'a T` does not outlive the data it
points at
 --> src/lib.rs:1:19
  |
1 | struct Ref<'a, T>(&'a T);
  |                    ^^^^^^
```

Because T can be any type, T could be a reference or a type that holds
one or more references, each of which could have their own lifetimes. Rust
can't be sure T will live as long as 'a.

Fortunately, the error provides helpful advice on how to specify the lifetime bound in this case:

```
consider adding an explicit lifetime bound `T: 'a` so that the reference type
`&'a T` does not outlive the data it points at
```

Listing 19-17 shows how to apply this advice by specifying the lifetime
bound when we declare the generic type T.

```
struct Ref<'a, T: 'a>(&'a T);
```

*Listing 19-17: Adding lifetime bounds on T to specify that any references in T live at least
as long as 'a*

This code now compiles because the T: 'a syntax specifies that T can be
any type, but if it contains any references, the references must live at least as
long as 'a.

We could solve this problem in a different way, as shown in the definition
of a StaticRef struct in Listing 19-18, by adding the 'static lifetime bound on
T. This means if T contains any references, they must have the 'static lifetime.

```
struct StaticRef<T: 'static>(&'static T);
```

*Listing 19-18: Adding a 'static lifetime bound to T to constrain T to types that have only
'static references or no references*

Because 'static means the reference must live as long as the entire program, a type that contains no references meets the criteria of all references
living as long as the entire program (because there are no references). For
the borrow checker concerned about references living long enough, there
is no real distinction between a type that has no references and a type that
has references that live forever: both are the same for determining whether
or not a reference has a shorter lifetime than what it refers to.

Inference of Trait Object Lifetimes

In "Using Trait Objects That Allow for Values of Different Types" on
page 369, we discussed trait objects, consisting of a trait behind a

reference, that allow us to use dynamic dispatch. We haven't yet discussed what happens if the type implementing the trait in the trait object has a lifetime of its own. Consider Listing 19-19 where we have a trait Red and a struct Ball. The Ball struct holds a reference (and thus has a lifetime parameter) and implements trait Red. We want to use an instance of Ball as the trait object Box<Red>.

src/main.rs

```
trait Red { }

struct Ball<'a> {
    diameter: &'a i32,
}

impl<'a> Red for Ball<'a> { }

fn main() {
    let num = 5;

    let obj = Box::new(Ball { diameter: &num }) as Box<Red>;
}
```

Listing 19-19: Using a type that has a lifetime parameter with a trait object

This code compiles without any errors, even though we haven't explicitly annotated the lifetimes involved in obj. This code works because there are rules for working with lifetimes and trait objects:

- The default lifetime of a trait object is 'static.
- With &'a Trait or &'a mut Trait, the default lifetime of the trait object is 'a.
- With a single T: 'a clause, the default lifetime of the trait object is 'a.
- With multiple clauses like T: 'a, there is no default lifetime; we must be explicit.

When we must be explicit, we can add a lifetime bound on a trait object like Box<Red> using the syntax Box<Red + 'static> or Box<Red + 'a>, depending on whether the reference lives for the entire program or not. As with the other bounds, the syntax adding a lifetime bound means that any implementor of the Red trait that has references inside the type must have the same lifetime specified in the trait object bounds as those references.

Next, let's look at some other advanced features that manage traits.

Advanced Traits

We first covered traits in "Traits: Defining Shared Behavior" on page 178, but as with lifetimes, we didn't discuss the more advanced details. Now that you know more about Rust, we can get into the nitty-gritty.

Specifying Placeholder Types in Trait Definitions with Associated Types

Associated types connect a type placeholder with a trait such that the trait method definitions can use these placeholder types in their signatures. The implementor of a trait will specify the concrete type to be used in this type's place for the particular implementation. That way, we can define a trait that uses some types without needing to know exactly what those types are until the trait is implemented.

We've described most of the advanced features in this chapter as being rarely needed. Associated types are somewhere in the middle: they're used more rarely than features explained in the rest of the book but more commonly than many of the other features discussed in this chapter.

One example of a trait with an associated type is the Iterator trait that the standard library provides. The associated type is named Item and stands in for the type of the values the type implementing the Iterator trait is iterating over. In "The Iterator Trait and the next Method" on page 271 , we mentioned that the definition of the Iterator trait is as shown in Listing 19-20.

```
pub trait Iterator {
    type Item;

    fn next(&mut self) -> Option<Self::Item>;
}
```

Listing 19-20: The definition of the Iterator trait that has an associated type Item

The type Item is a placeholder type, and the next method's definition shows that it will return values of type Option<Self::Item>. Implementors of the Iterator trait will specify the concrete type for Item, and the next method will return an Option containing a value of that concrete type.

Associated types might seem similar to generics, in that the latter allow us to define a function without specifying what types it can handle. So why use associated types?

Let's examine the difference between the two concepts with an example from Chapter 13 that implements the Iterator trait on the Counter struct. In Listing 13-21 on page 276, we specified that the Item type was u32:

src/lib.rs
```
impl Iterator for Counter {
    type Item = u32;

    fn next(&mut self) -> Option<Self::Item> {
        // --snip--
```

This syntax seems comparable to that of generics. So why not just define the Iterator trait with generics, as shown in Listing 19-21?

```
pub trait Iterator<T> {
    fn next(&mut self) -> Option<T>;
}
```

Listing 19-21: A hypothetical definition of the Iterator trait using generics

The difference is that when using generics, as in Listing 19-21, we must annotate the types in each implementation; because we can also implement `Iterator<String>` for `Counter` or any other type, we could have multiple implementations of `Iterator` for `Counter`. In other words, when a trait has a generic parameter, it can be implemented for a type multiple times, changing the concrete types of the generic type parameters each time. When we use the `next` method on `Counter`, we would have to provide type annotations to indicate which implementation of `Iterator` we want to use.

With associated types, we don't need to annotate types because we can't implement a trait on a type multiple times. In Listing 19-20 with the definition that uses associated types, we can only choose what the type of `Item` will be once, because there can only be one `impl Iterator for Counter`. We don't have to specify that we want an iterator of `u32` values everywhere that we call `next` on `Counter`.

Default Generic Type Parameters and Operator Overloading

When we use generic type parameters, we can specify a default concrete type for the generic type. This eliminates the need for implementors of the trait to specify a concrete type if the default type works. The syntax for specifying a default type for a generic type is `<PlaceholderType=ConcreteType>` when declaring the generic type.

A great example of a situation where this technique is useful is with operator overloading. *Operator overloading* is customizing the behavior of an operator (such as +) in particular situations.

Rust doesn't allow you to create your own operators or overload arbitrary operators. But you can overload the operations and corresponding traits listed in `std::ops` by implementing the traits associated with the operator. For example, in Listing 19-22 we overload the + operator to add two `Point` instances together. We do this by implementing the `Add` trait on a `Point` struct.

src/main.rs

```
use std::ops::Add;

#[derive(Debug, PartialEq)]
struct Point {
    x: i32,
    y: i32,
}

impl Add for Point {
    type Output = Point;

    fn add(self, other: Point) -> Point {
        Point {
            x: self.x + other.x,
            y: self.y + other.y,
        }
    }
}
```

```
fn main() {
    assert_eq!(Point { x: 1, y: 0 } + Point { x: 2, y: 3 },
            Point { x: 3, y: 3 });
}
```

Listing 19-22: Implementing the Add trait to overload the + operator for Point instances

The add method adds the x values of two Point instances and the y values of two Point instances to create a new Point. The Add trait has an associated type named Output that determines the type returned from the add method.

The default generic type in this code is within the Add trait. Here is its definition:

```
trait Add<RHS=Self> {
    type Output;

    fn add(self, rhs: RHS) -> Self::Output;
}
```

This code should look generally familiar: a trait with one method and an associated type. The new part is RHS=Self: this syntax is called *default type parameters*. The RHS generic type parameter (short for "right-hand side") defines the type of the rhs parameter in the add method. If we don't specify a concrete type for RHS when we implement the Add trait, the type of RHS will default to Self, which will be the type we're implementing Add on.

When we implemented Add for Point, we used the default for RHS because we wanted to add two Point instances. Let's look at an example of implementing the Add trait where we want to customize the RHS type rather than using the default.

We have two structs, Millimeters and Meters, holding values in different units. We want to add values in millimeters to values in meters and have the implementation of Add do the conversion correctly. We can implement Add for Millimeters with Meters as the RHS, as shown in Listing 19-23.

src/lib.rs

```
use std::ops::Add;

struct Millimeters(u32);
struct Meters(u32);

impl Add<Meters> for Millimeters {
    type Output = Millimeters;

    fn add(self, other: Meters) -> Millimeters {
        Millimeters(self.0 + (other.0 * 1000))
    }
}
```

Listing 19-23: Implementing the Add trait on Millimeters to add Millimeters to Meters

To add Millimeters and Meters, we specify impl Add<Meters> to set the value of the RHS type parameter instead of using the default of Self.

You'll use default type parameters in two main ways:

- To extend a type without breaking existing code
- To allow customization in specific cases most users won't need

The standard library's Add trait is an example of the second purpose: usually, you'll add two like types, but the Add trait provides the ability to customize beyond that. Using a default type parameter in the Add trait definition means you don't have to specify the extra parameter most of the time. In other words, a bit of implementation boilerplate isn't needed, making it easier to use the trait.

The first purpose is similar to the second but in reverse: if you want to add a type parameter to an existing trait, you can give it a default to allow extension of the functionality of the trait without breaking the existing implementation code.

Fully Qualified Syntax for Disambiguation: Calling Methods with the Same Name

Nothing in Rust prevents a trait from having a method with the same name as another trait's method, nor does Rust prevent you from implementing both traits on one type. It's also possible to implement a method directly on the type with the same name as a method from a trait.

When calling methods with the same name, you'll need to tell Rust which one you want to use. Consider the code in Listing 19-24 where we've defined two traits, Pilot and Wizard, that both have a method called fly. We then implement both traits on a type Human that already has a method named fly implemented on it. Each fly method does something different.

src/main.rs

```rust
trait Pilot {
    fn fly(&self);
}

trait Wizard {
    fn fly(&self);
}

struct Human;

impl Pilot for Human {
    fn fly(&self) {
        println!("This is your captain speaking.");
    }
}

impl Wizard for Human {
    fn fly(&self) {
        println!("Up!");
    }
}
```

```
impl Human {
    fn fly(&self) {
        println!("*waving arms furiously*");
    }
}
```

Listing 19-24: Two traits are defined to have a fly method and are implemented on the Human type, and a fly method is implemented on Human directly.

When we call fly on an instance of Human, the compiler defaults to calling the method that is directly implemented on the type, as shown in Listing 19-25.

src/main.rs

```
fn main() {
    let person = Human;
    person.fly();
}
```

Listing 19-25: Calling fly on an instance of Human

Running this code will print *waving arms furiously*, showing that Rust called the fly method implemented on Human directly.

To call the fly methods from either the Pilot trait or the Wizard trait, we need to use more explicit syntax to specify which fly method we mean. Listing 19-26 demonstrates this syntax.

src/main.rs

```
fn main() {
    let person = Human;
    Pilot::fly(&person);
    Wizard::fly(&person);
    person.fly();
}
```

Listing 19-26: Specifying which trait's fly method we want to call

Specifying the trait name before the method name clarifies to Rust which implementation of fly we want to call. We could also write Human::fly(&person), which is equivalent to the person.fly() that we used in Listing 19-26, but this is a bit longer to write if we don't need to disambiguate.

Running this code prints the following:

```
This is your captain speaking.
Up!
*waving arms furiously*
```

Because the fly method takes a self parameter, if we had two *types* that both implemented one *trait*, Rust could figure out which implementation of a trait to use based on the type of self.

However, associated functions that are part of traits don't have a self parameter. When two types in the same scope implement that trait, Rust can't figure out which type you mean unless you use *fully qualified syntax*, which is the most specific we can be when calling a function. For example, the Animal trait in Listing 19-27 has the associated function baby_name, the implementation of Animal for the struct Dog, and the associated function baby_name defined on Dog directly.

```rust
trait Animal {
    fn baby_name() -> String;
}

struct Dog;

impl Dog {
    fn baby_name() -> String {
        String::from("Spot")
    }
}

impl Animal for Dog {
    fn baby_name() -> String {
        String::from("puppy")
    }
}

fn main() {
    println!("A baby dog is called a {}", Dog::baby_name());
}
```

Listing 19-27: A trait with an associated function and a type with an associated function of the same name that also implements the trait

This code is for an animal shelter that wants to name all puppies Spot, which is implemented in the baby_name associated function that is defined on Dog. The Dog type also implements the trait Animal, which describes characteristics that all animals have. Baby dogs are called puppies, and that is expressed in the implementation of the Animal trait on Dog in the baby_name function associated with the Animal trait.

In main, we call the Dog::baby_name function, which calls the associated function defined on Dog directly. This code prints the following:

```
A baby dog is called a Spot
```

This output isn't what we wanted. We want to call the baby_name function that is part of the Animal trait that we implemented on Dog so the code prints A baby dog is called a puppy. The technique of specifying the trait name that we used in Listing 19-26 doesn't help here; if we change main to the code in Listing 19-28, we'll get a compilation error.

```rust
fn main() {
    println!("A baby dog is called a {}", Animal::baby_name());
}
```

Listing 19-28: Attempting to call the baby_name function from the Animal trait, but Rust doesn't know which implementation to use

Because `Animal::baby_name` is an associated function rather than a method, and thus doesn't have a `self` parameter, Rust can't figure out which implementation of `Animal::baby_name` we want. We'll get this compiler error:

```
error[E0283]: type annotations required: cannot resolve `_: Animal`
  --> src/main.rs:20:43
   |
20 |     println!("A baby dog is called a {}", Animal::baby_name());
   |                                           ^^^^^^^^^^^^^^^^^^
   |
   = note: required by `Animal::baby_name`
```

To disambiguate and tell Rust that we want to use the implementation of `Animal` for `Dog`, we need to use fully qualified syntax. Listing 19-29 demonstrates how to use fully qualified syntax.

src/main.rs

```rust
fn main() {
    println!("A baby dog is called a {}", <Dog as Animal>::baby_name());
}
```

Listing 19-29: Using fully qualified syntax to specify that we want to call the baby_name function from the `Animal` trait as implemented on `Dog`

We're providing Rust with a type annotation within the angle brackets, which indicates we want to call the `baby_name` method from the `Animal` trait as implemented on `Dog` by saying that we want to treat the `Dog` type as an `Animal` for this function call. This code will now print what we want:

```
A baby dog is called a puppy
```

In general, fully qualified syntax is defined as follows:

```
<Type as Trait>::function(receiver_if_method, next_arg, ...);
```

For associated functions, there would not be a receiver: there would only be the list of other arguments. You could use fully qualified syntax everywhere that you call functions or methods. However, you're allowed to omit any part of this syntax that Rust can figure out from other information in the program. You need to use this more verbose syntax only when there are multiple implementations that use the same name and Rust needs help to identify which implementation you want to call.

Using Supertraits to Require One Trait's Functionality Within Another Trait

Sometimes, you might need one trait to use another trait's functionality. In this case, you need to rely on the dependent trait's also being implemented. The trait you rely on is a *supertrait* of the trait you're implementing.

For example, let's say we want to make an `OutlinePrint` trait with an `outline_print` method that will print a value framed in asterisks. That is, given a `Point` struct that implements `Display` to result in `(x, y)`, when we call `outline_print` on a `Point` instance that has 1 for x and 3 for y, it should print the following:

```
**********
*        *
* (1, 3) *
*        *
**********
```

In the implementation of `outline_print`, we want to use the `Display` trait's functionality. Therefore, we need to specify that the `OutlinePrint` trait will work only for types that also implement `Display` and provide the functionality that `OutlinePrint` needs. We can do that in the trait definition by specifying `OutlinePrint: Display`. This technique is similar to adding a trait bound to the trait. Listing 19-30 shows an implementation of the `OutlinePrint` trait.

src/main.rs

```rust
use std::fmt;

trait OutlinePrint: fmt::Display {
    fn outline_print(&self) {
        let output = self.to_string();
        let len = output.len();
        println!("{}", "*".repeat(len + 4));
        println!("*{}*", " ".repeat(len + 2));
        println!("* {} *", output);
        println!("*{}*", " ".repeat(len + 2));
        println!("{}", "*".repeat(len + 4));
    }
}
```

Listing 19-30: Implementing the `OutlinePrint` trait that requires the functionality from `Display`

Because we've specified that `OutlinePrint` requires the `Display` trait, we can use the `to_string` function that is automatically implemented for any type that implements `Display`. If we tried to use `to_string` without adding a colon and specifying the `Display` trait after the trait name, we'd get an error saying that no method named `to_string` was found for the type `&Self` in the current scope.

Let's see what happens when we try to implement `OutlinePrint` on a type that doesn't implement `Display`, such as the `Point` struct:

src/main.rs

```rust
struct Point {
    x: i32,
    y: i32,
}

impl OutlinePrint for Point {}
```

We get an error saying that `Display` is required but not implemented:

```
error[E0277]: the trait bound `Point: std::fmt::Display` is not satisfied
  --> src/main.rs:20:6
   |
20 | impl OutlinePrint for Point {}
   |      ^^^^^^^^^^^^ `Point` cannot be formatted with the default formatter;
try using `:?` instead if you are using a format string
   |
   = help: the trait `std::fmt::Display` is not implemented for `Point`
```

To fix this, we implement `Display` on `Point` and satisfy the constraint that `OutlinePrint` requires, like so:

src/main.rs

```
use std::fmt;

impl fmt::Display for Point {
    fn fmt(&self, f: &mut fmt::Formatter) -> fmt::Result {
        write!(f, "({}, {})", self.x, self.y)
    }
}
```

Then implementing the `OutlinePrint` trait on `Point` will compile successfully, and we can call `outline_print` on a `Point` instance to display it within an outline of asterisks.

Using the Newtype Pattern to Implement External Traits on External Types

In "Implementing a Trait on a Type" on page 179, we mentioned the orphan rule that states we're allowed to implement a trait on a type as long as either the trait or the type are local to our crate. It's possible to get around this restriction using the *newtype pattern*, which involves creating a new type in a tuple struct. (We covered tuple structs in "Using Tuple Structs Without Named Fields to Create Different Types" on page 84.) The tuple struct will have one field and be a thin wrapper around the type we want to implement a trait for. Then the wrapper type is local to our crate, and we can implement the trait on the wrapper. *Newtype* is a term that originates from the Haskell programming language. There is no runtime performance penalty for using this pattern, and the wrapper type is elided at compile time.

As an example, let's say we want to implement `Display` on `Vec<T>`, which the orphan rule prevents us from doing directly because the `Display` trait and the `Vec<T>` type are defined outside our crate. We can make a `Wrapper` struct that holds an instance of `Vec<T>`; then we can implement `Display` on `Wrapper` and use the `Vec<T>` value, as shown in Listing 19-31.

src/main.rs

```
use std::fmt;

struct Wrapper(Vec<String>);
```

```
impl fmt::Display for Wrapper {
    fn fmt(&self, f: &mut fmt::Formatter) -> fmt::Result {
        write!(f, "[{}]", self.0.join(", "))
    }
}

fn main() {
    let w = Wrapper(vec![String::from("hello"), String::from("world")]);
    println!("w = {}", w);
}
```

Listing 19-31: Creating a Wrapper *type around* Vec<String> *to implement* Display

The implementation of Display uses self.0 to access the inner Vec<T>, because Wrapper is a tuple struct and Vec<T> is the item at index 0 in the tuple. Then we can use the functionality of the Display type on Wrapper.

The downside of using this technique is that Wrapper is a new type, so it doesn't have the methods of the value it's holding. We would have to implement all the methods of Vec<T> directly on Wrapper such that the methods delegate to self.0, which would allow us to treat Wrapper exactly like a Vec<T>. If we wanted the new type to have every method the inner type has, implementing the Deref trait (discussed in "Treating Smart Pointers Like Regular References with the Deref Trait" on page 311) on the Wrapper to return the inner type would be a solution. If we don't want the Wrapper type to have all the methods of the inner type—for example, to restrict the Wrapper type's behavior—we would have to implement just the methods we do want manually.

Now you know how the newtype pattern is used in relation to traits; it's also a useful pattern even when traits are not involved. Let's switch focus and look at some advanced ways to interact with Rust's type system.

Advanced Types

The Rust type system has some features that we've mentioned in this book but haven't yet discussed. We'll start by discussing newtypes in general as we examine why newtypes are useful as types. Then we'll move on to type aliases, a feature similar to newtypes but with slightly different semantics. We'll also discuss the ! type and dynamically sized types.

 The next section assumes you've read "Using the Newtype Pattern to Implement External Traits on External Types" on page 439.

Using the Newtype Pattern for Type Safety and Abstraction

The newtype pattern is useful for tasks beyond those we've discussed so far, including statically enforcing that values are never confused and indicating the units of a value. You saw an example of using newtypes to indicate units in Listing 19-23: recall that the Millimeters and Meters structs wrapped u32 values in a newtype. If we wrote a function with a parameter of type Millimeters, we couldn't compile a program that accidentally tried to call that function with a value of type Meters or a plain u32.

Another use of the newtype pattern is in abstracting away some implementation details of a type: the new type can expose a public API that is different from the API of the private inner type if we used the new type directly to restrict the available functionality, for example.

Newtypes can also hide internal implementation. For example, we could provide a People type to wrap a HashMap<i32, String> that stores a person's ID associated with their name. Code using People would only interact with the public API we provide, such as a method to add a name string to the People collection; that code wouldn't need to know that we assign an i32 ID to names internally. The newtype pattern is a lightweight way to achieve encapsulation to hide implementation details, which we discussed in "Encapsulation That Hides Implementation Details" on page 366.

Creating Type Synonyms with Type Aliases

Along with the newtype pattern, Rust provides the ability to declare a *type alias* to give an existing type another name. For this we use the type keyword. For example, we can create the alias Kilometers to i32 like so:

```
type Kilometers = i32;
```

Now, the alias Kilometers is a *synonym* for i32; unlike the Millimeters and Meters types we created in Listing 19-23, Kilometers is not a separate, new type. Values that have the type Kilometers will be treated the same as values of type i32:

```
type Kilometers = i32;

let x: i32 = 5;
let y: Kilometers = 5;

println!("x + y = {}", x + y);
```

Because Kilometers and i32 are the same type, we can add values of both types and we can pass Kilometers values to functions that take i32 parameters. However, using this method, we don't get the type-checking benefits that we get from the newtype pattern discussed earlier.

The main use case for type synonyms is to reduce repetition. For example, we might have a lengthy type like this:

```
Box<Fn() + Send + 'static>
```

Writing this lengthy type in function signatures and as type annotations all over the code can be tiresome and error prone. Imagine having a project full of code like that in Listing 19-32.

```
let f: Box<Fn() + Send + 'static> = Box::new(|| println!("hi"));

fn takes_long_type(f: Box<Fn() + Send + 'static>) {
    // --snip--
}

fn returns_long_type() -> Box<Fn() + Send + 'static> {
    // --snip--
}
```

Listing 19-32: Using a long type in many places

A type alias makes this code more manageable by reducing the repetition. In Listing 19-33, we've introduced an alias named Thunk for the verbose type and can replace all uses of the type with the shorter alias Thunk.

```
type Thunk = Box<Fn() + Send + 'static>;

let f: Thunk = Box::new(|| println!("hi"));

fn takes_long_type(f: Thunk) {
    // --snip--
}

fn returns_long_type() -> Thunk {
    // --snip--
}
```

Listing 19-33: Introducing a type alias Thunk to reduce repetition

This code is much easier to read and write! Choosing a meaningful name for a type alias can help communicate your intent as well (*thunk* is a word for code to be evaluated at a later time, so it's an appropriate name for a closure that gets stored).

Type aliases are also commonly used with the Result<T, E> type for reducing repetition. Consider the std::io module in the standard library. I/O operations often return a Result<T, E> to handle situations when operations fail to work. This library has a std::io::Error struct that represents all possible I/O errors. Many of the functions in std::io will be returning Result<T, E> where the E is std::io::Error, such as these functions in the Write trait:

```
use std::io::Error;
use std::fmt;

pub trait Write {
    fn write(&mut self, buf: &[u8]) -> Result<usize, Error>;
    fn flush(&mut self) -> Result<(), Error>;

    fn write_all(&mut self, buf: &[u8]) -> Result<(), Error>;
    fn write_fmt(&mut self, fmt: fmt::Arguments) -> Result<(), Error>;
}
```

The Result<..., Error> is repeated a lot. As such, std::io has this type of alias declaration:

```
type Result<T> = Result<T, std::io::Error>;
```

Because this declaration is in the std::io module, we can use the fully qualified alias std::io::Result<T>—that is, a Result<T, E> with the E filled in as std::io::Error. The Write trait function signatures end up looking like this:

```
pub trait Write {
    fn write(&mut self, buf: &[u8]) -> Result<usize>;
    fn flush(&mut self) -> Result<()>;

    fn write_all(&mut self, buf: &[u8]) -> Result<()>;
    fn write_fmt(&mut self, fmt: Arguments) -> Result<()>;
}
```

The type alias helps in two ways: it makes code easier to write *and* it gives us a consistent interface across all of std::io. Because it's an alias, it's just another Result<T, E>, which means we can use any methods that work on Result<T, E> with it, as well as special syntax like the ? operator.

The Never Type That Never Returns

Rust has a special type named ! that's known in type theory lingo as the *empty type* because it has no values. We prefer to call it the *never type* because it stands in the place of the return type when a function will never return. Here is an example:

```
fn bar() -> ! {
    // --snip--
}
```

This code is read as "the function bar returns never." Functions that return never are called *diverging functions*. We can't create values of the type ! so bar can never possibly return.

But what use is a type you can never create values for? Recall the code from Listing 2-5 on page 28; we've reproduced part of it here in Listing 19-34.

```
let guess: u32 = match guess.trim().parse() {
    Ok(num) => num,
    Err(_) => continue,
};
```

Listing 19-34: A match with an arm that ends in continue

At the time, we skipped over some details in this code. In "The match Control Flow Operator" on page 102, we discussed that match arms must all return the same type. So, for example, the following code doesn't work:

```
let guess = match guess.trim().parse() {
    Ok(_) => 5,
    Err(_) => "hello",
}
```

The type of guess in this code would have to be an integer *and* a string, and Rust requires that guess have only one type. So what does continue return? How were we allowed to return a u32 from one arm and have another arm that ends with continue in Listing 19-34?

As you might have guessed, continue has a ! value. That is, when Rust computes the type of guess, it looks at both match arms, the former with a value of u32 and the latter with a ! value. Because ! can never have a value, Rust decides that the type of guess is u32.

The formal way of describing this behavior is that expressions of type ! can be coerced into any other type. We're allowed to end this match arm with continue because continue doesn't return a value; instead, it moves control back to the top of the loop, so in the Err case, we never assign a value to guess.

The never type is useful with the panic! macro as well. Remember the unwrap function that we call on Option<T> values to produce a value or panic? Here is its definition:

```
impl<T> Option<T> {
    pub fn unwrap(self) -> T {
        match self {
            Some(val) => val,
            None => panic!("called `Option::unwrap()` on a `None` value"),
        }
    }
}
```

In this code, the same thing happens as in the match in Listing 19-34: Rust sees that val has the type T and panic! has the type !, so the result of the overall match expression is T. This code works because panic! doesn't produce a value; it ends the program. In the None case, we won't be returning a value from unwrap, so this code is valid.

One final expression that has the type ! is a loop:

```
print!("forever ");

loop {
    print!("and ever ");
}
```

Here, the loop never ends, so ! is the value of the expression. However, this wouldn't be true if we included a break, because the loop would terminate when it got to the break.

Dynamically Sized Types and the Sized Trait

Due to Rust's need to know certain details, such as how much space to allocate for a value of a particular type, there is a corner of its type system that
can be confusing: the concept of *dynamically sized types*. Sometimes referred
to as *DSTs* or *unsized types*, these types let us write code using values whose
size we can know only at runtime.

Let's dig into the details of a dynamically sized type called str, which
we've been using throughout the book. That's right, not &str, but str on its
own is a DST. We can't know how long the string is until runtime, meaning
we can't create a variable of type str, nor can we take an argument of type
str. Consider the following code, which does not work:

```
let s1: str = "Hello there!";
let s2: str = "How's it going?";
```

Rust needs to know how much memory to allocate for any value of a particular type, and all values of a type must use the same amount of memory. If
Rust allowed us to write this code, these two str values would need to take up
the same amount of space. But they have different lengths: s1 needs 12 bytes
of storage and s2 needs 15. This is why it's not possible to create a variable
holding a dynamically sized type.

So what do we do? In this case, you already know the answer: we make
the types of s1 and s2 a &str rather than a str. Recall that in "String Slices"
on page 75, we said the slice data structure stores the starting position
and the length of the slice.

So although a &T is a single value that stores the memory address of
where the T is located, a &str is *two* values: the address of the str and its
length. As such, we can know the size of a &str value at compile time: it's
twice the length of a usize. That is, we always know the size of a &str, no
matter how long the string it refers to is. In general, this is the way in which
dynamically sized types are used in Rust: they have an extra bit of metadata
that stores the size of the dynamic information. The golden rule of dynamically sized types is that we must always put values of dynamically sized types
behind a pointer of some kind.

We can combine str with all kinds of pointers: for example, Box<str>
or Rc<str>. In fact, you've seen this before but with a different dynamically
sized type: traits. Every trait is a dynamically sized type we can refer to by
using the name of the trait. In "Using Trait Objects That Allow for Values
of Different Types" on page 369, we mentioned that to use traits as trait
objects, we must put them behind a pointer, such as &Trait or Box<Trait>
(Rc<Trait> would work too).

To work with DSTs, Rust has a particular trait called the Sized trait to
determine whether or not a type's size is known at compile time. This trait
is automatically implemented for everything whose size is known at compile
time. In addition, Rust implicitly adds a bound on Sized to every generic
function. That is, a generic function definition like this:

```
fn generic<T>(t: T) {
    // --snip--
}
```

is actually treated as though we had written this:

```
fn generic<T: Sized>(t: T) {
    // --snip--
}
```

By default, generic functions will work only on types that have a known size at compile time. However, you can use the following special syntax to relax this restriction:

```
fn generic<T: ?Sized>(t: &T) {
    // --snip--
}
```

A trait bound on ?Sized is the opposite of a trait bound on Sized: we would read this as "T may or may not be Sized." This syntax is only available for Sized, not any other traits.

Also note that we switched the type of the t parameter from T to &T. Because the type might not be Sized, we need to use it behind some kind of pointer. In this case, we've chosen a reference.

Next, we'll talk about functions and closures!

Advanced Functions and Closures

Finally, we'll explore some advanced features related to functions and closures, which include function pointers and returning closures.

Function Pointers

We've talked about how to pass closures to functions; you can also pass regular functions to functions! This technique is useful when you want to pass a function you've already defined rather than defining a new closure. Doing this with function pointers will allow you to use functions as arguments to other functions. Functions coerce to the type fn (with a lowercase *f*), not to be confused with the Fn closure trait. The fn type is called a *function pointer*. The syntax for specifying that a parameter is a function pointer is similar to that of closures, as shown in Listing 19-35.

src/main.rs

```
fn add_one(x: i32) -> i32 {
    x + 1
}

fn do_twice(f: fn(i32) -> i32, arg: i32) -> i32 {
    f(arg) + f(arg)
}
```

```
fn main() {
    let answer = do_twice(add_one, 5);

    println!("The answer is: {}", answer);
}
```

Listing 19-35: Using the fn type to accept a function pointer as an argument

This code prints The answer is: 12. We specify that the parameter f in do_twice is an fn that takes one parameter of type i32 and returns an i32. We can then call f in the body of do_twice. In main, we can pass the function name add_one as the first argument to do_twice.

Unlike closures, fn is a type rather than a trait, so we specify fn as the parameter type directly rather than declaring a generic type parameter with one of the Fn traits as a trait bound.

Function pointers implement all three of the closure traits (Fn, FnMut, and FnOnce), so you can always pass a function pointer as an argument for a function that expects a closure. It's best to write functions using a generic type and one of the closure traits so your functions can accept either functions or closures.

An example of where you would want to only accept fn and not closures is when interfacing with external code that doesn't have closures: C functions can accept functions as arguments, but C doesn't have closures.

As an example of where you could use either a closure defined inline or a named function, let's look at a use of map. To use the map function to turn a vector of numbers into a vector of strings, we could use a closure, like this:

```
let list_of_numbers = vec![1, 2, 3];
let list_of_strings: Vec<String> = list_of_numbers
    .iter()
    .map(|i| i.to_string())
    .collect();
```

Or we could name a function as the argument to map instead of the closure, like this:

```
let list_of_numbers = vec![1, 2, 3];
let list_of_strings: Vec<String> = list_of_numbers
    .iter()
    .map(ToString::to_string)
    .collect();
```

Note that we must use the fully qualified syntax that we talked about in "Advanced Traits" on page 430 because there are multiple functions available named to_string. Here, we're using the to_string function defined in the ToString trait, which the standard library has implemented for any type that implements Display.

Some people prefer this style, and some people prefer to use closures. They end up compiling to the same code, so use whichever style is clearer to you.

Returning Closures

Closures are represented by traits, which means you can't return closures directly. In most cases where you might want to return a trait, you can instead use the concrete type that implements the trait as the return value of the function. But you can't do that with closures because they don't have a concrete type that is returnable; you're not allowed to use the function pointer fn as a return type, for example.

The following code tries to return a closure directly, but it won't compile:

```
fn returns_closure() -> Fn(i32) -> i32 {
    |x| x + 1
}
```

The compiler error is as follows:

```
error[E0277]: the trait bound `std::ops::Fn(i32) -> i32 + 'static:
std::marker::Sized` is not satisfied
  -->
   |
1 | fn returns_closure() -> Fn(i32) -> i32 {
   |                         ^^^^^^^^^^^^^^ `std::ops::Fn(i32) -> i32 +
'static` does not have a constant size known at compile-time
   |
   = help: the trait `std::marker::Sized` is not implemented for
`std::ops::Fn(i32) -> i32 + 'static`
   = note: the return type of a function must have a statically known size
```

The error references the Sized trait again! Rust doesn't know how much space it will need to store the closure. We saw a solution to this problem earlier. We can use a trait object:

```
fn returns_closure() -> Box<Fn(i32) -> i32> {
    Box::new(|x| x + 1)
}
```

This code will compile just fine. For more about trait objects, refer to "Using Trait Objects That Allow for Values of Different Types" on page 369.

Summary

Whew! Now you have some features of Rust in your toolbox that you won't use often, but you'll know they're available in very particular circumstances. We've introduced several complex topics so that when you encounter them in error message suggestions or in other peoples' code, you'll be able to recognize these concepts and syntax. Use this chapter as a reference to guide you to solutions.

Next, we'll put everything we've discussed throughout the book into practice and do one more project!

20

FINAL PROJECT: BUILDING A MULTITHREADED WEB SERVER

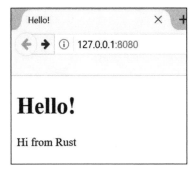

It's been a long journey, but we've reached the end of the book. In this chapter, we'll build one more project together to demonstrate some of the concepts we covered in the final chapters, as well as recap some earlier lessons.

For our final project, we'll make a web server that says "Hello!" and looks like Figure 20-1 in a web browser.

Figure 20-1: Our final shared project

Here is the plan to build the web server:

1. Learn a bit about TCP and HTTP.
2. Listen for TCP connections on a socket.
3. Parse a small number of HTTP requests.
4. Create a proper HTTP response.
5. Improve the throughput of our server with a thread pool.

But before we get started, we should mention one detail: the method we'll use won't be the best way to build a web server with Rust. A number of production-ready crates are available on *https://crates.io/* that provide more complete web server and thread pool implementations than we'll build.

However, our intention in this chapter is to help you learn, not to take the easy route. Because Rust is a systems programming language, we can choose the level of abstraction we want to work with and can go to a lower level than is possible or practical in other languages. We'll write the basic HTTP server and thread pool manually so you can learn the general ideas and techniques behind the crates you might use in the future.

Building a Single-Threaded Web Server

We'll start by getting a single-threaded web server working. Before we begin, let's look at a quick overview of the protocols involved in building web servers. The details of these protocols are beyond the scope of this book, but a brief overview will give you the information you need.

The two main protocols involved in web servers are the *Hypertext Transfer Protocol (HTTP)* and the *Transmission Control Protocol (TCP)*. Both protocols are *request-response* protocols, meaning that a *client* initiates requests and a *server* listens to the requests and provides a response to the client. The contents of those requests and responses are defined by the protocols.

TCP is the lower-level protocol that describes the details of how information gets from one server to another but doesn't specify what that information is. HTTP builds on top of TCP by defining the contents of the requests and responses. It's technically possible to use HTTP with other protocols, but in the vast majority of cases, HTTP sends its data over TCP. We'll work with the raw bytes of TCP and HTTP requests and responses.

Listening to the TCP Connection

Our web server needs to listen to a TCP connection, so that's the first part we'll work on. The standard library offers a std::net module that lets us do this. Let's make a new project in the usual fashion:

```
$ cargo new hello --bin
    Created binary (application) `hello` project
$ cd hello
```

Now enter the code in Listing 20-1 in *src/main.rs* to start. This code will listen at the address 127.0.0.1:7878 for incoming TCP streams. When it gets an incoming stream, it will print Connection established!.

src/main.rs

```
use std::net::TcpListener;

fn main() {
❶ let listener = TcpListener::bind("127.0.0.1:7878").unwrap();

❷ for stream in listener.incoming() {
❸     let stream = stream.unwrap();

❹     println!("Connection established!");
    }
}
```

Listing 20-1: Listening for incoming streams and printing a message when we receive a stream

Using TcpListener, we can listen for TCP connections at the address 127.0.0.1:7878 ❶. In the address, the section before the colon is an IP address representing your computer (this is the same on every computer and doesn't represent the authors' computer specifically), and 7878 is the port. We've chosen this port for two reasons: HTTP is normally accepted on this port, and 7878 is *rust* typed on a telephone.

The bind function in this scenario works like the new function in that it will return a new TcpListener instance. The reason the function is called bind is that in networking, connecting to a port to listen to is known as "binding to a port."

The bind function returns a Result<T, E>, which indicates that binding might fail. For example, connecting to port 80 requires administrator privileges (nonadministrators can listen only on ports higher than 1024), so if we tried to connect to port 80 without being an administrator, binding wouldn't work. As another example, binding wouldn't work if we ran two instances of our program and so had two programs listening to the same port. Because we're writing a basic server just for learning purposes, we won't worry about handling these kinds of errors; instead, we use unwrap to stop the program if errors happen.

The incoming method on TcpListener returns an iterator that gives us a sequence of streams ❷ (more specifically, streams of type TcpStream). A single *stream* represents an open connection between the client and the server. A *connection* is the name for the full request and response process in which a client connects to the server, the server generates a response, and the server closes the connection. As such, TcpStream will read from itself to see what the client sent and then allow us to write our response to the stream. Overall, this for loop will process each connection in turn and produce a series of streams for us to handle.

For now, our handling of the stream consists of calling unwrap to terminate our program if the stream has any errors ❸; if there aren't any errors, the program prints a message ❹. We'll add more functionality for the success case in the next listing. The reason we might receive errors from the `incoming` method when a client connects to the server is that we're not actually iterating over connections. Instead, we're iterating over *connection attempts*. The connection might not be successful for a number of reasons, many of them operating system specific. For example, many operating systems have a limit to the number of simultaneous open connections they can support; new connection attempts beyond that number will produce an error until some of the open connections are closed.

Let's try running this code! Invoke `cargo run` in the terminal and then load *127.0.0.1:7878* in a web browser. The browser should show an error message like "Connection reset," because the server isn't currently sending back any data. But when you look at your terminal, you should see several messages that were printed when the browser connected to the server!

```
    Running `target/debug/hello`
Connection established!
Connection established!
Connection established!
```

Sometimes, you'll see multiple messages printed for one browser request; the reason might be that the browser is making a request for the page as well as a request for other resources, like the *favicon.ico* icon that appears in the browser tab.

It could also be that the browser is trying to connect to the server multiple times because the server isn't responding with any data. When `stream` goes out of scope and is dropped at the end of the loop, the connection is closed as part of the `drop` implementation. Browsers sometimes deal with closed connections by retrying, because the problem might be temporary. The important factor is that we've successfully gotten a handle to a TCP connection!

Remember to stop the program by pressing CTRL-C when you're done running a particular version of the code. Then restart `cargo run` after you've made each set of code changes to make sure you're running the newest code.

Reading the Request

Let's implement the functionality to read the request from the browser! To separate the concerns of first getting a connection and then taking some action with the connection, we'll start a new function for processing connections. In this new `handle_connection` function, we'll read data from the TCP stream and print it so we can see the data being sent from the browser. Change the code to look like Listing 20-2.

src/main.rs

❶ `use std::io::prelude::*;`
`use std::net::TcpStream;`
`use std::net::TcpListener;`

```
fn main() {
    let listener = TcpListener::bind("127.0.0.1:7878").unwrap();
```

```
        for stream in listener.incoming() {
            let stream = stream.unwrap();

      ❷ handle_connection(stream);
        }
}

fn handle_connection(❸mut stream: TcpStream) {
  ❹ let mut buffer = [0; 512];

  ❺ stream.read(&mut buffer).unwrap();

  ❻ println!("Request: {}", String::from_utf8_lossy(&buffer[..]));
}
```

Listing 20-2: Reading from the TcpStream and printing the data

We bring std::io::prelude into scope to get access to certain traits that let us read from and write to the stream ❶. In the for loop in the main function, instead of printing a message that says we made a connection, we now call the new handle_connection function and pass the stream to it ❷.

In the handle_connection function, we've made the stream parameter mutable ❸. The reason is that the TcpStream instance keeps track of what data it returns to us internally. It might read more data than we asked for and save that data for the next time we ask for data. It therefore needs to be mut because its internal state might change; usually, we think of "reading" as not needing mutation, but in this case we need the mut keyword.

Next, we need to actually read from the stream. We do this in two steps: First, we declare a buffer on the stack to hold the data that is read in ❹. We've made the buffer 512 bytes, which is big enough to hold the data of a basic request and sufficient for our purposes in this chapter. If we wanted to handle requests of an arbitrary size, buffer management would need to be more complicated; we'll keep it simple for now. We pass the buffer to stream .read, which will read bytes from the TcpStream and put them in the buffer ❺.

Second, we convert the bytes in the buffer to a string and print that string ❻. The String::from_utf8_lossy function takes a &[u8] and produces a String from it. The "lossy" part of the name indicates the behavior of this function when it sees an invalid UTF-8 sequence: it will replace the invalid sequence with ◆, the U+FFFD REPLACEMENT CHARACTER. You might see replacement characters for characters in the buffer that aren't filled by request data.

Let's try this code! Start the program and make a request in a web browser again. Note that we'll still get an error page in the browser, but our program's output in the terminal will now look similar to this:

```
$ cargo run
   Compiling hello v0.1.0 (file:///projects/hello)
    Finished dev [unoptimized + debuginfo] target(s) in 0.42 secs
     Running `target/debug/hello`
Request: GET / HTTP/1.1
Host: 127.0.0.1:7878
User-Agent: Mozilla/5.0 (Windows NT 10.0; WOW64; rv:52.0) Gecko/20100101
```

```
Firefox/52.0
Accept: text/html,application/xhtml+xml,application/xml;q=0.9,*/*;q=0.8
Accept-Language: en-US,en;q=0.5
Accept-Encoding: gzip, deflate
Connection: keep-alive
Upgrade-Insecure-Requests: 1
```

Depending on your browser, you might get slightly different output. Now that we're printing the request data, we can see why we get multiple connections from one browser request by looking at the path after `Request: GET`. If the repeated connections are all requesting /, we know the browser is trying to fetch / repeatedly because it's not getting a response from our program.

Let's break down this request data to understand what the browser is asking of our program.

A Closer Look at an HTTP Request

HTTP is a text-based protocol, and a request takes this format:

```
Method Request-URI HTTP-Version CRLF
headers CRLF
message-body
```

The first line is the *request line* that holds information about what the client is requesting. The first part of the request line indicates the *method* being used, such as `GET` or `POST`, which describes how the client is making this request. Our client used a `GET` request.

The next part of the request line is /, which indicates the *Uniform Resource Identifier (URI)* the client is requesting: a URI is almost, but not quite, the same as a *Uniform Resource Locator (URL)*. The difference between URIs and URLs isn't important for our purposes in this chapter, but the HTTP spec uses the term URI, so we can just mentally substitute URL for URI here.

The last part is the HTTP version the client uses, and then the request line ends in a *CRLF sequence*. (CRLF stands for *carriage return* and *line feed*, which are terms from the days of typewriters!) The CRLF sequence can also be written as \r\n, where \r is a carriage return and \n is a line feed. The CRLF sequence separates the request line from the rest of the request data. Note that when the CRLF is printed, we see a new line start rather than \r\n.

Looking at the request line data we received from running our program so far, we see that `GET` is the method, / is the request URI, and `HTTP/1.1` is the version.

After the request line, the remaining lines starting from `Host:` onward are headers. `GET` requests have no body.

Try making a request from a different browser or asking for a different address, such as *127.0.0.1:7878/test*, to see how the request data changes.

Now that we know what the browser is asking for, let's send back some data!

Writing a Response

Now we'll implement sending data in response to a client request. Responses have the following format:

```
HTTP-Version Status-Code Reason-Phrase CRLF
headers CRLF
message-body
```

The first line is a *status line* that contains the HTTP version used in the response, a numeric status code that summarizes the result of the request, and a reason phrase that provides a text description of the status code. After the CRLF sequence are any headers, another CRLF sequence, and the body of the response.

Here is an example response that uses HTTP version 1.1, has a status code of 200, an OK reason phrase, no headers, and no body:

```
HTTP/1.1 200 OK\r\n\r\n
```

The status code 200 is the standard success response. The text is a tiny successful HTTP response. Let's write this to the stream as our response to a successful request! From the handle_connection function, remove the println! that was printing the request data and replace it with the code in Listing 20-3.

src/main.rs

```
fn handle_connection(mut stream: TcpStream) {
    let mut buffer = [0; 512];

    stream.read(&mut buffer).unwrap();

❶   let response = "HTTP/1.1 200 OK\r\n\r\n";

❷   stream.write(response.as_bytes()❸).unwrap();
❹   stream.flush().unwrap();
}
```

Listing 20-3: Writing a tiny successful HTTP response to the stream

The first new line defines the response variable that holds the success message's data ❶. Then we call as_bytes on our response to convert the string data to bytes ❸. The write method on stream takes a &[u8] and sends those bytes directly down the connection ❷.

Because the write operation could fail, we use unwrap on any error result as before. Again, in a real application you would add error handling here. Finally, flush will wait and prevent the program from continuing until all the bytes are written to the connection ❹; TcpStream contains an internal buffer to minimize calls to the underlying operating system.

With these changes, let's run our code and make a request. We're no longer printing any data to the terminal, so we won't see any output other than the output from Cargo. When you load *127.0.0.1:7878* in a web browser, you should get a blank page instead of an error. You've just hand-coded an HTTP request and response!

Returning Real HTML

Let's implement the functionality for returning more than a blank page. Create a new file, *hello.html*, in the root of your project directory, not in the *src* directory. You can input any HTML you want; Listing 20-4 shows one possibility.

hello.html

```html
<!DOCTYPE html>
<html lang="en">
  <head>
    <meta charset="utf-8">
    <title>Hello!</title>
  </head>
  <body>
    <h1>Hello!</h1>
    <p>Hi from Rust</p>
  </body>
</html>
```

Listing 20-4: A sample HTML file to return in a response

This is a minimal HTML5 document with a heading and some text. To return this from the server when a request is received, we'll modify handle _connection as shown in Listing 20-5 to read the HTML file, add it to the response as a body, and send it.

src/main.rs

```rust
❶ use std::fs::File;
// --snip--

fn handle_connection(mut stream: TcpStream) {
    let mut buffer = [0; 512];
    stream.read(&mut buffer).unwrap();

    let mut file = File::open("hello.html").unwrap();

    let mut contents = String::new();
    file.read_to_string(&mut contents).unwrap();

❷ let response = format!("HTTP/1.1 200 OK\r\n\r\n{}", contents);

    stream.write(response.as_bytes()).unwrap();
    stream.flush().unwrap();
}
```

Listing 20-5: Sending the contents of hello.html as the body of the response

We've added a line at the top to bring the standard library's File into scope ❶. The code for opening a file and reading the contents should look familiar; we used it in Chapter 12 when we read the contents of a file for our I/O project in Listing 12-4 on page 231.

Next, we use format! to add the file's contents as the body of the success response ❷.

Run this code with cargo run and load *127.0.0.1:7878* in your browser; you should see your HTML rendered!

Currently, we're ignoring the request data in buffer and just sending back the contents of the HTML file unconditionally. That means if you try requesting *127.0.0.1:7878/something-else* in your browser, you'll still get back this same HTML response. Our server is very limited and is not what most web servers do. We want to customize our responses depending on the request and only send back the HTML file for a well-formed request to /.

Validating the Request and Selectively Responding

Right now, our web server will return the HTML in the file no matter what the client requested. Let's add functionality to check that the browser is requesting / before returning the HTML file and return an error if the browser requests anything else. For this we need to modify handle_connection, as shown in Listing 20-6. This new code checks the content of the request received against what we know a request for / looks like and adds if and else blocks to treat requests differently.

src/main.rs

```
// --snip--

fn handle_connection(mut stream: TcpStream) {
    let mut buffer = [0; 512];
    stream.read(&mut buffer).unwrap();

❶  let get = b"GET / HTTP/1.1\r\n";

❷  if buffer.starts_with(get) {
        let mut file = File::open("hello.html").unwrap();

        let mut contents = String::new();
        file.read_to_string(&mut contents).unwrap();

        let response = format!("HTTP/1.1 200 OK\r\n\r\n{}", contents);

        stream.write(response.as_bytes()).unwrap();
        stream.flush().unwrap();
❸  } else {
        // some other request
    }
}
```

Listing 20-6: Matching the request and handling requests to / differently than other requests

First, we hardcode the data corresponding to the / request into the get variable ❶. Because we're reading raw bytes into the buffer, we transform get into a byte string by adding the b"" byte string syntax at the start of the content data. Then we check whether `buffer` starts with the bytes in `get` ❷. If it does, it means we've received a well-formed request to `/`, which is the success case we'll handle in the `if` block that returns the contents of our HTML file.

If `buffer` does *not* start with the bytes in `get`, it means we've received some other request. We'll add code to the `else` block ❸ in a moment to respond to all other requests.

Run this code now and request *127.0.0.1:7878*; you should get the HTML in *hello.html*. If you make any other request, such as *127.0.0.1:7878/something-else*, you'll get a connection error like those you saw when running the code in Listings 20-1 and 20-2.

Now let's add the code in Listing 20-7 to the `else` block to return a response with the status code 404, which signals that the content for the request was not found. We'll also return some HTML for a page to render in the browser indicating the response to the end user.

src/main.rs

```
// --snip--

} else {
❶  let status_line = "HTTP/1.1 404 NOT FOUND\r\n\r\n";
❷  let mut file = File::open("404.html").unwrap();
    let mut contents = String::new();

    file.read_to_string(&mut contents).unwrap();

    let response = format!("{}{}", status_line, contents);

    stream.write(response.as_bytes()).unwrap();
    stream.flush().unwrap();
}
```

Listing 20-7: Responding with status code 404 and an error page if anything other than / was requested

Here, our response has a status line with status code 404 and the reason phrase `NOT FOUND` ❶. We're still not returning headers, and the body of the response will be the HTML in the file *404.html* ❷. You'll need to create a *404.html* file next to *hello.html* for the error page; again feel free to use any HTML you want or use the example HTML in Listing 20-8.

404.html

```
<!DOCTYPE html>
<html lang="en">
  <head>
    <meta charset="utf-8">
    <title>Hello!</title>
  </head>
  <body>
    <h1>Oops!</h1>
    <p>Sorry, I don't know what you're asking for.</p>
  </body>
</html>
```

Listing 20-8: Sample content for the page to send back with any 404 response

With these changes, run your server again. Requesting *127.0.0.1:7878* should return the contents of *hello.html*, and any other request, like *127.0.0.1:7878/foo*, should return the error HTML from *404.html*.

A Touch of Refactoring

At the moment, the `if` and `else` blocks have a lot of repetition: they're both reading files and writing the contents of the files to the stream. The only differences are the status line and the filename. Let's make the code more concise by pulling out those differences into separate `if` and `else` lines that will assign the values of the status line and the filename to variables; we can then use those variables unconditionally in the code to read the file and write the response. Listing 20-9 shows the resulting code after replacing the large `if` and `else` blocks.

src/main.rs

```
// --snip--

fn handle_connection(mut stream: TcpStream) {
    // --snip--

    let (status_line, filename) = if buffer.starts_with(get) {
        ("HTTP/1.1 200 OK\r\n\r\n", "hello.html")
    } else {
        ("HTTP/1.1 404 NOT FOUND\r\n\r\n", "404.html")
    };

    let mut file = File::open(filename).unwrap();
    let mut contents = String::new();

    file.read_to_string(&mut contents).unwrap();

    let response = format!("{}{}", status_line, contents);

    stream.write(response.as_bytes()).unwrap();
    stream.flush().unwrap();
}
```

Listing 20-9: Refactoring the `if` and `else` blocks to contain only the code that differs between the two cases

Now the `if` and `else` blocks only return the appropriate values for the status line and filename in a tuple; we then use destructuring to assign these two values to `status_line` and `filename` using a pattern in the `let` statement, as discussed in Chapter 18.

The previously duplicated code is now outside the `if` and `else` blocks and uses the `status_line` and `filename` variables. This makes it easier to see the difference between the two cases, and it means we have only one place to update the code if we want to change how the file reading and response writing work. The behavior of the code in Listing 20-9 will be the same as that in Listing 20-8.

Awesome! We now have a simple web server in approximately 40 lines of Rust code that responds to one request with a page of content and responds to all other requests with a 404 response.

Currently, our server runs in a single thread, meaning it can only serve one request at a time. Let's examine how that can be a problem by simulating some slow requests. Then we'll fix it so our server can handle multiple requests at once.

Turning Our Single-Threaded Server into a Multithreaded Server

Right now, the server will process each request in turn, meaning it won't process a second connection until the first is finished processing. If the server received more and more requests, this serial execution would be less and less optimal. If the server receives a request that takes a long time to process, subsequent requests will have to wait until the long request is finished, even if the new requests can be processed quickly. We'll need to fix this, but first, we'll look at the problem in action.

Simulating a Slow Request in the Current Server Implementation

We'll look at how a slow-processing request can affect other requests made to our current server implementation. Listing 20-10 implements handling a request to */sleep* with a simulated slow response that will cause the server to sleep for 5 seconds before responding.

src/main.rs

```
use std::thread;
use std::time::Duration;
// --snip--

fn handle_connection(mut stream: TcpStream) {
    // --snip--

    let get = b"GET / HTTP/1.1\r\n";
 ❶ let sleep = b"GET /sleep HTTP/1.1\r\n";

    let (status_line, filename) = if buffer.starts_with(get) {
        ("HTTP/1.1 200 OK\r\n\r\n", "hello.html")
 ❷ } else if buffer.starts_with(sleep) {
     ❸ thread::sleep(Duration::from_secs(5));
     ❹ ("HTTP/1.1 200 OK\r\n\r\n", "hello.html")
    } else {
        ("HTTP/1.1 404 NOT FOUND\r\n\r\n", "404.html")
    };

    // --snip--
}
```

Listing 20-10: Simulating a slow request by recognizing /sleep and sleeping for 5 seconds

This code is a bit messy, but it's good enough for simulation purposes. We created a second request sleep ❶, whose data our server recognizes. We added an else if after the if block to check for the request to /*sleep* ❷. When that request is received, the server will sleep for 5 seconds ❸ before rendering the successful HTML page ❹.

You can see how primitive our server is: real libraries would handle the recognition of multiple requests in a much less verbose way!

Start the server using cargo run. Then open two browser windows: one for *http://127.0.0.1:7878* and the other for *http://127.0.0.1:7878/sleep*. If you enter the / URI a few times, as before, you'll see it respond quickly. But if you enter /*sleep* and then load /, you'll see that / waits until sleep has slept for its full 5 seconds before loading.

There are multiple ways we could change how our web server works to avoid having more requests back up behind a slow request; the one we'll implement is a thread pool.

Improving Throughput with a Thread Pool

A *thread pool* is a group of spawned threads that are waiting and ready to handle a task. When the program receives a new task, it assigns one of the threads in the pool to the task, and that thread will process the task. The remaining threads in the pool are available to handle any other tasks that come in while the first thread is processing. When the first thread is done processing its task, it's returned to the pool of idle threads, ready to handle a new task. A thread pool allows you to process connections concurrently, increasing the throughput of your server.

We'll limit the number of threads in the pool to a small number to protect us from Denial of Service (DoS) attacks; if we had our program create a new thread for each request as it came in, someone making 10 million requests to our server could create havoc by using up all our server's resources and grinding the processing of requests to a halt.

Rather than spawning unlimited threads, we'll have a fixed number of threads waiting in the pool. As requests come in, they'll be sent to the pool for processing. The pool will maintain a queue of incoming requests. Each of the threads in the pool will pop off a request from this queue, handle the request, and then ask the queue for another request. With this design, we can process *N* requests concurrently, where *N* is the number of threads. If each thread is responding to a long-running request, subsequent requests can still back up in the queue, but we've increased the number of long-running requests we can handle before reaching that point.

This technique is just one of many ways to improve the throughput of a web server. Other options you might explore are the fork/join model and the single-threaded async I/O model. If you're interested in this topic, you can read more about other solutions and try to implement them in Rust; with a low-level language like Rust, all of these options are possible.

Before we begin implementing a thread pool, let's talk about what using the pool should look like. When you're trying to design code, writing the client interface first can help guide your design. Write the API of the code so it's structured in the way you want to call it; then implement the functionality within that structure rather than implementing the functionality and then designing the public API.

Similar to how we used test-driven development in the project in Chapter 12, we'll use compiler-driven development here. We'll write the code that calls the functions we want, and then we'll look at errors from the compiler to determine what we should change next to get the code to work.

Code Structure If We Could Spawn a Thread for Each Request

First, let's explore how our code might look if it did create a new thread for every connection. As mentioned earlier, this isn't our final plan due to the problems with potentially spawning an unlimited number of threads, but it is a starting point. Listing 20-11 shows the changes to make to main to spawn a new thread to handle each stream within the for loop.

src/main.rs

```
fn main() {
    let listener = TcpListener::bind("127.0.0.1:7878").unwrap();

    for stream in listener.incoming() {
        let stream = stream.unwrap();

        thread::spawn(|| {
            handle_connection(stream);
        });
    }
}
```

Listing 20-11: Spawning a new thread for each stream

As you learned in Chapter 16, thread::spawn will create a new thread and then run the code in the closure in the new thread. If you run this code and load */sleep* in your browser, then */* in two more browser tabs, you'll indeed see that the requests to */* don't have to wait for */sleep* to finish. But as we mentioned, this will eventually overwhelm the system because you'd be making new threads without any limit.

Creating a Similar Interface for a Finite Number of Threads

We want our thread pool to work in a similar, familiar way so that switching from threads to a thread pool doesn't require large changes to the code that uses our API. Listing 20-12 shows the hypothetical interface for a ThreadPool struct we want to use instead of thread::spawn.

src/main.rs

```
fn main() {
    let listener = TcpListener::bind("127.0.0.1:7878").unwrap();
 ❶  let pool = ThreadPool::new(4);

    for stream in listener.incoming() {
        let stream = stream.unwrap();
```

```
❷ pool.execute(|| {
      handle_connection(stream);
  });
}
}
```

Listing 20-12: Our ideal `ThreadPool` *interface*

We use `ThreadPool::new` to create a new thread pool with a configurable number of threads, in this case four ❶. Then, in the `for` loop, `pool.execute` has a similar interface as `thread::spawn` in that it takes a closure the pool should run for each stream ❷. We need to implement `pool.execute` so it takes the closure and gives it to a thread in the pool to run. This code won't yet compile, but we'll try so the compiler can guide us in how to fix it.

Building the ThreadPool Struct Using Compiler-Driven Development

Make the changes in Listing 20-12 to *src/main.rs*, and then let's use the compiler errors from cargo check to drive our development. Here is the first error we get:

```
$ cargo check
    Compiling hello v0.1.0 (file:///projects/hello)
error[E0433]: failed to resolve. Use of undeclared type or module `ThreadPool`
  --> src\main.rs:10:16
   |
10 |     let pool = ThreadPool::new(4);
   |                ^^^^^^^^^^^^^^^^ Use of undeclared type or module
`ThreadPool`

error: aborting due to previous error
```

Great! This error tells us we need a `ThreadPool` type or module, so we'll build one now. Our `ThreadPool` implementation will be independent of the kind of work our web server is doing. So, let's switch the `hello` crate from a binary crate to a library crate to hold our `ThreadPool` implementation. After we change to a library crate, we could also use the separate thread pool library for any work we want to do using a thread pool, not just for serving web requests.

Create a *src/lib.rs* that contains the following, which is the simplest definition of a `ThreadPool` struct that we can have for now:

src/lib.rs
```
pub struct ThreadPool;
```

Then create a new directory, *src/bin*, and move the binary crate rooted in *src/main.rs* into *src/bin/main.rs*. Doing so will make the library crate the primary crate in the *hello* directory; we can still run the binary in *src/bin/main.rs* using cargo run. After moving the *main.rs* file, edit it to bring the library crate in and bring `ThreadPool` into scope by adding the following code to the top of *src/bin/main.rs*:

```
extern crate hello;
use hello::ThreadPool;
```

This code still won't work, but let's check it again to get the next error that we need to address:

```
$ cargo check
   Compiling hello v0.1.0 (file:///projects/hello)
error[E0599]: no function or associated item named `new` found for type
`hello::ThreadPool` in the current scope
  --> src/bin/main.rs:13:16
   |
13 |     let pool = ThreadPool::new(4);
   |                ^^^^^^^^^^^^^^^^ function or associated item not found in
`hello::ThreadPool`
```

This error indicates that next we need to create an associated function named `new` for `ThreadPool`. We also know that `new` needs to have one parameter that can accept 4 as an argument and should return a `ThreadPool` instance. Let's implement the simplest `new` function that will have those characteristics:

```
pub struct ThreadPool;

impl ThreadPool {
    pub fn new(size: usize) -> ThreadPool {
        ThreadPool
    }
}
```

We chose usize as the type of the size parameter, because we know that a negative number of threads doesn't make any sense. We also know we'll use this 4 as the number of elements in a collection of threads, which is what the usize type is for, as discussed in "Integer Types" on page 36.

Let's check the code again:

```
$ cargo check
   Compiling hello v0.1.0 (file:///projects/hello)
warning: unused variable: `size`
  --> src/lib.rs:4:16
   |
4  |     pub fn new(size: usize) -> ThreadPool {
   |                ^^^^
   |
   = note: #[warn(unused_variables)] on by default
   = note: to avoid this warning, consider using `_size` instead

error[E0599]: no method named `execute` found for type `hello::ThreadPool` in
the current scope
  --> src/bin/main.rs:18:14
```

```
18 |          pool.execute(|| {
   |                       ^^^^^^^
```

Now we get a warning and an error. Ignoring the warning for a moment, the error occurs because we don't have an execute method on ThreadPool. Recall from "Creating a Similar Interface for a Finite Number of Threads" on page 462 that we decided our thread pool should have an interface similar to thread::spawn. In addition, we'll implement the execute function so it takes the closure it's given and gives it to an idle thread in the pool to run.

We'll define the execute method on ThreadPool to take a closure as a parameter. Recall from "Storing Closures Using Generic Parameters and the Fn Traits" on page 264 that we can take closures as parameters with three different traits: Fn, FnMut, and FnOnce. We need to decide which kind of closure to use here. We know we'll end up doing something similar to the standard library thread::spawn implementation, so we can look at what bounds the signature of thread::spawn has on its parameter. The documentation shows us the following:

```
pub fn spawn<F, T>(f: F) -> JoinHandle<T>
    where
        F: FnOnce() -> T + Send + 'static,
        T: Send + 'static
```

The F type parameter is the one we're concerned with here; the T type parameter is related to the return value, and we're not concerned with that. We can see that spawn uses FnOnce as the trait bound on F. This is probably what we want as well, because we'll eventually pass the argument we get in execute to spawn. We can be further confident that FnOnce is the trait we want to use because the thread for running a request will only execute that request's closure one time, which matches the Once in FnOnce.

The F type parameter also has the trait bound Send and the lifetime bound 'static, which are useful in our situation: we need Send to transfer the closure from one thread to another and 'static because we don't know how long the thread will take to execute. Let's create an execute method on ThreadPool that will take a generic parameter of type F with these bounds:

src/lib.rs

```
impl ThreadPool {
    // --snip--

    pub fn execute<F>(&self, f: F)
        where
            F: FnOnce()❶ + Send + 'static
    {

    }
}
```

We still use the () after FnOnce ❶ because this FnOnce represents a closure that takes no parameters and doesn't return a value. Just like function definitions, the return type can be omitted from the signature, but even if we have no parameters, we still need the parentheses.

Again, this is the simplest implementation of the execute method: it does nothing, but we're trying only to make our code compile. Let's check it again:

```
$ cargo check
    Compiling hello v0.1.0 (file:///projects/hello)
warning: unused variable: `size`
 --> src/lib.rs:4:16
  |
4 |     pub fn new(size: usize) -> ThreadPool {
  |                ^^^^
  |
  = note: #[warn(unused_variables)] on by default
  = note: to avoid this warning, consider using `_size` instead

warning: unused variable: `f`
 --> src/lib.rs:8:30
  |
8 |     pub fn execute<F>(&self, f: F)
  |                              ^
  |
  = note: to avoid this warning, consider using `_f` instead
```

We're receiving only warnings now, which means it compiles! But note that if you try cargo run and make a request in the browser, you'll see the errors in the browser that we saw at the beginning of the chapter. Our library isn't actually calling the closure passed to execute yet!

NOTE   *A saying you might hear about languages with strict compilers, such as Haskell and Rust, is "If the code compiles, it works." But this saying is not universally true. Our project compiles, but it does absolutely nothing! If we were building a real, complete project, this would be a good time to start writing unit tests to check that the code compiles and has the behavior we want.*

Validating the Number of Threads in new

We'll continue to get warnings because we aren't doing anything with the parameters to new and execute. Let's implement the bodies of these functions with the behavior we want. To start, let's think about new. Earlier, we chose an unsigned type for the size parameter, because a pool with a negative number of threads makes no sense. However, a pool with zero threads also makes no sense, yet zero is a perfectly valid usize. We'll add code to check that size is greater than zero before we return a ThreadPool instance and have the program panic if it receives a zero by using the assert! macro, as shown in Listing 20-13.

src/lib.rs

```
impl ThreadPool {
    /// Create a new ThreadPool.
```

```
///
/// The size is the number of threads in the pool.
///
❶ /// # Panics
///
/// The `new` function will panic if the size is zero.
pub fn new(size: usize) -> ThreadPool {
  ❷ assert!(size > 0);

      ThreadPool
  }

  // --snip--
}
```

Listing 20-13: Implementing `ThreadPool::new` *to panic if size is zero*

We've added some documentation for our ThreadPool with doc comments. Note that we followed good documentation practices by adding a section that calls out the situations in which our function can panic ❶, as discussed in Chapter 14. Try running cargo doc --open and clicking the ThreadPool struct to see what the generated docs for new look like!

Instead of adding the assert! macro as we've done here ❷, we could make new return a Result as we did with Config::new in the I/O project in Listing 12-9 on page 239. But we've decided in this case that trying to create a thread pool without any threads should be an unrecoverable error. If you're feeling ambitious, try to write a version of new with the following signature to compare both versions:

```
pub fn new(size: usize) -> Result<ThreadPool, PoolCreationError> {
```

Creating Space to Store the Threads

Now that we have a way to know we have a valid number of threads to store in the pool, we can create those threads and store them in the ThreadPool struct before returning it. But how do we "store" a thread? Let's take another look at the thread::spawn signature:

```
pub fn spawn<F, T>(f: F) -> JoinHandle<T>
    where
        F: FnOnce() -> T + Send + 'static,
        T: Send + 'static
```

The spawn function returns a JoinHandle<T>, where T is the type that the closure returns. Let's try using JoinHandle too and see what happens. In our case, the closures we're passing to the thread pool will handle the connection and not return anything, so T will be the unit type ().

The code in Listing 20-14 will compile but doesn't create any threads yet. We've changed the definition of ThreadPool to hold a vector of thread::JoinHandle<()> instances, initialized the vector with a capacity of size, set up a `for` loop that will run some code to create the threads, and returned a `ThreadPool` instance containing them.

```
❶ use std::thread;

pub struct ThreadPool {
  ❷ threads: Vec<thread::JoinHandle<()>>,
}

impl ThreadPool {
    // --snip--
    pub fn new(size: usize) -> ThreadPool {
        assert!(size > 0);

      ❸ let mut threads = Vec::with_capacity(size);

        for _ in 0..size {
            // create some threads and store them in the vector
        }

        ThreadPool {
            threads
        }
    }

    // --snip--
}
```

Listing 20-14: Creating a vector for `ThreadPool` to hold the threads

We've brought `std::thread` into scope in the library crate ❶, because we're using `thread::JoinHandle` as the type of the items in the vector in `ThreadPool` ❷.

Once a valid size is received, our `ThreadPool` creates a new vector that can hold size items ❸. We haven't used the `with_capacity` function in this book yet, which performs the same task as `Vec::new` but with an important difference: it preallocates space in the vector. Because we know we need to store size elements in the vector, doing this allocation up front is slightly more efficient than using `Vec::new`, which resizes itself as elements are inserted.

When you run `cargo check` again, you'll get a few more warnings, but it should succeed.

A Worker Struct Responsible for Sending Code from the ThreadPool to a Thread

We left a comment in the `for` loop in Listing 20-14 regarding the creation of threads. Here, we'll look at how we actually create threads. The standard library provides `thread::spawn` as a way to create threads, and `thread::spawn` expects to get some code the thread should run as soon as the thread is created. However, in our case, we want to create the threads and have them *wait* for code that we'll send later. The standard library's implementation of threads doesn't include any way to do that; we have to implement it manually.

We'll implement this behavior by introducing a new data structure between the `ThreadPool` and the threads that will manage this new behavior.

We'll call this data structure Worker, which is a common term in pooling implementations. Think of people working in the kitchen at a restaurant: the workers wait until orders come in from customers, and then they're responsible for taking those orders and filling them.

Instead of storing a vector of JoinHandle<()> instances in the thread pool, we'll store instances of the Worker struct. Each Worker will store a single JoinHandle<()> instance. Then we'll implement a method on Worker that will take a closure of code to run and send it to the already running thread for execution. We'll also give each worker an id so we can distinguish between the different workers in the pool when logging or debugging.

Let's make the following changes to what happens when we create a ThreadPool. We'll implement the code that sends the closure to the thread after we have Worker set up in this way:

1. Define a Worker struct that holds an id and a JoinHandle<()>.
2. Change ThreadPool to hold a vector of Worker instances.
3. Define a Worker::new function that takes an id number and returns a Worker instance that holds the id and a thread spawned with an empty closure.
4. In ThreadPool::new, use the for loop counter to generate an id, create a new Worker with that id, and store the worker in the vector.

If you're up for a challenge, try implementing these changes on your own before looking at the code in Listing 20-15.

Ready? Here is Listing 20-15 with one way to make the preceding modifications.

src/lib.rs

```
use std::thread;

pub struct ThreadPool {
❶ workers: Vec<Worker>,
}

impl ThreadPool {
    // --snip--
    pub fn new(size: usize) -> ThreadPool {
        assert!(size > 0);

        let mut workers = Vec::with_capacity(size);

    ❷ for id in 0..size {
         ❸ workers.push(Worker::new(id));
        }

        ThreadPool {
            workers
        }
    }
    // --snip--
}
```

```
❹ struct Worker {
      id: usize,
      thread: thread::JoinHandle<()>,
  }

  impl Worker {
    ❺ fn new(id: usize) -> Worker {
        ❻ let thread = thread::spawn(|| {});

          Worker {
            ❼ id,
            ❽ thread,
          }
      }
  }
```

Listing 20-15: Modifying ThreadPool *to hold* Worker *instances instead of holding threads directly*

We've changed the name of the field on ThreadPool from threads to workers because it's now holding Worker instances instead of JoinHandle<()> instances ❶. We use the counter in the for loop ❷ as an argument to Worker::new, and we store each new Worker in the vector named workers ❸.

External code (like our server in *src/bin/main.rs*) doesn't need to know the implementation details regarding using a Worker struct within ThreadPool, so we make the Worker struct ❹ and its new function ❺ private. The Worker::new function uses the id we give it ❼ and stores a JoinHandle<()> instance ❽ that is created by spawning a new thread using an empty closure ❻.

This code will compile and will store the number of Worker instances we specified as an argument to ThreadPool::new. But we're *still* not processing the closure that we get in execute. Let's look at how to do that next.

Sending Requests to Threads via Channels

Now we'll tackle the problem that the closures given to thread::spawn do absolutely nothing. Currently, we get the closure we want to execute in the execute method. But we need to give thread::spawn a closure to run when we create each Worker during the creation of the ThreadPool.

We want the Worker structs that we just created to fetch code to run from a queue held in the ThreadPool and send that code to its thread to run.

In Chapter 16, you learned about *channels*—a simple way to communicate between two threads—which would be perfect for this use case. We'll use a channel to function as the queue of jobs, and execute will send a job from the ThreadPool to the Worker instances, which will send the job to its thread. Here is the plan:

1. The ThreadPool will create a channel and hold on to the sending side of the channel.

2. Each Worker will hold on to the receiving side of the channel.

3. We'll create a new Job struct that will hold the closures we want to send down the channel.

4. The execute method will send the job it wants to execute down the sending side of the channel.

5. In its thread, the Worker will loop over its receiving side of the channel and execute the closures of any jobs it receives.

Let's start by creating a channel in ThreadPool::new and holding the sending side in the ThreadPool instance, as shown in Listing 20-16. The Job struct doesn't hold anything for now but will be the type of item we're sending down the channel.

src/lib.rs
```
// --snip--
use std::sync::mpsc;

pub struct ThreadPool {
    workers: Vec<Worker>,
    sender: mpsc::Sender<Job>,
}

struct Job;

impl ThreadPool {
    // --snip--
    pub fn new(size: usize) -> ThreadPool {
        assert!(size > 0);

      ❶ let (sender, receiver) = mpsc::channel();

        let mut workers = Vec::with_capacity(size);

        for id in 0..size {
            workers.push(Worker::new(id));
        }

        ThreadPool {
            workers,
          ❷ sender,
        }
    }
    // --snip--
}
```

Listing 20-16: Modifying ThreadPool to store the sending end of a channel that sends Job instances

In ThreadPool::new, we create our new channel ❶ and have the pool hold the sending end ❷. This will successfully compile, still with warnings.

Let's try passing a receiving end of the channel into each worker as the thread pool creates the channel. We know we want to use the receiving end in the thread that the workers spawn, so we'll reference the receiver parameter in the closure. The code in Listing 20-17 won't quite compile yet.

src/lib.rs
```
impl ThreadPool {
    // --snip--
```

```
    pub fn new(size: usize) -> ThreadPool {
        assert!(size > 0);

        let (sender, receiver) = mpsc::channel();

        let mut workers = Vec::with_capacity(size);

        for id in 0..size {
    ❶     workers.push(Worker::new(id, receiver));
        }

        ThreadPool {
            workers,
            sender,
        }
    }
    // --snip--
}

// --snip--

impl Worker {
    fn new(id: usize, receiver: mpsc::Receiver<Job>) -> Worker {
        let thread = thread::spawn(|| {
    ❷     receiver;
        });

        Worker {
            id,
            thread,
        }
    }
}
```

Listing 20-17: Passing the receiving end of the channel to the workers

We've made some small and straightforward changes: we pass the receiving end of the channel into `Worker::new` ❶, and then we use it inside the closure ❷.

When we try to check this code, we get this error:

```
$ cargo check
   Compiling hello v0.1.0 (file:///projects/hello)
error[E0382]: use of moved value: `receiver`
  --> src/lib.rs:27:42
   |
27 |             workers.push(Worker::new(id, receiver));
   |                                          ^^^^^^^^ value moved here in
previous iteration of loop
   |
   = note: move occurs because `receiver` has type `std::sync::mpsc::Receiver<
Job>`, which does not implement the `Copy` trait
```

The code is trying to pass receiver to multiple Worker instances. This won't work, as you'll recall from Chapter 16: the channel implementation that Rust provides is multiple *producer*, single *consumer*. This means we can't just clone the consuming end of the channel to fix this code. Even if we could, that is not the technique we would want to use; instead, we want to distribute the jobs across threads by sharing the single receiver among all the workers.

Additionally, taking a job off the channel queue involves mutating the receiver, so the threads need a safe way to share and modify receiver; otherwise, we might get race conditions (as covered in Chapter 16).

Recall the thread-safe smart pointers discussed in Chapter 16: to share ownership across multiple threads and allow the threads to mutate the value, we need to use Arc<Mutex<T>>. The Arc type will let multiple workers own the receiver, and Mutex will ensure that only one worker gets a job from the receiver at a time. Listing 20-18 shows the changes we need to make.

src/lib.rs

```
use std::sync::Arc;
use std::sync::Mutex;
// --snip--

impl ThreadPool {
    // --snip--
    pub fn new(size: usize) -> ThreadPool {
        assert!(size > 0);

        let (sender, receiver) = mpsc::channel();

    ❶ let receiver = Arc::new(Mutex::new(receiver));

        let mut workers = Vec::with_capacity(size);

        for id in 0..size {
            workers.push(Worker::new(id, Arc::clone(&receiver)❷));
        }

        ThreadPool {
            workers,
            sender,
        }
    }

    // --snip--
}

impl Worker {
    fn new(id: usize, receiver: Arc<Mutex<mpsc::Receiver<Job>>>) -> Worker {
        // --snip--
    }
}
```

Listing 20-18: Sharing the receiving end of the channel among the workers using Arc and Mutex

In `ThreadPool::new`, we put the receiving end of the channel in an `Arc` and a `Mutex` ❶. For each new worker, we clone the `Arc` to bump the reference count so the workers can share ownership of the receiving end ❷.

With these changes, the code compiles! We're getting there!

Implementing the execute Method

Let's finally implement the execute method on `ThreadPool`. We'll also change `Job` from a struct to a type alias for a trait object that holds the type of closure that execute receives. As discussed in "Creating Type Synonyms with Type Aliases" on page 441, type aliases allow us to make long types shorter. Look at Listing 20-19.

```
// --snip--

type Job = Box<FnOnce() + Send + 'static>;

impl ThreadPool {
    // --snip--

    pub fn execute<F>(&self, f: F)
        where
            F: FnOnce() + Send + 'static
    {
      ❶ let job = Box::new(f);

      ❷ self.sender.send(job).unwrap();
    }
}

// --snip--
```

Listing 20-19: Creating a `Job` type alias for a `Box` that holds each closure and then sending the job down the channel

After creating a new `Job` instance using the closure we get in execute ❶, we send that job down the sending end of the channel ❷. We're calling `unwrap` on send for the case that sending fails. This might happen if, for example, we stop all our threads from executing, meaning the receiving end has stopped receiving new messages. At the moment, we can't stop our threads from executing: our threads continue executing as long as the pool exists. The reason we use `unwrap` is that we know the failure case won't happen, but the compiler doesn't know that.

But we're not quite done yet! In the worker, our closure being passed to `thread::spawn` still only *references* the receiving end of the channel. Instead, we need the closure to loop forever, asking the receiving end of the channel for a job and running the job when it gets one. Let's make the change shown in Listing 20-20 to `Worker::new`.

```
// --snip--

impl Worker {
```

```
fn new(id: usize, receiver: Arc<Mutex<mpsc::Receiver<Job>>>) -> Worker {
    let thread = thread::spawn(move || {
        loop {
            let job = receiver.lock()❶.unwrap()❷.recv()❸.unwrap()❹;

            println!("Worker {} got a job; executing.", id);

            (*job)();
        }
    });

    Worker {
        id,
        thread,
    }
}
```

Listing 20-20: Receiving and executing the jobs in the worker's thread

Here, we first call lock on the receiver to acquire the mutex ❶, and then we call unwrap to panic on any errors ❷. Acquiring a lock might fail if the mutex is in a *poisoned* state, which can happen if some other thread panicked while holding the lock rather than releasing the lock. In this situation, calling unwrap to have this thread panic is the correct action to take. Feel free to change this unwrap to an expect with an error message that is meaningful to you.

If we get the lock on the mutex, we call recv to receive a Job from the channel ❸. A final unwrap moves past any errors here as well ❹, which might occur if the thread holding the sending side of the channel has shut down, similar to how the send method returns Err if the receiving side shuts down.

The call to recv blocks, so if there is no job yet, the current thread will wait until a job becomes available. The Mutex<T> ensures that only one Worker thread at a time is trying to request a job.

Theoretically, this code should compile. Unfortunately, the Rust compiler isn't perfect yet, and we get this error:

```
error[E0161]: cannot move a value of type std::ops::FnOnce() +
std::marker::Send: the size of std::ops::FnOnce() + std::marker::Send cannot
be statically determined
  --> src/lib.rs:63:17
   |
63 |                 (*job)();
   |                 ^^^^^^
```

This error is fairly cryptic because the problem is fairly cryptic. To call a FnOnce closure that is stored in a Box<T> (which is what our Job type alias is), the closure needs to move itself *out* of the Box<T> because the closure takes ownership of self when we call it. In general, Rust doesn't allow us to move a value out of a Box<T> because Rust doesn't know how big the value inside the Box<T> will be: recall in Chapter 15 that we used Box<T> precisely because we had something of an unknown size that we wanted to store in a Box<T> to get a value of a known size.

As you saw in Listing 17-15 on page 379, we can write methods that use the syntax self: Box<Self>, which allows the method to take ownership of a Self value stored in a Box<T>. That's exactly what we want to do here, but unfortunately Rust won't let us: the part of Rust that implements behavior when a closure is called isn't implemented using self: Box<Self>. So Rust doesn't yet understand that it could use self: Box<Self> in this situation to take ownership of the closure and move the closure out of the Box<T>.

Rust is still a work in progress with places where the compiler could be improved, but in the future, the code in Listing 20-20 should work just fine. People just like you are working to fix this and other issues! After you've finished this book, we would love for you to join in.

But for now, let's work around this problem using a handy trick. We can tell Rust explicitly that in this case we can take ownership of the value inside the Box<T> using self: Box<Self>; then, once we have ownership of the closure, we can call it. This involves defining a new trait FnBox with the method call_box that will use self: Box<Self> in its signature, defining FnBox for any type that implements FnOnce(), changing our type alias to use the new trait, and changing Worker to use the call_box method. These changes are shown in Listing 20-21.

src/lib.rs

```
❶ trait FnBox {
    ❷ fn call_box(self: Box<Self>);
  }

❸ impl<F: FnOnce()> FnBox for F {
      fn call_box(self: Box<F>) {
      ❹ (*self)()
      }
  }

❺ type Job = Box<FnBox + Send + 'static>;

  // --snip--

  impl Worker {
      fn new(id: usize, receiver: Arc<Mutex<mpsc::Receiver<Job>>>) -> Worker {
          let thread = thread::spawn(move || {
              loop {
                  let job = receiver.lock().unwrap().recv().unwrap();

                  println!("Worker {} got a job; executing.", id);

                ❻ job.call_box();
              }
          });

          Worker {
              id,
              thread,
```

```
      }
    }
  }
```

Listing 20-21: Adding a new trait FnBox to work around the current limitations of Box<FnOnce()>

First, we create a new trait named FnBox ❶. This trait has the one method call_box ❷, which is similar to the call methods on the other Fn* traits except that it takes self: Box<Self> to take ownership of self and move the value out of the Box<T>.

Next, we implement the FnBox trait for any type F that implements the FnOnce() trait ❸. Effectively, this means that any FnOnce() closures can use our call_box method. The implementation of call_box uses (*self)() to move the closure out of the Box<T> and call the closure ❹.

We now need our Job type alias to be a Box of anything that implements our new trait FnBox ❺. This will allow us to use call_box in Worker when we get a Job value instead of invoking the closure directly ❻. Implementing the FnBox trait for any FnOnce() closure means we don't have to change anything about the actual values we're sending down the channel. Now Rust is able to recognize that what we want to do is fine.

This trick is very sneaky and complicated. Don't worry if it doesn't make perfect sense; someday, it will be completely unnecessary.

With the implementation of this trick, our thread pool is in a working state! Give it a cargo run and make some requests:

```
$ cargo run
   Compiling hello v0.1.0 (file:///projects/hello)
warning: field is never used: `workers`
 --> src/lib.rs:7:5
  |
7 |     workers: Vec<Worker>,
  |     ^^^^^^^^^^^^^^^^^^^^^
  |
  = note: #[warn(dead_code)] on by default

warning: field is never used: `id`
  --> src/lib.rs:61:5
   |
61 |     id: usize,
   |     ^^^^^^^^^
   |
   = note: #[warn(dead_code)] on by default

warning: field is never used: `thread`
  --> src/lib.rs:62:5
   |
62 |     thread: thread::JoinHandle<()>,
   |     ^^^^^^^^^^^^^^^^^^^^^^^^^^^^^^^
   |
   = note: #[warn(dead_code)] on by default
```

```
      Finished dev [unoptimized + debuginfo] target(s) in 0.99 secs
        Running `target/debug/hello`
Worker 0 got a job; executing.
Worker 2 got a job; executing.
Worker 1 got a job; executing.
Worker 3 got a job; executing.
Worker 0 got a job; executing.
Worker 2 got a job; executing.
Worker 1 got a job; executing.
Worker 3 got a job; executing.
Worker 0 got a job; executing.
Worker 2 got a job; executing.
```

Success! We now have a thread pool that executes connections asynchronously. There are never more than four threads created, so our system won't get overloaded if the server receives a lot of requests. If we make a request to */sleep*, the server will be able to serve other requests by having another thread run them.

After learning about the while let loop in Chapter 18, you might be wondering why we didn't write the worker thread code as shown in Listing 20-22.

src/lib.rs

```
// --snip--

impl Worker {
    fn new(id: usize, receiver: Arc<Mutex<mpsc::Receiver<Job>>>) -> Worker {
        let thread = thread::spawn(move || {
            while let Ok(job) = receiver.lock().unwrap().recv() {
                println!("Worker {} got a job; executing.", id);

                job.call_box();
            }
        });

        Worker {
            id,
            thread,
        }
    }
}
```

Listing 20-22: An alternative implementation of Worker::new using while let

This code compiles and runs but doesn't result in the desired threading behavior: a slow request will still cause other requests to wait to be processed. The reason is somewhat subtle: the Mutex struct has no public unlock method because the ownership of the lock is based on the lifetime of the MutexGuard<T> within the LockResult<MutexGuard<T>> that the lock method returns. At compile time, the borrow checker can then enforce the rule that a resource guarded by a Mutex cannot be accessed unless we hold the lock. But this implementation can also result in the lock being held longer than intended if we don't think carefully about the lifetime of the MutexGuard<T>. Because the values in the while expression remain in scope for the duration of the block, the lock remains held for the duration of the call to job.call_box(), meaning other workers cannot receive jobs.

By using loop instead and acquiring the lock and a job within the block rather than outside it, the MutexGuard returned from the lock method is dropped as soon as the let job statement ends. This ensures that the lock is held during the call to recv, but it is released before the call to job.call_box(), allowing multiple requests to be serviced concurrently.

Graceful Shutdown and Cleanup

The code in Listing 20-21 is responding to requests asynchronously through the use of a thread pool, as we intended. We get some warnings about the workers, id, and thread fields that we're not using in a direct way that reminds us we're not cleaning up anything. When we use the less elegant CTRL-C method to halt the main thread, all other threads are stopped immediately as well, even if they're in the middle of serving a request.

Now we'll implement the Drop trait to call join on each of the threads in the pool so they can finish the requests they're working on before closing. Then we'll implement a way to tell the threads they should stop accepting new requests and shut down. To see this code in action, we'll modify our server to accept only two requests before gracefully shutting down its thread pool.

Implementing the Drop Trait on ThreadPool

Let's start with implementing Drop on our thread pool. When the pool is dropped, our threads should all join to make sure they finish their work. Listing 20-23 shows a first attempt at a Drop implementation; this code won't quite work yet.

src/lib.rs

```
impl Drop for ThreadPool {
    fn drop(&mut self) {
    ❶ for worker in &mut self.workers {
        ❷ println!("Shutting down worker {}", worker.id);

        ❸ worker.thread.join().unwrap();
        }
    }
}
```

Listing 20-23: Joining each thread when the thread pool goes out of scope

First, we loop through each of the thread pool workers ❶. We use &mut for this because self is a mutable reference, and we also need to be able to mutate worker. For each worker, we print a message saying that this particular worker is shutting down ❷, and then we call join on that worker's thread ❸. If the call to join fails, we use unwrap to make Rust panic and go into an ungraceful shutdown.

Here is the error we get when we compile this code:

```
error[E0507]: cannot move out of borrowed content
  --> src/lib.rs:65:13
   |
65 |             worker.thread.join().unwrap();
   |             ^^^^^^ cannot move out of borrowed content
```

The error tells us we can't call join because we only have a mutable borrow of each worker and join takes ownership of its argument. To solve this issue, we need to move the thread out of the Worker instance that owns thread so join can consume the thread. We did this in Listing 17-15 on page 379: if Worker holds an Option<thread::JoinHandle<()>> instead, we can call the take method on the Option to move the value out of the Some variant and leave a None variant in its place. In other words, a Worker that is running will have a Some variant in thread, and when we want to clean up a Worker, we'll replace Some with None so the Worker doesn't have a thread to run.

So we know we want to update the definition of Worker like this:

src/lib.rs

```
struct Worker {
    id: usize,
    thread: Option<thread::JoinHandle<()>>,
}
```

Now let's lean on the compiler to find the other places that need to change. Checking this code, we get two errors:

```
error[E0599]: no method named `join` found for type `std::option::Option<std::
thread::JoinHandle<()>>` in the current scope
  --> src/lib.rs:65:27
   |
65 |             worker.thread.join().unwrap();
   |                           ^^^^

error[E0308]: mismatched types
  --> src/lib.rs:89:13
   |
89 |             thread,
   |             ^^^^^^
   |             |
   |             expected enum `std::option::Option`, found struct
`std::thread::JoinHandle`
   |             help: try using a variant of the expected type:
`Some(thread)`
   |
   = note: expected type `std::option::Option<std::thread::JoinHandle<()>>`
              found type `std::thread::JoinHandle<_>`
```

Let's address the second error, which points to the code at the end of `Worker::new`; we need to wrap the `thread` value in `Some` when we create a new `Worker`. Make the following changes to fix this error:

src/lib.rs

```
impl Worker {
    fn new(id: usize, receiver: Arc<Mutex<mpsc::Receiver<Job>>>) -> Worker {
        // --snip--

        Worker {
            id,
            thread: Some(thread),
        }
    }
}
```

The first error is in our `Drop` implementation. We mentioned earlier that we intended to call `take` on the `Option` value to move `thread` out of `worker`. The following changes will do so:

src/lib.rs

```
impl Drop for ThreadPool {
    fn drop(&mut self) {
        for worker in &mut self.workers {
            println!("Shutting down worker {}", worker.id);

❶          if let Some(thread) = worker.thread.take() {
❷              thread.join().unwrap();
            }
        }
    }
}
```

As discussed in Chapter 17, the `take` method on `Option` takes the `Some` variant out and leaves `None` in its place. We're using `if let` to destructure the `Some` and get the thread ❶; then we call `join` on the thread ❷. If a worker's thread is already `None`, we know that worker has already had its thread cleaned up, so nothing happens in that case.

Signaling to the Threads to Stop Listening for Jobs

With all the changes we've made, our code compiles without any warnings. But the bad news is that this code doesn't function the way we want it to yet. The key is the logic in the closures run by the threads of the `Worker` instances: at the moment, we call `join`, but that won't shut down the threads because they `loop` forever looking for jobs. If we try to drop our `ThreadPool` with our current implementation of `drop`, the main thread will block forever waiting for the first thread to finish.

To fix this problem, we'll modify the threads so they listen for either a `Job` to run or a signal that they should stop listening and exit the infinite loop. Instead of `Job` instances, our channel will send one of these two enum variants.

```
enum Message {
    NewJob(Job),
    Terminate,
}
```

This `Message` enum will either be a `NewJob` variant that holds the `Job` the thread should run, or it will be a `Terminate` variant that will cause the thread to exit its loop and stop.

We need to adjust the channel to use values of type `Message` rather than type `Job`, as shown in Listing 20-24.

```
pub struct ThreadPool {
    workers: Vec<Worker>,
 ❶ sender: mpsc::Sender<Message>,
}

// --snip--

impl ThreadPool {
    // --snip--

    pub fn execute<F>(&self, f: F)
        where
            F: FnOnce() + Send + 'static
    {
        let job = Box::new(f);

      ❷ self.sender.send(Message::NewJob(job)).unwrap();
    }
}

// --snip--

impl Worker {
 ❸ fn new(id: usize, receiver: Arc<Mutex<mpsc::Receiver<Message>>>) -> Worker {

        let thread = thread::spawn(move ||{
            loop {
              ❹ let message = receiver.lock().unwrap().recv().unwrap();

                match message {
                  ❺ Message::NewJob(job) => {
                        println!("Worker {} got a job; executing.", id);

                      ❻ job.call_box();
                    },
                  ❼ Message::Terminate => {
                        println!("Worker {} was told to terminate.", id);

                      ❽ break;
                    },
                }
            }
        }
```

```
    });

    Worker {
        id,
        thread: Some(thread),
    }
  }
}
```

Listing 20-24: Sending and receiving Message *values and exiting the loop if a* Worker *receives* Message::Terminate

To incorporate the Message enum, we need to change Job to Message in two places: the definition of ThreadPool ❶ and the signature of Worker::new ❸. The execute method of ThreadPool needs to send jobs wrapped in the Message::NewJob variant ❷. Then, in Worker::new where a Message is received from the channel ❹, the job will be processed ❻ if the NewJob variant is received ❺, and the thread will break out of the loop ❽ if the Terminate variant is received ❼.

With these changes, the code will compile and continue to function in the same way as it did after Listing 20-21. But we'll get a warning because we aren't creating any messages of the Terminate variety. Let's fix this warning by changing our Drop implementation to look like Listing 20-25.

src/lib.rs

```
impl Drop for ThreadPool {
    fn drop(&mut self) {
        println!("Sending terminate message to all workers.");

        for _ in &mut self.workers {
          ❶ self.sender.send(Message::Terminate).unwrap();
        }

        println!("Shutting down all workers.");

        for worker in &mut self.workers {
            println!("Shutting down worker {}", worker.id);

            if let Some(thread) = worker.thread.take() {
              ❷ thread.join().unwrap();
            }
        }
    }
}
```

Listing 20-25: Sending Message::Terminate *to the workers before calling* join *on each worker thread*

We're now iterating over the workers twice: once to send one Terminate message for each worker ❶ and once to call join on each worker's thread ❷. If we tried to send a message and join immediately in the same loop, we couldn't guarantee that the worker in the current iteration would be the one to get the message from the channel.

To better understand why we need two separate loops, imagine a scenario with two workers. If we used a single loop to iterate through each worker, on the first iteration, a terminate message would be sent down the channel and join called on the first worker's thread. If that first worker was busy processing a request at that moment, the second worker would pick up the terminate message from the channel and shut down. We would be left waiting on the first worker to shut down, but it never would because the second thread picked up the terminate message. Deadlock!

To prevent this scenario, we first put all of our Terminate messages on the channel in one loop; then we join on all the threads in another loop. Each worker will stop receiving requests on the channel once it gets a terminate message. So, we can be sure that if we send the same number of terminate messages as there are workers, each worker will receive a terminate message before join is called on its thread.

To see this code in action, let's modify main to accept only two requests before gracefully shutting down the server, as shown in Listing 20-26.

src/bin/main.rs

```
fn main() {
    let listener = TcpListener::bind("127.0.0.1:7878").unwrap();
    let pool = ThreadPool::new(4);

    for stream in listener.incoming().take(2) {
        let stream = stream.unwrap();

        pool.execute(|| {
            handle_connection(stream);
        });
    }

    println!("Shutting down.");
}
```

Listing 20-26: Shut down the server after serving two requests by exiting the loop

You wouldn't want a real-world web server to shut down after serving only two requests. This code just demonstrates that the graceful shutdown and cleanup is in working order.

The take method is defined in the Iterator trait and limits the iteration to the first two items at most. The ThreadPool will go out of scope at the end of main, and the drop implementation will run.

Start the server with cargo run, and make three requests. The third request should error, and in your terminal you should see output similar to this:

```
$ cargo run
   Compiling hello v0.1.0 (file:///projects/hello)
    Finished dev [unoptimized + debuginfo] target(s) in 1.0 secs
     Running `target/debug/hello`
Worker 0 got a job; executing.
Worker 3 got a job; executing.
Shutting down.
Sending terminate message to all workers.
```

```
Shutting down all workers.
Shutting down worker 0
Worker 1 was told to terminate.
Worker 2 was told to terminate.
Worker 0 was told to terminate.
Worker 3 was told to terminate.
Shutting down worker 1
Shutting down worker 2
Shutting down worker 3
```

You might see a different ordering of workers and messages printed.

We can see how this code works from the messages: workers 0 and 3 got the first two requests, and then on the third request, the server stopped accepting connections. When the ThreadPool goes out of scope at the end of main, its Drop implementation kicks in, and the pool tells all workers to terminate. The workers each print a message when they see the terminate message, and then the thread pool calls join to shut down each worker thread.

Notice one interesting aspect of this particular execution: the ThreadPool sent the terminate messages down the channel, and before any worker received the messages, we tried to join worker 0. Worker 0 had not yet received the terminate message, so the main thread blocked waiting for worker 0 to finish. In the meantime, each of the workers received the termination messages. When worker 0 finished, the main thread waited for the rest of the workers to finish. At that point, they had all received the termination message and were able to shut down.

Congrats! We've now completed our project; we have a basic web server that uses a thread pool to respond asynchronously. We're able to perform a graceful shutdown of the server, which cleans up all the threads in the pool. See *https://www.nostarch.com/Rust/* to download the full code for this chapter for reference.

We could do more here! If you want to continue enhancing this project, here are some ideas:

- Add more documentation to ThreadPool and its public methods.
- Add tests of the library's functionality.
- Change calls to unwrap to more robust error handling.
- Use ThreadPool to perform some task other than serving web requests.
- Find a thread pool crate on *https://crates.io/* and implement a similar web server using the crate instead. Then compare its API and robustness to the thread pool we implemented.

Summary

Well done! You've made it to the end of the book! We want to thank you for joining us on this tour of Rust. You're now ready to implement your own Rust projects and help with other peoples' projects. Keep in mind that there is a welcoming community of other Rustaceans who would love to help you with any challenges you encounter on your Rust journey.

A

KEYWORDS

The following list contains keywords that are reserved for current or future use by the Rust language. As such, they cannot be used as identifiers, such as names of functions, variables, parameters, struct fields, modules, crates, constants, macros, static values, attributes, types, traits, or lifetimes.

Keywords Currently in Use

The following keywords currently have the functionality described.

as perform primitive casting, disambiguate the specific trait containing an item, or rename items in use and extern crate statements

break exit a loop immediately

const define constant items or constant raw pointers

continue   continue to the next loop iteration

crate   link an external crate or a macro variable representing the crate in which the macro is defined

else   fallback for if and if let control flow constructs

enum   define an enumeration

extern   link an external crate, function, or variable

false   Boolean false literal

fn   define a function or the function pointer type

for   loop over items from an iterator, implement a trait, or specify a higher-ranked lifetime

if   branch based on the result of a conditional expression

impl   implement inherent or trait functionality

in   part of for loop syntax

let   bind a variable

loop   loop unconditionally

match   match a value to patterns

mod   define a module

move   make a closure take ownership of all its captures

mut   denote mutability in references, raw pointers, or pattern bindings

pub   denote public visibility in struct fields, impl blocks, or modules

ref   bind by reference

return   return from function

Self   a type alias for the type implementing a trait

self   method subject or current module

static   global variable or lifetime lasting the entire program execution

struct   define a structure

super   parent module of the current module

trait   define a trait

true   Boolean true literal

type   define a type alias or associated type

unsafe   denote unsafe code, functions, traits, or implementations

use   import symbols into scope

where   denote clauses that constrain a type

while   loop conditionally based on the result of an expression

Keywords Reserved for Future Use

The following keywords do not have any functionality but are reserved by Rust for potential future use.

- `abstract`
- `alignof`
- `become`
- `box`
- `do`
- `final`
- `macro`
- `offsetof`
- `override`
- `priv`
- `proc`
- `pure`
- `sizeof`
- `typeof`
- `unsized`
- `virtual`
- `yield`

B

OPERATORS AND SYMBOLS

This appendix contains a glossary of Rust's syntax, including operators and other symbols that appear by themselves or in the context of paths, generics, trait bounds, macros, attributes, comments, tuples, and brackets.

Operators

Table B-1 contains the operators in Rust, an example of how the operator would appear in context, a short explanation, and whether that operator is overloadable. If an operator is overloadable, the relevant trait to use to overload that operator is listed.

Table B-1: Operators

Operator	Example	Explanation	Overloadable?
!	`ident!(...)`, `ident!{...}`, `ident![...]`	Macro expansion	
!	`!expr`	Bitwise or logical complement	`Not`
!=	`var != expr`	Nonequality comparison	`PartialEq`
%	`expr % expr`	Arithmetic remainder	`Rem`
%=	`var %= expr`	Arithmetic remainder and assignment	`RemAssign`
&	`&expr`, `&mut expr`	Borrow	
&	`&type`, `&mut type`, `&'a type`, `&'a mut type`	Borrowed pointer type	
&	`expr & expr`	Bitwise AND	`BitAnd`
&=	`var &= expr`	Bitwise AND and assignment	`BitAndAssign`
&&	`expr && expr`	Logical AND	
*	`expr * expr`	Arithmetic multiplication	`Mul`
*=	`var *= expr`	Arithmetic multiplication and assignment	`MulAssign`
*	`*expr`	Dereference	
*	`*const type`, `*mut type`	Raw pointer	
+	`trait + trait`, `'a + trait`	Compound type constraint	
+	`expr + expr`	Arithmetic addition	`Add`
+=	`var += expr`	Arithmetic addition and assignment	`AddAssign`
,	`expr, expr`	Argument and element separator	
-	`- expr`	Arithmetic negation	`Neg`
-	`expr - expr`	Arithmetic subtraction	`Sub`
-=	`var -= expr`	Arithmetic subtraction and assignment	`SubAssign`
->	`fn(...) -> type`, `|...| -> type`	Function and closure return type	
.	`expr.ident`	Member access	
..	`..`, `expr..`, `..expr`, `expr..expr`	Right-exclusive range literal	
..	`..expr`	Struct literal update syntax	
..	`variant(x, ..)`, `struct_type { x, .. }`	"And the rest" pattern binding	
...	`expr...expr`	In a pattern: inclusive range pattern	
/	`expr / expr`	Arithmetic division	`Div`
/=	`var /= expr`	Arithmetic division and assignment	`DivAssign`
:	`pat: type`, `ident: type`	Constraints	
:	`ident: expr`	Struct field initializer	
:	`'a: loop {...}`	Loop label	
;	`expr;`	Statement and item terminator	

Operator	Example	Explanation	Overloadable?
;	[...; len]	Part of fixed-size array syntax	
<<	expr << expr	Left-shift	Shl
<<=	var <<= expr	Left-shift and assignment	ShlAssign
<	expr < expr	Less than comparison	PartialOrd
<=	expr <= expr	Less than or equal to comparison	PartialOrd
=	var = expr, ident = type	Assignment/equivalence	
==	expr == expr	Equality comparison	PartialEq
=>	pat => expr	Part of match arm syntax	
>	expr > expr	Greater than comparison	PartialOrd
>=	expr >= expr	Greater than or equal to comparison	PartialOrd
>>	expr >> expr	Right-shift	Shr
>>=	var >>= expr	Right-shift and assignment	ShrAssign
@	ident @ pat	Pattern binding	
^	expr ^ expr	Bitwise exclusive OR	BitXor
^=	var ^= expr	Bitwise exclusive OR and assignment	BitXorAssign
|	pat | pat	Pattern alternatives	
|	expr | expr	Bitwise OR	BitOr
|=	var |= expr	Bitwise OR and assignment	BitOrAssign
||	expr || expr	Logical OR	
?	expr?	Error propagation	

Non-operator Symbols

The following tables contain all non-letters that don't function as operators; that is, they don't behave like a function or method call.

Table B-2 shows symbols that appear on their own and are valid in a variety of locations.

Table B-2: Stand-Alone Syntax

Symbol	Explanation
'ident	Named lifetime or loop label
...u8, ...i32, ...f64, ...usize, etc.	Numeric literal of specific type
"..."	String literal
r"...", r#"..."#, r##"..."##, etc.	Raw string literal; escape characters not processed
b"..."	Byte string literal; constructs a [u8] instead of a string

(continued)

Table B-2: (continued)

Symbol	Explanation
`br"..."`, `br#"..."#`, `br##"..."##`, etc.	Raw byte string literal; combination of raw and byte string literal
`'...'`	Character literal
`b'...'`	ASCII byte literal
`|...| expr`	Closure
`!`	Always empty bottom type for diverging functions
`_`	"Ignored" pattern binding; also used to make integer literals readable

Table B-3 shows symbols that appear in the context of a path through the module hierarchy to an item.

Table B-3: Path-Related Syntax

Symbol	Explanation
`ident::ident`	Namespace path
`::path`	Path relative to the crate root (i.e., an explicitly absolute path)
`self::path`	Path relative to the current module (i.e., an explicitly relative path)
`super::path`	Path relative to the parent of the current module
`type::ident`, `<type as trait>::ident`	Associated constants, functions, and types
`<type>::...`	Associated item for a type that cannot be directly named (e.g., `<&T>::...`, `<[T]>::...`, etc.)
`trait::method(...)`	Disambiguating a method call by naming the trait that defines it
`type::method(...)`	Disambiguating a method call by naming the type for which it's defined
`<type as trait>::method(...)`	Disambiguating a method call by naming the trait and type

Table B-4 shows symbols that appear in the context of using generic type parameters.

Table B-4: Generics

Symbol	Explanation
`path<...>`	Specifies parameters to generic type in a type (e.g., `Vec<u8>`)
`path::<...>`, `method::<...>`	Specifies parameters to generic type, function, or method in an expression; often referred to as turbofish (e.g., `"42".parse::<i32>()`)
`fn ident<...> ...`	Define generic function

Symbol	Explanation
`struct ident<...> ...`	Define generic structure
`enum ident<...> ...`	Define generic enumeration
`impl<...> ...`	Define generic implementation
`for<...> type`	Higher-ranked lifetime bounds
`type<ident=type>`	A generic type where one or more associated types have specific assignments (e.g., `Iterator<Item=T>`)

Table B-5 shows symbols that appear in the context of constraining generic type parameters with trait bounds.

Table B-5: Trait-Bound Constraints

Symbol	Explanation
`T: U`	Generic parameter `T` constrained to types that implement `U`
`T: 'a`	Generic type `T` must outlive lifetime `'a` (meaning the type cannot transitively contain any references with lifetimes shorter than `'a`)
`T : 'static`	Generic type `T` contains no borrowed references other than `'static` ones
`'b: 'a`	Generic lifetime `'b` must outlive lifetime `'a`
`T: ?Sized`	Allow generic type parameter to be a dynamically sized type
`'a + trait,` `trait + trait`	Compound type constraint

Table B-6 shows symbols that appear in the context of calling or defining macros and specifying attributes on an item.

Table B-6: Macros and Attributes

Symbol	Explanation
`#[meta]`	Outer attribute
`#![meta]`	Inner attribute
`$ident`	Macro substitution
`$ident:kind`	Macro capture
`$(...)...`	Macro repetition

Table B-7 shows symbols that create comments.

Table B-7: Comments

Symbol	Explanation
`//`	Line comment
`//!`	Inner line doc comment
`///`	Outer line doc comment

(continued)

Table B-7: (continued)

Symbol	Explanation
/*...*/	Block comment
/*!...*/	Inner block doc comment
/**...*/	Outer block doc comment

Table B-8 shows symbols that appear in the context of using tuples.

Table B-8: Tuples

Symbol	Explanation
()	Empty tuple (aka unit), both literal and type
(expr)	Parenthesized expression
(expr,)	Single-element tuple expression
(type,)	Single-element tuple type
(expr, ...)	Tuple expression
(type, ...)	Tuple type
expr(expr, ...)	Function call expression; also used to initialize tuple structs and tuple enum variants
ident!(...), ident!{...}, ident![...]	Macro invocation
expr.0, expr.1, etc.	Tuple indexing

Table B-9 shows the contexts in which curly brackets are used.

Table B-9: Curly Brackets

Context	Explanation
{...}	Block expression
Type {...}	struct literal

Table B-10 shows the contexts in which square brackets are used.

Table B-10: Square Brackets

Context	Explanation
[...]	Array literal
[expr; len]	Array literal containing len copies of expr
[type; len]	Array type containing len instances of type
expr[expr]	Collection indexing; overloadable (Index, IndexMut)
expr[..], expr[a..], expr[..b], expr[a..b]	Collection indexing pretending to be collection slicing, using Range, RangeFrom, RangeTo, or RangeFull as the "index"

C

DERIVABLE TRAITS

 In various places in the book, we've discussed the derive attribute, which you can apply to a struct or enum definition. The derive attribute generates code that will implement a trait with its own default implementation on the type you've annotated with the derive syntax.

In this appendix, we provide a reference of all the traits in the standard library that you can use with derive. Each section covers:

- What operators and methods deriving this trait will enable
- What the implementation of the trait provided by derive does
- What implementing the trait signifies about the type
- The conditions in which you're allowed or not allowed to implement the trait
- Examples of operations that require the trait

If you want different behavior than that provided by the derive attribute, consult the standard library documentation for each trait for details on how to manually implement them.

The rest of the traits defined in the standard library can't be implemented on your types using derive. These traits don't have sensible default behavior, so it's up to you to implement them in the way that makes sense for what you're trying to accomplish.

An example of a trait that can't be derived is Display, which handles formatting for end users. You should always consider the appropriate way to display a type to an end user. What parts of the type should an end user be allowed to see? What parts would they find relevant? What format of the data would be most relevant to them? The Rust compiler doesn't have this insight, so it can't provide appropriate default behavior for you.

The list of derivable traits provided in this appendix is not comprehensive: libraries can implement derive for their own traits, making the list of traits you can use derive with truly open-ended. Implementing derive involves using a procedural macro, which is covered in Appendix D.

Debug for Programmer Output

The Debug trait enables debug formatting in format strings, which you indicate by adding :? within {} placeholders.

The Debug trait allows you to print instances of a type for debugging purposes, so you and other programmers using your type can inspect an instance at a particular point in a program's execution.

The Debug trait is required, for example, in use of the assert_eq! macro. This macro prints the values of instances given as arguments if the equality assertion fails so programmers can see why the two instances weren't equal.

PartialEq and Eq for Equality Comparisons

The PartialEq trait allows you to compare instances of a type to check for equality and enables use of the == and != operators.

Deriving PartialEq implements the eq method. When PartialEq is derived on structs, two instances are equal only if *all* fields are equal, and the instances are not equal if any fields are not equal. When derived on enums, each variant is equal to itself and not equal to the other variants.

The PartialEq trait is required, for example, with the use of the assert_eq! macro, which needs to be able to compare two instances of a type for equality.

The Eq trait has no methods. Its purpose is to signal that for every value of the annotated type, the value is equal to itself. The Eq trait can only be applied to types that also implement PartialEq, although not all types that implement PartialEq can implement Eq. One example of this is floating point number types: the implementation of floating point numbers states that two instances of the not-a-number (NaN) value are not equal to each other.

An example of when Eq is required is for keys in a HashMap<K,V> so the HashMap<K,V> can tell whether two keys are the same.

PartialOrd and Ord for Ordering Comparisons

The PartialOrd trait allows you to compare instances of a type for sorting purposes. A type that implements PartialOrd can be used with the <, >, <=, and >= operators. You can only apply the PartialOrd trait to types that also implement PartialEq.

Deriving PartialOrd implements the partial_cmp method, which returns an Option<Ordering> that will be None when the values given don't produce an ordering. An example of a value that doesn't produce an ordering, even though most values of that type can be compared, is the not-a-number (NaN) floating point value. Calling partial_cmp with any floating point number and the NaN floating point value will return None.

When derived on structs, PartialOrd compares two instances by comparing the value in each field in the order in which the fields appear in the struct definition. When derived on enums, variants of the enum declared earlier in the enum definition are considered less than the variants listed later.

The PartialOrd trait is required, for example, for the gen_range method from the rand crate that generates a random value in the range specified by a low value and a high value.

The Ord trait allows you to know that for any two values of the annotated type, a valid ordering will exist. The Ord trait implements the cmp method, which returns an Ordering rather than an Option<Ordering> because a valid ordering will always be possible. You can only apply the Ord trait to types that also implement PartialOrd and Eq (and Eq requires PartialEq). When derived on structs and enums, cmp behaves the same way as the derived implementation for partial_cmp does with PartialOrd.

An example of when Ord is required is when storing values in a BTreeSet<T>, a data structure that stores data based on the sort order of the values.

Clone and Copy for Duplicating Values

The Clone trait allows you to explicitly create a deep copy of a value, and the duplication process might involve running arbitrary code and copying heap data. See "Ways That Variables and Data Interact: Clone" on page 65 for more information on Clone.

Deriving Clone implements the clone method, which when implemented for the whole type, calls clone on each of the parts of the type. This means all the fields or values in the type must also implement Clone to derive Clone.

An example of when Clone is required is when calling the to_vec method on a slice. The slice doesn't own the type instances it contains, but the vector returned from to_vec will need to own its instances, so to_vec calls clone on each item. Thus, the type stored in the slice must implement Clone.

The Copy trait allows you to duplicate a value by only copying bits stored on the stack; no arbitrary code is necessary. See "Stack-Only Data: Copy" on page 65 for more information on Copy.

The Copy trait doesn't define any methods to prevent programmers from overloading those methods and violating the assumption that no arbitrary code is being run. That way, all programmers can assume that copying a value will be very fast.

You can derive Copy on any type whose parts all implement Copy. You can only apply the Copy trait to types that also implement Clone, because a type that implements Copy has a trivial implementation of Clone that performs the same task as Copy.

The Copy trait is rarely required; types that implement Copy have optimizations available, meaning you don't have to call clone, which makes the code more concise.

Everything possible with Copy you can also accomplish with Clone, but the code might be slower or have to use clone in places.

Hash for Mapping a Value to a Value of Fixed Size

The Hash trait allows you to take an instance of a type of arbitrary size and map that instance to a value of fixed size using a hash function. Deriving Hash implements the hash method. The derived implementation of the hash method combines the result of calling hash on each of the parts of the type, meaning all fields or values must also implement Hash to derive Hash.

An example of when Hash is required is in storing keys in a HashMap<K,V> to store data efficiently.

Default for Default Values

The Default trait allows you to create a default value for a type. Deriving Default implements the default function. The derived implementation of the default function calls the default function on each part of the type, meaning all fields or values in the type must also implement Default to derive Default.

The Default::default function is commonly used in combination with the struct update syntax discussed in "Creating Instances from Other Instances with Struct Update Syntax" on page 84. You can customize a few fields of a struct and then set and use a default value for the rest of the fields by using ..Default::default().

The Default trait is required when you use the method unwrap_or_default on Option<T> instances, for example. If the Option<T> is None, the method unwrap_or_default will return the result of Default::default for the type T stored in the Option<T>.

D

MACROS

We've used macros like `println!` throughout this book but haven't fully explored what a macro is and how it works. This appendix explains macros as follows:

- What macros are and how they differ from functions
- How to define a declarative macro to do metaprogramming
- How to define a procedural macro to create custom `derive` traits

We're covering the details of macros in an appendix because they're still evolving in Rust. Macros have changed and, in the near future, will change at a quicker rate than the rest of the language and standard library since Rust 1.0, so this section is more likely to become out-of-date than the rest of the book. Due to Rust's stability guarantees, the code shown here will continue to work with future versions, but there may be additional capabilities or easier ways to write macros that weren't available at the time of this publication. Bear that in mind when you try to implement anything from this appendix.

The Difference Between Macros and Functions

Fundamentally, macros are a way of writing code that writes other code, which is known as *metaprogramming*. In Appendix C, we discussed the derive attribute, which generates an implementation of various traits for you. We've also used the println! and vec! macros throughout the book. All of these macros *expand* to produce more code than the code you've written manually.

Metaprogramming is useful for reducing the amount of code you have to write and maintain, which is also one of the roles of functions. However, macros have some additional powers that functions don't have.

A function signature must declare the number and type of parameters the function has. Macros, on the other hand, can take a variable number of parameters: we can call println!("hello") with one argument or println!("hello {}", name) with two arguments. Also, macros are expanded before the compiler interprets the meaning of the code, so a macro can, for example, implement a trait on a given type. A function can't, because it gets called at runtime and a trait needs to be implemented at compile time.

The downside to implementing a macro instead of a function is that macro definitions are more complex than function definitions because you're writing Rust code that writes Rust code. Due to this indirection, macro definitions are generally more difficult to read, understand, and maintain than function definitions.

Another difference between macros and functions is that macro definitions aren't namespaced within modules like function definitions are. To prevent unexpected name clashes when using external crates, you have to explicitly bring the macros into the scope of your project at the same time as you bring the external crate into scope, using the #[macro_use] annotation. The following example would bring all the macros defined in the serde crate into the scope of the current crate:

```
#[macro_use]
extern crate serde;
```

If extern crate was able to bring macros into scope by default without this explicit annotation, you would be prevented from using two crates that happened to define macros with the same name. In practice, this conflict doesn't occur often, but the more crates you use, the more likely it is.

There is one last important difference between macros and functions: you must define or bring macros into scope *before* you call them in a file, whereas you can define functions anywhere and call them anywhere.

Declarative Macros with macro_rules! for General Metaprogramming

The most widely used form of macros in Rust are *declarative macros*. These are also sometimes referred to as *macros by example*, macro_rules! *macros*, or just plain *macros*. At their core, declarative macros allow you to write something similar to a Rust match expression. As discussed in Chapter 6, match expressions are control structures that take an expression, compare the resulting value of the expression to patterns, and then run the code associated with the matching pattern. Macros also compare a value to patterns that have code associated with them; in this situation, the value is the literal Rust source code passed to the macro, the patterns are compared with the structure of that source code, and the code associated with each pattern is the code that replaces the code passed to the macro. This all happens during compilation.

To define a macro, you use the macro_rules! construct. Let's explore how to use macro_rules! by looking at how the vec! macro is defined. Chapter 8 covered how we can use the vec! macro to create a new vector with particular values. For example, the following macro creates a new vector with three integers inside:

```
let v: Vec<u32> = vec![1, 2, 3];
```

We could also use the vec! macro to make a vector of two integers or a vector of five string slices. We wouldn't be able to use a function to do the same because we wouldn't know the number or type of values up front.

Let's look at a slightly simplified definition of the vec! macro in Listing D-1.

```
❶ #[macro_export]
❷ macro_rules! vec {
    ❸ ( $( $x:expr ),* ) => {
        {
            let mut temp_vec = Vec::new();
          ❹ $(
              ❺ temp_vec.push($x❻);
            )*
          ❼ temp_vec
        }
    };
}
```

Listing D-1: A simplified version of the vec! macro definition

NOTE *The actual definition of the vec! macro in the standard library includes code to pre-allocate the correct amount of memory up front. That code is an optimization that we don't include here to make the example simpler.*

The #[macro_export] annotation ❶ indicates that this macro should be made available whenever the crate in which we're defining the macro is imported. Without this annotation, even if someone depending on this crate uses the #[macro_use] annotation, the macro wouldn't be brought into scope.

We then start the macro definition with macro_rules! and the name of the macro we're defining *without* the exclamation mark ❷. The name, in this case vec, is followed by curly brackets denoting the body of the macro definition.

The structure in the vec! body is similar to the structure of a match expression. Here we have one arm with the pattern ($($x:expr),*), followed by =>

and the block of code associated with this pattern ❸. If the pattern matches, the associated block of code will be emitted. Given that this is the only pattern in this macro, there is only one valid way to match; any other will be an error. More complex macros will have more than one arm.

Valid pattern syntax in macro definitions is different than the pattern syntax covered in Chapter 18 because macro patterns are matched against Rust code structure rather than values. Let's walk through what the pieces of the pattern in Listing D-1 mean; for the full macro pattern syntax, see the reference at *https://doc.rust-lang.org/stable/reference/macros.html*.

First, a set of parentheses encompasses the whole pattern. Next comes a dollar sign ($) followed by a set of parentheses, which captures values that match the pattern within the parentheses for use in the replacement code. Within $() is $x:expr, which matches any Rust expression and gives the expression the name $x.

The comma following $() indicates that a literal comma separator character could optionally appear after the code that matches the code captured in $(). The * following the comma specifies that the pattern matches zero or more of whatever precedes the *.

When we call this macro with vec![1, 2, 3];, the $x pattern matches three times with the three expressions 1, 2, and 3.

Now let's look at the pattern in the body of the code associated with this arm: the temp_vec.push() code ❺ within the $()* part ❹❼ is generated for each part that matches $() in the pattern, zero or more times depending on how many times the pattern matches. The $x ❻ is replaced with each expression matched. When we call this macro with vec![1, 2, 3];, the code generated that replaces this macro call will be the following:

```
let mut temp_vec = Vec::new();
temp_vec.push(1);
temp_vec.push(2);
temp_vec.push(3);
temp_vec
```

We've defined a macro that can take any number of arguments of any type and can generate code to create a vector containing the specified elements.

Given that most Rust programmers will *use* macros more than *write* macros, we won't discuss macro_rules! any further. To learn more about how to write macros, consult the online documentation or other resources, such as "The Little Book of Rust Macros" at *https://danielkeep.github.io/tlborm/book/index.html*.

Procedural Macros for Custom derive

The second form of macros is called *procedural macros* because they're more like functions (which are a type of procedure). Procedural macros accept some Rust code as an input, operate on that code, and produce some Rust code as an output rather than matching against patterns and replacing the code with other code as declarative macros do. At the time of this writing, you can only define procedural macros to allow your traits to be implemented on a type by specifying the trait name in a derive annotation.

We'll create a crate named hello_macro that defines a trait named HelloMacro with one associated function named hello_macro. Rather than making our crate users implement the HelloMacro trait for each of their types, we'll provide a procedural macro so users can annotate their type with #[derive(HelloMacro)] to get a default implementation of the hello_macro function. The default implementation will print Hello, Macro! My name is TypeName!, where TypeName is the name of the type on which this trait has been defined. In other words, we'll write a crate that enables another programmer to write code like Listing D-2 using our crate.

src/main.rs

```
extern crate hello_macro;
#[macro_use]
extern crate hello_macro_derive;

use hello_macro::HelloMacro;

#[derive(HelloMacro)]
struct Pancakes;

fn main() {
    Pancakes::hello_macro();
}
```

Listing D-2: The code a user of our crate will be able to write when using our procedural macro

This code will print Hello, Macro! My name is Pancakes! when we're done. The first step is to make a new library crate, like this:

```
$ cargo new hello_macro --lib
```

Next, we'll define the HelloMacro trait and its associated function:

src/lib.rs

```
pub trait HelloMacro {
    fn hello_macro();
}
```

We have a trait and its function. At this point, our crate user could implement the trait to achieve the desired functionality, like so:

```
extern crate hello_macro;

use hello_macro::HelloMacro;

struct Pancakes;

impl HelloMacro for Pancakes {
    fn hello_macro() {
        println!("Hello, Macro! My name is Pancakes!");
```

```
    }
}

fn main() {
    Pancakes::hello_macro();
}
```

However, they would need to write the implementation block for each type they wanted to use with `hello_macro`; we want to spare them from having to do this work.

Additionally, we can't yet provide a default implementation for the `hello_macro` function that will print the name of the type the trait is implemented on: Rust doesn't have reflection capabilities, so it can't look up the type's name at runtime. We need a macro to generate code at compile time.

The next step is to define the procedural macro. At the time of this writing, procedural macros need to be in their own crate. Eventually, this restriction might be lifted. The convention for structuring crates and macro crates is as follows: for a crate named `foo`, a custom derive procedural macro crate is called `foo_derive`. Let's start a new crate called `hello_macro_derive` inside our `hello_macro` project:

```
$ cargo new hello_macro_derive --lib
```

Our two crates are tightly related, so we create the procedural macro crate within the directory of our `hello_macro` crate. If we change the trait definition in `hello_macro`, we'll have to change the implementation of the procedural macro in `hello_macro_derive` as well. The two crates will need to be published separately, and programmers using these crates will need to add both as dependencies and bring them both into scope. We could instead have the `hello_macro` crate use `hello_macro_derive` as a dependency and reexport the procedural macro code. But the way we've structured the project makes it possible for programmers to use `hello_macro` even if they don't want the derive functionality.

We need to declare the `hello_macro_derive` crate as a procedural macro crate. We'll also need functionality from the syn and quote crates, as you'll see in a moment, so we need to add them as dependencies. Add the following to the *Cargo.toml* file for `hello_macro_derive`:

*hello_macro_derive
/Cargo.toml*

```
[lib]
proc-macro = true

[dependencies]
syn = "0.11.11"
quote = "0.3.15"
```

To start defining the procedural macro, place the code in Listing D-3 into your *src/lib.rs* file for the `hello_macro_derive` crate. Note that this code won't compile until we add a definition for the `impl_hello_macro` function.

```
❶ extern crate proc_macro;
❷ extern crate syn;
  #[macro_use]
❸ extern crate quote;

  use proc_macro::TokenStream;

❹ #[proc_macro_derive(HelloMacro)]
❺ pub fn hello_macro_derive(input: TokenStream) -> TokenStream {
      // Construct a string representation of the type definition
❻     let s = input.to_string();

      // Parse the string representation
❼     let ast = syn::parse_derive_input(&s).unwrap();

      // Build the impl
❽     let gen = impl_hello_macro(&ast);

      // Return the generated impl
❾     gen.parse().unwrap()
  }
```

Listing D-3: Code that most procedural macro crates will need to have for processing Rust code

Notice the way we've split the functions in Listing D-3; this will be the same for almost every procedural macro crate you see or create, because it makes writing a procedural macro more convenient. What you choose to do in the place where the impl_hello_macro function is called ❽ will be different depending on your procedural macro's purpose.

We've introduced three new crates: proc_macro ❶, syn ❷ (available from *https://crates.io/crates/syn/*), and quote ❸ (available from *https://crates.io/crates/quote/*). The proc_macro crate comes with Rust, so we didn't need to add that to the dependencies in *Cargo.toml*. The proc_macro crate allows us to convert Rust code into a string containing that Rust code. The syn crate parses Rust code from a string into a data structure that we can perform operations on. The quote crate takes syn data structures and turns them back into Rust code. These crates make it much simpler to parse any sort of Rust code we might want to handle: writing a full parser for Rust code is no simple task.

The hello_macro_derive function ❺ will get called when a user of our library specifies #[derive(HelloMacro)] on a type. The reason is that we've annotated the hello_macro_derive function here with proc_macro_derive ❹ and specified the name, HelloMacro, which matches our trait name; that's the convention most procedural macros follow.

This function first converts the input from a TokenStream to a String by calling to_string ❻. This String is a string representation of the Rust code for which we are deriving HelloMacro. In the example in Listing D-2, s will have the String value struct Pancakes; because that is the Rust code we added the #[derive(HelloMacro)] annotation to.

At the time of this writing, you can only convert a TokenStream to a string. A richer API will exist in the future.

Now we need to parse the Rust code String into a data structure that we can then interpret and perform operations on. This is where syn comes into play. The parse_derive_input function in syn takes a String and returns a DeriveInput struct representing the parsed Rust code ❼. The following code shows the relevant parts of the DeriveInput struct we get from parsing the string struct Pancakes;:

```
DeriveInput {
    // --snip--

    ident: Ident(
        "Pancakes"
    ),
    body: Struct(
        Unit
    )
}
```

The fields of this struct show that the Rust code we've parsed is a unit struct with the ident (identifier, meaning the name) of Pancakes. There are more fields on this struct for describing all sorts of Rust code; check the syn documentation for DeriveInput at *https://docs.rs/syn/0.11.11/syn/struct .DeriveInput.html* for more information.

At this point, we haven't defined the impl_hello_macro function ❽, which is where we'll build the new Rust code we want to include. But before we do, note that the last part of this hello_macro_derive function uses the parse function from the quote crate to turn the output of the impl_hello_macro function back into a TokenStream ❾. The returned TokenStream is added to the code that our crate users write, so when they compile their crate, they'll get extra functionality that we provide.

You might have noticed that we're calling unwrap to panic if the calls to the parse_derive_input or parse functions fail here. Panicking on errors is necessary in procedural macro code because proc_macro_derive functions must return TokenStream rather than Result to conform to the procedural macro API. We've chosen to simplify this example by using unwrap; in production code, you should provide more specific error messages about what went wrong by using panic! or expect.

Now that we have the code to turn the annotated Rust code from a TokenStream into a String and a DeriveInput instance, let's generate the code that implements the HelloMacro trait on the annotated type:

hello_macro_derive /src/lib.rs

```
fn impl_hello_macro(ast: &syn::DeriveInput) -> quote::Tokens {
❶  let name = &ast.ident;
❷  quote! {
```

```
        impl HelloMacro for #name❸ {
    ❹ fn hello_macro() {
        ❺ println!("Hello, Macro! My name is {}", stringify!❻(#name));
        }
    }
}
}
```

We get an `Ident` struct instance containing the name (identifier) of the annotated type using `ast.ident` ❶. The code in Listing D-2 specifies that the name will be `Ident("Pancakes")`.

The `quote!` macro ❷ lets us write the Rust code that we want to return and convert it into `quote::Tokens`. This macro also provides some very cool templating mechanics; we can write `#name`, and `quote!` will replace it with the value in the variable named `name`. You can even do some repetition similar to the way regular macros work. Check out the quote crate's docs at *https://docs.rs/quote/* for a thorough introduction.

We want our procedural macro to generate an implementation of our `HelloMacro` trait for the type the user annotated, which we can get by using `#name` ❸. The trait implementation has one function, `hello_macro` ❹, whose body contains the functionality we want to provide: printing `Hello, Macro!` `My name is` and then the name of the annotated type ❺.

The `stringify!` macro used here ❻ is built into Rust. It takes a Rust expression, such as `1 + 2`, and at compile time turns the expression into a string literal, such as `"1 + 2"`. This is different from `format!` or `println!`, which evaluate the expression and then turn the result into a `String`. There is a possibility that the `#name` input might be an expression to print literally, so we use `stringify!`. Using `stringify!` also saves an allocation by converting `#name` to a string literal at compile time.

At this point, `cargo build` should complete successfully in both `hello_macro` and `hello_macro_derive`. Let's hook up these crates to the code in Listing D-2 to see the procedural macro in action! Create a new binary project in your *projects* directory using `cargo new --bin pancakes`. We need to add `hello_macro` and `hello_macro_derive` as dependencies in the pancakes crate's *Cargo.toml*. If you're publishing your versions of `hello_macro` and `hello_macro_derive` to *https://crates.io/*, they would be regular dependencies; if not, you can specify them as path dependencies as follows:

```
[dependencies]
hello_macro = { path = "../hello_macro" }
hello_macro_derive = { path = "../hello_macro/hello_macro_derive" }
```

Put the code from Listing D-2 into *src/main.rs*, and run `cargo run`: it should print `Hello, Macro! My name is Pancakes`! The implementation of the `HelloMacro` trait from the procedural macro was included without the pancakes crate needing to implement it; the `#[derive(HelloMacro)]` added the trait implementation.

The Future of Macros

In the future, Rust will expand declarative and procedural macros. Rust will use a better declarative macro system with the `macro` keyword and will add more types of procedural macros for more powerful tasks than just `derive`. These systems are still under development at the time of this publication; please consult the online Rust documentation for the latest information.

INDEX

Symbols and Numbers

+ (addition operator), 38, 137–138, 492
& (ampersand), 17, 492
<> (angle brackets), 494–495
   for specifying lifetime
      parameters, 191
   for specifying type parameters, 130,
      172, 173
-> (arrow), 46–47, 492
* (asterisk), 492
   dereference operator, 68,
      311–315, 416
   glob operator, 124–125
   multiplication operator, 38
@ (at operator), 410–411, 493
: (colon), 492–493, 495
   for struct fields, 82
   for trait bounds, 183
{} (curly brackets), 496
   for function bodies, 6, 15
   as placeholders in the `println!`
      macro, 18
   scope creation, 45, 71
/ (division operator), 38, 492
. (dot), 492
   for method syntax, 91
   for struct field access, 82
   for tuple element access, 40
:: (double colon), 494
   for associated functions, 94
   for enum variants, 96
   for namespacing, 111
" (double quote), 39, 493
- (hyphen)
   for negation, 492
   for subtraction, 38, 492
+ (multiple trait bound syntax), 183, 492
! (never type), 443–444, 494
() (parentheses), 496
   for function parameters, 6, 15
   for tuples, 39–40
? (question mark operator), 159–161, 493

% (remainder operator), 38, 492
; (semicolon), 6, 493
' (single quote), 493–494
   for characters, 39
   for lifetime parameter names, 190
[] (square brackets), 496
   for array creation, 41
   for element access, 41, 131–132
_ (underscore), 494
   as a catchall pattern, 28, 106–107,
      403–405
   as a visual separator in integer
      literals, 37
| (vertical pipe), 493–494
   in closure definitions, 261
   in patterns, 398
1:1 threading model, 343

A

ABI (application binary interface), 420
abort, 150
addition
   of custom types, 432–434
   of number types, 38
   of strings, 137–138
addition operator (+), 38, 137–138, 492
ahead-of-time compiled, 7
ampersand (&), 17, 492
angle brackets (<>), 494–495
   for specifying lifetime
      parameters, 191
   for specifying type parameters, 130,
      172, 173
API (Application Programming
      Interface), xxvi, 4
application binary interface (ABI), 420
Arc<T> type, 361–362, 473–474
arguments, 43
arms
   in if expressions, 49
   in match expressions, 24, 103

array data type, 40–42
    invalid element access, 41–42
    iterating over elements of, 54–55
    slices of, 78–79
arrow (->), 46–47, 492
as_bytes method, 73–74
assert_eq! macro, 208–210
assert! macro, 205–208
assert_ne! macro, 210
associated function, 16, 93–94
associated types, 431–432
associative array. *See* HashMap<K, V> type
asterisk (*), 492
    dereference operator, 68, 311–315, 416
    glob operator, 124–125
    multiplication operator, 38
at operator (@), 410–411, 493
atomically reference counted, 361–362
automatic dereferencing, 92
automatic referencing, 92

B

backtrace, 151–153
binary crate, 8, 19, 233
binary target, 302
blanket implementations, 186
blocking, 345
Boolean data type, 39, 50
borrow checker, 188–189, 190
borrowing, 68–73
Box<T> type, 306–311
break keyword, 27–28
buffer overread, 151
Build Tools for Visual Studio, 3
byte literal syntax, 37, 74

C

*const T, 415–417, 492
Cargo, xxiv, 7–11
    commands
        build, 9
        check, 10
        doc, 22, 287–288
        install, 302–303
        login, 294
        new, 8, 14
        publish, 294–296
        run, 10, 299

test, 202–205, 215–220, 289, 301–302
        update, 21
        yank, 296
    extending with custom commands, 303
    workspaces, 297–302
Cargo.lock, 9, 20–21
Cargo.toml
    dependencies section, 9, 19
    package section, 8, 294–295
    profile section, 286–287
    updating crate versions in, 21
carriage return, 454
cfg (configuration) attribute, 221
channels, 349–355, 470–474
character data type, 39
client, 450
clone method
    deep copy creation, 65
    trade-offs of, 236
Clone trait, 499–500
closed channel, 350
closures, 258–270
    capturing the environment with, 268–270, 274–275
    returning, 448
    running in threads, 344
    type inference in, 263–264
cmp method, 23
coherence, 180
collections, 129–147
collect method, 143, 229
colon (:), 492–493
    for struct fields, 82
    for trait bounds, 183
command line arguments, accepting, 228–231
command line notation, 2
comments, 48, 287–290, 467
compiler-driven development, 462
compiling
    with Cargo, 7–11
    in release mode, 10–11
    with rustc, 6–7
compound data types, 39–42
concurrency, 341–364
concurrent programming, 341
configuration (cfg) attribute, 221
connection, 451–54
cons list, 308–311

constants, 34
  vs. static variables, 421–422
  vs. variables, 34
constructor, 319
consume, 272–273
consuming adaptors, 272–273
continue keyword, 28–29
contracts, 163
control flow, 48–55
Copy trait, 5, 499–500
crate, 9
  binary vs. library, 8, 19
  license of, 295
  publishing, 294–296
  updating versions, 21
  using as a dependency, 21–22
  yanking, 296
crates.io, 287–296
  documentation comments, 287–288
  publishing to, 295–296
  removing from, 296
  setting up an account on, 294
CRLF sequence, 454
CTRL-C, 27, 53, 452, 479
curly brackets ({}), 496
  for function bodies, 6, 15
  as placeholders in the println!
      macro, 18
  scope creation, 45, 71

D

dangling pointer, 72
dangling reference, 72–73, 187–189,
      193–194
data race, 70–71, 422
data types, 36–42
  annotation of, 25, 36
  compound, 39–42
  scalar, 36–39
deadlock, 343, 362, 484
Debug trait, 89–90, 498
declarative macros, 502–504
deep copy, 64–65
Default trait, 500
default type parameters, 432–434
dependencies section in *Cargo.toml*, 9, 19
dependency, 7, 19
deref coercion, 138, 315–317
DerefMut trait, 316–317
Deref trait, 311–317, 440
derive annotation, 88–90, 497–500

destructor, 319
destructuring
  of enums, 400–401
  of references, 402
  of structs, 399–400
  of tuples, 40
Dickinson, Emily, 231
Dijkstra, Edsger W., 201
Display trait, 89
diverging functions, 443
division operator (/), 38, 492
doc tests, 289
documentation
  comments, 287–290, 467
  offline for Rust, 4
  tests, 289
  viewing a crate's, 22
  writing, 287–290
dot (.), 492
  for method syntax, 91
  for struct field access, 82
  for tuple element access, 40
double colon (::), 494
  for associated functions, 94
  for enum variants, 96
  for namespacing, 111
double free error, 63, 319
double quote ("), 39, 493
Doyle, Sir Arthur Conan, 281
drop function, 62
Drop trait, 65, 317–320, 479–481
dynamically sized type (DST), 445–446
dynamic dispatch, 374

E

else if expression, 50–51
else keyword, 49
empty type, 443–444, 494
encapsulation, 366–368
entry method, 145–147
Entry type, 145–147
enumerate method, 74
enums, 95–108
  defining, 96
  instantiating, 96
  variants of, 96
environment, 269
environment variables, 249–254
eprintln! macro, 255–256
Eq trait, 498
error handling, 149–166

executable file, 6–7
executing code, 6–7
exit status code, 239–240
expect method, 17–18, 26, 157–158
expressions, 44–46
extern crate, 21–22
extern functions, 420–421

F

fearless concurrency, 342
FFI (Foreign Function Interface), 420
field init shorthand, 83
fields, 82
files, 231–232
floating-point data types, 38
fn keyword, 15
FnMut trait, 265, 269, 447, 465
FnOnce trait, 265, 269, 447, 465
Fn trait, 265, 269, 447, 465
fn type, 446–447
Foreign Function Interface (FFI), 420
for keyword
    loop, 54–55
    in trait implementations, 179–180
format! macro, 138
from function
    on the From trait, 160
    on String, 60–61, 136
fully qualified syntax, 434–437, 447
functional programming, 257
function pointers, 446–447
functions, 42–47
    arguments to, 43
    bodies, statements, and expressions
        in, 44–46
    with multiple return values using a
        tuple, 67–68
    parameters of, 43–44
    public vs. private, 119
    returning early from, 46
    with return values, 46–47

G

Gallant, Andrew, 228
Gamma, Erich, 366
garbage collector (GC), 61
generics, 167–178, 199
    default types for, 432–434
    in enum definitions, 174–175
    in function definitions, 170–173

in method definitions, 175–177
performance of, 177–178
in struct definitions, 173–174
get method
    on HashMap<K, V>, 144
    on Vec<T>, 131–132
getter, 165
Git, 8, 11
global variables, 421–422
grapheme clusters, 140, 142
green threads, 343
grep, 227
guarding, 356
guessing game, 13–30

H

hash. See HashMap<K, V> type
hasher, 147
hashing function, 142, 147
hash map. See HashMap<K, V> type
HashMap<K, V> type, 142–147
    entry method on, 145–147
    get method on, 144
    insert method on, 142–143
    iterating over, 144–145
    new function on, 142–143
hash table. See HashMap<K, V> type
Hash trait, 500
heap
    allocating on, 58
    and the stack, 58–59
Helm, Richard, 366
Hoare, Tony, 100
HTTP (Hypertext Transfer Protocol),
        450, 454–456
hyphen (-)
    for negation, 492
    for subtraction, 38, 492

I

IDE (Integrated Development
        Environment), xxiv, 4
if keyword, 48–52
if let syntax, 107–108
ignore attribute, 219–220
immutabity. See mutability
impl keyword
    for defining associated functions,
        93–94
    for defining methods, 91
    for implementing traits, 179–180

indexing syntax, 131–132
indirection, 310–311
inheritance, 368–369
input lifetimes, 196
input/output (io) library, 15, 231–232
installation of Rust, 1–4
instance, 82
integer data types, 36–38
    numeric operations with, 38
    signed, 36–37
    type suffixes of, 37
    unsigned, 36–37
Integrated Development Environment
    (IDE), xxiv, 4
integration tests, 222–225
interfaces. *See* traits
interior mutability, 323–332, 362
invalidated variable, 64
io (input/output) library, 15, 231–232
IpAddr type, 96–98
irrefutable patterns, 395–396
isize type
    architecture dependent size of, 37
    indexing collection with, 38
iterator adaptors, 273–274, 280–281
iterators, 270–277
    creating with iter method, 73–74
    enumerate method on, 74
    next method on, 271–272
    performance of, 281–283
iter method, 73–74

J

Johnson, Ralph, 366
JoinHandle type, 345

K

Kay, Alan, 365
keywords, 32, 487–489

L

last in, first out ordering, 58
lazy evaluation, 264, 270
len method, 74
let keyword, 16
library crate, 7, 8, 19, 110
license, 295
license identifier value, 295

lifetimes, 187–199
    annotation of, 190–195
    bounds, 428–429
    elision, 195–198
    inferring for trait objects, 429–430
    subtyping, 423–428
line feed, 454
linker, 2–3
Linux installation of Rust, 2–3
Little Book of Rust Macros, The, 504
lock, 356–359
loop keyword, 26–27, 53

M

*mut T, 415–417, 492
macOS installation of Rust, 2–3
macro_export annotation, 503
macro_rules! macro, 502–503
macros, 501–510
    declarative, 502–504
    procedural, 504–509
macro_use annotation, 502–503
main function, 5–6
mangling, 421
map. *See* HashMap<K, V> type
match expression, 102–107
    exhaustiveness of, 106
    handling comparison results with,
        23–24
    handling Result values with, 28–29
match guard, 156, 408–410
memoization, 264
memory leak, 332
message passing, 349–355
metaprogramming, 502
methods
    defined on enums, 99
    defined on structs, 90–93
method syntax, 91
M:N threading model, 343
mock object, 325–330
mod keyword, 110–112
modules, 109–127
    moving to other files, 112–118
    root, 118
monomorphization, 177–178
move keyword, 269–270, 347–349
moving ownership, 62–64
    vs. borrowing, 68–73
    with function calls, 66
    with function return values, 66–68

multiple producer, single consumer
(mpsc), 350, 354, 473
multiple trait bound syntax (+),
183, 492
multiplication, 38
Mutex<T> type, 356–362, 473–474,
478–479
mut keyword
making a reference mutable with,
69–71
making a variable mutable with, 33
mutability
of references, 69–71
of variables, 32–33
mutual exclusion, 356

N

never type (!), 443–444, 494
new function
on HashMap<K, V>, 142–143
on String, 135–136
on Vec<T>, 130
new project setup, using cargo, 14
newtype pattern, 439–441
null, 100–102
numeric operations, 38

O

object, 366, 370. *See also*
HashMap<K, V> type
object-oriented programming (OOP),
365–387
object-safe traits, 374–375, 383
operator overloading, 432–434
operators, 491–493
optimizations, 10–11
Option<T> enum, 100–102
Ordering type, 23
Ord trait, 499
orphan rule, 180, 439
output lifetimes, 196
ownership, 57–79
and functions, 66–68
rules, 59

P

package section in *Cargo.toml*, 8, 294–295
panicking, 42

panic! macro, 150–153, 161–165
parallel programming, 341
parameters, 43–44
parentheses, (()), 496
for function parameters, 6, 15
for tuples, 39–40
parse method, 25
PartialEq trait, 498
PartialOrd trait, 499
PATH system variable, 2, 3, 302–303
patterns, 389–411
binding to values with, 104–105
in for loops, 392–393
in function parameters, 394
in if let syntax, 107, 390–391
in let statements, 393–394
in match expressions, 102–103, 390
refutable vs. irrefutable, 395–396
in while let syntax, 392
pointer, 305
dangling, 72
to data on the heap, 58
raw, 415–417
smart, 305–339
poisoned mutex, 475
polymorphism, 368
prelude, 15
primitive obsession, 235
println! macro, 6, 18
privacy rules, 121
private functions, 119
procedural macros, 504–509
process, 342
proc_macro crate, 507
profiles, 286–287
profile section in *Cargo.toml*, 286–287
propagating errors, 158–161
pub keyword, 119–121
public
API, 120, 290–293
vs. private functions, 119
pub use, 290–293
push method, 131, 137
push_str method, 61, 137

Q

question mark operator (?),
159–161, 493
quote crate, 507–509

R

race conditions, 70, 343
RAII (Resource Acquisition Is
        Initialization), 62
rand crate, 19, 21–23
random number functionality, 19,
        21–23
Range type, 55
raw pointers, 415–417
Rc<T> type, 320–323, 330–339
read_line method, 16–17
receiver, 350
recoverable errors, 149
recursive types, 308–311
re-export, 290–293
RefCell<T> type, 323–339
reference counting, 306, 320–323,
        361–362
reference cycles, 332–339
references
        for accessing data from multiple
                places, 17
        and borrowing, 68–73
        creating in patterns, 407–408
        dangling, 72–73
        dereferencing, 68
        mutability of, 69–71, 73
        rules of, 73
refutable patterns, 395–396
registry, 20, 287–296
release mode, 10–11
release profiles, 286–287
remainder operator (%), 38, 492
request line, 454
request-response protocol, 450
Resource Acquisition Is Initialization
        (RAII), 62
Result<T, E> type, 17, 153–161
        expect method on, 17–18, 26,
                157–158
        vs. panic!, 161–165
        type aliases for, 442–443
        unwrap method on, 157–158
        unwrap_or_else method on, 239
return keyword, 46
return values
        of functions, 46–47
        multiple using a tuple, 67–68
rev method, 55
ripgrep, 228, 302–303
RLS (Rust Language Server), xxiv
root module, 118

.rs file extension, 5
running code, 6–7
runtime, 343
Rustaceans, 3–4
rustc, 3, 5, 6–7
rustfmt, xxiv, 6
Rust Language Server (RLS), xxiv
Rustonomicon, The, 133, 339, 363
rustup commands, 1–4
        doc, 4
        uninstall, 3
        update, 3

S

scalar data types, 36–39, 65–66
scope, 60
SCREAMING_SNAKE_CASE, 421
Self keyword, 374–375
self parameter, 90
Semantic Versioning (SemVer), 19, 296
semicolon (;), 6, 493
Send trait, 362–363, 423, 465
sequence, 55
server, 450
shadowing, 25, 34–36
shallow copy, 64
shared-state concurrency, 355–362
should_panic attribute, 212–215
signed integer types, 36–37
single quote ('), 493–494
        for characters, 39
        for lifetime parameter names, 190
?Sized, 446
Sized trait, 445–446, 448
slice type, 73–79
        of array, 78–79
        string slices, 75–78
smart pointer, 305–339
        Box<T> type, 306–311
        Rc<T> type, 320–323, 330–339
        RefCell<T> type, 323–339
snake case, 42
Software Package Data Exchange
        (SPDX), 295
square brackets ([]), 496
        for array creation, 41
        for element access, 41, 131–132
stack
        and the heap, 58–59
        last in, first out ordering, 58
        popping off of, 58
        pushing onto, 58

standard error (stderr), 254–256
standard output (stdout), 254–256
statements, 44–46
state objects, 376
state pattern, 376–384
statically typed, 36
static dispatch, 374
'static lifetime, 198–199, 421, 429,
        430, 465
static method, 16, 93–94
static variables, 421–422
status line, 455
stderr (standard error), 254–256
stdin function, 16
stdout (standard output), 254–256
&str (string slice type), 75–78
stream, 451–453
stringify! macro, 509
string literal, 60
    storage in the binary of, 61
    of string slice type, 75–78
string slice type (&str), 75–78
String type, 60–61, 135–142
    as_bytes method on, 73–74
    bytes method on, 141–142
    chars method on, 141
    concatenation with +, 137–138
    from function on, 60–61, 136
    indexing into, 139–140
    internal structure of, 62–63,
        139–140
    iterating over, 141–142
    len method on, 74
    new function on, 135–136
    parse method on, 25
    push method on, 137
    push_str method on, 61, 137
    slicing, 140–141
    trim method on, 25
    UTF-8 encoding of, 136
Stroustrup, Bjarne, 282
structs, 81–94
    defining, 81–82
    field init shorthand, 83
    fields, 82
    instantiating, 81–82
    ownership of data, 85–86
    tuple, 84–85, 439–440
    unit-like, 85
    update syntax, 84
subtraction, 38, 492
super keyword, 125–127

supertraits, 437–439
symbols, 493–496
syn crate, 507–508
Sync trait, 362–363, 423

T

TCP (Transmission Control Protocol),
        450–452
test attribute, 202–203
test double, 325
test-driven development (TDD), 244
test functions, 202–205
tests, 201–226
    custom failure messages for,
        210–212
    filtering, 219
    ignoring, 219–220
    integration, 222–225
    organizing, 220–225
    of private functions, 221–222
    running, 215–220
    unit, 220–222
    writing, 201–215
thread pool, 461–485
threads, 342–349
    creating with spawn, 344, 462–463
    joining, 345
    pausing with sleep, 344
thunk, 442
Tom's Obvious, Minimal Language
        (TOML), 8
to_string method, 136, 186
trait bounds, 182–187, 199
    conditionally implementing
        methods with, 185–187
    fixing the largest function with,
        183–185
trait objects, 369–375, 448
    dynamic dispatch, 374
    inferring lifetimes of, 429–430
    object safety, 374–375
traits, 178–187
    associated types in, 431–432
    default implementations of, 181–182
    defining, 178–179
    implementing, 179–180
    unsafe, 422–423
Transmission Control Protocol (TCP),
        450–452
transmitter, 350
trim method, 25

tuple data type, 39–40, 67–68
tuple structs, 84–85, 439–440
type alias, 441–443, 474
type annotation, 25, 36
type inference, 24
type suffixes, 37

U

underscore (_), 494
    as a catchall pattern, 28, 106–107,
        403–405
    as a visual separator in integer
        literals, 37
Unicode Scalar Value, 39, 139–141
Uniform Resource Identifier
        (URI), 454
Uniform Resource Locator (URL), 454
unit-like structs, 85
unit tests, 220–222
unrecoverable errors, 149–153
unrolling, 283
unsafe, 414–423
    functions, 417–420
    superpowers, 414, 423
    traits, 422–423
unsigned integer types, 36–37
unsized type, 445–446
unwinding, 150
unwrap method, 157–158
unwrap_or_else method, 239
URI (Uniform Resource
        Identifier), 454
URL (Uniform Resource Locator), 454
use keyword, 22, 123–127
user input, 15
usize type
    architecture-dependent size of, 37
    indexing collection with, 38
UTF-8 encoding, 136, 139–140

V

variables
    vs. constants, 34
    global, 421–422
    mutability, 32–33
    shadowing, 25, 34–36
    static, 421–422
    storing values in, 15–16
variants, 96
vec! macro, 130
vector. *See* Vec<T> type
Vec<T> type, 130–134
    get method on, 131–132
    iterating over, 133–134
    new function on, 130
    push method on, 131
vertical pipe (|), 493–494
    in closure definitions, 261
    in patterns, 398
Visual Studio, 3
Vlissides, John, 366

W

weak reference, 334–335
Weak<T> type, 334–339
where clause, 183
while loop, 53–54
Windows installation of Rust, 3
workspaces, 297–302

Y

yanking, 296

Z

zero-cost abstractions, xxv, 282–283
zero-overhead, 282

The Rust Programming Language is set in New Baskerville, Futura, Dogma, and TheSansMono Condensed. This book was printed and bound at Sheridan Books, Inc. in Chelsea, Michigan. The paper is 60# Finch Offset, which is certified by the Forest Stewardship Council (FSC).

The book uses a layflat binding, in which the pages are bound together with a cold-set, flexible glue and the first and last pages of the resulting book block are attached to the cover. The cover is not actually glued to the book's spine, and when open, the book lies flat and the spine doesn't crack.